Learn Spanish for Beginners

This Book Includes:

The Complete Course With Short Stories, Easy Phrases, Words in Context and Grammar for Spanish Language Learning from Beginners to Intermediate Level.

[Michael Navarro]

Text Copyright © [Michael Navarro]

Legal & Disclaimer

Table of Contents

Spanish Short Stories for Beginners

Learn Spanish for Beginners the Fast Way

Learn Spanish in your car 1001 common Phrases for Beginners

Spanish Short Stories for Intermediate Level

Learn Spanish for intermediate Level Fast Way

1001 Top Spanish Words in Context

Spanish Short Stories for Beginners

Learn Spanish Easily with 12 Simple and Captivating Common and Noble Stories.

[Michael Navarro]

Introduction

So you want to learn Spanish? Then you're about to embark on one of the most rewarding, interesting and fun adventures of your life. The Spanish language is one of the most spoken languages on Earth, spreading over 20 countries where it holds the status of official language, this means that over 450 million people around the world have Spanish as their native tongue. If you include the millions more who are actively learning the language, then Spanish is one of the most used and useful languages anyone needs to learn.

Learning is a process that usually takes time and motivation from the learner. To that end, it's necessary to count on a tool that will help you make the very first step towards understanding. This is where *Spanish Short Stories for Beginners* proves useful. *Spanish Short Stories for Beginners* was designed with the learner in mind so you won't have any trouble enjoying its content.

This book compiles 12 entertaining and easy-to-read stories that take place in a wide range of settings. You'll see how certain vocabulary is used at school, at the doctor's, when talking about family members, pets and so on. The stories use basic vocabulary so that you can easily understand what's being talked about. At the end of each story, there's a brief summary of the story, both in Spanish and English. Wrapping up every chapter, a glossary of the most important words is provided along with translations.

The conversation method is used in every chapter, so you'll see the Spanish language in action! There's no better way to learn a foreign language that seeing how native speakers use it daily. Don't hesitate to return to some parts of the story if you feel you didn't catch the idea. Take a look at the word that you don't understand and look it up in the glossary, chances are you'll find it and now you'll be able to read it confidently. Remember that when you're beginning to learn a new language, you might find some terms and ideas difficult to comprehend, this doesn't mean that you should give up.

We encourage to have a positive attitude and a lot of motivation. Concentrate on each story and submerge yourself in what you're reading. Spanish is a fun language and this book makes it even funnier and easier!

Chapter 1: Greetings and Basic Vocabulary

Era un **día como cualquier otro** para Juan. Juan es un **muchacho alto**, de **cabello corto** y de **tez** muy **blanca**. A Juan no le **gusta levantarse temprano** pero tiene que hacerlo, ya que él tiene que ir a la **escuela**. Sus **padres siempre** lo animan a ser **puntual** y **responsable**, pero Juan a veces no los **escucha**. **Bostezando** y **estirándose**, se sienta en la **cama**. Unos instantes después, él **baja** las **escaleras** hacia el **baño** para **tomar una ducha**, cuando **de repente** ve a su **madre**.

La mamá de Juan se levanta mucho más temprano que Juan. Ella va a trabajar a las 10 de la mañana, pero ella se levanta más temprano para tener listo el desayuno. El abuelo de Juan también se levanta temprano. Los fines de semana, cuando Juan no va a estudiar, él ayuda en la cocina a hacer el desayuno. Hoy día Juan tiene que ir a estudiar.

"**¡Buenos días, hijo!**" – Dice su mamá con **voz** muy **alta**. – "!**Me alegro** que te hayas levantado **a tiempo**!

"¡Buenos días, **mamá!** – **responde** Juan.

"El **desayuno** ya está **listo** en la **mesa**" – **Anuncia** su mamá.

"**Gracias**, pero tomaré una ducha **primero**"

Juan camina hacia el baño. El baño de la casa se encuentra en el segundo piso y el dormitorio de Juan se encuentra en el tercer piso. Cuando Juan finalmente llega al baño, él intenta abrir la puerta. Pero Juan no se había **dado cuenta** que la **luz** del **baño** estaba **encendida** y que también **había ruidos** que salían del baño. Eran ruidos **familiares**, como la de una voz **cantando**. Era la **hermana** de Juan que había entrado a tomarse una ducha mucho antes de que Juan se levantara.

La hermana de Juan se llama Luisa. Luisa es una muchacha joven. Ella es mayor que Juan por tres años. Amos asisten a la misma escuela, pero Luisa está en tres grados más adelante que Juan.

"¿Vas a **tardar?**" – Juan **pregunta** a su hermana.

Pero Juan no escucha ninguna **respuesta**. Tal parece que su hermana no lo **puede** escuchar. Juan puede escuchar que hay música que viene dentro del baño. La hermana de Juan trajo la radio al baño. Eso puede ser peligroso. La hermana de Juan tiene una pequeña radio en su habitación que ella puede llevar a cualquier lugar. Es por eso que ella no puede escucharlo. Entonces Juan decide **tocar la puerta** del baño con fuerza y pregunta **una vez más**:

"**¿Cuánto tiempo** vas a estar en el baño? Yo **también quiero** tomar una ducha"

Finalmente su hermana responde:

"Juan, **dame** unos 15 **minutos** más"

"¡¿15 minutos?! ¡Pero no puedo **esperar** 15 minutos, se me va hacer muy tarde para la escuela!" – dice Juan.

Juan no tiene otra **opción** más que esperar a que su hermana salga del baño antes que sea muy tarde para la escuela. Pero Juan sabe muy bien que, en ocasiones, su hermana toma una ducha por más de 15 minutos.

Su hermana puede llegar tarde a la escuela pero tal parece que eso no le importa. Sus padres le han dicho ya varias veces que ella debe tomar una ducha en sólo 10 minutos. En ocasiones, su novio viene a recogerla. Tal vez por eso ella se está tomando más tiempo de lo usual. Normalmente, cuando su novio viene a recogerla, ellos van a ala escuela en el auto de su novio. De esa manera, ellos llegan rápido a la escuela.

Juan decide sentarse en las escaleras a esperar a que su hermana acabe de bañarse. Mientras Juan está sentado esperando por su hermana, él escucha la voz de su papá que le dice:

"Tendrás que irte a la escuela sin ducharte hoy día, hijo"

"¡Buenos días, **papá**!" – dice Juan.

"**Felizmente**, yo ya tomé una ducha. ¿Por qué no vas a **cambiarte** de **ropa** y **desayunas**?"

"Pero papá, yo quería tomar una ducha primero" – Se **queja** Juan

"Tendrás que esperar a tu hermana, entonces" – dice **jocosamente** el papá de Juan.

Es **obvio** que Juan tendrá que ir a la escuela sin ducharse. Juan no está **acostumbrado** a ir a la escuela sin ducharse. **Derrotado**, Juan sube a su **habitación**, se cambia de ropa y luego **baja** las **escaleras nuevamente** para ir al **comedor** dónde su desayuno le espera. Es un desayuno que a él le **encanta**. **Avena** con **cereal** y **gofres** con **mucha miel**.

Su mamá sabe cómo levantarle el ánimo. Gofres es el desayuno favorito de Juan. A Juan le gusta tanto los gofres que en ocasiones él ha pedido a su mamá que ponga gofres en su lonchera. Ahora, en el desayuno, Juan le pide que ponga bastante miel a los gofres.

"**Buenos días**, Juan" – dice la **abuela** de Juan.

"Buenos días, abuela" – responde Juan. - ¡**Muchas gracias** por los gofres, mamá, son mis **favoritos**!"

"**De nada**, hijo" – responde su mamá.

Juan **come** tan **rápido como puede** su desayuno y se **alista** para **ir** a la escuela. Él **sabe** que si no llega temprano, puede **meterse en problemas**. Pero no se **preocupa** mucho ya que **hoy día** su papá lo llevará en su **auto**.

El auto que su papá tiene es uno nuevo. A Juan le parece muy bonito el carro de su papá. Su papá compró ese auto hace sólo unos meses. Juan también sueña con comprarse un auto cuando él crezca. Pero antes de eso, él tiene que aprender a conducir. Todo eso es lo que piensa mientras toma su desayuno. Después de unos minutos, su mamá le dice que se apure porque puede llegar tarde.

"Ya **terminé**, mamá"

"Entonces entra al auto de tu papá ya" – responde la mamá de Juan.

Juan sale **corriendo** del comedor. Sale tan rápido que se **olvida** su **lonchera**. Pero felizmente, su mamá le **avisa** y Juan **regresa** para **coger** su lonchera. Con un **beso**, se **despide** de su mamá y de su abuela.

"**Adiós**, mamá"

"**Adiós,** hijo, **pórtate bien**" – responde su mamá

"**Nos vemos luego**" – **grita** su abuela

"Entra al auto, hijo" – le dice su papá.

"Ahí voy" – dice Juan

Juan **abre** la puerta, entra al auto, se **abrocha** el cinturón y se **pone cómodo**. Su papá **hace lo mismo** pero **además pone música**. Juan **conoce** muy bien esa **canción**. Es una canción que el papá de Juan siempre pone cuando va a **trabajar**.

"**Sube el volumen**, papá"

"**Claro**, hijo"

A Juan también le gusta mucho la canción, por eso le dice a su papá que suba el volumen. Ir en el auto de su papá es también algo que le encanta Juan. Desde que él era **pequeño**, su papá llevaba a toda la familia de **paseo** a la **playa** en el auto. Hoy día, él no está en camino a la playa. Lo mejor de todo es que cuando él va a la escuela en al auto de su papá, el viaje no toma más de 20 minutos, lo que **asegura** que Juan llegará no sólo a tiempo a la escuela, pero también mucho **más temprano** que sus **compañeros**.

La escuela a la que Juan va es una escuela muy grande. La escuela también es antigua. En la escuela de Juan, los profesores enseñan muy bien y a Juan le gusta ir a esa escuela. Él tiene muchos amigos en esta escuela. Una de las cosas que a Juan le gusta de esta escuela es que hay bastantes cosas que hacer, tiene un campo de futbol enorme y sus amigos siempre le ayudan con su tarea si él necesita tarea.

Finalmente, Juan y su papá llegan a la escuela. Su papá lo **deja** en la escuela pero antes le dice:

"¡**Hasta pronto**, hijo! ¡**Nos vemos** en la casa!"

A lo que Juan responde: "¿Vendrás a **recogerme después de clases**?"

"No podré, hijo. ¿Puedes **tomar el bus**?" – responde su papá.

"Claro, papá" – dice Juan.

"¿Tienes **suficiente** para el **pasaje de bus**?" – pregunta el papá de Juan.

"Sí, mi mamá me dio **dinero** para el bus"

Juan se despide de su papá y entra a la escuela. **Como era de esperarse**, no hay muchos **alumnos** aún, pero Juan sabe que **pronto** sus compañeros de clase **llegarán**. Él sabe que será un día **divertido** en la escuela.

La hora de entrada en la escuela de Juan es a las 8:30 de la mañana. Juan llegó hoy día media hora antes de la hora de entrada. Normalmente, no hay nadie a esa hora más que algunos profesores y a veces, algunos alumnos que les gusta llegar temprano. Juan tiene toda la escuela para él. Mientras él espera a que las clases comiencen, él se pone a jugar en el campo de fútbol. De repente, él ve una figura que viene de adentro de la escuela.

"Juan, ¿qué haces aquí tan temprano?"

Juan escucha una voz que viene desde dentro de la escuela. Es su **mejor amigo**, Andrés.

"Vine en el auto de mi papá y él me dejó aquí en la escuela" – responde Juan

"¿Quieres venir a **jugar** conmigo mientras **esperamos** a los **demás**?" – le dice Andrés

"Claro, ¡**Vamos ya!**"

Resumen de la historia

Un muchacho de 14 años llamado Juan empieza su día queriendo tomar una ducha pero se da cuenta que su hermana está en baño y tomará demasiado tiempo, así que decide salir a la escuela sin tomarse una ducha. Después del desayuno, Juan sube al auto de papá. El viaje en el auto de su papá es tan rápido que Juan llega a la escuela mucho antes que sus otros compañeros de clase. Finalmente, él escucha a un compañero llamándolo, por lo que Juan entra a jugar con él.

Summary of the story

A 14-year-old boy called Juan starts his day wanting to have a shower but he realizes that his sister is in the bathroom and will take a long time, so he decides to go to school without taking a shower. After breakfast, Juan gets into his father's car. The trip in his dad's car is so fast that Juan arrives at school way earlier than his other classmates. Finally, he hears one of his classmates calling him, so Juan enters to play with him.

- **Día:** día
- **Como cualquier otro:** Like any other
- **Muchacho:** Boy
- **Alto:** Tall
- **Cabello:** Hair
- **Corto:** Short
- **Tez:** Skin
- **Blanca:** White
- **Gusta:** Like
- **Levantarse:** Get up
- **Temprano:** Early
- **Escuela:** School
- **Padres:** Parents
- **Siempre:** Always
- **Puntual:** Punctual
- **Responsable:** Responsible
- **Escucha:** Listen
- **Bostezando:** Yawning
- **Estirándose:** Stretching
- **Cama:** Bed
- **Baja:** Go down
- **Escaleras**: Stairs
- **Baño:** Bathroom
- **Tomar una ducha:** Take a shower
- **De repente:** Suddenly
- **Buenos días:** Good morning
- **Hijo:** Son

- **Voz:** Voice
- **Alta:** High
- **Me alegro:** I'm glad
- **A tiempo:** On-time
- **Mamá:** Mother
- **Responde:** Answers
- **Desayuno:** Breakfast
- **Listo:** Ready
- **Mesa:** Table
- **Anuncia:** Announces
- **Gracias:** Thank you
- **Primero:** First
- **Dado cuenta:** Realized
- **Luz:** Light
- **Baño:** Bathroom
- **Encendida:** On
- **Había:** There were
- **Ruidos:** Noises
- **Familiares:** Familiar
- **Cantando:** Singing
- **Hermana:** Sister
- **Tardar:** Take long
- **Pregunta:** Ask
- **Respuesta:** Answer
- **Puede:** Can
- **Tocar la puerta:** Knock on the door
- **Una vez más:** One more time
- **Cuánto tiempo:** How long
- **También:** Also
- **Quiero:** Want
- **Dame:** Give me
- **Minutos:** Minutes
- **Esperar:** Wait

- **Opción:** Option
- **Papá:** Dad
- **Felizmente:** Thankfully
- **Cambiarte:** Change
- **Ropa:** Clothe
- **Desayunas:** Have breakfast
- **Queja:** Complain
- **Jocosamente:** Jokingly
- **Obvio:** Obvious
- **Acostumbrado:** Used to
- **Derrotado:** Defeated
- **Habitación:** Bedroom
- **Nuevamente:** Again
- **Comedor:** Dining room
- **Encanta:** Love
- **Avena:** Oatmeal
- **Cereal:** Cereal
- **Gofres:** Waffles
- **Mucha:** A lot
- **Miel:** Honey
- **Abuela:** Grandmother
- **Muchas gracias:** Thank you very much
- **Favoritos:** Favorite
- **De nada:** You're welcome
- **Come:** Eat
- **Rápido:** Fast
- **Como puede:** As you can
- **Alista:** Get ready
- **Ir:** Go
- **Sabe:** Know
- **Meterse en problemas:** Get into trouble
- **Preocupa:** Worry
- **Hoy día:** Today

- **Auto:** Car
- **Terminé:** Finish
- **Corriendo:** Running
- **Olvida:** Forget
- **Lonchera:** Lunch
- **Avisa:** Tell
- **Regresa:** Return
- **Coger:** Pick up/ Take
- **Beso:** Kiss
- **Despide:** Say goodbye
- **Adiós:** Goodbye
- **Pórtate bien:** Behave yourself
- **Nos vemos luego:** See you later
- **Grita:** Yell
- **Abre:** Open
- **Abrocha el cinturón:** Fasten the seatbelt
- **Ponte cómodo:** Get comfortable
- **Hace lo mismo:** Do the same
- **Además:** Also
- **Pone música:** Play music
- **Conoce:** Know
- **Trabajar:** Work
- **Sube el volumen:** Turn up the volume
- **Claro:** Sure
- **Pequeño:** Little
- **Paseo:** Trip
- **Playa:** Beach
- **Más temprano:** Earlier
- **Compañeros:** Classmates
- **Finalmente:** Finally
- **Deja:** Let
- **Recogerme:** Pick me up
- **Después de clases:** After school

- **Tomar el bus:** Take the bus
- **Suficiente:** Enough
- **Pasaje de bus:** Bus fare
- **Dinero:** Money
- **Como era de esperarse:** As it was expected
- **Alumnos:** Students
- **Pronto:** Soon
- **Llegarán:** Come
- **Divertido:** Fun
- **Mejor amigo:** Best friend
- **Jugar:** lay
- **Esperamos:** Wait
- **Demás:** others
- **¡Vamos ya!:** Let's go!

Chapter 2: Numbers

Rosa fue al **supermercado** al que siempre iba cada vez que **necesitaba** hacer las compras para la **semana**. Rosa es una mujer muy **organizada**. Ella siempre escribe en una **libreta** lo que va a **comprar** ese día en el supermercado para no **olvidarse**. **Usualmente**, ella va a comprar todos los **martes**, ya que es él día en que ella no trabaja. Comprar para la semana puede ser una **tarea** muy **difícil**, pero **afortunadamente** rosa ya se acostumbró a hacerlo **sola**.

Rosa vive en una zona muy tranquila de la ciudad. A ella le gusta vivir aquí. Ella se mudó a este vecindario hace tres años. Cerca de su vecindario ella puede encontrar el supermercado. El supermercado al que Rosa va todos los martes es un supermercado nuevo.

Rosa se **alista**, coge su bolsa y toma el bus. La **estación del bus** está a solo 1 **cuadra** de la casa de Rosa.

"¡Buenos días!" – dice Rosa al **chofer** del bus

"¡Buenos días!" - responde el chofer a Rosa

"¿Cuánto está el **pasaje de bus**?" – pregunta Rosa

"Está 1 dólar con **veinte centavos**"

Con una **sonrisa** en el **rostro**, Rosa saca su **billetera** y **empieza** a buscar unas cuantas **monedas** para **pagar** el pasaje del bus. Pero no **encuentra** ninguna **moneda**.

El pasaje de bus es muy barato. Rosa ha escuchado que en otras ciudades el pasaje está el doble o incluso más. El pasaje de bus en la anterior ciudad en la que Rosa vivía costaba 2 dólares. A veces, el pasaje subía de precio sin razón.

"¡O, no! ¡De seguro **olvidé** las monedas antes de **salir** de casa!" – **Piensa** Rosa **dentro de sí misma.**

Después de buscar en su billetera por alguna moneda, Rosa no encuentra ninguna. **Felizmente**, Rosa había **guardado** unos **billetes** en su billetera. Ella tiene que preguntar ahora si se aceptan billetes.

"¿Tiene **cambio** de 10?"

El chofer **mueve** la **cabeza**, **indicándole** que sí, él sí tiene **suficiente** cambio para un billete de diez dólares. Después de dar el **cambio** a Rosa, el chofer le indica que **tome un asiento**.

"**Disfrute del viaje**" – dice el chofer.

A veces, Rosa quisiera comprarse un auto. La verdad es que comprarse un auto está fuera de los planes de Rosa ya que un auto puede ser muy caro. Varias veces, Rosa ha preguntado a sus amigos e incluso a algunos familiares lo que costaría comprar un auto nuevo, pero vez tras vez, ella ha ido recibiendo la misma respuesta: es demasiado caro comprarse un **auto** nuevo.

Eso no **significa** que Rosa se ha rendido. Ella sigue ahorrando para comprarse un auto nuevo. ¿Qué hay de autos usados? Bueno, Rosa solía tener un auto usado hace varios años. Ella solía usarlo para ir a **trabajar**. Después de que ella dejo su trabajo, ella vendió ese auto. Con el dinero de la venta, ella se compró un departamento en la zona donde ella ahora está viviendo.

Ella se prometió a sí misma que no volvería a comprarse una ut usado. ¿Por qué? Porque el **auto** que Rosa solía usar para ir a trabajar tenía bastantes fallas. Ella tenía que llevarlo constantemente al taller y ella usualmente pagaba bastante dinero para tener el carro reparado.

Ella no quería volver a gastar tanto **dinero** para reparar un **auto**. Así que cuando ella empezó a vivir en su nuevo apartamento, ella dejó de pensar en **conducir**. Ella no puede dejar de fantasear sobre cómo sería su viaje si tuviese un **auto**.

Mientras Rosa está sentada en el bus, **se le ocurre** coger su lista de compras y ver que **artículos** comprará para la semana. Es una **lista** muy **larga**. Ella compra **teniendo en mente** a sus **dos hijos** y también a sus **tres mascotas**. Rosa empieza a leer de la lista:

- "Un **kilogramo** de **azúcar**
- **Medio kilogramo** de **sal**
- **Cinco latas** de **atún enlatado**
- 250 kilogramos de **ajo**
- 4 **kilos** de **cebolla**
- Un **kilo y medio** de **plátano**..."

Rosa para de **leer** su lista y se **da cuenta** que su **teléfono celular** empezó a **sonar**. El teléfono de Rosa es un teléfono **muy moderno**, pero Rosa aún no **sabe usarlo** muy bien. Por eso, le toma un poco de tiempo **responder** la llamada. Cuando **finalmente** Rosa **contesta**, una **voz** muy **familiar** se escucha **diciendo**:

"Hola, Rosa, **soy** Mariana"

Rosa **sonríe** y responde – "Mariana, ¡**qué gusto** escuchar de ti!

"Gracias, Rosa quiero **contarte** que **acabo de mudarme** a una **nueva casa** y **pensaba** que tal vez **te gustaría visitarme**" – dice Mariana

"**Me encantaría. ¿Dónde estás viviendo ahora?**

"Mi **nueva dirección** es 452 calle Las Palmeras"

"¿Es esa **realmente** tu **dirección**? Yo vivo en la 862 de la **misma** calle. Eso **significa** que ahora somos **vecinas**" - dice Rosa.

"Así es. Bueno vecina, tengo que **colgar** la llamada. Estoy **cocinando**. Te **llamo luego**"

Muy **alegre**, Rosa **guarda** su **celular** en su bolsillo. Han pasado **tantos años desde** que ella y Mariana se **encuentran**. ¡Y ahora **resulta** que son vecinas! Sólo 4 cuadras las **separa**.

"Eso es **sólo** 7 u 8 minutos **caminando**. En **bicicleta** sólo me tomaría 5 **minutos** o **incluso menos**." – piensa Rosa.

Pero **antes** de **seguir**, ella tiene que **anotar** el **número** de Mariana. Rosa no quiere **olvidarse** del número de Mariana, así que ella lo anota **de inmediato**. El número de Mariana es un poco **largo**. Pero Rosa lo anota **de todas maneras**. El número es 252 555 7812. Después de anotar el número, **Rosa ve por la ventana** y **se da cuenta** que está **a punto de llegar** al supermercado. Sólo **tres paraderos de bus** más.

En el camino al supermercado, Rosa puede notar que hay **muchísimas personas saliendo** a **estudiar** o **trabajar. A mitad del camino** hacia el supermercado, hay una escuela enorme. No es la primera vez que ella ve esta escuela, pero es la primera vez que ve que hay bastantes alumnos. Muchos de ellos son jóvenes y niños. Ella empieza a recordad como era su vida cuando ella estaba también ene colegio. Ella se graduó de la escuela hace muchos años. Ahora son sus sobrinos los que van a la escuela. Ellos no van a esta escuela pero ellos han estado **pensando** en mudarse a esta zona también. Si ellos se llagan a mudar aquí, entonces tendrán que **asistir** a esta escuela. Rosa aun no puede dejar de asombrarse por la **cantidad** de alumnos que ve.

"De seguro hay más de **dos mil quinientos alumnos**."

En el bus también hay **bastantes** personas. Muchas de las personas que están el bus **con** a Rosa están en camino al trabajo. El bus en el cual Rosa está tiene **por lo menos** 50 **asientos**. **Eso significa** que hay **capacidad** para 50 personas. Rosa está **contenta** de haber encontrado un asiento **disponible**.

"Sólo falta un paradero para el supermercado" – **anuncia** el chofer.

Rosa se **prepara** para bajar del bus. Ella se **levanta** de su asiento pero todo el cambio que el chofer le dio se le **cae** y todas las **monedas ruedan** a varios **lugares** del bus.

"¡No puede ser! Por favor, **ayúdenme** a **recoger** mis monedas" – dice Rosa **preocupadamente**.

"Recuerde que le di ocho dólares con ochenta centavos de cambio" – le dice el chofer.

"Gracias"

Todas las personas se levantan de sus asientos para ayudar **amablemente** a recoger las monedas de Rosa. Ellos entregan las monedas a Rosa y Rosa les **agradece**.

"**Acá** hay 4 monedas" – dice un pasajero

"**Aquí** le **traje** 16 monedas" – dice otro pasajero

Poco a poco, Rosa recupera todas las monedas que se le cayeron.

"**Llegamos** al supermercado" – anuncia el chofer

Rosa guarda su dinero, **baja** del bus y **da las gracias** al chofer. El paradero del supermercado es muy limpio. Ahora ella tiene que **entrar** al supermercado y **comprar** todo lo que **necesita**.

"Espero poder **encontrar** lo que tengo que **comprar**; **si no**, **tendré** que ir al **centro comercial** que está a 20 minutos **de aquí**"

Ella se acerca a la puerta del mercado y se da cuenta que está cerrada. Ella no entiende por qué el mercado está cerrado. Entonces, una persona se le acerca y le dice que no se preocupe.

"El mercado no está cerrado."

"Entonces, ¿qué ocurrió? ¿Por qué esta puerta está cerrada?"

"Es porque están reparando las tuberías de las tiendas que están cerca a estas puertas. Las han cerrado para que no haya accidentes."

"Entonces, ¿cómo puedo entrar al mercado si las puertas están cerradas?"

"Tiene que seguir caminando. Si sigue caminando usted encontrará otras puertas. Esas puertas deben seguir abiertas."

"Muchas gracias por ayudarme"

"De nada"

Rosa sigue caminando y, tal como la persona le había dicho, ella encuentra dos puertas grandes. Esas dos puertas grandes estaban abiertas y todas las personas que quieran entrar al mercado tenían que entrar por esas puertas.

Rosa entra y empieza a comprar todo lo que ella escribo en la lista. Felizmente, ella encuentra todos los productos. Aunque ella no ha vivido tanto tiempo aquí como sus otros vecinos, ella ya conoce dónde comprar y que productos son los mejores.

Después de terminar de comprar todos los productos, ella tiene que tomar el bus de regreso a casa. Ella sale del mercado y va al paradero de bus. Ella espera 1 bus que llegue. Finalmente el bus llega. Rosa aun no puede dejar de pensar en cómo sería su vida si tuviera un auto.

Al final, Rosa vuelve a casa con todas las compras. Ella empieza a ordenar y a seguir con los quehaceres de la casa.

Resumen de la historia

Rosa es una mujer que decide ir al supermercado para comprar lo que ella necesita para la semana. Durante su viaje al supermercado, ella recibe una llamada que la distrae. Ella se prepara para bajar del bus, pero desafortunadamente, todo su dinero se cae al suelo. Los otros pasajeros amablemente la ayudan a recuperar todo su dinero. Finalmente ella baja del bus para ir a comprar al supermercado

Summary of the story

Rosa is a woman who decided to go to the supermarket to buy what she needs for the week. During her trip to the supermarket, she receives a call that distracts her. She then gets ready to get off the bus, but unfortunately, all her money falls to the ground. The other passengers kindly help her and she recovers all her money. She finally gets off the bus to go to the supermarket.

- **Supermercado: Supermarket**
- **Necesitaba: Need**
- **Semana: Week**
- **Organizada: Organized**
- **Libreta: Notebook**
- **Comprar: buy**
- **Olvidarse: forget**
- **Usualmente: usually**
- **Martes: Tuesdays**
- **Tarea: Task**
- **Difícil: difficult**
- **Afortunadamente: fortunately**
- **Alista: gets ready**
- **Estación de bus: bus stop**
- **Cuadra: block**
- **Chofer: driver**
- **Pasaje de bus: bus fare**
- **Veinte: twenty**
- **Centavos: cents**
- **Sonrisa: smile**
- **Rostro: face**
- **Billetera: wallet**

- Empieza: starts
- Monedas: coins
- Pagar: pay
- Encuentra: finds
- Olvidé: I forgot
- Salir: go out
- Piensa: thinks
- Dentro de sí misma: within herself
- Después: after
- Felizmente: fortunately
- Guardado: kept
- Billetes: bills
- Cambio: change
- Mueve: move
- Cabeza: head
- Indicándole: indicating to her
- Suficiente: enough
- Tome un asiento: have a seat
- Disfrute del viaje: enjoy the trip
- Mientras: while
- Se le ocurre: It occurred to her
- Artículos: Items
- Lista: list
- Larga: long
- Teniendo en mente: having in mind
- Dos: two
- Hijos: children
- Tres: three
- Mascotas: pets
- Kilogramo: kilogram
- Azúcar: sugar
- Medio kilogramo: half a kilogram
- Sal: salt

- Cinco: five
- Latas: cans
- Atún enlatado: canned tuna
- Ajo: garlic
- Kilos: kilos
- Cebolla: onion
- Un kilo y medio: a kilogram and a half
- Plátano: banana
- Leer: read
- Da cuenta: realizes
- Teléfono celular: cellphone
- Sonar: rings
- Muy: very
- Moderno: modern
- Sabe: knows
- Usarlo: use it
- Responder: answer
- Finalmente: finally
- Voz: voice
- Familiar: familiar
- Diciendo: saying
- Soy: I am
- Sonríe: smile
- ¡Qué gusto!: how nice!
- Contarte: tell you
- Acabo de mudarme: I have already moved
- Nueva: new
- Casa: house
- Pensaba: thought
- Te gustaría: would you like
- Visitarme: visit me
- Me encantaría: I'd love to
- Donde estás viviendo: where are you living

- Ahora: now
- Dirección: address
- Realmente: really
- Calle: street
- Significa: means
- Vecinas: neighbors
- Colgar: hang up
- Cocinando: cooking
- Llamo: call
- Luego: later
- Alegre: happy
- Guarda: keep
- Celular: cellphone
- Tantos años: so many years
- Desde: since
- Encuentra: meet
- Resulta: turns out
- Sólo: only
- Caminando: walking
- Bicicleta: bicycle
- Minutos: minutes
- Incluso menos: even less
- Antes: before
- Seguir: continue
- Anotar: write down
- Numero: number
- Olvidarse: forget
- De inmediato: immediately
- Largo: long
- De todas maneras: anyway
- Ve por la ventana: look through the window
- A punto de llegar: about to arrive
- Paraderos de bus: bus stops

- En el camino: on the way
- Muchísimas: too many
- Personas: people
- Saliendo: going out
- Estudiar: study
- Trabajar: work
- A mitad del camino: halfway through
- Bastantes: a lot
- Con: with
- Por lo menos: at least
- Asientos: seats
- Eso significa: that means
- Capacidad: capacity
- Disponible: available
- Prepara: gets ready
- Levanta: gets up
- Cae: falls
- Monedas: coins
- Ruedan: roll
- Lugares: places
- Ayúdenme: help me
- Recoger: pick up
- Preocupadamente: worryingly
- Todas: all
- Amablemente: kindly
- Agradece: thanks
- Acá: here
- Aquí: here
- Traje: bring
- Poco a poco: Little by little
- Llegamos: we have arrived
- Baja: get off
- Da las gracias: give thanks

- **Entrar: go in**
- **Comprar: buy**
- **Necesita: needs**
- **Encontrar: finds**
- **Si no: if not**
- **Tendré: have to**
- **Centro comercial: mall**
- **De aquí: from here**

Chapter 3: Past tense

El pequeño José está **sentado** en la **sala**. **A pesar** de que sólo tiene 8 años, José es un niño muy **curioso**. A él le encanta ver el **álbum de fotos** de sus **abuelos**. A él le gusta mucho ver las **fotos** ya que parecen **de otro mundo**. Las **ropas** que las **personas** usan en esas fotos le parecen a José muy **raras** y también muy **divertidas**. ¡Algunas fotos incluso están en **blanco y negro**!

José **llama** a su abuelo para que le pueda **explicar** cuando se **tomaron** esas fotos:

"¿Por qué las fotos están en blanco y negro?" – pregunta José **curiosamente**

"Es porque estas fotos son muy **antiguas**, José." – responde su abuelo.

José ve más fotos y continúa preguntando a su abuelo sobre ellas. José encuentra una foto en la que **aparece** su abuelo. A José le gusta mucho esa foto.

"¿Qué **estabas** haciendo aquí, abuelo?"

El abuelo de José **coge** la foto y la **acerca** a su rostro. Desafortunadamente, con el pasar de los años, el abuelo de José ha estado **perdiendo** la **vista**. El abuelo de José tiene 80 años y ahora necesita **lentes** para poder **ver** bien. Felizmente, no tiene ningún otro **problema** de **salud**. Después de ver la foto por unos **segundos**, el abuelo de José empieza a explicar lo que él hacía en esa foto.

"Era mi **primer** día de **escuela** cuando era un niño. Recuerdo que era un día muy **caluroso**. Por eso me ves con **pantalones cortos** y un **polo**. En esta foto estaba cogiendo mis **libros** de la escuela también"

"¿Dónde era tu **colegio**, abuelo?" – pregunta José

"Mi colegio se encontraba ubicado a sólo 15 minutos de aquí. Yo iba **caminando**. Después, compré una **bicicleta** y empecé a manejar mi **bicicleta** al colegio" – responde el abuelo

"¿Qué pasó con tu **bicicleta**? ¿La **regalaste**?" – pregunta José

"Usé mi bicicleta por varios años. Mi papá me **ayudaba** a **repararla**, él fue quien me **enseñó** a manejarla. Después de mucho tiempo, finalmente mi bicicleta se **malogró** y no pude **usarla** más."

"¿La **botaste**, abuelo?"

"Sí, José"

José **sigue** mirando las fotos. Después de voltear **algunas páginas**, él **para** a ver una foto que **llama** su **atención**. Es una foto **grande**. A pesar de ser una foto muy grande, solo aparecen dos personas. Una de esas personas es una **mujer**, es una mujer muy **alta** y **delgada**. Lleva puesto un **vestido** muy **largo** y de color **blanco**. Con mucha curiosidad, José pregunta una vez más a su abuelo.

"¿Quién es ella, abuelo?"

"Ella es tu **abuela**, José" – responde el abuelo

"¿Ese eres tú, abuelo?" – pregunta José una vez más

"Sí, así es. Esa foto la tomamos cuando tu abuela y yo nos **casamos** hace 42 años. Aún me **acuerdo** mucho de ese día. Yo **estaba** muy **nervioso** y tu abuela también lo estaba. La **boda** fue en el **jardín** de esta **casa**. Había muchos **invitados**. **Nuestros amigos** y **familiares** nos **trajeron** muchos **regalos**. Lo **disfrutamos** bastante.

"¿Es verdad que las personas **bailan** en una boda?" – pregunta José

"Es cierto"

"¿Y ustedes también bailaron?"- pregunta José

"¡Nosotros bailamos por **horas**! Las bodas son **ocasiones** muy **alegres** y **divertidas**. A tu abuela le **encantaba** bailar. Ella **escogió** las canciones para la boda." – responde el abuelo"

El abuelo de José encuentra una foto muy **peculiar**. El abuelo piensa que tal vez esa foto le gusta a José ya que alguien muy **familiar aparece** en esa foto. ¿Podrá José **darse cuenta** de quién se trata?

"Mira la siguiente foto. ¿Puedes **adivinar** quién es la persona que aparece en la foto?" – le dice el abuelo a José

José se queda mirando la foto **detenidamente**. La examina una y otra vez, pero tal parece que él no puede adivinar quién es, así que José ahora pregunta.

"¿Quién es ese niño?"

"Es tu papá. Tomé esta foto cuando tu papá tenía 10 años. Él se **parecía** mucho a ti"

El álbum de fotos que José tiene en sus manos es muy grande. Las fotos que ve lo dejan **maravillado**. Al abuelo de José le gusta recordar los viejos tiempos cuando él era **joven**. Es verdad que han pasado muchos años, pero el abuelo de José aún **mantiene** esa misma **energía** que tenía cuando era sólo un niño.

"Este fue el **primer** auto que compré. Lo compré cuando tenía 20 años" – añade el abuelo

José escucha con mucha atención a su abuelo. Se **sorprende** que su abuelo sepa tanto sobre bicicletas, autos, su papá. ¡A José le parece que el abuelo ha vivido desde **siempre**!

"En ese entonces, no teníamos internet. Si queríamos buscar **información**, teníamos que ir a la **biblioteca**. Tampoco teníamos **televisión** ni **cable**" – añade el abuelo.

"¿Y no se **aburrían**?" – pregunta José

"Para nada. Nos gustaba salir a **caminar** y **jugar** con nuestros **amigos**. Cuando **llegábamos** a casa, **leíamos** un **libro** o **escuchábamos** la **radio**" – responde el abuelo

Es increíble que el abuelo de José aún pueda **recordar** todas estas cosas. Es como si todos los recuerdos estuviesen **intactos** en su cabeza. Ahora, el abuelo empieza a **mostrarle** como se usaba la radio. El abuelo de José aún mantiene su **antigua radio** en la sala, así que no es **difícil** encontrarla. José ayuda a su abuelo a **limpiar** la antigua radio y la **conectan**. Es una radio muy grande, de color **marrón** y con tan sólo dos **botones**. Tiene una **antena** muy larga y José **no tiene idea** de porque una **radio** necesita **antena**. El abuelo le explica que es para **captar** la señal de radio.

Después de **conectarla**, intentan **encenderla**. **Lamentablemente**, la radio ya no **funciona**. La radio dejó de funcionar hace muchos años. Pero el abuelo pensó que esta vez sí iba a funcionar.

"Mejor **sigamos** viendo **más** fotos, abuelo" – dice José

"¿**De verdad** quieres seguir viendo las fotos, José? – pregunta el abuelo.

"Sí. **Es divertido** cuando tú me **cuentas tus historias**, abuelo"

El abuelo de José le cuenta más **historias** sobre lo que él hacía cuando era un niño. El abuelo le cuenta que antes, ellos tenían que viajar en barco en lugar de avión. A José eso le parece muy extraño. Él nunca ha viajado en avión. ¿Qué tan extraño es? Bueno, José le empieza a preguntar cómo eran los barcos cuando él era joven.

"¿Eran los barcos muy grandes, como en las **películas**?"

"No todos. Si ibas muy lejos e iban **bastantes personas**, entonces los barcos eran muy **grandes**. Pero si sólo ibas a pescar, entonces los barcos eran **pequeños**."

"¿Tú sabías **conducir** un barco?"

"No, José. Nunca aprendí a conducir un barco"

"¿Por qué no?"

"Porque es muy difícil"

"Pero, ¿sabes pescar?"

"Eso sí. Incluso le enseñé a tu papá a **pescar**"

"Mi papá también me enseño a pescar. Él me llevaba todos los domingos al lago para pescar"

El **abuelo** de José ahora le pregunta a su nieto como hace él las cosas. José es un **niño** muy **inteligente**. José corre a traer a su abuelo su reporte de notas y le hace ver que él ha aprobado todas las **materias**.

"Muy bien José. Me alegro por ti"

"Gracias, abuelo"

El **abuelo** de José va a la cocina y empieza a buscar las galletas que él había guardado ayer. Él las había comprado pensando en José. A José le gusta mucho las galletas de chocolate. Por eso, el abuelo compro bastantes galletas de chocolate para compartir con José. Lo que José no sabe es que al **abuelo** también le gustan mucho las galletas de chocolate.

El **abuelo** encuentra las galletas y empieza a poner algunas en un plato. También, él empieza a preparar leche. José ama las galletas con chocolate. El **abuelo** las lleva donde está José y ambos se ponen a comer.

"¿Dónde compraste estas galletas, **abuelo**?" – pregunta José

"Las compré en el **supermercado**. Tu mamá me ayudó a comprarlas"

"¿Ella te **ayudó** a comprarlas? ¿Cómo?"

"Ella me dio el **dinero** para comprarlas. Estas galletas están un poco caras"

"¿Cuánto cuestan estas **galletas**, abuelo?"

"No te lo puedo decir. Recuerdo que en mis tiempos, las **galletas** no estaban tan caras. Tu podías comprar galletas en todos lados y eran muy baratas"

"¿También había galletas de chocolate en tus tiempos, abuelo?"

"Déjame contarte sobre eso"

"Dime abuelo"

"En mis tiempos no habían muchas galletas de chocolate, pero si habían galletas de vainilla. Las galletas de chocolates, aunque pocas, eran baratas"

"¿Quién te compraba las galletas de **chocolate**, abuelo?"

"Me las compraba mi mamá. Luego yo empecé a **trabajar** y yo mismo empecé a comprármelas"

"¡Vaya, abuelo! Yo también quiero trabajar para comprarme galletas"

"No te preocupes, cuando crezcas vas a poder trabajar y comprar todas las galletas que quieras"

"Quiero crecer ya abuelo"

"No desesperes. Crecerás"

"¿En qué **trabajabas abuelo**?"

44

"Yo reparaba los techos de las **casas** y también los **baños** de las casas"

"¿Era difícil reparar los techos de las casas y los baños también?"

"Sí. Para reparar los **techos** de las casas, tienes que subir con una escalera al techo y ver cuál es el problema. Puedes tener una accidente si no tienes cuidado."

"¿Tú has tenido algún accidente mientras reparabas los techos, abuelo?"

"Sí, una vez me caí del techo de una casa. La casa era muy alta"

"¿Qué pasó después, abuelo?"

"Tuvieron que llevarme al **hospital**"

"¡Vaya! ¿Y dejaste de trabajar después de tu **accidente**?"

"No, después que salir del hospital seguí trabajando reparando los techos de las casas"

"Pero abuelo, ¿no volviste a tener una **accidente**?"

"Nunca más volví a tener un accidente, José. En realidad, a mí me gustaba reparar los techos de las casas. Era más fácil que reparar los baños de las casas"

"¿Tú fuiste quien reparó el baño de nuestra **casa, abuelo**?"

"No. Tu papá fue quien reparó el baño de la casa. Yo le enseñé a reparar el baño de la casa hace mucho tiempo"

"¿Por qué mi papá se demoró mucho tiempo en reparar el **baño**?"

"Porque no quería obedecerme. Él no quería seguir mis **instrucciones**."

"¿Me puedes enseñar a mí a reparar el **baño**, abuelo?"

"Claro. Verás que es muy fácil reparar el **baño**, José. Sólo tienes que usar guantes y traer todas las **herramientas** que vamos a usar."

"Yo sé dónde mi papá guarda todas sus **herramientas**. Si quieres podemos ir a verlas. ¿Quieres que te muestre, abuelo?"

"Claro. Vamos a verlas"

Resumen de la historia

José es un niño muy curioso que un día encuentra el álbum de fotos de sus abuelos. Asombrado por las fotos que ve en el álbum, José llama a su abuelo para que le ayude a entender lo que está pasando en las fotos. El abuelo de José le cuenta la historia detrás de algunas fotos y le muestra como encender una radio antigua. Después de ver que la radio no funciona, José y su abuelo continúan viendo más fotos del álbum. Al final, José y su abuelo continúan hablando sobre cómo era la vida en el tiempo del abuelo y como él enseño muchas cosas al papá de José

Summary of the story

José is a very curious kid that one day finds his grandparents' photo album. Amazed at the pictures he sees in the album, José calls his grandfather to help him understand what's going on in the pictures. José's grandfather tells him the stories behind some pictures and shows him how to turn on an old radio. After realizing that the radio doesn't work, José and his grandfather continue seeing more pictures from the album. In the end, José and his grandfather continue talking about how life was in the days of his granddad and how he taught José's dad many things.

- **Sentado: seated**
- **Sala: living room**
- **A pesar: even though**
- **Curioso: curious**
- **Álbum de fotos: photo album**
- **Abuelos: grandparents**
- **Fotos: pictures**
- **De otro mundo: from another world**
- **Ropas: clothes**
- **Personas: people**
- **Raras: rare**
- **Divertidas: funny**
- **Blanco y negro: black and white**
- **Llama: call**
- **Explicar: explain**
- **Tomaron: took**
- **Curiosamente: curiously**
- **Antiguas: old**
- **Aparece: appear**
- **Estabas: were**
- **Coge: took**
- **Acerca: approach**
- **Perdiendo: losing**
- **Vista: sight**
- **Lentes: glasses**

- Ver: see
- Problema: problem
- Salud: health
- Segundos: seconds
- Primer: first
- Escuela: school
- Caluroso: warm
- Pantalones cortos: short pants
- Polo: T-shirt
- Colegio: school
- Caminando: walking
- Bicicleta: bicycle
- Regalaste: give
- Ayudaba: help
- Repararla: fix
- Enseñó: taught
- Malogró: broke down
- Usarla: use it
- Botaste: threw away
- Sigue: continue
- Algunas: some
- Páginas: pages
- Para: stop
- Atención: attention
- Grande: big
- Alta: tall
- Delegada: thin
- Mujer: woman
- Vestido: dress
- Largo: long
- Abuela: grandmother
- Casamos: got married
- Acuerdo: remember

- Estaba: was
- Nervioso: nervous
- Boda: wedding
- Jardín: garden
- Casa: house
- Invitados: invited
- Nuestros: our
- Amigos: friends
- Familiares: relatives
- Trajeron: brought
- Regalos: gifts
- Disfrutamos: enjoyed
- Bailan: dance
- Horas: hours
- Ocasiones: occasions
- Alegres: joyful
- Encantaba: loved
- Escogió: chose
- Peculiar: peculiar
- Familiar: familiar
- Darse cuenta: realize
- Adivinar: guess
- Detenidamente: attentively
- Parecía: looked like
- Maravillado: amazed
- Joven: young
- Mantiene: keep
- Energía: energy
- Primer: first
- Sorprende: surprise
- Siempre: forever
- Información: information
- Biblioteca: library

- Televisión: TV
- Cable: cable
- Aburrían: got bored
- Caminar: walk
- Jugar: play
- Llegábamos: arrived
- Leíamos: read
- Libro: books
- Escuchábamos: listened to
- Radio: radio
- Intactos: intact
- Mostrarle: show it
- Antigua: old
- Radio: radio
- Difícil: difficult
- Limpiar: clean
- Conectan: connect
- Marrón: brown
- Botones: buttons
- Antena: antena
- No tiene idea: doesn't have an idea
- Captar: catch
- Conectarla: plug it
- Encenderla: turn it on
- Lamentablemente: unfortunately
- Funciona: works
- Sigamos: continue
- Más: more
- De verdad: really
- Cuentas: tell
- Tus: your
- Historias: stories

Chapter 4: Members of the Family

Sara estaba **haciendo** la tarea que la **profesora** de **Ciencias Sociales** dejó a la clase. Sara es una niña muy **inteligente**. Ella siempre **presenta** sus tareas **a tiempo** y normalmente no tiene ningún **problema** en hacerlas. Pero en esta ocasión, a Sara le parece que la tarea que dejó la profesora de Ciencias Sociales es un **poco complicada**. El tema es **sencillo**: el **árbol genealógico**. Pero la tarea **requiere** que Sara **investigue** sobre su **familia**. ¿A quién puede pedir **ayuda** Sara?

Felizmente, la mamá de Sara entra a la **habitación** de su hija y le pregunta si todo va bien con la tarea.

"**¿Cómo te va con** la tarea, hija? ¿Ya la terminaste?" – pregunta la mamá de Sara

"Bueno, **tengo** una tarea que no **puedo** hacer" - responde Sara

"¿Y cuál es esa tarea?"

Sara **saca** su **cuaderno** y le **muestra** a su mamá lo que la profesora le dejó. Su mamá sabe **exactamente** como **ayudar** a su hija. Primero le dice que vaya a coger una **hoja de papel** y un **lápiz**. Después de encontrar donde escribir, Sara le pregunta a su mamá como hacer un árbol genealógico.

"Bueno, hacer un árbol genealógico es sencillo. Déjame **explicarte**. Lo primero que tienes que hacer es **dibujar** el **tronco**. En el tronco, tienes que escribir el **nombre** de uno de **nuestros antepasados**."

Esa es una nueva **palabra** para Sara. Ella jamás había **escuchado** la palabra "**antepasado**". Curiosa como siempre, Sara le pregunta a su mamá.

"¿Qué significa antepasado?" – pregunta Sara

"Es una persona de la cual nosotros **descendemos**. Es decir, una persona que vivió mucho antes que nosotros y que es **parte** de nuestra familia" - responde la mamá de Sara.

Sara se pone a pensar.

"¿Qué nombre puedo **poner aquí**, entonces?"

"Puedes poner el nombre del abuelo"- responde su mamá

El abuelo de Sara es la persona con más **edad** que Sara conoce. Él tiene 87 años. A Sara eso le parece bastantes años. Sara se acuerda muy bien del nombre de su abuelo. Su abuelo se llama Raúl.

"Después de poner el nombre del abuelo, tienes que poner el nombre de tu **abuela**. Esos son los nombres de los abuelos de parte de tu papá. Mis padres son tus abuelos." – añade la mamá de Sara.

"Entonces ya tengo cuatro nombres"

"Ahora **dibuja** las **ramas** del árbol. En estas ramas tienes que escribir mi nombre y también el nombre de tu papá. Recuerda que tu papá no es **hijo único**, él tiene **hermanos**. ¿Te acuerdas cuántos **hermanos** tiene tu papá?" – le dice la mamá a Sara.

"Sí. Mi papá me dijo que él tiene 2 **hermanos** más. Él también me dijo que él es el **hermano mayor**"

"¿Te acuerdas de los nombres de los hermanos de tu papá?" – pregunta la mamá de Sara

"Sí. Juan y Fabricio." – responde Sara

"Ellos son tus **tíos**. Tienes que escribir sus nombres en las ramas que salen de los nombres de tus abuelos. Escribe sus nombres **cerca** del nombre de tu papá"

Sara **obedece** a su mamá y escribe los nombres de sus abuelos y sus tíos, pero el árbol aún no está **completo**.

"Ahora tienes que escribir mi nombre en otra rama."

"Ya lo hice, mamá" – le dice Sara.

Sara recuerda también que su mamá no tiene **hermanos** ni **hermanas**, así que no necesita dibujar otras ramas que salgan de los nombres de sus abuelos. ¿Qué es lo que tiene que hacer ahora Sara?

Su mamá le dice: "Ahora tienes que poner el nombre de todos tus **primos**"

¿El nombre de todos sus primos? Sara tiene bastantes primos. Son **muchísimos**. Ella sabe que su tío Juan tiene 3 **hijos** y 2 **hijas**. Entonces ahí van 5 primos de parte del tío Juan. El tío Fabricio sólo tiene 2 **hijas**.

Sara se acuerda muy bien del nombre de sus primas ya que ellas vienen a jugar con Sara durante las **vacaciones de verano**. Pero ella no se acuerda del nombre de sus primos.

"¿Cómo se llaman los hijos de mi tío Juan, mamá?" – pregunta Sara

"Ellos se llaman Luis, Ricardo y Emilio. Emilio es **el mayor** de todos." – responde su mamá

Sara se pone a **escribir** los nombres de sus primos. ¿**Faltará** algo que poner en el árbol genealógico? Bueno, aunque Sara es todavía una niña, ella ya es **tía**. Su primo Emilio está **casado** y tiene 1 hijo. Por lo tanto, Sara dibuja una rama que sale del nombre de Emilio y escribe el nombre de su **sobrino**.

"Ahora tienes que poner tu nombre debajo del nombre de tu papá y yo" – le dice su mamá

"Ahorita lo pongo"

"¿Quién más falta en la familia?" – pregunta la mamá de Sara

"¡Mi **hermano**!" – dice Sara.

Sara tiene un **hermano mayor** de 17 años. Él también estudia en la misma escuela que Sara. Sara escribe el nombre de su hermano y el **suyo** para así acabar la tarea.

"Ahora tienes que **pintarlo** con muchos **colores**"

La mamá de Sara le compró a su hija muchísimos **lápices de colores nuevos** hace sólo una **semana**. Ya llegó la hora de usarlos.

"¿De qué **color** vas a **pintar** el **árbol**? – pregunta la mamá

"Pintaré el tronco de marrón y las ramas también. Las hojas las **pintaré** de verde. También quiero **dibujar** el **cielo** y algunas **nubes**. Y unos **pajaritos** con sus **nidos** en el árbol." – responde Sara.

"Muy bien, te dejo haciendo tu tarea. Tengo que volver a la sala. Cuando termines de hacer toda tu tarea, me avisas." – añade su mamá

La mamá de Sara se va contenta de la habitación de su hija después de haberla ayudado con su tarea. Sara le agradece a su mamá y le dice que no **cierre** la **puerta**. A Sara le gusta **pintar**, así que tal parece ella va a **disfrutar** pintar su árbol genealógico.

Resumen de la historia

La profesora de Sara ha dejado a la clase la tarea de dibujar un árbol genealógico. Para ello, Sara pide la ayuda de su mamá. Su mamá le ayuda haciéndole recordar de todos sus familiares incluyendo sus tíos, primos e incluso hermano. Sara agradece la ayuda de su mamá y se pone a pintar el árbol genealógico con los lápices de colores que su mamá la había regalado

Summary of the story

Sara's teacher has left an assignment that consists of drawing a family tree. To that end, Sara asks her mother help. Her mom helps her reminding her of all the relatives including hers uncles, cousins and even brother. Sara thanks her mom's help and begins painting the family tree with the color pencils her mom had given her.

- **Haciendo: doing**
- **Profesora: teacher**
- **Ciencias Sociales: Social studies**
- **Inteligente: smart**
- **Presenta: presents**

- A tiempo: on time
- Problema: problem
- Poco: a little
- Complicada: compicated
- Sencillo: easy
- Árbol genealógico: family tree
- Requiere: requires
- Investigue: investigate
- Familia: family
- Ayuda: help
- Habitación: bedroom
- Como te va con: how's it going with
- Tengo: have
- Puedo: can
- Saca: take out
- Cuaderno: notebook
- Muestra: show
- Exactamente: exactly
- Ayudar: help
- Hoja de papel: paper sheet
- Lápiz: pencil
- Explicarte: explain to you
- Dibujar: draw
- Tronco: trunk
- Nuestros: our
- Antepasados: ancestors
- Palabra: word
- Escuchado: heard
- Descendemos: we descend
- Parte: part
- Poner: put
- Aquí: here
- Edad: age

- Abuela: grandmother
- Ramas: branches
- Hijo único: only child
- Hermanos: siblings
- Hermano mayor: older brother
- Cerca: near
- Obedece: obeys
- Completo: complete
- Hermanos: brothers
- Hermanas: sisters
- Muchísimos: too many
- Hijos: sons
- Hijas: daughters
- Vacaciones de verano: summer vacation
- El mayor: the eldest
- Escribir: write
- Faltará: missing
- Tía: aunt
- Casado: Married
- Sobrino: nephew
- Suyo: hers
- Pintarlo: paint it
- Colores: colors
- Lápices de colores: color pencils
- Nuevos: new
- Semana: week
- Color: color
- Pintar: paint
- Árbol: tree
- Pintaré: will paint
- Cielo: sky
- Nubes: clouds
- Pajaritos: birds

- **Nidos:** nests
- **Cierre:** close
- **Puerta:** door
- **Pintar:** paint
- **Disfrutar:** enjoy

Chapter 5: School Vocabulary

Diego y sus **compañeros de clase** están **conversando** en el **aula** mientras esperan que la profesora **venga**. En esta ocasión, la profesora se está **demorando** más de lo normal. Diego tiene 13 años y es un **nuevo estudiante**. Sus padres se acaban de **mudar** a esta ciudad y Diego aún no ha hecho muchos **amigos** en esta nueva escuela.

A Diego le gusta mucho su nueva escuela. Es **grande** y **espaciosa**. Tiene bastantes aulas. Parece nueva. Los **profesores** son muy **amables** y los compañeros lo tratan bien. Lo mejor de todo es que esta escuela está cerca de la casa de Diego. La anterior escuela a la que Diego **asistía** estaba muy **lejos** de su casa. A veces, le **tomaba** a Diego **media hora** en **llegar** a la escuela. Ahora, él puede venir a la escuela **incluso** en **bicicleta**.

Ser un nuevo estudiante puede ser muy **estresante**. Tus compañeros no te **conocen** y no conoces a tus profesores ni las **materias** que vas a tener. La materia que Diego debería tener ahora es **matemáticas**. Pero la profesora aún no llega.

"¿De dónde vienes, Diego?" – le pregunta uno de sus compañeros

"Vengo de Málaga" – responde Diego

"¿Cuándo te mudaste a esta ciudad?"

"Hace sólo dos **semanas**"

Diego sabe muy bien que la materia de matemáticas es muy importante. Por eso, él siempre hace su tarea a tiempo.

"¿Hiciste la **tarea** de matemáticas?" – pregunta el compañero a Diego

"Sí. Estaba **sencilla**. ¿Tú la hiciste?" – responde Diego

"Sí la hice. Pero al principio no entendía la tarea. Tuve que pedir ayuda a mi papá. Él también me ayudó a **estudiar** para el **examen** de hoy" – añade el compañero

"¿Qué? ¿**Había** un examen hoy día?" – exclama Diego

"Claro que sí. ¿No te **acuerdas**?"

Diego **nunca** deja de hacer su tarea. En esta ocasión, Diego hizo su tarea pero se olvidó de estudiar para el examen de matemáticas. ¿Qué hará Diego ahora? ¿Podrá estudiar todo en los pocos minutos que quedan para el examen?

"No te **preocupes**, puedes **copiar** de mi examen" – escucha Diego decir a su compañero

¿**Copiar**? A Diego nunca le ha agradado la idea de copiar de sus compañeros. Sus padres siempre le han enseñado a ser **honesto**. Por eso, **a pesar** de que Diego no ha estudiado para el examen de matemáticas, él no copiará.

"No quiero copiar. No me **gusta** copiar en el examen. Pero al menos sé que si la profesora no viene, no tomaremos el examen." – dice Diego

"Eso no es cierto"

"¿A qué te refieres?"

"Si la profesora no viene, entonces una **profesora sustituta** vendrá a la clase y tomará el examen." – dice el compañero a Diego

"¿En serio? ¡Vaya! **Intentaré** estudiar lo más que pueda ahora mismo."

La profesora sustituta entra al salón unos minutos después. Ella **explica** a la clase que la profesora de matemáticas no pudo venir y que ella va a **reemplazarla** hoy día. Después de tomar la **asistencia** a todos los alumnos, ella pasa a **recoger** las tareas. Luego, empieza a **escribir** en la **pizarra**. El tema de hoy día es **fracciones**, un tema que Diego conoce muy bien.

Diego y sus compañeros escriben en el cuaderno lo que la profesora explica y después sacan los libros de matemáticas de sus **mochilas**. La profesora escribe algunos **ejercicios** en la pizarra y saca al frente a varios estudiantes para que **resuelvan** los **problemas**. Diego saca una **nota aprobatoria**. Él nunca **desaprueba** matemáticas.

Llegó la hora del examen. La hora pasa **volando**. Los alumnos entregan los exámenes a la profesora y uno por uno se van **retirando** de la clase. **Suena** el **timbre** y llega la hora del **receso**.

En el **receso**, Diego y sus compañeros **empiezan** a **conversar** sobre el examen y sobre otras cosas:

"¿Qué te pareció el examen, Diego?" – pregunta un compañero

"No estudié así que me pareció un poco **difícil**" – dice Diego

Después de conversar sobre el examen. Empiezan a hablar sobre las materias que más les gusta.

"A mí me gusta **Literatura**, es muy fácil. Sólo te mandan a **leer** y ya"

"A mí me gusta **Química** porque puedes ir al laboratorio a ver experimentos"

"Durante mis **vacaciones de verano**, estuve leyendo varios **libros de historia**, así que la materia que me gusta más es **Historia**"

Diego y sus compañeros **escuchan** el timbre nuevamente. Esta vez suena para avisar que el receso se ha acabado. ¿Qué clase tienen ahora Diego y sus demás compañeros?

"Tenemos **Gimnasia**"

"¿Dónde está el **gimnasio**?" – pregunta Diego

"Está cerca del **laboratorio**, al frente del **club de Francés**" – responde su compañero

"¿Tú estás en el equipo de **baloncesto**, verdad?" – pregunta Diego

"Sí, soy parte del equipo de **baloncesto** y también parte del club de **Francés**. Son **actividades extracurriculares**." – responde el compañero de Diego.

"¿Actividades extracurriculares?"

"Sí. Son actividades en las que te puedes inscribir para que seas partes de clubes o **equipos deportivos**. Todas las actividades extracurriculares son después de clases."

No había actividades extracurriculares en la anterior escuela de Diego. Pero ahora él tiene la oportunidad de ser parte de cualquier club o equipo que él quiera. ¿Cuál podría escoger? Hay muchos clubs y a Diego le gustan bastantes cosas.

Su mamá le ha estado **enseñando** a **cocinar** así que él puede entrar al **club de cocina**. Diego sabe que cocinar puede ser muy **divertido**. Pero a Diego también le gusta el **ajedrez**. ¿Habrá un club de ajedrez en su nueva escuela? Para saberlo, Diego tiene que preguntar a los profesores **encargados** de los clubes o al **coordinador de actividades extracurriculares**.

Después de clases, Diego espera fuera de la **oficina** del **coordinador encargado** de las actividades extracurriculares.

"¿Cuáles son las actividades extracurriculares **disponibles**?" – pregunta Diego al coordinador

"La escuela tiene muchas actividades extracurriculares disponibles para todos los estudiantes. Si te **interesa** el deporte, entonces puedes unirte al club de **atletismo**. El club de atletismo entrena todos los **lunes**, **miércoles** y **viernes después de clases**. El club de **fútbol** entrena los **martes** y los **jueves**. El club de **baloncesto** entrena los **lunes** y los **viernes**." – le responde el coordinador

"¿Son esos todas las actividades?"

"Claro que no, mira, tengo una **lista** aquí que quisiera darte para que de esa manera escojas la actividad extracurricular que tú quieras. **Llévate** la lista a casa y **mañana** me dices lo que has **escogido**. ¿**Vale**?"

"Suena bien. Muchas gracias, coordinador"

La lista es **increíblemente** larga. Escritos en la lista están los nombres de los varios clubes que la escuela tiene. El club de cocina, de ajedrez, de natación, de francés, de decatlón, de matemáticas, de fotografía, de **radio estudiantil** y muchos más.

Para saber que escoger, Diego decide preguntar a su mamá. Ella le ayudará a escoger a que club unirse. Por el momento, Diego tiene que subir al **bus escolar** para regresar a casa. No será un viaje tan largo, pero Diego no puede esperar.

Resumen de la historia

Diego se ha mudado con su familia desde Málaga a una nueva ciudad, lo que significa que Diego es un nuevo estudiante en su escuela. Él se olvida de estudiar para el examen de matemáticas, pero no se preocupa. Después de las clases, Diego escucha que hay actividades extracurriculares disponibles para todos los alumnos en su nueva escuela. Diego decide hablar con el coordinador de actividades extracurriculares y éste le da la lista de actividades disponibles. Finalmente, Diego se lleva la lista a su casa para que su mamá lo ayude a decidir.

Summary of the story

Diego and his family have moved from Malaga to a new city, which means that Diego is a new student in his school. He forgets to study for his math exam, but he doesn't worry. After classes, Diego hears that there are extracurricular activities available to all students. Diego decides to talk with the coordinator of extracurricular activities and he gives Diego the list of available activities. Finally, Diego takes the list home so that his mom can help him decide

- **Compañeros de clase: classmates**
- **Conversando: talking**
- **Aula: classroom**
- **Venga: comes**
- **Demorando: delaying**
- **Nuevo: new**
- **Estudiante: student**
- **Mudar: move**
- **Amigos: friends**
- **Grande: big**
- **Espaciosa: spacious**
- **Profesores: teachers**
- **Amables: kind**
- **Asistía: attended**
- **Lejos: far**

- Tomaba: took
- Media hora: half an hour
- Llegar: arrive
- Incluso: even
- Bicicleta: bicycle
- Estresante: stressing
- Materias: subjects
- Matemáticas: math
- Semanas: weeks
- Tarea: assignment
- Sencilla: easy
- Estudiar: study
- Examen: exam/test
- Había: there was
- Acuerdas: remember
- Nunca: never
- Preocupes: worry
- Copiar: cheat
- Honesto: honest
- A pesar: even though
- Gusta: likes
- Profesora sustituta: substitute teacher
- Intentaré: will try
- Explica: explain
- Reemplazarla: replace
- Asistencia: attendance
- Recoger: pick up
- Escribir: write
- Pizarra: blackboard
- Fracciones: fractions
- Mochilas: backpacks
- Ejercicios: problems (Of math)
- Resuelvan: solve

- Problemas: problems
- Nota aprobatoria: passing grade
- Desaprueba: fail
- Volando: flying
- Retirando: going out
- Suena: sounds
- Timbre: bell
- Receso: lunch
- Empiezan: start
- Conversar: talk
- Difícil: hard
- Literatura: literature
- Leer: read
- Química: chemistry
- Gimnasia: gymnastics
- Gimnasio: gyn
- Laboratorio: lab
- Club de francés: French club
- Baloncesto: basketball
- Actividades extracurriculares: extracurricular activities
- Equipos deportivos: sport team
- Enseñando: teaching
- Cocinar: cook
- Club de cocina: cooking club
- Divertido: fun
- Ajedrez: chess
- Encargado: in charge
- Coordinador de actividades extracurriculares: extracurricular activities coordinator
- Oficina: office
- Coordinador: coordinator
- Disponibles: available
- Interesa: interest
- Atletismo: athletics

- **Lunes: Monday**
- **Miércoles: Wednesday**
- **Viernes: Friday**
- **Después de clases: after classes**
- **Futbol: soccer**
- **Martes: Tuesday**
- **Jueves: Thursday**
- **Lista: list**
- **Llévate: take it**
- **Mañana: tomorrow**
- **Escogido: chosen**
- **¿Vale?: Ok?**
- **Increíblemente: incredibly**
- **Radio estudiantil: student radio**
- **Bus escolar: school bus**

Chapter 6: Parts of the House

Pamela ha **invitado** a sus amigas a una **pijamada** esta noche. Sus padres le dieron el **permiso** para hacer la pijamada. La única **condición** es que todas tienen que **portarse** bien y no hacer mucho **ruido** después de la **media noche**. Pamela **aceptó** la condición e invito a 5 amigas. Todas ellas estudian en la misma escuela.

Pamela les dijo que **vinieran** a las 4 de la tarde. Les dijo **también** que no **cenaran** porque en su casa iban a invitar la cena a todas. ¿Qué **hicieron** de cena en la casa de Pamela? Hicieron **espagueti**. La mama de Pamela aún está **preparando** el espagueti y no estará **listo** hasta dentro de una hora.

Por mientras, Pamela les **dice** a sus amigas que suban a su **habitación**. Suben las **escaleras** y **después** entran a la **habitación** de Pamela. En la habitación de Pamela, una de sus amigas le **pregunta** dónde está el baño.

"**¿Puedo entrar** tu baño, Pamela?"

"**Claro, sígueme**. Te **mostraré** donde queda el baño" – responde Pamela

El baño está muy **cerca** de la habitación de Pamela. La **amiga** de Pamela se queda **sorprendida** por todo lo que ve dentro del baño.

"¿Qué son todas estas **cremas**?"

"Esta es una **botella** de **champú**. Mi papá la **usa** cuando se **baña**." – responde Pamela

"¿Y esto es una **pasta dental**? Es una **marca** que nunca he **visto**" – pregunta **sorprendida** la amiga de Pamela

"Mi mamá lo compró en un **supermercado lejos** de aquí" – le dice Pamela

La **bañera**, la **ducha**, los **grifos** y los **espejos**. Todos están muy **limpios**.

"Debe haberles tomado **muchísimo** tiempo haber **limpiado** todo el baño" – **exclama** la amiga de Pamela.

Después de haber **usado** el baño, Pamela y su amiga vuelven a la **habitación;** sus amigas están conversando y riéndose. Antes de que Pamela pueda preguntar algo, el **gato** de Pamela entra a la habitación **maullando**.

Todas las migas de Pamela se quedan **mirándolo** y quieren **acariciarlo**. El gato de Pamela se llama Tomás. Es un gato muy **gordo** y muy **peludo**. Las amigas de Pamela **corren** a acariciarlo.

"¡Qué **tierno** gatito!" – dicen las amigas de Pamela

Tomás **ve** que todas las amigas de Pamela quieren **agarrarlo** y **huye asustado**. Él sale de la habitación de Pamela y sube las **escaleras** hacia el **ático**. Pamela les dice que no suban, pero ellas no **escuchan** y suben al ático.

El ático es un lugar muy **oscuro** y las amigas de Pamela no pueden ver nada. Por eso, se **asustan** y salen del ático. Las amigas de Pamela se **disculpan** con ella y **caminan nuevamente** hacia su habitación.

Antes de que puedan entrar a la habitación de Pamela nuevamente, ellas **escuchan** una voz. La voz **proviene** del **primer piso**. Es la **voz** de la mamá de Pamela. La mamá de Pamela está **llamando** a todas las chicas para que vengan a la cocina.

"Pamela, quizás puedas **mostrar** la casa a tus amigas. La cena puede **tardar** un poco." – les dice la mamá de Pamela.

"Claro, mamá, no hay problema. Vengan, les **mostraré** la casa" – responde Pamela.

Pamela empieza **llevándolas afuera** de la casa.

"Este es el **jardín**. Aquí mi mamá y mi hermana **plantan** y **cuidan** de las plantas y los **árboles** que **crecen**. A mi mamá le gusta la **jardinería**, así que ella **siempre** está **trayendo** nuevas **flores**."

"Esas **flores** son muy **bonitas**" – dice una de las amigas de Pamela

"Esas flores son **jazmines**. Si siguen caminando, verán **margaritas** y **dientes de león**." – dice Pamela

"¿Y qué son estas **herramientas**, Pamela?"

"Son los **útiles de jardinería** de mi mamá. Los ha **dejado** acá porque **de seguro** va a seguir **trabajando**" – responde Pamela

"¡Los **árboles** son **enormes**!"

"Pasaron muchos años para que **finalmente crezcan** tan **altos** como lo son ahora" – señala Pamela.

Después de ver el jardín de la casa de Pamela, Pamela las lleva **adentro** de la casa. ¿Qué es lo **primero** que ven cuando ellas entran a la casa? Bueno, es la **sala**. En la sala de Pamela, ellas pueden ver que la familia de Pamela tiene muchos **muebles**. Los **sofás** parecen nuevos. Tal parece que a la familia de Pamela también le gusta mucho el **arte**, ya que hay varias **pinturas** y **retratos**.

Ellas también notan que el **televisor** que hay en la sala de Pamela es muy **antiguo**. Hay una **mesa pequeña** al **centro** de la sala. El **teléfono de casa** está en una **esquina** y la **alfombra** esta debajo de la mesa.

Las amigas de Pamela **aprovechan** el **momento** y se sientan en los **muebles**.

"Si **quieren**, podemos ver televisión más tarde." – les dice Pamela

"Yo quisiera ver televisión de **después** de la cena" – responde una de ellas

Pamela pasa a mostrarles la **cocina**. Su mamá aún sigue **preparando** la cena. Ellas ven que la cocina está llena de muchos **instrumentos**.

"¿**Alguna** de ustedes sabe **cocinar**?" – pregunta la mamá de Pamela

"Sí, yo **sé** cocinar" – responde una de las amigas de Pamela.

"Yo también sé cocinar" – responde otra

"¿Y qué les gusta cocinar?" – pregunta la mamá una vez más

"A mí me encanta preparar **postres**. Mi mamá me **ayuda** a hacerlos y nos **divertimos** mucho cuando los hacemos. Nuestro postre **favorito** es el **pastel de chocolate.**"

Pamela les dice que es hora de **subir** las escaleras una vez más para ver las **demás** habitaciones en la casa. Ellas ya **conocen** el baño. Pamela les muestra la habitación de su **hermana mayor**.

La hermana mayor de Pamela se llama Elsa. Elsa está en su habitación **jugando videojuegos**. Antes de entrar a la habitación de Elsa, Pamela **toca** la puerta. Elsa **sale** de su habitación y les **permite entrar**.

Por unos minutos, Pamela y sus amigas **juegan videojuegos** en la habitación de Elsa. Luego, Pamela les dice para **continuar**.

"¿Qué hay **detrás** de esa puerta, Pamela? – **pregunta** una de las chicas

"Ese es la **habitación** de mis **padres**. No podemos entrar allí." – responde Pamela.

Cerca de la puerta de la habitación de sus padres, las amigas de Pamela ven que hay una pequeña **cama**.

"¿Quién **duerme** ahí?"

"Esa es la **cama** de Tomás"

"¿No tiene **frío** en la **noche**?"

"No creo. A veces Tomás entra a mi habitación y duerme en mi cama."

Pamela les quiere mostrar el ático pero sus amigas están un poco asustadas por la **oscuridad**. Pamela les dice que esta vez ella **encenderá** la luz para que ellas no tengan tanto **miedo**.

"Aquí en el ático **guardamos** todas las **herramientas** que mi papá usa. También hay una escalera y antiguos **artefactos** que ya no usamos."

Al final del ático hay una pequeña **ventana**. Desde esa ventana ese puede ver todas las casas de la cuadra. **Finalmente**, Pamela les dice que es hora de bajar y ver el **comedor**. Pamela y sus amigas bajan y encuentran el **comedor** muy **desordenado**.

"¿Podrían ayudarme a **limpiarlo**, por favor?" – pregunta la mamá de Pamela

"No hay problema. Le ayudaremos" – responden

Pamela y todas sus amigas limpian la mesa, ordenan las cosas que estaban sobre la mesa y traen los **cubiertos** y las **tazas**. La mamá de Pamela trae los **vasos** y también el **azúcar** y las **servilletas**.

"La cena ya va a estar listo dentro de poco chicas. Pueden **sentarse** en la mesa"

"Mamá, podemos ver televisión hasta que la cena esté lista" – pregunta Pamela.

"Está bien. Pero tienen que venir cuando les llame. ¿Vale?"

"Ok, mamá. Lo haremos." – le dice Pamela.

Las chicas van corriendo a la sala y **encienden** el televisor.

"¿Qué quieren ver?" – pregunta Pamela

"Hay un **programa** muy **divertido** en el canal 4."

"Sí, yo **también** quiero verlo"

"Pon ese programa, Pamela"

"Está bien. Lo haré" – les dice Pamela

Pamela enciende el televisor y **pone** el canal 4. El programa está **a punto** de **comenzar**. Es un programa de **comedia** muy **popular** donde Pamela vive. Después de 15 minutos, la mamá de Pamela las llama para cenar.

"¡La cena ya está lista! ¡Es hora de cenar!"

Resumen de la historia

Pamela ha invitado a 5 amigas de su escuela a su casa para una pijamada. Mientras ellas esperan a que la cena esté lista, la mamá de Pamela les dice que vayan a ver las partes de la casa. Empezando con el jardín, todas ellas se sorprenden al ver todas las cosas que Pamela, su mamá y su hermana hacen para mantener la casa muy bonita. Al final, la mamá de Pamela les pide ayuda para limpiar el comedor y después todas ellas van a cenar.

Summary of the story

Pamela has invited 5 friends to her house for a slumber party. While they're waiting for dinner to be ready, Pamela's mom tells them to go to see the parts of the house. Beginning with the garden, all of them are surprised at the things Pamela, her mother, and her sister do to keep the house very beautiful. In the end, Pamela's mom asks them for help in cleaning the dining room and then all of them have dinner.

- **Invitado: invited**
- **Pijamada: slumber party**
- **Permiso: permission**
- **Condición: condition**
- **Portarse: behave**
- **Ruido: noise**
- **Medianoche: midnight**
- **Aceptó: accepted**
- **Viniera: come**
- **También: also**
- **Hicieron: made**
- **Espagueti: spaghetti**
- **Preparando: making**
- **Listo: ready**
- **Por mientras: in the meantime**
- **Dice: say**
- **Habitación: bedroom/room**
- **Pregunta: ask**
- **Puedo: can**
- **Entrar: enter/get in**
- **Claro: sure**
- **Sígueme: follow me**
- **Mostraré: show**
- **Carca: near**
- **Amiga: friend**
- **Sorprendida: surprised**
- **Cremas: creams**
- **Botella: bottle**
- **Champú: shampoo**
- **Usa: use**
- **Baña: bathes**
- **Pasta dental: toothpaste**
- **Marca: Brand**

- Visto: seen
- Supermercado: supermarket
- Lejos: far
- Bañera: bath
- Ducha: shower
- Grifos: faucet/tap
- Espejos: mirrors
- Limpios: clean
- Muchísimo: too much
- Limpiado: cleaned
- Exclama: exclaim
- Usado: used
- Gato: cat
- Maullando: meowing
- Mirándolo: watching him
- Acariciarlo: pet him
- Gordo: fat
- Peludo: furry
- Corren: run
- Tierno: cute
- Ve: see
- Agarrarlo: grab him
- Huye: run away
- Asustado: scared
- Escaleras: stairs
- Ático: attic
- Escuchan: hear
- Oscuro: dark
- Asustan: be afraid
- Disculpan: say sorry
- Proviene: comes from
- Primer piso: first floor
- Llamando: calling
- Mostrar: show
- Tardar: delay
- Llevándolas: taking them

- Afuera: outside
- Plantan: plant
- Cuidan: take care of
- Jardín: garden
- Arboles: trees
- Crece: grow
- Jardinería: gardening
- Siempre: always
- Trayendo: bringing
- Flores: flowers
- Bonitas: beautiful
- Jazmines: jasmines
- Margaritas: daisies
- Dientes de león: dandelion
- Herramientas: tools
- Útiles de jardinería: gardening tools
- Dejado: left
- De seguro: surely
- Trabajando: working
- Árboles: trees
- Enormes: large
- Finalmente: finally
- Crezcan: grow
- Altos: tall
- Adentro: inside
- Primero: first
- Sala: living room
- Muebles: furniture
- Sofás: sofas
- Arte: art
- Pinturas: paintings
- Retratos: portraits
- Televisor: TV
- Antiguo: old
- Mesa: table
- Pequeña: small

- Centro: center
- Teléfono de casa: home phone
- Esquina: corner
- Alfombra: carpet
- Aprovechan: take advantage of
- Momento: moment
- Quieren: want
- Después: after
- Cocina: kitchen
- Preparando: making
- Instrumentos: tools
- Alguna: some
- Cocinar: cook
- Sé: know
- Postres: desserts
- Ayuda: help
- Divertimos: have fun
- Favorito: favorite
- Pastel: cake
- Chocolate: chocolate
- Subir: go up
- Demás: other
- Conocen: know
- Hermana mayor: older sister
- Jugando: playing
- Videojuegos: videogames
- Toca: knock
- Sale: go out
- Permite: allow
- Entrar: enter
- Continuar: continue
- Detrás: behind
- Pregunta: ask
- Padres: parents
- Cerca: near
- Cama: bed

- Duerme: sleep
- Frio: cold
- Guardamos: store
- Herramientas: tools
- Artefactos: artifacts
- Ventana: window
- Finalmente: finally
- Comedor: dining room
- Desordenado: messy
- Límpialo: clean it
- Cubiertos: cutlery
- Tazas: cups
- Vasos: glasses
- Azúcar: sugar
- Servilletas: napkins
- Sentarse: sit down
- Encienden: turn on
- Programa: program
- Divertido: funny
- También: also
- Pone: put on
- A punto: about to
- Comenzar: begin
- Comedia: comedy
- Popular: popular

Chapter 7: Food

Alicia **está en camino** al **mercado** con su **mejor amiga**, Laura. Ellas están **yendo** para **comprar** lo que **necesitan** para **hacer** el **almuerzo** de esta **tarde**. A Alicia le **gusta** ir al mercado con su **mamá** todos los **fines de semana**, así que ella **fines de semana dónde** y qué comprar. Ella sabe dónde **encontrar** las **mejores ofertas** y también **productos** de **calidad**.

Por otro lado, Laura no tiene la **costumbre** de ir al mercado. Ella sólo va de **vez en cuando**. Laura le **dice** a Alicia que **tal vez** ella no será de mucha ayuda al **momento** de hacer las compras, pero Alicia le dice que no se **preocupe**. Alicia está **contenta** de que Laura le **acompañe** al mercado.

Después de **tomar** el bus que les **deja** en el mercado, ambas chicas empiezan a **conversar** sobre lo que necesitan traer del mercado.

"Estaba **pensando** en hacer una **lasaña**" – dice Alicia

"¿Qué eso no es muy **difícil** de hacer?" – **pregunta** Laura

"Sí lo es. Pero no te preocupes, mi mamá y mi tía me **enseñaron** a hacer lasaña." – responde Alicia.

"La lasaña **viene** de Italia, ¿verdad? ¿Cómo piensas **conseguir** todos los **ingredientes**?" – dice Laura

"Mi tía me **mostró** algunos **lugares** donde puedo **encontrar** los ingredientes. Están un poco **caros**, pero **vale la pena comprarlos**."

"¿Por qué **simplemente** no usas ingredientes **más baratos**?"

"Porque no saldrá **igual**. Los ingredientes son lo más **importante** para hacer la lasaña. Mientras de mayor calidad sean los ingredientes, mejor saldrá la lasaña."

Laura y Alicia bajan del bus en el **paradero**. Se **dirigen** hacia el mercado y **empiezan** a hacer las compras.

"¿Qué **necesitamos** comprar **primero** para hacer la lasaña?" – pregunta Laura

"Necesitamos comprar el **queso** y el **tomate**" – responde Alicia

"¿Dónde compraremos los tomates y el queso? Yo no **conozco** muy bien el mercado"

"Yo conozco muy bien este mercado. **Ven**, te mostraré donde compro el queso y los tomates."

Caminan por unos 5 minutos. El mercado es **increíblemente grande**. En el mercado hay muchas **secciones**: la **sección de carnes, de frutas, de vegetales, de abarrotes, de ferretería, de comida**

marina, **de juguetes, de golosinas** y más. Muchas personas e incluso **familias** enteras vienen a este mercado para hacer sus compras. Incluso **turistas** del **extranjero visitan** este mercado porque saben que aquí hay **buenos precios**.

Alicia y Laura **encuentran** la sección de frutas vegetales. En esta sección, los **vendedores venden** una gran **variedad** de frutas y también de vegetales frescas y a buen precio. Alicia le **da un vistazo** a todos los vegetales que se están vendiendo aquí. **Zanahoria, perejil, frijoles, alverjitas, brócoli, maíz, zapallo, camote** y muchos más. En esta ocasión, Alicia **solamente** ha venido a comprar queso y tomate.

Pero antes de comprar, Alicia mira la **lista de compras** nuevamente y se da cuenta que **en realidad** ella debe comprar más que solamente tomate y queso en la sección de vegetales. Ella también debe comprar perejil, **cebolla** y otros más.

"Buenos días. ¿Me podría dar **medio kilogramo** de cebolla, por favor?"

"Claro, no hay problema. Aquí tiene. Medio kilogramo de cebolla. ¿**Desea** algo más? – pregunta el vendedor

"Sí, también quisiera 250 **miligramos** de perejil, un **cuarto de kilo** de **ajo** y un **kilo** de tomate."

"Aquí tiene. ¿Algo más?"

"¿Vende **queso Parmesano**?"

"Sí, vendo queso Parmesano. ¿Cuánto desea?"

"Deme medio kilo, por favor"

Después de **conseguir** todo lo que necesitan en la sección de vegetales, Alicia y Laura se dirigen ahora a la sección de carnes. La sección de carnes es **más grande que** la sección de vegetales. En esta sección, varios **tipos** de carnes son vendidos. Aquí Alicia y Laura **encontraran carne de res, de pollo, de cabra, de conejo** e incluso encontrarán **carne de pescado.** Como el mercado está cerca de la **bahía**, es muy fácil **traer** pescado **fresco**.

"Laura, ¿podrías tú esta vez **preguntar** si venden carne de res?" – le dice Alicia a Laura.

"Claro. ¿Cuánto **quieres** que pida?"

"Pide 2 kilos de carne de res, por favor."

Una vez **comprada** la carne de res, ellas ahora se **dirigen** a la sección de abarrotes. En la sección de abarrotes las personas que vienen a este mercado podrán encontrar **sal, azúcar, jabones, champús, aceite, pimienta, arroz e incluso comida de mascotas**, entre muchas otras cosas más.

"Buenos días, señoritas. ¿En qué puedo ayudarlas?" – pregunta el vendedor de la tienda de abarrotes.

"Buenos días. Estamos **buscando** una **botella** de **aceite**."

"Tengo botellas de medio litro, un litro y 3 litros. ¿Cuál desea?"

"De un litro, por favor"

"Aquí tiene. ¿Algo mas en que pueda ayudarla?"

"Quisiera un **bolsa** de **sal** y también un kilo de azúcar"

"Esta es lo que pidió, señorita, tome."

"Muchas gracias"

"Gracias a usted"

Después de comprar en la sección de abarrotes, Laura le dice a Alicia para ir a la sección de golosinas. Alicia le pregunta:

"¿La sección de golosinas? ¿Por qué quieres ir a la sección de golosinas?"

"Se me ha **antojado** unos **caramelos** y unas **barras de chocolate**." – responde Laura

"¿Tienes **dinero** para comprar esas golosinas?" – pregunta Alicia

"Sí. ¿Vamos?"

"Ok, vamos"

Alicia y Laura van a la sección de golosinas y se quedan **asombradas** por toda la **variedad** de golosinas que encuentran en esa sección. Hay muchas golosinas con **diferentes** precios. Finalmente, Laura ve unos chocolates **riquísimos**.

"¿Cuánto cuestan estas barras de chocolate?"

"Cuestan 6 **dólares**"

"Deme dos, por favor"

Tal parece que Alicia y Lara **acabaron** de hacer todas las compras para hacer la lasaña. Antes de irse, dan un **último vistazo** a la **lista de compras** para así saber si se han olvidado de algo o no. Después de ver que no les falta comprar nada más, ellas **salen** del supermercado y se van al **paradero de bus** que está **al frente del** mercado. Allí, las chicas esperan hasta que venga el bus.

El bus se demora un poco pero finalmente **llega**. **Ambas** jóvenes se suben y Laura le empieza a preguntar a Alicia como es que ella **aprendió** a preparar lasaña.

"Mi tía viene de Italia. Ella me **enseñó** a preparar cuando yo era una **niña**. Para que a lasaña te salga bien, tienes que **escoger** bien los ingredientes y también tienes que tener todas los **útiles de cocina** que vas a usar."

"¿Qué hay del **horno** y las **bandejas**?" – pregunta Laura

"Eso también. En mi casa yo tengo un **horno** lo suficientemente **grande** como para preparar bastantes **porciones** de lasaña." – responde Alicia

"¿Cuánto te demoras en preparar una lasaña?" – pregunta Laura

"A mí sólo me toma alrededor de 3 horas. Pero la carne tiene que cocinarse muy bien antes de **ponerla** en la lasaña"

"Quisiera ayudarte a hacer a lasaña, Alicia; pero no sé cómo hacerla."

"No te preocupes, tú puedes ver como hago la lasaña. Así aprenderás a hacerla también."

"Gracias"

Las chicas siguen **conversando** en el bus mientras este las lleva a casa. El viaje es un poco largo. Ambas se ponen a conversar de lo que está pasando en la escuela y de las tareas. También conversan sobre lo que ellas saben cocinar y lo que no saben hacer. La verdad es que aunque Laura no sabe hacer lasaña, ella si sabe hacer **postres**.

A Alicia siempre le han **fascinado** los postres. Por ello, ellas **hacen un acuerdo**. Hoy día, Alicia enseñará a Laura a hacer lasaña, y Laura luego enseñará a Alicia a hacer **deliciosos** postres.

"¿Es difícil hacer postres? – pregunta Alicia

"**Depende de** que postre quieres hacer. Por ejemplo, a mí me salen muy bien los cheesecakes y los **pies de manzana**. Son muy fáciles de hacer" – responde Laura.

"Yo quisiera que me enseñes a hacer postres. ¿Cuándo estás **disponible** para que me enseñes?

"Puede ser la **siguiente semana**."

"Necesito traer ingredientes?"

"Primero tenemos que **pensar** en qué vamos a hacer. Si es un cheesecake, entonces no necesitarás traer ingredientes ya que yo tengo ingredientes que **sobraron** de la anterior ocasión que hice un cheesecake."

¿Y si quisiera hacer un pie?"

"Entonces sí **tendrías** que traer los ingredientes. También hay que pensar en donde lo vamos a hacer"

"¿No podemos hacerlo en tu casa?"

"Sí podemos hacerlo en mi casa. Pero tengo que pedir permiso a mis padres primero y no sé si a ellos les **gustará** la **idea**."

"¿Por qué no?"

"Porque la **anterior** ocasión que hice un postre, hice **demasiado desorden** y me **olvidé** de limpiar la cocina"

"¡O, vaya! No te preocupes, yo te puedo ayudar a limpiar"

"¡Gracias! Déjame preguntar a mis padres primero y cuando ellos me den permiso, yo te lo hago saber."

"Genial. Estaré **esperando**"

De esa manera el trato queda hecho. Amabas tienen sus propios **talentos** y saben muy bien cómo usarlos. Eso es lo bueno de tener buenas amigas, siempre se puede **contar** con ellas en todo momento.

Resumen de la historia

Alicia y Laura son dos muchachas que están yendo al mercado a comprar todos los ingredientes que necesitan para hacer una lasaña. Alicia sabe hacer la lasaña pero Laura no sabe nada; es más, ella casi nunca viene a este mercado, por ello, ella no sabe dónde comprar. Alicia le pide que ella la acompañé y después de comprar todos los ingredientes para la lasaña, ambas suben al bus que las llevará a casa. Al final, Alicia se enteré que Laura sabe hacer postres, por lo que ambas hacen un trato para que Laura enseñe a Alicia a hacer postres, tal como Alicia enseñará a hacer la lasaña a Laura.

Summary of the story

Alicia and Laura are two young girls that are going to the market to buy all the ingredients that they need to make a lasagna. Alicia knows how to make lasagna but Laura doesn't; what is more, she hardly ever goes to this market, that's why she doesn't know where to buy. Alicia asks her to go with her and after buying all the ingredients for the lasagna, both get on the bus that will take them home. In the end, Alicia gets to know that Laura knows how to make desserts, so both make a deal: Laura will teach Alicia how to make desserts just as Alicia will teach Laura to make lasagna.

- **Está en camino: on their way**
- **Mercado: market**
- **Mejor amiga: best friend**
- **Yendo: going**
- **Comprar: buying**
- **Necesitan: need**
- **Hacer: do**
- **Almuerzo: lunch**
- **Tarde: afternoon**

- Gusta: like
- Mamá: mom
- Fines de semana: weekend
- Dónde: where
- Encontrar: find
- Mejores: best
- Ofertas: offers
- Productos: products
- Calidad: quality
- Costumbre: habit
- De vez en cuando: often
- Dice: say
- Tal vez : maybe
- Momento: moment
- Preocupe: worry
- Contenta: content
- Acompañe: accompany
- Tomar: take
- Deja: leave
- Conversar: talk
- Pensando: think
- Lasaña: lasagna
- Difícil: difficult
- Pregunta: ask
- Enseñaron: taught
- Viene: come
- Conseguir: get
- Ingredientes: ingredients
- Mostró: show
- Lugares: places
- Encontrar: find
- Caros: expensive
- Comprarlos: buy them

- Vale la pena: worth it
- Simplemente: simply
- Más baratos: cheaper
- Igual: same
- Importante: important
- Paradero: stop
- Dirigen: headed for
- Empiezan: start
- Necesitamos: need
- Queso: cheese
- Tomate: tomato
- Conozco: know
- Ven: come
- Caminan: walk
- Increíblemente: incredibly
- Grande: big
- Secciones: sections
- Sección de carnes: meat section
- Frutas: fruits
- Vegetales: vegetables
- Ferretería: hardware store
- Comida marina: seafood
- Juguetes: toys
- Golosinas: candies
- Familias: families
- Turistas: tourists
- Del Extranjero: from abroad
- Visitan: visit
- Buenos: good
- Precios: prices
- Vendedores : sellers
- Encuentran: find
- Venden: sell

- Variedad: variety
- Da un vistazo: take a look at
- Zanahoria: carrot
- Perejil: parsley
- Frijoles: beans
- Alverjitas: peas
- Brócoli: bróccoli
- Maíz: corn
- Zapallo: pumpkin
- Camote: sweet potato
- Solamente: only
- Lista de compras: shopping list
- En realidad: in reality
- Cebolla: onion
- Medio kilogramo: half a kilogram
- Desea: wish
- Miligramos: miligrams
- Cuarto de kilo: quarter of kilogram
- Ajo: garlic
- Kilo: kilo
- Queso parmesano: parmesan cheese
- Conseguir: get
- Más grande que: bigger than
- Tipos: types
- Carne de pescado: fish meat
- Encontraran : find
- Carne de res: beef
- Pollo: chicken
- Cabra: goat
- Conejo: rabbit
- Bahía: bay
- Traer: bring
- Fresco: fresh

- Preguntar: ask
- Quieres: want
- Comprada: sold
- Sal: salt
- Azúcar: sugar
- Jabones: soaps
- Champús: shampoos
- Aceite: oil
- Pimienta: pepper
- Arroz: rice
- Comida de mascotas: pet food
- Buscando: searching
- Botella: bottle
- Bolsa: bag
- Muchas gracias: thank you very much
- Antojado: craving
- Caramelos: candies
- Barras de chocolate: chocolate bars
- Dinero: money
- Asombradas: surprised
- Variedad: variety
- Diferentes: different
- Riquísimos: very delicious
- Dólares: dollars
- Tal parece: it seems that
- Acabaron: finish
- Último: last
- Vistazo: look
- Salen: go out
- Paradero de bus: bus stop
- Al frente del: in front of
- Llega: arrives
- Ambas: both

- Aprendió: learnt
- Enseñó: taught
- Niña: kid
- Escoger: choose
- Útiles de cocina: cooking tools
- Horno: oven
- Bandejas: trays
- Grande: big
- Porciones: portions
- Ponerla: put it
- Conversando: talking
- Postres: desserts
- Hacen un acuerdo: make a deal
- Deliciosos: delicious
- Depende de: depends on
- Pies de manzana: Apple pies
- Disponible: available
- Siguiente: next
- Semana: week
- Pensar: think
- Sobraron: left
- Tendrías: you would have
- Gustará: will like
- Idea: idea
- Anterior: last
- Demasiado: too much
- Desorden: mess
- Olvidé: forgot
- Esperando: waiting
- Talentos: talents
- Contar con: count on

Chapter 8: Musical Instruments

Andrés es un **muchacho** de 17 años que **disfruta** mucho tocar la **guitarra**. Él es **parte** del club de **música** de su **escuela secundaria**. Andrés le **dedica** varias horas a **practicar** la guitarra. Él practica con el club todos días después de clases.

La guitarra que Andrés **toca** es una guitarra que su papá le **regaló** hace un **mes**. Andrés no sabe cuánto **costó** lo guitarra pero él **piensa** que la guitarra pudo haber costado bastante dinero. La guitarra es **nueva** y muy **bonita**.

Todos sus amigos le han estado **diciendo** que la guitarra que él tiene es una muy buena guitarra. Él ya **sabe** cómo tocarla. Andrés sabe cómo tocar las canciones más **populares**.

Hoy día es **miércoles**, lo que **significa** que Andrés **tendrá** que **quedarse** para la práctica. Después de su **última** clase del día, él se dirige al **salón de música**. Lo mejor de todo es que Andrés tiene muchos amigos en el club de música. Su **mejor amigo**, José, también está en el club de música, aunque él no toca la guitarra **sino más bien** la **batería**.

Andrés sale tan rápido como puede de su clase y **corre hacia** el salón de música y lo **encuentra vacío**. Es **raro**. Hoy día **hay práctica**. ¿Dónde están todos?

Sin darse cuenta, Andrés escucha una voz. Es el **profesor** de música.

"¿Qué haces aquí **tan temprano**, Andrés?

"**Vengo** para la práctica"

"**Entiendo**. ¿Pero por qué **viniste** tan temprano?"

"¿Tan temprano? Si siempre hemos tenido practica a esta hora, profesor."

"Creo que no te has enterado que el día doy la práctica será **más tarde**"

"¿Más tarde? ¿A qué hora será la practica?"

"La práctica será en dos horas"

"¡Dos horas! ¿Qué voy a hacer **durante** esas dos horas?"

"Buenos, **puedes** ir **practicando** con tu guitarra o puedes **regresar luego**."

"Quisiera **quedarme** a practicar. Voy al **baño** y **regreso** para practicar"
"Vale"

Andrés sale del aula de música y va al baño. Él no entiende cómo es que no se **enteró** que la práctica de hoy día iba a **empezar** más tarde.

Después de salir del baño, **saca** su celular de su **bolsillo** y **llama** a José para que le haga **compañía**

"¿Dónde estás, José?"

"Estoy en el **gimnasio**. **¿Qué pasó?**"

"Estoy **afuera** del aula de música. No hay **nadie** en el salón **excepto** por mí y el profesor"

"¿Qué no **sabías** que la práctica iba a empezar tarde hoy día?"

"No lo sabía. ¿Quieres venir para **conversar** un **rato**?"

"Sí. Pero tengo que quedarme un rato más aquí en el gimnasio."

"¿Cuánto tiempo más vas a quedarte en el gimnasio?"

"Por lo menos **media hora más**"

"Vale. No hay problema, te puedo **esperar**. Me encontrarás dentro del aula de música."

"Vale"

Andrés **cuelga** la llamada y **entra** al salón de música. **Dentro**, se da con la **sorpresa** que el profesor no está sólo. Otra **compañera** también está dentro del salón con él. La compañera de Andrés también es parte del club de música y ella sabe tocar el **piano**.

Ella empieza a tocar una **canción de cuna** que Andrés **nunca antes** había **escuchado**. Lo raro de todo esto es que, **a pesar de que** ellos son parte del club de música, ellos nunca han conversado antes. Por eso, Andrés se **presenta**.

"Hola, me llamo Andrés"

"Hola, Andrés. **Me llamó** Lucía."

"¡Sabes tocar muy bien el piano!"

"¡Gracias! Tú también sabes tocar muy bien la guitarra"

"¿De veras piensas eso?"

"Sí. Te he visto tocar la guitarra **varias veces** y **creo** que debes practicar bastante para tocar así. Mi **hermano menor** también sabe tocar la guitarra pero él no toca tan bien como tú"

El profesor también quiere **unirse** a la conversación, pero **antes** de hacerlo, él empieza a tocar la **flauta** que está en su **mesa**. Después de tocar la flauta, el profesor **explica** que cuando él estaba en la secundaria, él también tocaba la guitarra.

"Cuando yo estaba **estudiando** en la secundaria, me **gustaba** mucho la música. Aprendí a tocar varios **instrumentos, grandes** y **pequeños**"

"¿Qué instrumentos sabe tocar usted, profesor?" – pregunta Lucia

"Bueno, Lucía, yo empecé **tocando** la **batería**."

"¿Cómo José?" – dice Andrés

"Así es. Yo tocaba la batería **todos los días**. **Recuerdo** que la **primera** batería que **toqué** era una batería que **pertenecía** a mi papá. Él era **baterista** de una **banda de rock**."

"¿De veras?" – pregunta Lucía

"Así es. Mi mamá era la **vocalista** de esa banda."

"Vaya, profesor. Veo que usted viene de una familia musical" – dice Andrés.

"Creo que sí"

"**¿Aprendió** a tocar más instrumentos, verdad?"

"Por supuesto. Después de aprender a tocar la batería, empecé a aprender a tocar la guitarra. No fue **fácil**. Tuve que practicar por varias horas, pero valió la pena. Después de dos años, ya sabía tocar la guitarra como un **profesional**. La **tuba** fue el siguiente instrumento que aprendí. Mi hermano tocaba la **trompeta** y yo a veces lo **acompañaba** a sus **prácticas**."

"Si su hermano sabía tocar la trompeta, ¿por qué **escogió** usted la tuba?"

"Porque quería **probar algo diferente**. La tuba era mucho más grande y **pesada** que la trompeta. Además, era la primera **vez** que tocaba un instrumento de viento. La **lira** fue mucho más sencilla."

"¿Aprendió a tocar **guitarra eléctrica**?"

"Un amigo de mi papá sabía tocar la guitarra eléctrica muy bien y él me regaló la suya cuando estaba aprendiendo a tocar. Para tocar una guitarra eléctrica, necesitas tener un **amplificador** y el amplificador que venía con la guitarra eléctrica que el amigo de mi papá me regaló estaba **malograda**. Tuve que **comprar** una nueva. En ese entonces yo no sabía que los amplificadores de guitarra eléctrica pueden costar muy caros"

"¿Aún recuerda como tocar la guitarra eléctrica?"

"Claro que sí"

"¿Podría enseñarme?"

"Primero tendría que ver si ya has aprendido a tocar la guitarra **acústica** los suficiente como para poder enseñare a tocar una eléctrica."

"Yo ya sé tocar la guitarra acústica profesor. Escuche"

Andrés se pone a tocar la guitarra acústica que **trajo** des su casa. El profesor le pide que toque una canción que es muy **difícil**. Andrés se pone un poco **nervioso** pero luego empieza a tocar la guitarra muy bien. No se **equivoca** para nada. El profesor lo mira **asombrado** y se da cuenta que Andrés sabe tocar muy bien la guitarra.

"Te salió muy bien, Andrés" – dice Lucía

"Gracias"

"Eso es cierto, Andrés. Te salió muy bien" – dice el profesor

"Entonces, ¿va a enseñarme como tocar la guitarra eléctrica?"

"Lo haré, pero no podrá ser hoy día. ¿Qué te parece el **viernes**?"

"Me parece bien"

"Profesor, ¿usted nunca **aprendió** a tocar el piano?"

"Sí sé cómo tocar el piano. Pero no **practico** tanto como antes. Tal vez me he estado **olvidando** un poco."

"¿Quisiera **escuchar** como toco, profesor?" – pregunta Lucía

"Claro, te escucho"

Lucía también está un poco nerviosa. Esta vez, el profesor no ha escogido ninguna canción para que ella toque. Lucía escoge la canción que ella quiere tocar. Es una **balada**. El profesor **reconoce** esa balada ya que es una balada un poco antigua.

Lucía sigue tocando el piano hasta que la canción **acaba**. El profesor y Andrés **aplauden**.

"Muy bien hecho, Lucía" – dice el profesor

"Sí, te salió muy bien" – dice Andrés

"Gracias. Estuve practicando." – responde Lucía

Lucía, al igual que Andrés, practica todos los días. En su caso, su mamá le enseñó a tocar el piano. Su mamá también es una muy buena **pianista**. Por eso, es sólo **natural** que Lucía quiera **pertenecer** al club de música.

"Lucía, tú has estado en este club de música por mucho tiempo." – hace notar el profesor

"Así es. Me gusta mucho ser parte del club de música. Es muy **divertido** y **aprendo** muchas cosas nuevas también."

"No sabía que habías estado en este club por bastante tiempo." – dice Andrés

Antes que Lucía pueda decir algo, José, el amigo de Andrés, **llega** al salón. Antes de entrar al aula, José toca la puerta y saluda.

"Hola. Buenas tardes a todos. ¿Puedo **pasar**?" – pregunta José

"Claro, pasa José" – responde el profesor

"Hola, Andrés. Hola Lucía. ¿Qué estaban haciendo?"

"Estábamos conversando sobre como el profesor sabe tocar muchos instrumentos musicales" - dice Andrés

"¡Qué genial! Sabía que el profesor sabía tocar la guitarra y la batería. ¿También sabe tocar más instrumentos?"

"La música es mi **pasión**, José." – le dice el profesor

"Tú sabes tocar la batería, ¿verdad?" – pregunta Lucía

"Sí."

"¿Sabes tocar la batería muy bien?"

"Yo creo que sí. ¿Quieres escuchar cómo toco?"

"Claro que sí"

"¿Dónde está la batería?"

José se **sienta** en la **silla cerca** de la **batería** y **coge** las **baquetas**. Antes de tocar la batería, José **limpia** las baquetas y se **acomoda**.

"Andres, ¿por qué mejor no tocamos los dos **juntos**?"

"Suena bien"

Ambos muchachos tocan sus instrumentos. **Parecen** una banda de rock cuando ellos dos tocan. Lucía también se une y les sigue con el piano. Después de la canción. El profesor aplaude.

"Esa fue una excelente **tocada**, muchachos."

"Gracias, profesor"

"Deberían formar una banda de rock"

"¿De verdad piensa eso usted?"

"Claro, pero no se olviden que tienen que seguir practicando más."

"Entendemos, profesor."

"Muy bien. Ya falta poco para que la clase comience. ¿Qué tal si ustedes siguen practicando mientras yo reparo los instrumentos **defectuosos**?"

"Ok, profesor"

Mientras el profesor va a limpiar y **repara** los instrumentos de la clase de música, Andrés, José y Lucía se ponen a conversar sobre la idea del profesor de formar una banda de rock. Ellos **acuerdan** juntarse **nuevamente** este fin de semana en la casa de José.

"Los **esperaré** a las 10 de la mañana. No se olviden."

Resumen de la historia

Andrés es un muchacho de 17 años que está en el club de música de su escuela secundaria. Hoy día, el club de música tiene práctica, pero Andrés se da con la sorpresa que no hay nadie presente cuando él llega al aula de música. El profesor explica a Andrés que la práctica será en 2 horas. Mientras ambos esperan a que comience la práctica, Lucía y José llegan para conversar y tocar sus instrumentos. Al final, el profesor sugiere que ellos tres se junten y formen una banda de rock.

Summary of the story

Andrés is a 17-year-old kid that is part of his high school music club. Today, the music club has a rehearsal, but Andrés is surprised that there's no one when he gets to the music room. The teacher explains to Andrés that the practice will take place in 2 hours. While they're both waiting, Lucía and José arrive to talk and play their instruments. In the end, the teacher suggests that the three get together and form a rock band.

- **Muchacho: guy**
- **Disfruta: enjoys**
- **Guitarra: guitar**
- **Parte: part**
- **Música: music**
- **Escuela secundaria: high school**
- **Dedica: dedicate**
- **Practicar: rehearse**
- **Regaló: gave**
- **Toca: play**
- **Mes: month**
- **Costó: cost**
- **Piensa: thinks**
- **Nueva: new**
- **Bonita: beautiful**
- **Todos: everybody**
- **Diciendo: saying**
- **Sabe: knows**
- **Populares: popular**
- **Hoy día: today**
- **Significa: means**
- **Tendrá: will have to**
- **Quedarse: stay**
- **Última: last**
- **Salón de música: music room**
- **Mejor amigo: best friend**
- **Batería: drums**

- Sino más bien: rather
- Corre: runs
- Hacia: toward
- Encuentra: find
- Vacío: empty
- Raro: weird
- Hay: there is
- Práctica: rehearsal
- Profesor: teacher
- Tan: so
- Temprano: early
- Vengo: come
- Entiendo: understand
- Viniste: come
- Más tarde: later
- Durante: during
- Puedes: you can
- Practicando: rehearsing
- Regresar: come back
- Luego: later
- Quedarme: stay
- Baño: bathroom
- Regreso: come back
- Enteró: got to know
- Empezar: begin
- Saca: take out
- Bolsillo: pocket
- Llama: call
- Compañía: company
- Gimnasio: gym
- Qué pasó: what happened
- Afuera: outside
- Nadie: nobody
- Excepto: except
- Sabías: did you know

- Conversar: talk
- Rato: a while
- Media hora más: half an hour
- Esperar: wait
- Cuelga: hang up
- Entra: enter
- Dentro: inside
- Sorpresa: surprise
- Compañera: classmate
- Piano: piano
- Canción de cuna: lullaby
- Nunca: never
- Antes: before
- Escuchado: listen
- A pesar de que: even though
- Presenta: show
- Me llamó: my name is
- Varias: many
- Veces: times
- Creo: I think that
- Hermano menor: younger brother
- Unirse: join
- Antes: before
- Flauta: flute
- Mesa: table
- Explica: explain
- Estudiando: studying
- Gustaba: liked
- Instrumentos: instruments
- Grandes: big
- Pequeños: little
- Tocando: playing
- Batería: drums
- Todos los días: everyday
- Recuerdo: remember

- Primera: first
- Toqué: played
- Pertenecía: belonged
- Baterista: drummer
- Banda de rock: rock band
- Vocalista: vocalist
- Aprendió: learned
- Fácil: easy
- Profesional: proffesional
- Tuba: tuba
- Trompeta: trumpet
- Prácticas: rehearsals
- Acompañaba: accompanied
- Escogió: chose
- Probar: try
- Algo: something
- Diferente: different
- Pesada: heavy
- Vez: time
- Lira: lyre
- Guitarra eléctrica: electric guitar
- Amplificador: amplifier
- Malograda: broken down
- Comprar: buy
- Acústica: acoustic
- Trajo: brought
- Difícil: difficult
- Nervioso: nervous
- Equivoca: is wrong
- Asombrado: astonished
- Viernes: Friday
- Aprendió: learned
- Practico: rehearse
- Olvidando: forgetting
- Escuchar: listen

- Balada: ballad
- Reconoce: acknowledges
- Acaba: finish
- Aplauden: applaud
- Pianista: pianist
- Natural: natural
- Pertenecer: belong
- Divertido: fun
- Aprendo: learn
- Llega: arrive
- Pasar: come in
- Pasión: passion
- Sienta: sits
- Silla: chair
- Cerca: near
- Batería: drums
- Coge: takes
- Baquetas: drum sticks
- Limpia: cleans
- Acomoda: get comfortable
- Juntos: together
- Parecen: look like
- Tocada: play
- Defectuosos: broken down
- Repara: fix
- Acuerdan: agree
- Nuevamente: new
- Esperaré: wait

Chapter 9: Sports Vocabulary

Rodrigo sale a jugar **futbol** todos los días **después** del **colegio**. Su **rutina** es casi siempre la **misma**: él **viene** del colegio, hace su **tarea**, y luego se va a jugar futbol. Salir a jugar futbol es muy **fácil** para él ya que él **vive** en **frente** de dos **campos** de futbol muy grandes.

Rodrigo siempre ha jugado futbol desde que es un **niño**. A él siempre le ha gustado jugar ese **deporte** con sus amigos. A veces, sus amigos lo **llaman** para salir a jugar. Sus padres **permiten** que él juegue siempre y cuando él **sea responsable** con sus tareas y no llegue tarde a clases.

Todos los **vecinos** lo conocen muy bien. Aunque Rodrigo no es un jugador profesional, él **sueña** en **convertirse** en uno cuando sea **grande**. Hoy día, Rodrigo se está **alistando** para jugar con unos amigos que no ve desde hace mucho tiempo.

Los amigos de Rodrigo se llaman Ángel y Piero. Piero parece tener un poco de dificultad a la hora de **patear** la **pelota**. Rodrigo está **contento** de ayudarle.

"Piero, tienes que **apuntar** al **arco**. Tienes que patear fuerte la pelota."

"Pero es muy difícil apuntar, Rodrigo."

"No te preocupes. Mira, patea como yo pateo"

"Ok, lo haré"

Piero patea tan fuerte como puede. Él **tiro** salió **fenomenal**. Fue un **gol**. Rodrigo y Ángel **celebran** y **grita**. Pero Piero se sienta en el suelo y empieza a **quejarse** de **dolor**.

"¿Qué pasa, Piero?"

"Me duele mucho el pie. Esa pelota si estaba **dura**"

"La pelota no es tan dura. ¿De verdad te duele bastante?"

"Sí"

"Espera, creo que ya sé cuál es el problema aquí."

"¿En serio?"

"Sí. Tus **zapatillas**. Tus zapatillas son muy viejas. Están muy **desgastadas**. Tienes que usar zapatillas nuevas y que no estén tan desgastadas. Así no te dolerá tanto cuando patees la pelota."

"pero no tengo más zapatillas que estas"

"Yo te puedo **prestar** las **mías**. Tengo un par más de zapatillas que están en mi habitación. Espera acá mientras las traigo"

Rodrigo sale corriendo del campo de futbol para irse a buscar sus zapatillas. Felizmente, Rodrigo las encuentra. Su par de zapatillas extra estaban **debajo** de la cama. Cuando finalmente las encuentra, se da cuenta que las zapatillas están **sucias**.

Rodrigo las limpia rápidamente y se las lleva a Piero

"**Sácate** las zapatillas que tienes y **ponte** estas"

"¿me **quedarán**?"

"Yo creo que sí. Pruébatelas"

"Lo haré"

"¿Y qué tal?"

"Me quedan bien. Se siente diferente"

"¿Se siente mejor?"

"Se siente mucho mejor"

"Sigamos jugando ahora. Sigue pateando la pelota y yo iré al arco y taparé"

Piero patea la pelota varias veces y **anota** varios goles más. Los chicos continúan celebrando con él. Después de que Piero acabara de patear la pelota, le llega el **turno** a Ángel. Ángel sabe jugar tan bien como Rodrigo, por lo que Rodrigo tiene que **esforzarse** más al tapar cada vez que Ángel patea.

Así, el tiempo pasa volando y los tres muchachos juegan por 1 hora. Luego, Piero y Ángel preguntan a Rodrigo si él practica algún otro deporte.

"¿Qué otro deporte prácticas, Rodrigo? ¿Sólo juegas futbol o también sabes jugar otra cosa?"

"Futbol es lo que más me gusta. Yo lo juego todos los días. Pero también sé jugar **vóleibol**."

"¿Vóleibol? ¿Dónde juegas vóleibol?"

"Aquí en este campo deportivo"

"¿También se puede jugar vóleibol aquí en este campo?"

"Sí. Sólo tienes que traer los instrumentos y después de **ármalo**, juegas con tus amigos."

"¿Qué instrumentos tienes que traer para jugar vóleibol?"

"Tienes que traer tu **net**, tus **postes** y tu pelota de vóleibol"

"Genial. ¿Tú tienes una pelota de vóleibol?"

"Sí. Tengo 2, en realidad"

"Yo no sé jugar vóleibol para nada. Pero aparte del futbol, a mí me gusta jugar tenis."

"¿**Tenis**? ¿Dónde juegas tenis? ¡También vives cerca de un campo deportivo?"

"No. Para ir a jugar tenis, yo tengo que subir a un bus e ir hasta el centro de la ciudad"

"¡Vaya! ¿Cuánto tiempo te toma el viaje?"

"No mucho. Yo vivo cerca del centro de la ciudad así que sólo me toma alrededor de 15 minutos."

Piero se va a comprar una botella de agua mientras los chicos siguen conversando. En la **bodega**, la persona que está allí le pregunta qué tipo de bebida desea.

"¿No quisieras una bebida **energizante**?"

"No me gusta ese tipo de bebidas."

"¿Cuál deseas, entonces? ¿Una gaseosa?

"Vengo por una agua mineral"

"¿De qué tamaño?"

"¿Cuánto cuesta cada tamaño?"

"El tamaño pequeño cuesta 1 dólar, el mediano 2 dólares con 50 centavos y el grande cuesta 3 dólares con 50 centavos"

"Deme el **mediano**, por favor."

"Aquí tienes"

"Gracias"

Cuando Piero llega y se une a la conversación, escucha que los demás están conversando sobre los otros deportes que a ellos les gusta practicar. Piero está emocionado de decirles que él practica varios deportes.

"Yo practico **ciclismo**. Todos los fines de semana me voy con mi tío y mi hermano a manejar bicicleta. Nos vamos **lejos**."

"¿A qué hora salen de sus casas?"

"Salimos a las 9 de la mañana y regresamos a las 4 de la tarde"

"¡Vaya! Son varias horas"

"Sí. Es súper divertido porque puedes ver **paisajes** hermosos e ir a **lugares** que nunca has visto antes"

"Suena divertido. ¿Podría yo ir con ustedes?" – pregunta Ángel.

"¡Por supuesto! Puedes venir este **sábado** con nosotros. Partiremos a las 9 de la mañana"

"¿Qué debo traer?"

"Tienes que traer tu **bicicleta**, tu **casco**, tu **cadena** de seguridad, tus **luces**, y tu **teléfono** por si ocurre alguna emergencia. También trae tu **documento de identidad.**"

"Ok. Traeré todo eso este sábado"

"¿Qué hay de ti, Rodrigo? ¿No quisieras venir con nosotros este sábado a manejar bicicleta?"

"Me encantaría. Pero este sábado ya hice planes con unos amigos para ir a jugar futbol. La siguiente semana puedo ir a manejar con ustedes" – responde Rodrigo

"Vale. No te vayas a olvidar."

"No me olvidaré"

Los muchachos siguen conversando cuando de repente llegan bastantes personas adultas para jugar futbol en el campo deportivo. Las personas parecen muy rudas. Tal parece que ellos son jugadores profesionales. No es la primera vez que Rodrigo ve a jugadores profesionales de futbol en este campo de futbol, pero es la primera vez que los ve a ellos.

Las personas forman sus dos **equipos** pero se dan cuenta que necesitan unos cuantos más para estar **completos**. Por lo que llaman a los muchachos y los invitan a jugar. Los muchachos saben que a la mayoría de jugadores les gusta **apostar**. Pero los muchachos no quieren apostar ni tampoco tienen dinero.

Las personas les dicen que no hay problema y que pueden jugar sin apostar si ellos quieren. Al final, los muchos deciden no jugar y se quedan sentados conversando.

"Yo ya estoy cansado. No quisiera jugar con ellos"

"¿Por qué no vamos a jugar **básquetbol**?"

"¿También sabes jugar básquetbol, Rodrigo?"

"No. Pero tengo una pelota de básquetbol **guardada** en mi casa. Si quieren puedo traerla para jugar un poco de básquetbol"

"Suena bien. Tráela. No te demores mucho"

Rodrigo tiene muchísimas pelotas de futbol, vóleibol, básquetbol e incluso de tenis. Vivir en frente de dos enormes campos deportivos ha ayudado a Rodrigo a mantener un **estilo** de **vida sano** y **alegre**.

Rodrigo no encuentra la pelota de básquetbol. Él corre a preguntarle a su papá si es que ha visto la pelota. Su papá le dice que sí. La pelota está en su habitación. El papá de Rodrigo le da la **llave** de su habitación y Rodrigo entra para sacar el balón.

Rodrigo saca el balón y sale de su casa hacia el campo deportivo. Algunos de sus vecinos lo ven y le preguntan qué está haciendo.

"Estoy llevando mi balón de básquetbol para jugar con mis amigos"

"¿Podemos jugar contigo también?"

"Voy a preguntar a mis amigos"

Rodrigo siempre juega con sus **vecinos**. Pero en esta ocasión él está con Piero y ángel. Él sabe que Piero y Ángel jamás han jugado con los vecinos de Rodrigo y él no sabe si es una buena idea que Piero y Ángel jueguen con sus vecinos.

"Piero, ángel, mis vecinos quieren jugar con nosotros. ¿Les dejamos jugar?"

"No tengo problema. ¿Qué dices tú Piero?

"Yo tampoco tengo ningún problema. Que vengan a jugar."

Rodrigo los llama y ellos entran al campo deportivo. Son bastantes lo que entran a jugar. Durante media hora más, Piero, Ángel y Rodrigo y sus vecinos juegan básquetbol.

Al final de partido, los vecinos de Rodrigo le **agradecen** y se van del campo para comprar unas bebidas.

"Estuvo divertido, ¿verdad, muchachos?"

"Estuvo genial. La siguiente vez que estemos aquí, puedes llamarlos para que jueguen con nosotros una vez más"

"Yo les diré"

"¿Sabes qué hora es?"

"Son las 2 de la tarde"

Piero estaba preguntando la hora ya que él tiene que ir a almorzar. Rodrigo le dice que él puede comer en su casa si es que él desea. En realidad, Rodrigo invita a Piero y Ángel a comer en su casa.

"Vamos a mi casa a comer"

"Gracias, Rodrigo"

"De nada. Cuando estén adentro, no se olviden de **lavarse** bien las **manos** y de limpiar sus zapatillas"

"Yo quisiera bañarme"

"Ya te podrás bañar cuando llegues a casa. Por el momento sólo lávate las manos para que puedas comer"

"Vale"

"Vale, también quisiera **descansar**. Estoy muerto"

"En mi casa hay unos sofás en los que podrás sentarte, sólo espera a que entremos"

"Vale"

Los muchachos entran a la casa de Rodrigo y después de lavarse las manos, se ponen a comer. Luego de comer, los muchachos intentan **acordar** otro día para volver a jugar futbol. Piero **prefiere** los domingos, pero Ángel quiere los martes. Al final Rodrigo les dice que el campo deportivo está **ocupado** de lunes a viernes y que sólo los fines de semana está lo suficientemente vacío para que vengan a jugar.

Entonces, los tres acuerdan jugar el siguiente domingo. Esta vez, ángel piensa traer a su hermano menor, ya que a él también le gusta jugar mucho el fútbol.

"Si tu hermano sabe jugar muy bien y a él le gusta, entonces tráelo."

"Lo haré, tendremos que pedir permiso a nuestros padres, primero"

Y así, los muchachos acaban su conversación y salen nuevamente al campo de fútbol, esta vez ellos no jugarán. Simplemente van para ver como juegan las demás personas.

Resumen de la historia

Rodrigo es un muchacho a quien le encanta jugar futbol. Él lo juega todos los días después de hacer sus tareas. Él vive en frente de dos campos de fútbol enormes, por lo que le es fácil salir a jugar todos los días. Piero y Ángel, amigos de Rodrigo, vienen a jugar con él. Piero tiene un problema con sus zapatillas y Rodrigo le ayuda. Luego, se ponen a conversar sobre los otros deportes que ellos practican. Al final, los vecinos de Rodrigo vienen a jugar con ellos y después, Piero, Ángel y Rodrigo van a almorzar todos juntos en la casa de Rodrigo.

Summary of the story

Rodrigo is a kid who loves playing soccer. He plays it every day after doing his homework. He lives in front of two huge soccer field, so he doesn't have any problem getting there every day. Piero and Ángel, Rodrigo's friends have come to play with him. Piero has a problem with his shoes and Rodrigo helps him. Then they start talking about the other sports they play. In the end, Rodrigo's neighbors come to play with them and then, Piero, Ángel, and Rodrigo go to have lunch together in Rodrigo's house.

- **Futbol: soccer**
- **Después: after**
- **Colegio: school**
- **Rutina: routine**
- **Misma: same**
- **Viene: come**
- **Tarea: homework**

- Fácil: easy
- Vive: lives
- Frente: in front
- Campos: fields
- Niño: kid
- Deporte: sport
- Llaman: call
- Permiten: allow
- Responsable: responsible
- Sea: be
- Vecinos: neighbors
- Sueña: dreams
- Convertirse: become
- Grande: big
- Alistando: getting ready
- Patear: kick
- Pelota: ball
- Contento: content
- Apuntar: aim
- Arco: goal
- Fenomenal: phenomenal
- Tiro: shot
- Gol: goal
- Celebran: celebrate
- Grita: shout
- Quejarse: complain
- Dolor: pain
- Dura: tough
- Zapatillas: snickers
- Desgastadas: worn out
- Prestar: lend
- Mías: mine
- Debajo: under

- Sucias: dirty
- Sácate: take off
- Ponte: put on
- Quedarán: fit
- Anota: score
- Turno: turn
- Esforzarse: strive
- Vóleibol: volleyball
- Ármalo: set it up
- Net: net
- Postes: poles
- Tenis: tennis
- Bodega: store
- Energizante: energizing
- Mediano: médium-sized
- Ciclismo: cycling
- Lejos: far
- Paisajes: landscapes
- Lugares: places
- Sábado: Saturday
- Bicicleta:bycicle
- Casco: helmet
- Cadena: chain
- Luces: lights
- Teléfono: telephone
- Documento de identidad: identity document/ID card
- Equipos: teams
- Completos: complete
- Apostar: bet
- Básquetbol: basketball
- Guardada: stored
- Estilo: style
- Vida: life

- **Sano: healthy**
- **Alegre: happy**
- **Llave: key**
- **Vecinos: neighbors**
- **Agradecen: thank**
- **Lavarse: wash**
- **Manos: hands**
- **Descansar: rest**
- **Acordar: agree**
- **Prefiere: prefer**
- **Ocupado: busy**

Chapter 10: Shopping

Diana está **libre** el día de hoy ya que es **feriado**. En los feriados, ella sale con sus amigas a **pasear**. En esta ocasión, Diana y sus amigas han ido al **centro comercial** que está en el centro de la ciudad para comprar ropa y accesorios.

Diana las **recoge** en su auto y las lleva al centro comercial. Las amigas de Diana viven muy cerca de ella, así que ella no tiene ningún problema en recogerlas. Una de las amigas de Diana se demora un poco en salir. Pero al final ella sale de su casa y entra al auto de Diana.

Cuando finalmente llegan al centro comercial, Diana tiene que **estacionar** su auto pero ella no puede encontrar un lugar donde estacionarse. Ella pregunta a varias personas si hay un espacio disponible cerca de donde ellas están.

Al final, ella logra encontrar un espacio disponible y se estaciona. Diana les dice a sus amigas que **bajen** del auto y todas se dirigen al centro comercial. Dentro del centro comercial, ellas se quedan maravilladas por la **renovación** que se había llevado a cabo la semana pasada.

En los ojos de ellas, el centro comercial parece nuevo. Muchas de las tiendas que estaban en la entrada del centro comercial ya no están. Todas las tiendas han sido **movidas** a otros pisos u otros lugares.

"La tienda donde me gusta comprar **ropa** ya no está aquí" – dice Diana

"De seguro está cerca de aquí. ¿Por qué no preguntamos a uno de los **guardias** si ellos saben dónde está esa tienda?"

"Sí, hay que **preguntarle**"

Diana y sus amigas empiezan a buscar a un guardia de **seguridad** para preguntare sobre la tienda. Felizmente, encuentran a uno en sólo segundos.

"Buenos días, ¿sabe dónde está la tienda de ropas que estaba aquí cerca de la entrada?"

"La tienda que estaba allí fue movida al **segundo** piso. Ustedes pueden tomar el **ascensor** o pueden subir las escaleras."

"Muchas gracias, ¿dónde están las escaleras eléctricas?"

"Las escaleras eléctricas están cerca del **baño**"

"¿Y el ascensor?"

"El ascensor está cerca del baño también"

"Gracias nuevamente."

"De nada"

"Muy bien, chicas. Hay que encontrar las escaleras eléctricas."

Las escaleras eléctricas están un poco lejos de donde ellas están. Caminan por unos cuantos minutos, pero mientras van caminando, ellas van mirando todos los productos que están en las **vitrinas** de las tiendas. La variedad de las tiendas en este centro comercial es asombrosa.

Hay de todo un poco. Hay **tiendas de electrodomésticos, tiendas de celulares, tiendas de ropas, tiendas de muebles, tiendas para ropas de bebés, pastelerías, tiendas de bicicletas y ropa deportiva, casas de cambio** y mucho más.

Antes de ir a las escaleras eléctricas, una de las amigas de Diana se acerca a una de las tiendas.

"¿A dónde vas, María?"

"Estoy yendo a la tienda de electrónicos. Quiero preguntar por los precios de **cargadores** de celulares"

"Hay que entrar a la tienda, entonces, y preguntar al vendedor"

"Buenos días, ¿cómo le puedo ayudar?"

"Buenos días. Vengo por un cargador de celular."

"Aquí usted podrá encontrar el cargador que usted anda buscando. Sígame para mostrarle los cargadores que tenemos"

"¿Los cargadores están en oferta?"

"Sí, los cargadores tienen un **descuento especial** este mes."

"Quisiera llevarme este cargador"

"Genial. Sígame a la **ventanilla**, por favor"

"Vamos"

"El precio de este cargador es de 9 dólares y 25 centavos"

"Vale. ¿Acepta **tarjeta**?"

"¿Tiene tarjeta de **débito** o **crédito**?"

"Es una tarjeta de débito"

"Por favor **deslice** su tarjeta aquí e ingrese su **clave**."

"Ya está"

"Muy bien. ¿Desea una **bolsa** con para el cargador?"

"No. Llevaré el cargador en mi **cartera**."

"¿Desea algún otro producto?"

"No, gracias"

"Ok. Gracias por comprar aquí"

"Gracias"

La amiga de Diana pone el cargador de celular que acaba de comprar dentro de su cartera. Ella también guarda su tarjeta de débito dentro de su **billetera**. El cargador anterior que ella tenía se había malogrado después que le **cayera agua.** Ahora, con este nuevo cargador, ella podrá usar su celular cuando ella desee.

Las muchachas siguen caminando hasta que finalmente encuentran las escaleras eléctricas. Como dijo el guardia. Las escaleras estaban cerca de donde está el baño. Las chicas suben a las escaleras y llegan al segundo piso.

En el segundo piso de este centro comercial hay más tiendas que en el primer piso. La tienda de ropa que Diana estaba buscando se encuentra aquí. Antes de entrar, Diana busca su billetera para ver si tiene suficiente dinero. Dentro de su billetera, ella encuentra 300 dólares.

Diana y sus amigas entran a la tienda de ropa. En esta tienda hay de todo. Hay **zapatos, zapatos con tacones, blusas, pantalones largos y cortos, ropa interior, ropa para hombres y niños**. Lo único que no hay en esta tienda es ropa para **bebés.**

Diana vino para comprarse una blusa nueva. Después de buscar en la tienda por unos minutos, Diana cree que ella ha encontrado la blusa ideal. Es una **blusa** muy bonita y a ella le gusta, pero no sabe si le quedará.

Ella va al vestuario para probárselo y se da con la sorpresa de que no le queda. Pero no se preocupa porque ese vestido viene en varios **tamaños**. Diana le pide a una de sus amigas que traiga el mismo vestido pero en un tamaño diferente.

La amiga de Diana lo trae y se lo da a Diana. Diana se lo prueba y esta vez sí le **queda** perfectamente. Sale del vestuario con el vestido puesto y pregunta a sus amigas si se ve bien.

"¿Qué tal **luzco** en este vestido, chicas? ¿Les gusta?"

"Está muy bonito. Tienes buen gusto"

"Gracias"

"¿Cuánto cuesta ese vestido?"

"No lo sé. Tendré que preguntar a uno de los **vendedores**"

"¿Ese vestido no tiene ninguna **etiqueta**?"

"No he visto ninguna etiqueta en este vestido"

"Yo sí la veo. Aquí está."

"¿qué dice en la etiqueta?"

"Dice que fue hecha en China y que hay que lavarse con cuidado"

"¿Dice algo sobre el precio?"

"Déjame ver. Sí. Dice que el precio de este vestido es de 80 dólares"

"¿80 dólares?"

"Sí, así es"

"Me parece muy caro. ¿No hay algún otro vestido parecido a este que sea más barato?"

"Déjame buscar"

La amiga de Diana va a buscar un vestido que se parezca un poco al vestido que Diana se acaba de probar. Pero no encuentra ninguno parecido. Tal parece que si Diana quiere llevarse ese vestido, ella tendrá que pagar 80 dólares.

"Creo que mejor no lo compro. Me parece muy caro y creo que puedo **conseguir** otro vestido a menor precio"

"Tienes razón. Pero no hay que salir de la tienda todavía. Quiero buscar unos pantalones"

"No hay problema. Busquemos juntas."

Diana y sus amigas empiezan a buscar en la tienda de ropas unos pantalones que le queden a la amiga de Diana. La tienda de ropas es tan grande, que los pantalones tienen su propia sección.

Después de pasar 10 minutos buscando, la amiga de Diana siente que no encuentra nada que le guste. Salen de la tienda y van hacia la tienda de **muebles** a preguntar los precios de sofás.

Los sofás de la casa de Diana son muy viejos y están muy desgastados. Sus padres le pidieron que ella compre unos nuevos sofás. Ella no sabe cuánto pueden costar los sofás exactamente, por ello decide preguntar.

"Hola. Quería preguntar el precio de unos sofás nuevos"

"¿Tienes algún modelo en mente?"

"No. Sólo quiero saber el precio para saber si puedo llevármelo."

"Claro. Mira. Aquí tenemos **modelos** de sofás que sé que te van a encantar."

"¿Y cuánto esta este modelo?"

"Este modelo de sofá esta 120 dólares"

"Me parece un buen precio."

"Y eso no es todo. Si usted compra con una tarjeta de crédito, usted tendrá un 30% de **descuento**"

"¡Genial! Quisiera llevármelos"

"Por favor, sígame a la **ventanilla**"

"Vamos"

"Por favor, deslice su tarjeta de crédito aquí"

"Ya está"

"Parece que hubo un problema. No puedo **aceptar** su tarjeta."

"¿En serio? ¿Puedo deslizarla una vez más?

"Claro"

"Ya está. ¿Esta vez mi tarjeta fue aceptada?"

"Sí, su tarjeta fue aceptada. Disculpe el inconveniente"

"No se preocupe"

Algo que tal vez Dina y sus amigas se hayan olvidado es que los sofás son muy **pesados**, y para llevarlos, ellas tendrán que pedir ayuda a los encargados de la tienda. Felizmente, ellos las ayudan sin cobrar nada. Los empleados suben los sofás al carro de Diana y ella les da una **propina**.

Antes de irse del centro comercial, Diana desea comer algo en el restaurante del centro comercial. Las chicas vuelven a entrar al centro comercial y, debido a la renovación del centro comercial, no pueden encontrar la sección de restaurantes.

Nuevamente preguntan a un guardia de seguridad para que las ayude a encontrar el restaurante. Este guardia no sabe dónde se encuentra el restaurante que Diana está buscando. Diana teme que el restaurante al que ella siempre iba cuando venía al centro comercial haya dejado funcionar debido a la renovación.

Una de las migas de Diana se da cuenta que el restaurante está afuera del centro comercial. Lo que les llama la atención. Sin demora, las chicas van al restaurante y piden una hamburguesa para cada una. Diana también pide un burrito y unos tacos para llevar. Las amigas de Diana también quieren comer un helado.

"Yo pago el **helado**, chicas"

"Gracias, Diana"

"¿Tú no quieres helado?"

"¿Quisiera saber primero qué **sabores** tienen?"

"Bueno, yo sé que sabores tienen ya que yo siempre pido el helado cada vez que vengo a este restaurante"

"¿Cuáles son los sabores?"

"Los sabores que ellos tienen son **mora, fresa, vainilla, chocolate, piña y menta**"

"¡Vaya! Son varios sabores. No puedo escoger"

"Escoge un sabor que no hayas probado aun. Así probaras algo diferente"

"Ok. Aún no he probado el helado sabor a menta."

"Entonces, ¿pido ese sabor de helado?

"Sí, por favor"

Las chicas disfrutan de los helados por unos cuantos minutos más hasta que ven que ya es hora de partir. Es cierto que Diana no pudo comprar la blusa que ella quería, pero tal vez, la próxima vez que venga, el precio de ese vestido baje considerablemente.

Las chicas caminan hacia el auto de Diana. Diana muestra su boleto de compras para no pagar el estacionamiento. Las chicas se suben y ponen algo de música. Antes de partir, todas se ponen su cinturón de seguridad.

Antes de encender el auto, Diana les agradece.

"Muchas gracias por acompañarme"

"No te preocupes. La siguiente nos pasas la voz. Nos gustó salir contigo. Esperemos que se repita."

"No hay duda que las llamaré"

Finalmente, Diana enciende el auto, sale del **estacionamiento** del centro comercial y se dirige a casa.

Resumen de la historia

Diana y sus amigas se dirigen al centro comercial en el feriado. Diana tiene en mente comprar un vestido, pero lamentablemente cuando ella encuentra el vestido, el precio es demasiado caro para ella. Mientras tanto, las amigas de Diana van comprando cargadores y pantalones. Al final, Diana se acuerda que ella tiene que comprar sofás nuevos ya que los sofás que ella tiene en su casa son muy viejos y están muy desgastados. Después de comprarlos, los pone en su auto. Finalmente, ellas comen en un restaurante que antes estaba dentro del centro comercial para luego partir a casa.

Summary of the story

Diana and her friends go to the mall on a holiday. Diana has in mind buying a dress, but unfortunately, when she finds the dress, it's too expensive for her. Meanwhile, Diana's friends are buying chargers and pants. In the end, Diana remembers that she has to buy new sofas because the sofas that she has in her house are very old and worn-out. After buying them, she puts them in her car. Finally, they eat at a restaurant that used to be inside the mall and then go home.

- **Libre: free/available**
- **Feriado: holiday**
- **Pasear : hang out**
- **Centro comercial: mall**

- Recoge: pick up
- Estacionar: park
- Bajen: get off
- Renovación: renovation
- Movidas: moved
- Ropa: clothes
- Guardias: guards
- Preguntarle: ask him
- Seguridad: security
- Segundo: second
- Ascensor: lift
- Baño: bathroom
- Vitrinas: glass
- Electrodomésticos: home appliances
- Celulares: celphones
- Ropas: clothes
- Muebles: furniture
- Ropas de bebés: baby clothes
- Pastelerías: bakeries
- Deportiva: sport
- Casas de cambio: Currency Exchange office
- Cargadores: chargers
- Descuento: discount
- Especial: especial
- Ventanilla: counter
- Tarjeta: card
- Débito: debit
- Crédito: credit
- Deslice: swipe
- Clave: key
- Bolsa: bag
- Cartera: purse
- Billetera: wallet

- Cayera: fall
- Agua:water
- Bebés: babies
- Zapatos: shoes
- Zapatos con tacones: high heels
- Pantalones largos: long pants
- Pantalones cortos: short pants
- Ropa interior: underwear
- Ropa para hombres: men's clothes
- Blusa: blouse
- Tamaños: sizes
- Queda: fit
- Luzco: look
- Vendedores: sellers
- Etiqueta: label
- Conseguir: get
- Modelos: models/brands
- Descuento:discount
- Aceptar: accept
- Pesados: haeavy
- Propina: tip
- Helado: ice cream
- Sabores: flavors
- Mora: blackberry
- Fresa: strawberry
- Vainilla: vanilla
- Chocolate: chocolate
- Piña: pineapple
- Menta: mint
- Estacionamiento: parking

Chapter 11: Animals

El **zoológico** de la ciudad fue recientemente **inaugurado**. Muchas personas estaban esperando **ansiosamente** a que el zoológico esté abierto. Un nuevo zoológico significa un nuevo lugar dónde las familias pueden ir para **divertirse** y pasar unos momentos juntos. Además, todos los que entran al zoológico pueden aprender sobre los **animales** que **alberga**.

Es eso lo que hoy día Jorge, sus padres y su hermano menor están haciendo. Jorge se perdió el **paseo** al zoológico que su escuela había planeado el mes pasado, ya que él se había **enfermado**.

Ahora que está mejor, sus padres lo han traído a él y a su hermano menor a este zoológico. Y como el zoológico acaba de ser inaugurado, muchas de las **instalaciones** y **atracciones** del zoológico son nuevas.

Los animales nuevos que han traído son la **sensación**. Jorge está súper emocionado de ver el **león** y la **pantera**. Sus padres están más interesados en ver los **peces** y el **hermanito** de Jorge quiere ver las **aves**.

Ellos llegan al zoológico temprano. Hacen su **cola** y pagan la **entrada**. Como Jorge y su hermano son menores de edad, ellos pagan un precio especial; ellos tienen un **descuento**. No es así con los padres de Jorge; ellos pagan el precio completo.

La primera sección a la que ellos entran es la sección de los **primates**. Es nueva. Se ve que han traído más animales y los animales en esta sección son muestra de ello.

"Papá, ¿Esos son **monos**?"

"Así es hijo"

"No sabía que los monos pueden ser tan grandes"

"Estos no son cualquier mono, hijo. Estos son gorilas."

"¿Gorilas? Me dan mucho miedo"

"Son muy grandes y fuertes. No te acerques mucho a ellos"

"¿De dónde vienen los **gorilas**?"

"Los gorilas viene de la jungla"

"¿Comen mucho?"

"Sí. Ellos comen bastante"

"¿Qué otros animales hay en esta sección, papá?"

"En la sección de primates vas a encontrar varios tipos de monos, **orangutanes** y gorilas."

"Los monos parecen divertidos"

"Lo son. Pero siempre hay que tener cuidado a la hora de estar con animales"

"Entendido, papá"

"Si seguimos caminando, veremos más monos y más animales"

"¡Vamos!"

Mientras Jorge y su familia van caminando por la sección de primates, ellos ven más **simios** y se quedan maravillados por la gran variedad que hay. Todos estos animales tienen su propio espacio donde ellos pueden **jugar**, **comer** y **dormir**. Todos los animales de la sección de primates y de las demás secciones de este zoológico cuentan con cuidados especiales.

Muchos de los animales en este zoológico son animales que fueron **rescatados**. Aquí, ellos son cuidados y alimentados. También se les da la medicina que ellos necesitan para sentirse mejor.

La siguiente sección es la sección de las aves. Es la sección que el hermano de Jorge estaba esperando ver. El hermanito menor de Jorge se sorprende. Para entrar a la sección de aves, ellos tiene que entrar a una **jaula** enorme donde todas las aves se encuentran. Hay aves muy coloridas y el hermano de Jorge se anima a preguntar.

"Papá, ¿estás aves siempre hacen mucho ruido?"

"Así es hijo, es su manera de comunicarse"

"¿Cuántas aves crees que haya aquí?"

"Tal vez haya mil o más"

"¡Vaya! Yo también quisiera tener una ave de **mascota**."

"No hijo. Algunas aves no pueden ser mascotas"

"¿En serio? ¿Cómo cuáles?"

"Como por ejemplo, las aves no voladoras"

"¿Aves no voladoras? ¿Hay aves que no pueden volar?"

"Así es hijo, y creo que tú conoces un ave que no puede volar"

"No se me ocurre nada, papá"

"Bueno, el **pollo** y la **gallina** son aves que no pueden volar, por ejemplo. Ambas aves sirven de **alimento** para nosotros"

"No se me había ocurrido"

"Mira, afuera de la sección de aves hay otra ave que tampoco puede volar"

"¿Qué ave es esa?"

"Fíjate bien en que ave es y lo sabrás"

"¡Es un **pingüino**!"

"Exacto. Los pingüinos tampoco pueden volar, pero son excelentes nadadores. Algunos pingüinos viven en lugares donde hace mucho **frío**"

"¿Y cómo aguantan todo ese frío?"

"Los pingüinos tienen un **pelaje** especial que les ayuda a **mantenerse calientes**. Pero ellos también se **protegen** y se alimentan muy bien"

"Ellos comen **pescado**, ¿verdad, papá?"

"Como ellos son excelentes **nadadores**, ellos saben **cazar** pescado muy bien"

Después de esa **explicación**, Jorge y su familia se dirigen al **acuario** que está en el centro del zoológico. Los padres de Jorge querían venir a ver esta sección en especial ya que al papá de Jorge le gusta mucho los peces.

La mamá de Jorge solía tener una pequeña **pecera** en la sala de la casa. Ella cuidaba del acuario todos los días. Ella alimentaba a los peces y cambiaba el agua cada vez que era necesario. Ahora ella se queda **boquiabierta** al ver el inmenso acuario que hay en este zoológico.

Pero los peces no son los únicos que están en este acuario. **Cangrejos, moluscos, camarones, esponjas de mar, pulpos e incluso delfines** están en este acuario. Cada especie en un lugar diferente.

Mientras ellos caminan viendo el acuario, ellos pueden ver que hay **letreros** que explican lo que cada animal hace y cómo se comporta en su hábitat **salvaje**. Ellos leen con interés mientras que Jorge y su hermanito se quedan viendo un pulpo.

El pulpo parecía que estaba durmiendo. Jorge y su hermanito creen que ellos despertaron al pulpo. Ellos ven que el pulpo tiene muchos tentáculos y empiezan a contarlo. Todos estos tentáculos son muy largos pero el pulpo parece tener una forma muy divertida.

El pulpo se va nadando y aparece un cangrejo. Pero este cangrejo es más grande que los cangrejos que se ven en el mar. Este cangrejo se mueve rápido y sus largas **patas** lo ayudan a saltar.

Jorge ve un objeto de color naranja que está en el suelo del acuario y le pregunta a su papá qué es. Su papá le dice que esa cosa es un animal.

"¿Estás seguro que no lo has visto antes?" – pregunta su papá

"No creo que lo haya visto antes, papá" - responde Jorge

"¿Cuántas patas tiene?"

"Tiene 5"

"¿Qué forma tiene es e animal, hijo?"

"Se parece a una **estrella**"

"Entonces, ese animal debe ser..."

"¡Es una estrella de mar!"

"¡Así es! Es una **Estrella de mar**"

Jorge le dice a su hermanito que él ha encontrado una estrella de mar en el acuario. El hermanito de Jorge le pregunta dónde está y Jorge le señala dónde se encuentra la estrella de mar.

El acuario es una de las zonas más grandes del zoológico, por lo que le toma a la familia de Jorge alrededor de 20 minutos salir del acuario. Antes de salir, ellos toman tantas fotos como pueden de los animales y de los peces que ven. Los peces son de muchísimos colores y formas. Casi todos los animales del acuario son animales que Jorge y su familia jamás han visto.

Al salir del acuario, ellos encuentran al león. Es lo que Jorge quería ver desde que él llegó. El león está puesto en un espacio cerrado. Las personas pueden verlo a través de la **pared** de **vidrio transparente**. A algunas personas les da mucho miedo **acercarse** al león. Jorge también tiene un poco de miedo, pero igual se queda a ver al león. Él sabe bien que el león no puede hacerle daño siempre y cuando el león esté en su espacio y haya una pared de vidrio transparente.

El león **ruge** con mucha fuerza y las personas se quedan asombradas por su rugido. El hermanito de Jorge se **asusta** y empieza a llorar. Sus padres intentan calmarlo pero el niño sigue llorando.

Jorge se da cuenta de que su hermanito está llorando y va a comprar un helado afuera de la jaula del león, se lo trae a su hermano y su hermano deja de llorar. Todos siguen avanzando.

"Pensé que en este zoológico había serpientes" – dice Jorge

"Yo también" - dice la mama de Jorge

"A lo mejor hay que preguntar a alguien dónde están las **serpientes**" – dice el papá de Jorge

Antes de que puedan preguntar a alguien, ellos se topan con los cocodrilos. Están en un hábitat especial que parece un pantano. Los padres de Jorge quieren tomar una foto pero el cuidador les dice que las fotos están prohibidas en esta sección. Los padres de Jorge guardan sus cámaras y admiran al animal.

"¿Qué nos falta ver?" – pregunta el papá de Jorge

"Creo que no nos falta nada más por ver"

"Entonces, ¿qué les parece si vamos a comer algo?"

"Suena genial"

"Sí"

"Tenemos que encontrar el restaurante"

"Aquí hay un mapa que nos puede guiar al restaurante"

Dentro del zoológico hay un restaurante muy grande y muy bonito. Todas las familias son bienvenidas dentro del restaurante. Cuando finalmente la familia de Jorge encuentra el restaurante, ellos ven que el restaurante está decorado con muchas fotos y pinturas de animales salvajes. Incluso hay muñecos enormes de leones, **gacelas, tortugas y cebras**.

Los padres de Jorge empiezan a almorzar mientras que Jorge y su hermano van a jugar a los juegos **mecánicos** que están cerca del restaurante. Hay **carritos chocones, laberintos y toboganes**. Jorge y su hermanito se divierten bastante mientras juegan.

Después que los papás de Jorge acaban de comer, ellos llaman a sus hijos para que vengan a comer también. Después que toda la familia ha acabado de comer, ellos se preparan para salir del zoológico y regresar a casa.

Cerca de la puerta de salida del zoológico hay una tienda de reglaos muy bonita. Jorge insiste a su padre para comprar unos recuerdos del zoológico. Al principio, su papá no quiere entrar a la **tienda de regalos** ya que él cree que todo lo que venden allí está muy caro. Él le dice a Jorge que él no tiene suficiente dinero para comprar unos recuerdos dentro del zoológico.

La mamá de Jorge les dice que no hay problema en entrar al zoológico siempre y cuando no vayan a comprar algo muy caro. El papá de Jorge acepta y todos entran a la tienda de regaos.

"Mira papá. Hay un **oso de peluche** colgado aquí"

"Sí. Y es muy grande."

"¿Nos lo podemos llevar?"

"Hay que preguntar a tu mamá"

"Mamá, ¿puedes comprarme este oso de peluche?"

"Pero hijo, tú ya tienes dos osos de peluche en la casa"

"Sí, lo sé. Pero no tengo uno de este tamaño"

"Hijo, este oso de peluche es muy caro"

"Pero mamá, lo quiero"

"Hijo, tienes que entender que no tenemos para pagar por el oso"

"Ok, mamá"

"Mira, aquí hay otro oso de peluche que estoy segura que te va a gustar. Este oso de peluche está más barato también."

"A ver. Quiero verlo"

"Es un oso muy bonito"

"Es un oso panda, ¿verdad?"

"Sí, hijo"

A Jorge le gustan mucho los **osos pandas** y a su hermanito también, sus padres deciden comprar el oso panda para ambos. El papá de Jorge compra un gorro y la mamá de Jorge se compra un **llavero**.

De esa manera termina el día para la familia de Jorge. Todos salen muy contentos del zoológico. Jorge y su hermanito preguntan cuándo volverán.

"¿Podemos volver la siguiente semana, papá?"

"Si se portan bien, los traeré de nuevo al zoológico"

"¡Qué bien!"

Jorge y su hermano se ponen a jugar dentro del auto y la mamá y el papá de Jorge se **abrochan** los **cinturones**. El papá de Jorge enciende el auto y todos regresan a casa.

Resumen de la historia

Jorge no pudo ir al paseo que su escuela había organizado porque él estaba enfermo. Por esa razón, su familia planea un paseo al zoológico. Jorge y su familia encuentran diferentes secciones en todo el zoológico y se asombran por todos los animales nuevos que han traído. Después de ver los animales, Jorge y su familia almuerzan y van a la tienda de regalos. Al final, el papá de Jorge les promete volver la siguiente semana si ellos se portan bien.

Summary of the story

Jorge couldn't go on the trip his school had organized because he was sick. That's why his family plans a trip to the zoo. Jorge and his family find different sections in all the zoo and they're amazed at the new animals that have been brought. After seeing the animals, Jorge and his family have lunch and go to the gift store. In the end, Jorge's dad promises them to go back next week if they behave.

- **Zoológico: zoo**
- **Inaugurado: inaugurated**
- **Ansiosamente: anxiously**
- **Divertirse: have fun**
- **Animales: animals**
- **Alberga: hosts**
- **Enfermado: sick**
- **Paseo: trip**

- Instalaciones: installations
- Atracciones: attractions
- Sensación: sensation
- León: lion
- Pantera: panther
- Peces: fish
- Hermanito: younger brother
- Aves: bird
- Cola: queue
- Entrada: ticket
- Descuento: discount
- Primates: primates
- Monos: monkeys
- Gorilas: gorillas
- Orangutanes: orangutans
- Simios: apes
- Jugar: play
- Comer: eat
- Dormir: sleep
- Rescatados: rescued
- Jaula: cage
- Mascota: pet
- Pollo: chicken
- Gallina: hen
- Alimento: food
- Pingüino: penguin
- Frio: cold
- Pelaje: fur
- Mantenerse: keep
- Calientes: hot
- Protegen: protect
- Pescado: fish
- Nadadores: swimmers
- Cazar: hunt
- Explicación: explanation
- Acuario: aquarium

- Pecera: fish tank
- Boquiabierta: open
- Cangrejos: crab
- Moluscos: mollusks
- Camarones: shrimps
- Esponjas de mar: sea sponges
- Pulpos: octopuses
- Delfines: dolphines
- Letreros: signs
- Salvaje: wild
- Patas: feet
- Estrella: star
- Estrella de mar: starfish
- Pared: wall
- Vidrio: glass
- Transparente: transparent
- Acercarse: approach
- Ruge: roar
- Asusta: be afraid
- Serpientes: serpents
- Gacelas: gazelles
- Tortugas: turtles
- Cebras: zebras
- Mecánicos: mechanic
- Carritos chocones: bumper car
- Laberintos: mazes
- Toboganes: sledges
- Oso de peluche: teddy bear
- Tienda de regalos: gift shop
- Osos pandas: panda bear
- Llavero: key chain
- Abrochan: fasten
- Cinturones: belt

Chapter 12: Going to the Doctor

Era un tarde como **cualquier** otra para Fernando. El muchacho había ido a jugar fútbol con sus amigos después de hacer sus tareas. A él le **encantaba** jugar futbol con sus amigos. Aunque es verdad que él sabe jugar futbol muy bien, los **accidentes** pueden llegar a ocurrir de todas maneras.

Se **escuchó** un grito muy fuerte en el campo deportivo. Dos muchachos, uno de ellos Fernando, estaban **echados** en el suelo **quejándose** de dolor. Los demás muchachos **dejaron** de jugar y empezaron a **rodear** a los dos muchachos que se habían **golpeado**.

Fue un accidente, pero parecía **grave**. Fernando estaba **sangrando**, el otro muchacho estaba solo **llorando** de **dolor**. Uno de los amigos de Fernando que estaba jugando con él cuando el accidente pasó **llamó** a su mamá y le dijo sobre lo que había **ocurrido**. Su mamá fue **apresuradamente** al campo deportivo a ver a su hijo.

La mamá de Fernando entró al campo deportivo y ayudó a su hijo a **levantarse**. Es ahí cuando ella se dio cuenta que su hijo no podía **caminar**. La mamá de Fernando también llamo a unos de los padres del otro muchacho. Los padres del otro muchacho también vinieron al campo deportivo sólo unos minutos después.

Ambos muchachos fueron llevados al **hospital** tan rápido como se pudo. Después de estar en la sala de **urgencias** por unas horas, los muchachos se **recuperan** y vuelven a casa. Una **semana** después, ellos **vuelven** al doctor para **continuar** con el **chequeo** médico y ver su **avance**.

"Buenas tardes, doctor" – dice Fernando

"Buenas tardes. ¿Dónde está tu mamá?" – pregunta el doctor

"Mi mamá está por llegar. Ella está en camino"

"Mientras esperamos a tu mamá, ¿por qué no me cuentas lo que ocurrió?"

"Claro, doctor. Yo estaba jugando futbol con mis amigos en el campo deportivo que está cerca de mi casa. En una de las **jugadas**, yo pensé que había **pateado** muy fuerte el balón. En realidad, pateé a uno de mis amigos por accidente. El **golpe** que nos dimos fue tan fuerte que ambos nos caímos y nos raspamos las piernas contra el suelo. Cuando me di cuenta de que estaba sangrando, quería levantarme para ir a mi casa y buscar ayuda, pero se me hacía difícil levantarme."

"¿Qué parte de la pierna te golpeaste?"

"Fue el **tobillo**, doctor"

"¿Qué pasó después?"

"Nos quedamos en el **suelo** por unos minutos y nuestros amigos nos rodearon. Ellos intentaron **ayudarnos** pero no sabían que hacer. Uno de ellos llamó a mi mamá y le dijo que había tenido un **accidente**. Mi mamá vino al campo deportivo y ella también **intento** levantarme pero se dio cuenta que yo no podía caminar."

"¿Fue ella quien te **llevó** al hospital?"

"Sí. Ella me llevó al hospital."

"¿Qué te hicieron? ¿Estuviste en la sala de Urgencias?"

"Sí, doctor. Ahí, un **traumatólogo** me ayudó. Él me dio algunas **pastillas** para el **dolor** y también me vendó el tobillo.

"¿Te dijo que hicieras algunos **ejercicios** para **mejorar** la **movilidad** del **pie**?"

"Me dijo que sí me iba a dar ejercicios para hacer en casa. Pero por el momento tenía que **descansar** y **avisar** a mi **doctor de cabecera.**"

"Bueno, yo soy tu doctor de cabecera y déjame decirte que el accidente que tuviste no es muy grave"

"¿De veras, doctor?"

"Así es. Pero de todos modos tienes que descansar por una semana más. Que no sea grave no significa que puedes jugar **inmediatamente**."

"Lo sé, doctor. De todas maneras aun siento que no puedo jugar. Solamente caminar me duele, no me imagino cuánto me dolería si jugara futbol nuevamente."

"¿Trajiste los **medicamentos** que el traumatólogo te **recomendó**?"

"Sí, aquí están."

"Muy bien. Escucha. Seguirás tomando los medicamentos que el traumatólogo te dio, ¿ok? No **dejes** de tomarlos. Esos medicamentos son muy importantes. Ahora bien. Yo voy a **recomendarte** una **crema** contra el dolor."

"¿Dónde puedo **conseguir** esa crema, doctor?"

"La puedes conseguir en cualquier farmacia."

"¿Qué hará esa crema por mí, doctor?"

"Esa crema ayudará a que la **intensidad** del dolor **baje** considerablemente"

"Pero doctor, tengo una **herida** en varias partes de mi pierna. ¿Puedo **aplicarme** esa crema a pesar de las heridas que tengo?"

"Déjame ver tus heridas, por favor"

Fernando se quita la **venda** a la orden del doctor. Las vendas que rodean su pierna son muy largas. Cuando finalmente Fernando se quita las vendas, el doctor puede ver que las heridas que Fernando tiene no son tan grandes como lo eran la primera vez que vino hace una semana.

"Gracias, toma, acá tengo unas vendas para ti. Póntelas."

"Gracias, doctor"

"Veo que tu heridas no son tan graves como lo eran hace una semana. No hay **problema** en que te apliques la crema que te estoy dando. Recuerda **aplicar** esta crema a tu tobillo 3 veces por día. Todas las mañanas, después del almuerzo y antes de irte a dormir, ¿entendido?"

"Entendido doctor. ¿**Con cuanta frecuencia** debería cambiar muis vendas?"

"Debes **cambiártelas** una vez al día. De preferencia, cámbiatelas antes de irte a dormir"

"¿De vería usar un jabón **antibacteriano** para lavar las heridas?"

"No es necesario, pero si quieres usarlo, puedes hacerlo."

En ese momento, la puerta del doctor suena. Alguien está tocando la puerta del doctor. ¿Quién puede ser? Al doctor no le gusta que le **interrumpan** cuando está **atendiendo** a un paciente.

El doctor abre la puerta y es su **asistente** quien le dice que la mamá de Fernando acaba de llegar. El doctor le dice al asistente que deje pasar a la mamá de Fernando. La mamá de Fernando saluda al doctor y a su hijo, **toma asiento** y empieza a hablar con el doctor.

"Buenos días, doctor. Disculpe por la demora."

"No se preocupe, señora. Estaba conversando con su hijo sobre el accidente que tuvo hace una semana."

"Ya veo. Fue muy feo el accidente que Fernando y su amigo tuvieron."

"Lo sé. ¿Recuerda cuánto tiempo estuvieron en la sala de urgencias?"

"Creo que estuvimos por 2 horas, doctor"

"¿Y qué hicieron después?"

"Después de salir de la salas de urgencias, lo llevé a casa y le dije que descansara, tal como el doctor le había ordenado. "

"Bien. ¿Tiene usted alguna pregunta para mí?"

"Sí, doctor. ¿Cuánto tiempo tiene él que tener la venda puesta?"

"El accidente no fue tan grave, así que yo diría que en un mes él podrá quitarse las vendas. Pero si es que él no se **cuida** y no se **recupera**, entonces tendrá que seguir con las vendas por más tiempo"

"¿Tendrá que seguir un **tratamiento** de **rehabilitación**, doctor?"

"No creo. Normalmente recomendamos un tratamiento de rehabilitación cuando el accidente ha sido muy grave o cuando el paciente no puede mover su pierna. En el caso de Fernando, él aún puede mover su pierna y aunque ahora mismo es muy difícil caminar para él, él estará volverá a caminar en sólo dos semanas más sin necesidad de estar en rehabilitación"

"¿Debería él volver a jugar futbol?"

"No. Él no debe jugar futbol. Si él vuelve a jugar fútbol, podría tener un accidente de nuevo o no permitiría que su **lesión** sane correctamente, lo que causará más dolor y tal vez una lesión **permanente**."

"Entendido doctor"

Fernando mira a su mamá y su mama le da un **abrazo**. El doctor sabe muy bien que puede ser un poco difícil tenar un accidente, pero les asegura a los dos que no hay nada por lo que **preocuparse**.

El doctor toma asiento y empieza a **escribir** en una hoja de papel. Es la **receta médica**. Se lo da a la mamá de Fernando y les pide que lo compren inmediatamente.

El doctor también les dice a Fernando y a su mamá que él va a pedir una cita para **traumatología** para este fin de semana. Fernando y su mamá están de acuerdo. El doctor pasa a decirles lo que tienen que hacer.

"Tienen que ir a la cita con el traumatólogo. La cita ya está **programada** para este fin de semana. La cita es este sábado a las 11 de la mañana. Por favor, no se olviden de traer su receta médica que les estoy dando y no se olviden de decirle al doctor sobre el accidente."

"¿Cómo se llama el traumatólogo?"

"El nombre del doctor es: Pedro Abad"

"Muchas gracias, doctor"

"Eso sería todo por hoy. ¿Alguna pregunta más?"

"No doctor, no tengo ninguna otra pregunta"

Fernando y su mama agradecen al doctor por la atención que recibieron y se despiden de él. Al salir de la oficina del doctor, agradecen al asistente y también se despiden de él. Fernando vino en bus pero la mamá de Fernando vino en carro, por lo que ambos suben al auto.

Durante el regreso a casa, Fernando se queda **dormido**. Al llegar a casa, su mamá tiene que levantarlo ya ayudarlo a caminar hacia la puerta de la casa. El perro de Fernando se **alegra** de verlos pero su mamá intenta alejarlo para que el perro no toque la pierna de Fernando

Al entrar a la casa, la mamá de Fernando le dice que **descanse** y que vaya su habitación. La verdad es que Fernando se **aburre** mucho en su habitación y prefiere estar afuera con sus amigos. La mamá de Fernando piensa en algo muy ingeniosos.

Como ella sabe que su hijo prefiere estar afuera con sus amigos en lugar de estar todo el día en la casa. La mamá de Fernando pone una silla y una mesa en el jardín que está al frente de la casa y le dice a Fernando que vaya a sentarse ahí. Después, la mamá de Fernando llama a los amigos de Fernando para que vengan a jugar con él.

Muchos de los amigos de Fernando que vieron el accidente que tuvo vienen a ver como está. Algunos de ellos le traen **regalos** e incluso le traen **comida**. Otros traen unos juegos de mesa para jugar con Fernando.

La mamá de Fernando trae más sillas para que todos se sienten cómodos y hagan compañía a Fernando. Todos los amigos de Fernando tienen muchísimas preguntas.

"¿Te dolió mucho?"

"¿Cuánto tiempo estuviste en el hospital?"

"¿Cuándo volverás a jugar con nosotros?"

Fernando intenta responder todas las preguntas que puede, ¡pero son muchas! Algunos de sus amigos se sorprenden por las vendas que Fernando tiene. Uno de ellos incluso relata cómo una vez él también tuvo un accidente jugando fútbol.

Toda la tarde, Fernando y sus amigos se quedan conversando hasta que finalmente la mamá de Fernando le dice que es hora para cenar. Los amigos de Fernando saben que es hora de despedirse. Todos se dicen adiós y se van a casa.

Fernando **agradece** a su mamá y le da un abrazo. Tal parece que Fernando se olvidó del accidente que tuvo. Es cierto que tendrá que descansar por un mes, pero el tiempo pasa **volando**. Él sabe que en unas **pocas** semanas más él estará **jugando** una vez más con **todos** sus amigos.

Resumen de la historia

Fernando es un muchacho a quien le encanta jugar futbol después de hacer sus tareas. Lamentablemente, en esta ocasión, Fernando y su amigo tienen un accidente mientras ambos juegan futbol. Fernando y su amigo son llevados al hospital para ser revisados. Una semana después, Fernando vuelve con su mamá para el seguimiento con su doctor de cabecera. El doctor de cabera de Fernando le da instrucciones para que él siga cuando llegue a casa y también una nueva receta médica. Cuando Fernando y su mamá finalmente llegan a casa, Fernando, con la ayuda de su mamá, pasa el rato con sus amigos que vienen a visitarlo. Al final, Fernando agradece a su mamá y ambos ven a cenar.

Summary of the story

Fernando is a guy who loves playing soccer after doing his homework. Unfortunately, on this occasion, Fernando and his friend have an accident while both are playing soccer. Fernando and his friend are sent to the hospital to be checked. A week later, Fernando returns with his mom for a follow-up with his primary care physician. Fernando's doctor gives him instructions for him to follow and a new medical receipt. When Fernando and his mom finally get home, Fernando, with his mom's help, hangs out with his friends that are coming to visit him. In the end, Fernando thanks his mom and both have dinner.

- **Cualquier: any**
- **Encantaba: loved**
- **Accidentes: accidents**
- **Escuchó: heard**
- **Echados: laid**
- **Quejándose: complaining**
- **Dejaron: left**
- **Rodear: surround**
- **Golpeado: hit**
- **Grave: serious**
- **Sangrando: bleeding**
- **Llorando: crying**
- **Dolor: pain**
- **Llamó: called**
- **Ocurrido: happened**
- **Apresuradamente: in a hurry**
- **Levantarse: get up**
- **Caminar: walk**
- **Hospital: hospital**
- **Urgencias: urgencies**
- **Recuperan: recover**
- **Semana: week**
- **Vuelven: come back**
- **Continuar: continue**
- **Chequeo: check**

- Avance: follow up
- Jugadas: moves
- Pateado: kicked
- Golpe: hit
- Tobillo: ankle
- Suelo: ground
- Ayudarnos: help us
- Intento: try
- Llevó: brought
- Traumatólogo: traumatologist
- Pastillas: pills
- Dolor: pain
- Ejercicios: exercises
- Mejorar: improve
- Movilidad: mobility
- Pie: foot
- Descansar: rest
- Avisar: tell
- Doctor de cabecera: primary care physician
- Inmediatamente: immediately
- Medicamentos: medication
- Recomendó: recommended
- Dejes: leave
- Recomendarte: recommend
- Crema: cream
- Conseguir: get
- Intensidad: intensity
- Baje: decreases
- Herida: wound
- Aplicarme: apply it
- Venda: bandage
- Problema: problem
- Aplicar: apply

- Con cuanta frecuencia: how often
- Cambiártelas: change them
- Antibacteriano: antibacterial
- Interrumpan: interrump
- Atendiendo: attending
- Asistente: assistant
- Toma asiento: takes a seat
- Recupera: recovers
- Cuida: takes care of
- Tratamiento: treatment
- Rehabilitación: rehab
- Lesión: injury
- Permanente: permanently
- Abrazo: hug
- Preocuparse: worry
- Escribir: write
- Receta médica: medical receipt
- Traumatología: traumatology
- Programada: programed
- Dormido: slept
- Alegra: rejoices
- Descanse: rest
- Aburre: gets bored
- Regalos: gifts
- Comida: food
- Agradece: thanks
- Volando: flying
- Pocas: few
- Jugando: playing
- Todos: everyone

Conclusion

There are many goals you can set for yourself as a person. You can decide to grow your language skills by practicing the language that you prefer in any way you want it, but the key to success remains the same: perseverance. You see, sometimes, you might not have the time to read a whole book or lean all the grammar rules of a language, but that shouldn't stop you from trying to achieve your goal of proficiency and fluency. Try to practice every day, as little as you can, but don't give up easily. Don't quit just because you feel you can't.

Spanish Conversations is the tool you need to practice every day to understand not only how the language works, but also how the language is used on a daily basis by native speakers. This book was designed with you, the learner, in mind so that you can have a better understanding of what's being said and introduced in every chapter. Each chapter dealt with a specific topic and each story that's within it was produced to illustrate that point as much as possible, whether that topic is numbers, past tense, animals, parts of the house, sport vocabulary, school vocabulary and more.

Spanish Conversations' goal is to help you see how the language is used so that you can understand words in context and also imitate the example of native Spanish speakers. Because let's face it. The best examples of how to use the Spanish language comes from Spanish speakers themselves. They know how their language can be used in the many facets of life they encounter. Many of the phrases and terms this book uses have been verified by Spanish speakers themselves and they have given their approval. You can rest assured that what you are holding in your hands is a very modern and useful tool that anyone can use.

Learning Spanish might not seem easy at first. You might think that you're not making any progress, but don't despair. Every language learner has to come to terms with their own circumstances that might limit their advancement and then tackle them with optimism and confidence. Don't be shy to speak up. Show what you're learning so far. The best way to practice Spanish is if you use it, so don't stop speaking! At the same time, listen and continue learning. If your goal is fluency, then you understand that you need to continue growing in knowledge every day.

We know *Spanish Conversations* will prove to be the most useful tool in this path. You can have fun while learning, and improving every day.

Learn Spanish for Beginners the Fast Way

Grammar Lessons, Pronunciation, Rules, Reading and Writing. Spanish Made Easy with your Personal Coach

[Michael Navarro]

Introduction

Congratulations on purchasing "Learning Spanish for Beginners the Fast Way," and thank you for doing so. Globally, Spanish is a popular language spoken by many. Therefore, having excellent mastery of it can offer you unlimited opportunities. For instance, it can enable you to work in many Spanish-speaking countries, form networks for whatever purpose, and significantly fortify your resume to attract well-paying jobs, among other benefits. Getting this book puts you at the doorstep of actually learning the basics of the Spanish language, which will open you up to more in-depth learning.

That said, the following chapters will discuss the origin of Spanish speakers so that you may appreciate the roots of what you are going to learn. It will also discuss how you can understand Spanish speaking, which will provide you with an idea of how you can best learn the language. At this point, you will want to learn the small things that would enable one to understand the Spanish language.

After gathering the preambles of understanding of the language, you'll then learn how a personal coach can make your learning process easy and enjoyable. Even better, you get to know how you can outsource one and the importance of including such professionals in your training. Furthermore, you'll learn about what to consider when starting Spanish speaking lessons. The chapter will go on to explain the benefits accrued from learning Spanish.

You will then dive into what matters most. The core of the book will teach you basic grammar lessons, pronunciation rules, how to read and write in Spanish, and the Spanish grammar lessons to take. Lastly, you will learn how to work with a Spanish grammar narrator to understand the language.

There are a lot of books on this subject on the market; thanks again for choosing this one! Every detail was made to ensure it is full of as much useful information as possible; please enjoy!

Chapter 1: The Origin of Spanish Speakers

You will agree with me that, as one of the most popular and oldest languages, the Spanish language bears a vibrant and exciting history. Apart from that, it enhances communication in many parts of the world, and its richness brings about happiness among the human race at large. Without further ado, let's dig into the roots of Spanish for you to appreciate some of the milestones the language has overcome and, more importantly, generate some interest in you.

The Spanish language has its roots in 210 BC. It was derived from Latin and started being spoken in Burgos, north-central Spain during the 9th century and was of the archaic type. Due to some prevalent activities, such as wars, trade, and intermarriages taking place at that particular time, it was able to move toward the southward direction.

At the beginning of the 11th century, it had arrived in the southern side of Spain and cities, such as Madrid and Toledo. Its first written format was developed in Madrid City during the 14th century. Other written forms of the dialect were created in Toledo around the same time.

Spanish or Castilian, as referred by the Spaniards, was first installed as an official language in Spain toward the end of the 15th century. The same occurred after uniting the Aragon and Leone kingdoms, which eventually led to the spread of the language to different parts of the globe. Some of the notable countries that were influenced by this language include the Americas, Morocco, and other countries bordering Spain. Among them were some parts of the Mediterranean Sea, especially the southern part of it.

The earlier form of the language was known as old Spanish, which that was documented during the 15th century. Since then, a newer version has come into existence. These elements are generally referred to as "classical Spanish." The same is appended to the fact that there's the modernization of the language and its various achievements in the contemporary fields, such as the academic world.

Castilian, which is a variation of the original form of the language, originates from the northern and central regions of Spain and is widely spoken in these areas up to date. The consensus of developing the written form of the language was reached when different versions of the language started cropping up with no particular order. These brought about the standardization of the language. On the other hand, it dominated other dialects due to the significant exploits by the Castilians during the wars, such as the Reconquista.

Similarly, the Reconquista was also influential in the northern parts of Spain and also shifted southwards. Its words were heavily Arabic, and as a result of it heading south, it replaced many local languages found within this part of the country. Later, the language becomes extinct within Spain borders as a result of people adopting other variations of the Spanish language.

The Glosas Emillanenses was traditionally believed to have been in existence during the earlier centuries. It contained a lot of Spanish writings of that time and was consulted for various reasons. King Alfonso x Castile standardized the previous copies of the Castilian by developing universally acceptable forms. What he did was to collect several writers in his office and then oversaw their writing process. As a result, a lot of wealthy knowledge was generated in several fields. It is believed that learning from those sources was utilized to run the Spanish empire. For instance, laws written by these authors were used to determine cases in the realm. The astronomical knowledge was used in the advancement of the technical field in the empire, among other significant wealth of resources used to run the country.

Similarly, another individual by the name of Antonio de Nebrija created the fist grammar for the language. It formed the syntax for writing the language, which was of great help to both writers and readers as it created a basis for writing and understanding. He eventually gave it to Queen Isabella in the year 1942 because of her love for it. She believed that it was a valuable asset that brought about hegemony.

Similarities are there between the archaic and current forms of Spanish. This means that the readers can understand it from both readers. A current Spanish speaker can quickly flip through the old Spanish literature and be able to comprehend what is being said.

After several years of depending on the written formats of the language, the first Spanish academy opened up its doors in the late 18th century and came up with a standardized variation of the language. These brought about much understanding between the different players in the field. As such, writers could be able to develop their work based on a uniform standard; therefore, it enabled uniformity and general understanding within their audience.

The academy then produced its first kind of the Spanish language dictionary. The same enabled both the writers and readers to develop new vocabulary concerning the Spanish language. If one was in doubt regarding a particular word, they could quickly look for it in the dictionary. It also produced grammar for the language, which suggested they write syntax, grammatical rules, and pronunciations that should be used regarding the Spanish language. Currently, the academy continues to produce newer editions of the dictionary and grammar rules. Finally, you can access the said dictionary through the internet.

On a global scale, the Spanish language can be categorized as the second most spoken language after English and is also an official language of at least thirty countries. Another thing to note about the language is that it is mainly spoken in Mexico, which is home to the most active users of this dialect. Other countries with a significant number of Spanish speakers include Spain, Argentina, and America. The Spaniards refer to it as Espanola to contrast it from the rest of the languages and call it Castilian when differentiating it from the other standard dialects found within Spain.

The Advent of Spanish in the U.S.

This language gained entry into the United States as a result of colonizing Spain. Due to the constant interaction between the citizens of the two countries, the Spanish language infiltrated further into the American territory and almost influenced all its states. It also spread to other parts of the world through its colonies. After the end of the colonization period, the inhabitants of these states continued enforcing its use and even made it the national language through the enactment of policies that expanded the use of the language.

Also, immigrants from Spanish colonies found their way into the US mainland and continued to spread the language. And those who lived in the southwestern parts of America did not see the need for adopting English as the language since they believed that the American government had forcefully taken their land. Therefore, in retaliation, they maintained their culture and language and even spread it to other people around them.

Similarly, inhabitants of the US welcomed the idea of learning a new language, which brought in new changes. Also, as a result of intermarriages between the American citizens and those from Spanish-speaking countries led to multi-racial communities that were bilingual in nature, which further spread the language to places it had never reached.

Spanish in Other Parts of the World

Its Establishment in Africa

Its presence was first felt in Africa during the 18th century. The language was established in Guinea during a particular period when it became a Spaniard colony. Consequently, it was recognized as the national language after the country got liberated. It is also common in western parts of the Sahara because of its colonization by the Spanish.

In the Jew Population

After the Spanish government repatriated the Jewish community from its country in the year 1492, a new version of the Spanish language, known as Ladino, was born within them. It started and spread to other areas on its own and is still used by a declining number of speakers of the Jewish origin.

In the Pacific

The pacific, being part of the Chile Island, made people speak Spanish from 1888, particularly the Easter Island.

In Spain

Spain is the homeland of the Spanish language. It is here that language was conceived, brought up, and spread. This makes the language to continue to receive unwavering support and popularity. People here literary wake in it and sleep in it. The government and a majority of the private institutions use it as an official language of communication.

Other variations of the language have been allowed by parliament to be used in provinces, depending on their familiarity with them. The early forms of written Spanish in this country were witnessed as early as the 11th century. They comprised of texts borrowed from the Castile and Rioja. Literacy works done in Leones existed until the 14th century while that of the Aragonese stayed until the 15th century.

The Roots of the Spanish Dialects

Apart from Spain, the Spanish language has infiltrated a lot of countries on a global scale. Such include the Americas, the Philippines, and Mexico, among other popular nations; thus, developing different regional dialects with a common denominator based on Castilian. However, these dialects disagree on various instances of their phonology.

An example is a difference in the pronunciation of nouns that produce different sounds while speaking the language. Many of the native Spanish speakers use the Catalina variation of the language. It might sound a bit different from the Spanish expressed in the US.

Spain also has other forms of the language that can be used depending on which province one comes from. The United States, on the other hand, has its rendition of the Spanish language. For instance, it is more liberal, thus making it sound a bit sophisticated in comparison to the one that is spoken in Spain. However, there are no significant changes in the original version. It has maintained most of the rules associated with the language.

Chapter 2: Understanding Spanish Speaking

Your primary goal for purchasing this book is to learn how to speak Spanish, right? Just like any activity, understanding Spanish speaking requires some strategy. Doing so can considerably reduce your leaning time and curve. Besides, this would offer you a smooth learning experience.

To accomplish such, I have provided you with some steps that you might consider undertaking and some questions that can provoke your thinking to come up with appropriate strategies. Let's dive in!

What does understanding Spanish speaking mean to you?

To cut to the chase, this phrase refers to your ability to grasp the Spanish language and be able to express yourself in it. To succeed in this, you first need to internalize the language. Though quite a bit challenging, internalizing the individual words and phrases enables the mastering of connections between them. As a result, your brain will be able to accept the basic, as well as the complicated structures of the language, which leads us to the next question.

What is your motivation for learning Spanish?

I can say that, if it is to satisfy your curiosity, then you might be in for the wrong reason, which could eventually lead to failure.

You may ask why?

Here is the reason.

Curiosity, as well as interest, is a one-time factor that can quickly come and go. For example, you may show excitement at the start of the program. However, somewhere within the course, you may lose interest and develop cold feet. The same implies that you shall move to something else that you find interesting. Therefore, come up with a solid reason for the joining program.

Motivations, such as advancing your career and developing effective communication with the people who matter in your life should encourage you to learn the Spanish language. Also, your relocation to a Spanish-speaking country, for example, among other solid reasons, can bring about the necessity of learning the language.

After coming up with an adequate reason for studying the language, you can then plan yourself by doing some of the following things.

- Jot down a list of the learning resources at your disposal.

orm research of the learning resources at your disposal and e them down. Such includes available books, coach, and o lessons, among others. It is beneficial to do this since it can ificantly reduce the amount of time you may require to master the language.

There are tons of online and offline resources that can help you to learn Spanish. Therefore, you would better research on the best learning methods and what currently works for you. These can be attained through reading reviews.

Your list can be made up of the different categories of resources; for instance, those dealing with grammar that you can find on books, free blogs, and online courses. Add an extra column detailing all the YouTube channels and videos that you find useful. Investing in research at the beginning can certainly be helpful.

- Develop a list detailing all language basics.

As a beginner, having the basics of the language at your fingertips makes learning a lot easier. Besides that, it allows you to make simple introductory statements without much struggle. Spending part of your time internalizing some of the basics and phrasebook expressions lays the foundation for more elaborate conversations.

As a rule of thumb, the motivation for learning the language will provide you with guidance on what to emphasize. For instance, it wouldn't be prudent to master all the Spanish content relating to close relations, such as families. The same is crucial for business.

To that end, you should craft the list depending on what is relevant to you. You also need to go over it several times. That way, you can easily internalize the contents. You can also spend some of your time perusing the course and phrasebooks to determine the conversation content ingredients, which are useful and relevant in the context of these dialogues.

- Listen to a lot to Spanish conversations.

Build a habit of listening to Spanish discussions. Whether in your house, car, holiday, picnic, or any activity, make sure that Spanish sounds are a part of your day. The movies you watch, the music you listen to, and the TV programs that you watch can have Spanish content that is produced by native Spanish speakers. More importantly, keep listening to the language even if you do not comprehend what is talked about. These will eventually bring about familiarity with the language and sounds.

In doing so, the language will stick in your memory, paving the way for further instructions.

Apart from that, let us look at some of the pros and cons of some of the methods that you are going to use in your quest of understanding your Spanish speaking journey.

Applications and Software

Apps and software can quicken your mastery of the Spanish language by providing a platform to meet and interact with other learners and coaches, which can give you some essential tips.

Advantages

Most of the applications that offer the platform are free and easy to join, thus becoming affordable and convenient enough. With a Smartphone, computer, or tablet with a stable network, you are ready to start your lessons. The only thing you are required is to go to your application store and download the appropriate application you want. After that, install it and register yourself on the platform, which will only take less than ten minutes. Lastly, login in and start sharing knowledge with others on the platform. The process makes the whole learning process fun, exciting, and interactive. Additionally, you set reminders to alert you when lessons are due, thus maintaining your interest. They also reward you for any progress made, which makes you better focused and eager to learn more.

Disadvantages

Majority of the apps introduce you to the Spanish world. They also end up leaving you at that. For instance, they teach you regarding the basic grammar but refer you to a specific tutor for more in-depth learning. In doing so, you might end up paying for a course that you had not intended to do.

Group Classes

Advantages

They present a well-structured technique of learning the language. You need to introduce yourself to the agreed avenue then a teacher explains the concepts as you ask questions. Also, in this model, the students can be able to assist each other to understand the concepts. The students can also form after class groups to discuss further on whatever they have learned. The latter cements into your mind the lessons learned during the class.

Disadvantages

Classes can be quite expensive in terms of tuition payment and making it to the avenue. Also, your progress in learning the language is dependent on the slowest person in the group. Therefore, if you are a fast learner, you end up waiting on others concerning particular topics, unlike if you were studying alone with a personal coach.

Also, in most cases, the students do not maximally benefit from the provided lessons due to the slow rate and a significant number of students. For instance, a lesson of three hours might only allow you between five to ten minutes of actual speaking.

Majority of them do bench-warming; therefore, you end up getting nothing at the end of the program. For example, there are a lot of individuals who have undertaken Spanish lessons during their high school and college years. However, most of them have ended up with very little to show off. At the end of it, all this type of experience can be frustrating because of the time and finance wasted during that particular learning period.

Listening

This method entails listening to a variety of media, such as podcasts, radio, movies, TV, and audio courses.

Advantages

They present an elaborate process of becoming accustomed to Spanish sounds and phonetics, which can enable you to pronounce some of the basic phrases. Radio, television, and movies allow you to listen to what is appropriate and interests you. In attaining a conversational level, you can listen to such medium to improve on your vocabulary and comprehension capabilities.

Disadvantages

A significant disadvantage of the audio courses is that they are limited to particular areas of the language, such as speaking. On the other hand, movies, television, and radio medium forms require lots of exposure time and also not ideal for beginners who have little knowledge concerning Spanish grammar, etc. A lot of people may choose to have them as a background while concentrating on other things, hence reducing their effectiveness. Furthermore, they might require you to sacrifice your time off doing other duties so that you may focus on them. The same can be a difficult choice, especially those who are juggling between work and studies.

Textbooks

A textbook can also teach you how to speak Spanish.

Advantages

It offers the best way to learn Spanish grammar. It also puts everything under one roof, thus providing you with the needed convenience. Instead of testing with any available resource, you can schedule your learning process. For instance, you learn a concept and then practice it over and over again using the given exercises after every unit; therefore, it ensures that you fully understand the language.

Disadvantages

It is one of the oldest methods of learning a language and can become tiresome, especially among the millennials. Moreover, it requires a lot of patient and self-discipline and also the will to study. Using it alone can also be quite a challenge since there are no explanations of concepts that you cannot understand. People more often just read the first few chapters of the book before getting tired of it or drifting toward other lively and exciting things.

Going to Meet-ups

Such can involve online searches to sites such as meetup.com where you can meet fellow learners and be able to interact with one another.

Advantages

Going to such meet-ups is free; all you need is a computer and an internet, and you are good to go. You also get to meet with individuals at the same level and area as you and be able to share learning ideas. Moreover, there is a higher probability that someone in your group has answers to any difficult questions that you may have.

Disadvantages

This kind of arrangement favors the more talkative but not the shy ones. For instance, in a meet up consisting of ten plus attendees, only two to three confident speakers would do most of the talking while the rest would be listening to them. It can be ideal for a person who has already started speaking it and can communicate with another person.

Practicing With the People You Know

Advantages

To begin with, it is a free method; therefore, you do not incur any expenses. Also practicing out with a family member, relative, or friend might become less intimidating to you, compared to speaking with total strangers. Besides, the fact that they know you in person will allow them to offer you personalized assistance.

Disadvantages

One downside is that some of your friends or family members might shy away from telling you the truth or informing you about the mistakes you have committed. Moreover, a lot of the indigenous speakers of the language do not know the rules that govern their language. Therefore, everything you say might sound correct to them. Lastly, you can quickly revert to your own language without someone pointing the finger at you. After all, they are your buddies or family.

Online Spanish Coaches

Advantages

A professional coach has detailed knowledge concerning the language grammar, thus able to explain any differences between Spanish and English. Moreover, they can instill confidence to any of their shy leaners and coax them into speaking, ultimately becoming their hero and source of motivation.

Disadvantages

Online coaches come at a price, though not as expensive as the majority of people imagine. Additionally, finding an ideal tutor for your needs can be time-consuming since you will need to separate some wheat from the chaff. Some of the online platforms list all their tutors as five stars, hence complicating your search.

Language Exchanges

Advantages

It is free to join such forums. They will help you to get exposure to indigenous speakers from diverse Spanish-speaking nations. In the end, they can give you an idea concerning the different forms of the language, depending on the country of origin.

Disadvantages

It might take you a lot of time to find the right partner for your level and liking. More often, you will also utilize up to half of your interaction time speaking Spanish. This is due to their lack of English knowledge, which would also affect how they explain the concepts to you. The method also requires that you at least know how to speak the language.

Factors That Contribute to Learning Spanish

What are the factors that contribute to the understanding of Spanish speaking?

In learning how to speak Spanish, the following factors will contribute in a major way:

- How you practice speaking the language. It is a fact that the only sure way to understand how to speak a new language is by actually speaking it. The number of years you have spent in school studying the language grammar does not matter; what matters is putting it into practice through speaking.

  During the practice sessions, you must perform it loudly at your typical conversational volume. It is also essential to practice speaking to yourself. The action is a common occurrence among individuals who aspire to develop listening skills at a faster rate compared to how they talk about the language. Therefore, to eliminate this phenomenon, you may want to continue to practice the word even if you are alone to facilitate the speaking ability.

- Your consistency. To develop a good grasp of a new language, you need commitment and patience. Having a daily set time to practice the language will do more good to your mastery of the language, compared to doing it periodically or haphazardly.

- The time spent listening to Spanish. Being surrounded by Spanish sounds and literature expedites the learning process. Grammar alone cannot take the place of the language sounds and also cannot capture every bit of intonation and tone.

Chapter 3: Spanish Made Easy With Your Language Coach

As a beginner, you may find out that learning Spanish isn't as easy as you thought, right? But, worry not. A personal language coach can be handy in such cases. Not only can they facilitate your language learning process. They can also hold your hand all the way. The move will enable you to develop self-confidence in speaking the language and also act as an inspiration to you.

The same leads us to the following questions.

What Is Coaching?

Coaching entails the process of helping someone to learn a specific thing rather than teaching them. A coach, in most cases, holds the belief that the individual learner has all the answers to their questions. A coach will help you to maximize your performance; hence, you learn better. Coaching encompasses teaching, observation, and providing feedback.

Why Choose a Personal Coach to Aid Your Spanish Learning?

Selecting a personal trainer to take care of your learning needs can be informed from several reasons. To begin with, you may want to learn the language within the minimum time possible. Secondly, you may require a coach if you're going to have deeper insights concerning the language.

The trainer or coach will allow you to adjust the program, depending on your needs and level and what you can handle at any given time.

Who Can Be a Suitable Coach for Your Spanish Learning Needs?

- One who provides a convenient learning environment — This is to allows you to make the most out of the lessons by asking questions and receive replies without any distractions. Therefore, choose an instructor who is well-organized regarding their working environment. For instance, one who has a private office and can work without interference from family members and other things would be ideal. Also, it's vital to have an office and communication device, such as computers installed with high-speed internet to facilitate learning in case of an online coach.

- One needs to be a native speaker — Having a coach who is well-versed with Spanish makes it easy for you to learn easily. They will transfer their mastery of language to you, as they are the primary contacts who will guide you from the known to the unknown.

- Should be supportive and enthusiastic — A coach who loves what he/she does can transfer the same effect on you. Therefore, look for a coach who is happy to guide you and can offer you with any support that you need. In doing so, you would quickly learn how to listen and speak the language.

- Needs to have a personalized and student-focused approach — This enables him/her to develop an intimate learning relationship with you that is focused on your learning style. Identifying what matters to you and how you learn should be the main principle in learning the Spanish language. The same needs to guide the person who is going to coach you and also acts as an essential language empowering policy. This will also enable you to develop your confidence and skills within minimal time.

- Is an active listener and asks smart questions — A good listening coach can quickly identify your problem areas so that you can rectify it. Also, asking you quick questions would highlight your gray areas, as far as learning Spanish is concerned. These will enable them to start addressing the trouble areas.

- Respects their profession, thereby offering quality services — An excellent coach is dedicated to his line of duty and performs perfect work. Your ideal coach should be able to come up with things, such as your styles and skills profile to enable you to understand how you can learn best. They can also take you through a reflective process so that you can determine your current language acquisition methods and how they may work best for you.

- Has a suitable learning system — A system that makes the learning process fun is recommendable since it would eliminate the boredom that comes with overly complex systems. A fun system can also allow you to repeat the words as much as possible, which make them stick more.

How to Find a One-on-One Coach

If you are living in a Spanish-speaking country, finding a coach for your Spanish learning needs may not pose a significant challenge. However, when staying in a non-Spanish country, you may need to look for them or search for them through the internet. One way to initiate a physical search is through referrals or word of mouth.

The right one-on-one coach for you needs to be:

- Thoroughly trained and certified. Since it is a skill-based on scientific research. A well-trained coach needs to use evidence-based coaching models in their line of duty. Though it can be hard to ascertain if your coach has been trained, be sure to ask them about the courses they attended regarding their coaching of the language.

- Having the style of coaching that you appreciate. Some coaches can be quite intimidating and confrontational.

  On the other hand, there are warm and supportive coaches. Choose a suitable coach depending on your style and what works best for you. You can still ask them, their kind of style beforehand to avoid wastage of time or resources.

- One needs to own the right tools and methodologies. You would want a coach who has proven coaching methods and techniques at his disposal. You would not want someone who is just guessing what they are doing. These ensure that active learning takes place.

  Furthermore, you want to ensure that their coaching method goes down well with you and are in line with your goals or objectives.

- Within your budget. You don't want to enter into a contract with someone who will deplete your resources in the name of learning a new language. Therefore, do your homework and approach a coach who is within your budget limits to have an enjoyable learning experience. You will also need to find out if they can provide a return on your investment. The cheapest coaches might not be the appropriate choices for you since quality matters a lot, and you shouldn't forget that you are investing in yourself.

- Available for your learning needs. A good coach needs to be available for you when you are in a good headspace and are ready to learn. Also, several coaches only work during business hours, which can be quite a hassle, especially if you have another job during those hours.

  Additionally, find out their availability outside the learning sessions. For instance, can they answer some quick question or email from you? Or can they accommodate you if made some quick call to them?

- Having some success in their line of duty. You want to ensure that you get ROI. You can use any available data concerning them to gauge their success rates. You can also ask around regarding customer experience and how they have been able to transfer what they know to their students. Alternatively, you can have a word with one of their former clients and be able to discern what may be awaiting you.

- Having accountability and organization. The way an individual acts during the initial contact is the same way they are going to behave when working together. Therefore, for you determine their levels of organization and accountability, you can find out answers to the following questions. Was there any follow out regarding your application? How long did it take? Was the coach easily accessible, or you had to try a few times? Did the coach allocate you helpful resources?

How to Find an Online Personal Language Coach?

If you find a one-on-one coach, not fortunate to have Spanish friends or speakers to practice with, you can reach out to an online coach. Applications, such as the *italki*, among others, will connect you to coaches. Some of these professionals are from Latin America and Spain. The same can enable you to learn Spanish at a convenient time. Whether you learn at home or work, you'll find it to be suitable and at an affordable rate.

An efficient online coach needs to allow you to learn at your own pace. Therefore, the person cannot cover a lot within a limited period or jump ahead of you. They also need to teach you in Spanish and not English. Apart from that, they need to be able to use the learned terms repeatedly. The same is true until you can comprehend them before moving to a new concept. Therefore, having control over your coach would enable you to have a good grasp of the language. Don't forget that you are at liberty to fire your coach and hire a new one if they don't deliver according to your expectations.

Benefits of Online Coaching/Lessons

Online coaching and classes can present several benefits to you as a learner. Such include:

- The ability to set your objectives and be able to control the flow of lessons, depending on how fast you learn — Having a flexible learning process is an essential thing to your learning process, particularly with the current busy schedules.

- Cheaper and convenient compared to other methods of learning, as you will only require access to a computer and a reliable network to accomplish your mission — This enables you to quickly learn and start speaking Spanish at the comfort of your house with a native Spanish speaker.

- Comfortable environment — Arguably, there is no other place that might be more comfortable than your home. Online lessons provide you with the capabilities of attending the lessons while sipping your favorite coffee or lemonade. Besides, learning in a friendly environment, such as your home can make you feel calm, which can enable you to focus more on learning.

Chapter 4: Taking Spanish Speaking Lessons

After getting a gist about the history of Spanish and what its learning entails, it's now time to shift gears and get into the nitty-gritty of taking up the Spanish speaking lessons. To begin, a Spanish lesson comprises a list of instructions that can enable you to understand the language.

For you to access such guidelines, you must have a source.

Online and Offline Sources for Your Spanish Lessons

Taking a look at both the online and offline sources for your Spanish lessons yields several results which include the following.

- Reading books — These sources have been utilized since time immemorial and are still being used by many for reference purposes and practice. By reading books, you'll be familiarizing yourself with the basics of learning the Spanish language. That way, you'll be able to garner instrumental skills regarding how to speak the Spanish language. Also, you'll master the different uses of vowels. That way, you can apply them in your speech.

- Audio lessons — These lessons are mostly in the form of audiobooks and podcasts and can help you to have grasp specifics of the language since they are lesser targeted. The audio lessons will also assist you in comprehending how to put different sentences to use.

- Video lessons — In this format, you will watch as an instructor gives you lessons concerning the language

- Applications — Several applications can link you to Spanish tutors or an online platform where you can learn various Spanish lessons. Apart from that, we have those who can assist you in grammar and pronunciation.

- Learning partners — You can help your fellow learners and support each other to master the language. These can be through discussions and forums, among other avenues. When working with partners, you'll garner interesting lessons based on how to master vital elements of the Spanish language. Therefore, you can ensure that you're working with the right partner. In this case, it refers to someone who is willing to train you while amassing a source of knowledge on the same subject. Perhaps you can try to learn more about the language by partnering with a native speaker. That way, you can rest assured that you are garnering vital lessons about how to become pro!

- Group lessons — These sources have a similar format to class lessons where a coach or tutor takes a whole group through training sessions. You can ask any questions that can be answered during the sessions. A group lesson also plays a role in supporting your ability to master the language. With the group, you'll be in a position to learn fast. You'll also have the support of your team in assessing different uses of verbs and adverbs. With that said, your lessons should directly be appended to your requirements. In the learning process, you should also garner lessons based on how to use nouns and pronouns. To be successful in this, you also need to work with people who have the same goal. That way, you can master some of the basic Spanish lessons that the group offers.

- Native speakers as tutors — Through applications, you can link yourself with an online native speaker who can become your Spanish teacher. Alternatively, you can hire one near you to take you through the lessons on a face-to-face basis. Working with a native speaker allows you to master different languages. You'll be able to learn more about how to take the next steps involved in learning Spanish. You shall also learn about the requirements of speaking the Spanish language not only in school but also in other forums.

- Live training — you can also attend live online training sessions by native speakers via your computer. It can be free sessions like those offered by native speaker volunteers or paid versions done by professionals.

- Taking weekly audio Spanish lessons — just like the live pieces of training, you can also get free weekly audio lessons from volunteers and organizations. These groups are out there to provide you with free lessons. You can access such through your personal computer, phone, or radio.

- YouTube — There are tons of free video Spanish lessons on YouTube. Once inside this platform, you can select your favorite instructor and listen to them.

- Taking free online Spanish systems and courses — As a beginner, you can get tons of free online courses to start you off on your journey. Just make sure that you conduct a review of the course you are going to take. The same applies to all units you're willing to learn. It's better rather than wasting time on an outdated piece of material or one which makes your learning experience horrible.

What to consider when purchasing or signing up for a Spanish lesson?

- The tutor should have all the language tools. The requirements indicate that one should have the right software, too. In the case of software, it needs to have all the necessary language tools at its disposal. The same will enable you to quickly learn all the helpful expressions and the fundamental conversational Spanish.

- It offers the best value. I'm sure that you want a lesson that provides the best value for your money spent. Furthermore, attending such lessons is a life investment; therefore, you need a serious course that transforms you from a newbie to a master in the language.

- It's affordable for you. Make sure to purchase a class that you can easily afford without breaking the bank. If you are not financially stable, you can start with the free stuff and, when ready, graduate to the premium content. An ideal lesson is neither too expensive nor too cheap for you.

- It has different teaching format. Select a lesson or Spanish application with a teaching methodology that you are comfortable in. Different forms of the experiences do exist in the market; therefore, you need to select the one that you are comfortable in.

- The lessons have different levels. If you are a beginner, stick to the readings for starters and so on. Each level has its lessons, so make the right choice.

- This can be a free or paid lesson.-Before starting up, ascertain whether the course you are signing up is a free one, or you will be required to pay for it within a particular period or is a trial lesson. This can save you from starting a course then abandoning it halfway because of the monetary aspect, which can derail your learning or demoralize you from continuing to learn.

What constitutes a useful Spanish lesson?

A practical Spanish lesson has the following attributes.

- Has the needed ingredients — A well-thought-out lesson needs to have all the necessary components to guarantee its success. The one facilitating the learning process need to be proficient in their communication, whatever method they are using. Also, they should have the ability to explain the concepts using more than a single method to facilitate proper understanding. Moreover, a coach or tutor should be patient enough for you to understand.

- Include typical phrases — This enables the utilization of the concept immediately after class and also fosters the learning experience. In this regard, they have to use your standard pronunciation, spelling, sentence structure, grammar, and colloquialisms.

- Has constant repetitions to understand the language — Repetition of the common phrases will often be required during the lessons. The coach or tutor needs to be asking you or the class to repeat what they say. They can also utilize other things, such as word plays, role-play, and subtitles from the movies or television programs when the class breaks from intense learning.

- Should incorporate quizzes and tests — The lessons need to have some exams after every significant aspect learned. Also, the tutors need to give their students announced and surprise tests to understand how they are fairing on with the lesson. These would also help students to identify their weak areas and improve on them. These will also build your confidence in the learning progress, which is equally important.

- Needs to have rewards — A practical lesson is one that identifies where you have improved during the learning process and rewards you accordingly, which can act as a motivation for putting in more efforts. It should also determine if you are not making any progress so that additional coaching can be offered to you.

- Challenging — The lessons need to throw up some challenges within it to encourage the learning process. Once you overcome a specific problem, you can learn something new, which prepares you for an even more significant challenge, and the cycle continues. Besides, difficulties can break up the monotony that occurs when learning the same things over and over again.

- Engaging — A conversational lesson makes the language user-friendly. You will understand it quickly, thus allowing you to understand the concepts. Engaging content is also fun to learn since it brings liveliness and breaks up the monotony.

- Productive — A practical lesson needs to yield some positive results among the learners. For instance, more than half of the students should gain something after the lesson rather than sticking at the same levels

- Continuous — This means that the lesson should add value to what was taught before. This acts as building blocks to future lessons that you are going to undertake. With a positive attitude from both ends, an excellent learning experience is possible.

How to Prepare for Your First Spanish Lesson

Starting your Spanish can be challenging at times. Hence if you develop some worry about how things will go about, then you can try out some the following ideas to put things in line.

- Try out the vowels

    Gladly the Spanish language has got only five vowel sounds. One for every vocal in Spanish; therefore, each letter maintains its original sound no matter the circumstances. Therefore, try first to identify the messages with their corresponding sounds. A good practice is to try and pronounce the vocals correctly before lesson time. These will allow the consonant sounds to follow easily. When practicing, try to open your mouth and at the same time exaggerating the vowel shape while speaking them.

- Determine your feminine and masculine sides

    Spanish nouns have two forms that are feminine and masculine. Therefore, if a direct article is utilized, then you will need to determine whether to use the feminine or masculine article. More often, the nouns that you will learn at the beginning of the Spanish lessons will be alongside the direct article.

    Secondly, you will need to be patient since the Spanish verbs have different conjugations depending with whom you are interacting with. For instance, there is a distinct difference between respectful and familiar modes of address.

After learning a few concepts from the first-class make it a habit of repeating what you have learned. Constant practice can enable internalization of whatever has been leaned. These can be achieved by creating practicing opportunities. Such include:

- Making sure some sticky notes or index cards are at hand before attending your first lesson.

- Having pictures and corresponding Spanish names hung in your house or your favorite resting place to help you internalize them. You can also have their English translations written on the backside.

- After attending a few Spanish lessons, you can then turn the index cards to flashcards to also enable internalization.

- You can label all the objects inside your house and any other place you regularly spend your time. In this case, you can use sticky notes. They will help you in identifying them using Spanish names. You can eventually begin to remove the sticky notes once memorize the different names

How to maximally benefit from Spanish lessons

To gain maximum benefits from a Spanish language session, you can strive to do the following:

- Ask many questions to remove any doubts from your head
- Come up with a sizeable vocabulary which can increase language mastery
- Master all the elementary Spanish grammar to aid future lessons
- Understand spoken Spanish by using it to communicate
- Be consistent with language practice
- Ensure decent pronunciation
- like the language to increase its familiarity
- Attend the whole training program

How to Self-Master Spanish Lessons

Developing a mastery of Spanish by yourself is an intricate process that requires some specific steps or techniques, which include the following.

Choose Your Resources

How to go about acquiring the best Spanish resources and lessons. In this step, you should review the resources you are going to purchase. It's vital to make sure that you buy the best audio course, book, or online course and study the lessons. You need to include the audio component to get a hint of how Spanish words sound.

Regarding classes, you may take the Spanish lessons in the country where you live or decide to migrate to a Spanish speaking country or take a plunge into the online world to acquire your lessons. An alternative would be conducting an online tutor to teach you the language using a progressive curriculum.

Utilize Practical Study Methods

You can study yourself to identify the most suitable study method that may suit you. In the beginning, you may not know what is appropriate for you. Therefore, try to experiment with various techniques of learning

Spend the Required Time on the Lessons

In the process of trying out a self-study of the Spanish language, self-discipline comes up as a vital component that you need to incorporate in your study schedule. An appropriate learning program should one that requires you to practice the language daily. Sticking to such kind of program will enable you to grasp the basics which would act as the foundation to the higher levels.

You can also utilize idle time to your advantage by practicing how to read and write Spanish; for instance, time spends a while on the bus, queue, or relaxing. You can do this by writing the Spanish vocabulary on several cards which you can be removed from time to time during those time and try to memorize what is on them. Alternatively, you can always have a Spanish novel or textbook to read at a convenient time. Besides, listen to podcasts and audiotapes while doing other things such as driving to work, performing some manual duties, among other activities. Doing this will allow the language to stick. It'll also make the learning of the next courses easier.

In case you don't have sufficient time to create it. These can entail the cancellation of some chores to accommodate the program. You can cut off some unproductive activities from your daily schedules and allocate them to learning. In the long run, it would pay off since it is a long term investment thing.

Immersion

Another technique for self-learning Spanish is by total immersion. In this method, you immerse yourself among Spanish speaking persons and take the challenge of mastering it head-on and combining this method with other well-known techniques aid leaning. Examples of techniques you can utilize in immersion without actually having to travel to a Spanish speaking country include:

i) Watching Spanish videos daily: these videos must not necessarily be learning videos but can be from any subject or topic in Spanish. For instance, if you want to watch a Spanish video regarding cooking, you can google translate "cooking" into Spanish then copy and paste the results on to your browser. You will get so many Spanish cooking videos which you can watch at your convenience. These can provide you with the flow of the Spanish language and the words to use in topics and subjects that fancy you.

ii) Writing Spanish daily: you can juggle your mind through writing in Spanish for a few minutes daily. You can write a sentence or talk about how your day was using a new vocabulary learned that day. The same can reinforce whatever phrases or words acquired while stimulating your mind to start thinking in Spanish.

iii) Think in Spanish: It can be challenging at the start; but with constant practice, your abilities can skyrocket. You may achieve this by questioning yourself and try answering it in Spanish. By doing so, the various locations of your brain become stimulated and also helps to argument the already learned into a coherent, purposeful sentence or phrase.

iv) You may immerse into your favorite Spanish books. Since a lot of top novels and books have already been translated to Spanish, you may take your ideal edition in English and compare it with the translated version. These make it easy to understand what you are reading.

v) Form a habit of listening to Spanish audio: you can listen to your exciting topic. Doing this will familiarize you with the Spanish sounds and improve your grammar and vocabulary.

vi) Use music as a learning aid: some channels can translate songs that are in Spanish into English subtitles. Therefore, you can select your favorite song and start to listen while reading the texts that are both in Spanish and English. Utilizing a bit of your creativity, you can be able to create an immersive setting that can take care of your learning needs.

Chapter 5: Benefits of Learning Spanish

Ever wondered why you should take the challenge head-on and concentrate on learning Spanish? Having an excellent command of Spanish comes along with a bag of goodies. Here are several advantages of gaining Spanish knowledge

Benefits for the General Audience

- It introduces you to the world. Imagine being able to understand all those Spanish movies on cable TV or your favorite channel. Learning Spanish opens up new learning avenues where you will gain access to immense knowledge concerning life; for instance, you would be able to easily consume content found in Spanish books written by highly rated authors. Books that are in their original form provide more insight, unlike translated versions. Besides this, you will enjoy music from Spanish artists with comparative ease.

- Moreover, life can become easy when touring in overseas countries. Being able to understand the basic expressions and phrases will not only make your life more comfortable within the initial weeks and months but will also reduce your anxiety levels in case of any emergency. Apart from that, having the ability to give your cab driver the direction to your home and be able to offer him the correct sum of money without any assistance would also be an excellent experience.

- It provides you with employment opportunities. Understanding and speaking Spanish fluently gives you a chance to interact with more people than you had in your life. Therefore, you will become a potential asset for any employer who wishes to expand his business to international standards.

What is more, this language is one of the six languages recognized by the United States and is the third most utilized language in the media, which increases the possibility of you being employed. Also, a look at the gross domestic product in the Spanish-speaking countries and Latin America shows tremendous growth. Businesses are picking up everywhere, and the primary language used is Spanish.

Therefore, to increase your chances of becoming employed at any of this business or companies, an understanding of Spanish puts you ahead of the competition. Besides, in most cases, it is used to advertise current job opportunities; therefore, understanding it allows you to pitch jobs.

Also, bilingual persons earn up to 30 percent bonus salary compared to monolingual counterparts. For companies that mostly deal with international customers, bilingual workers are much appreciated.

- It makes your travels and adventures enjoyable. Due to its global popularity, studying Spanish can be a worthwhile endeavor. It will enable you to easily interact with the folks from these countries while traveling there. In doing so, you gain lots of experience and knowledge from the people you interact with. Lastly, you get can definitely experience a lovely time while crisscrossing these countries.

Moreover, enjoy speaking out fluent Spanish when touring the most beautiful Spanish destinations. Such include Costa Rica, Mexico, Argentina, and Peru, among others. Besides this, it makes you a confident traveler in these countries. For instance, imagine yourself pitching a business deal in Mexico City using an English presentation, while the rest speak in Spanish. After finishing your performance, you might also not be able to socialize around, and the locals might also avoid interacting with you. Another way of warming yourself to you prospective clients would be interacting with them in their language. Therefore, excellent knowledge of Spanish will enable you to win their hearts and, in the long run, make a successful business with them.

Also, relocating to other countries becomes comfortable with the knowledge of the language. Apart from that, the business which plans to expand to overseas markets is on a constant lookout for bilingual employees who are compensated well.

The lack of knowledge concerning the local language of the place you are going to visit handicaps you in a way since you would experience a communication breakdown, which might not be fun after all or might end up in a bad note.

- It maintains a healthy mind. When practicing a new activity that you have never done before, your mind and body perform some form of exercise. Studying a new language such as Spanish causes similar action. The importance of such exercises is to keep your brain at its level best and also helps eliminate some issues such as the decline in the mental abilities of a person. Scientists, on their part, have discovered that people reduced brain activities have a high chance of developing conditions such as Alzheimer. To minimize such occurrences on your part, you can choose to learn a language such as Spanish to improve your brain activity; thus maintaining it at a tip-top condition. Besides, it was identified that bilinguals had more advanced brain functions as a result of learning more than one language. Lastly, the acquiescence of a new language enlarges your language faculties. It, thereby, increases your hippocampus volumes. The same increases the size of the cortical. This would protect your brain from adversaries such as diseases and injuries

- Makes you a better person

  Having an in-depth knowledge of a second language like Spanish broadens your knowledge concerning other people's culture, values, likes, and dislikes, among other things. These will enable you to empathize with them in times of trouble and need and be able to read cues easily. Also, being bilingual can improve your mind theory and perception; both of which are necessary emotional and social skills, and Perception; both of which are necessary emotional and social skills.

- Will make you appreciate the pop industry

  Currently, top acts in the pop industry enlisting the Spanish language. Therefore, fluency in it will provide you access to top-notch entertainment. A lot of modern creatives have taken the dance floor by storm; for instance, it wouldn't be hard for you to hear some pitbull music chiming from speakers in a club. Also, big restaurants and brands such as Wal-Mart and Taco Bell are not being left behind by the craze. They, too, have infused some Spanish words in their welcoming comments to attract Hispanic clients. Therefore, if you need employment from such brands or just needed marvel at the Spanish pop-ups in these facilities, then I guess that you need to put on the work boots and get it going.

- It can act as occupational therapy. Though learning a new language can be beneficial to all ages, it can be particularly helpful to the elderly, who, in most cases, have free time at their disposal. Not only can the leaning of a new language help eliminate cognitive decline but will also help in the development of mnemonic devices, study strategies, and other resources. Apart from that, it adds emotion to the senior citizens' lives as the challenge of learning a new language comes along with its expectations. Also, the prospects of meeting new people, traveling to new destinations, and studying about new cultures can bring excitement into one's life.

- It can help you form a new romantic relationship. Being a popular language across the globe, Spanish can help you in finding a partner. Therefore, you can make efforts to learn Spanish if it interests you.

Benefits for Students

If you are a student, learning Spanish provides you with several advantages that include the following

- There is an increased chance of getting into your desired college. Several universities require those entering their institution to have the ability to speak more than a single dialect. The same applies to everyone who wants to join before enrolling. Other programs, like postgraduate courses, require fluency in a specific dialect since relevant research might not be published in English. Knowing a second language can provide you with a competitive edge during the admission process.

- It allows you to make new friends. One of the best strategies for acquiring new friends is by studying a new language. During the process of learning the skill, you will find tons of resources on the internet and offline sources. You can make friends with those you are sharing the resources with, both online and offline by having conversations concerning your shared interest in the Spanish culture and language.

- You have an increased chance of getting a scholarship to study abroad. Becoming a bilingual can immensely increase the chances of you winning an award to go and study abroad. An ability to speak Spanish fluently paves the way for study opportunities to some well-known universities in Latin America. Also, students with a fluent level of Spanish are allowed to join undergraduate and graduate programs in any Spanish-speaking nations.

  Moreover, students can engage themselves in local traditions and cultures.

- It sharpens one's cognitive skills. According to a study done by a student, the study of a language increases the scores of grad and college school exams. People who have the abilities to communicate using more than one language portray cognitive development in their various aspects of life. Such areas include mental flexibility, creativity, reasoning, and problem-solving. Also, studying a new language creates new neural formations in the brain and creates new connections that were not in mind before. Additionally, their encounter with different cultures makes them accept the diverse customs and way of life. These improve their ability to interact with persons from diverse backgrounds.

Chapter 6: Major Spanish Grammar Lessons to Consider

To learn the Spanish language, you must immerse yourself in it and learn everything, including grammar. You need to learn the basic principles of Spanish grammar. It is fundamental to build a strong block in the language. Here are some of the things you should learn.

Nouns Combined With Articles

A noun is a place, person, or a thing. In Spanish, a noun is preceded by the article, but the ending can change depending on the gender of the noun. When learning this language, you should learn the articles and understand which one comes before a particular noun. The nouns are determined by gender. You cannot predict the gender of any Spanish noun, so you must master the nouns and vocabulary words to know speak or write the language correctly.

A good example is the word "dress." Your first guess is that this word is female, but it is wrong; "dress" is a male noun. You need to memorize the articles with a noun instead of trying to guess them. One of the great tips to use when mastering the Spanish grammar is that feminine nouns mostly end with an "a," while masculine ones end with "o." They are similar to "an," "a," and "the" used in English. Examples include the following:

- El, which masculine singular
- La, which is feminine singular
- Los, which is masculine plural
- Las, which feminine plural

A noun also changes for a living thing, for example, a dress is *el vstido* and this never changes because it's a non-living thing. However, when refereeing to "the cat," you say *el gato*, which changes, depending on the cat's gender.

- *El gato* means the male cat.
- *La gata* means the female cat.

Nouns with a vowel in the end + S Las comidas
Noun with a consonant in the end + es
Los profesores

Learning the Plurals

Spanish plurals are not different from English plurals. You simply add an "s" or "es" at the end; however, you must also change the article when writing and speaking in plural. For a noun that ends with a vowel in Spanish, you add an s to change into plural. For example, *La camas* is the plural of *la cama*. It's the same thing in English where *bed* becomes *beds*, for example.

A noun that ends with a consonant in Spanish requires you to add an *es* and change the article to change it into plural.

El professor is changed to *Los profesores* (*the professor* becomes *the professors*)

The nouns, articles, and genders help you speak correct Spanish, and you can describe events in proper grammar. These are the pillars of learning Spanish like a native and enable you to communicate effectively.

Always ask yourself what the definition of the nouns and the articles are. The gender alterations of the word define how you can write in the plural and the articles to use with it.

Asking Questions in Spanish

In every language, you need to ask questions, especially when learning. Questions are also important in real life when you need help in directions or even when you have a conversation with someone. If the locals only speak Spanish, you must know how to ask questions.

When speaking, the voice inflection helps you ask a question. This means you simply raise the voice just before you end the sentence. The whole statement becomes a question because of the change of pitch. It works perfectly when communicating in Spanish verbally.

A written question in Spanish has two question marks, indicating a raising voice. One question mark is at the beginning of a sentence and another one at the end.

For example:

"*¿Qué significa esta palabra?*" and it means "*Where are you going?*"

In Spanish, there are interrogative words, which also referred to as the question words. They have a unique accent that makes it easy for the reader to know they are questions and not just ordinary statements. As a Spanish learner, it will take you a lot of practice to get familiar with common question words. Here are some examples:

¿Dónde está..? And it means, *where is...?*

¿Quién e..? Meaning, *Who is...?*

The Description Words

For you to express yourself in Spanish, you must know how to describe people, your surroundings, and places. You cannot write or speak Spanish unless you know the description words. Describing things is part of every language, and this is the part that carries most vocabularies. It's unlimited; you can enrich your language by learning as many descriptive words as you can.

Spanish descriptive sentences are not very different from English; you have to follow the same principles of grammar. The only difference is that, in Spanish, the noun comes before the adjective. This means learning to think the opposite when writing or speaking Spanish. For example:

Manos grandes, which means hands big.

Pelo largo, which means hair long.

To practice more Spanish description words, read books you know in English but are translated in Spanish. Since you already know the story, it will you identify useful phrases that you can use in descriptions. What's more, you get to learn more vocabulary words and use them.

Learning Basic Conjugation-Verbs

At this point, you are already familiar with questions, nouns, and descriptions. You are still a newbie in Spanish but on your way to learning how to speak and read like natives. However, for you to put everything together, you must also learn about verbs, and verbs cannot be used without conjugation.

Conjugating verbs make your language fluent. But, one incorrect conjugation will alter the whole meaning of a sentence. A good example is *Yo soy de Tejas*, which means, *"I am from Texas."* If the conjugation is changed, the sentence goes like, *Eres de Tejas*, which means, *"You are from Texas."*

As a beginner, do not stress yourself overmastering everything at the same time. Study and try to memorize as much as possible. Start with the basic ones and advance gradually to the present tense conjugations; they are the simplest and most important. Most conversations are in the present tense, so this will be helpful and prepare you for the other tenses.

For example:

"Good morning Mary, how are you."
"I am fine thank you."
"Glad you good, do you want to go out tonight?"
"No, I would like to stay indoors."

This conversation is an example of the everyday discussions people engage in the present tense. Present tense conjugation endings include:

- *"o"* when speaking about yourself
- *"a"* referring to someone else informally
- *"a"* refereeing to someone else formally
- *"Emos, imos, amos"* they referred to a group where you are included
- *"an"* refers to a group where you are not included.

The Stem-Changing Verbs

These are verbs consisting *-ar, -ir,* and *-er.* They are also known as shoe verbs; when a stem-changing verb is conjugated, it fits in the "shoe," and the vowel changes from single to double vowel. These groups of stem-changing verbs mainly speak about you, about someone informally or formally, or about a group where you are not included. They are the most used verbs in Spanish. So, getting familiar with them will help you get ready to learn future and past tense conjugations. As they say, practice makes perfect. Spend time practicing the conjugating stem-changing verbs, and use the shoe fitting trick so that you may know what to change.

The Spanish Tenses

Learning Spanish grammar and tenses is the primary way to speak and write this language correctly. What you should know is that it is not possible to learn everything right away. Get a general idea in the initial stages, and you will understand how to learn Spanish without feeling intimidated. Take time to familiarize yourself with different tenses.

Present Tense

Speaking in the present tense means speaking or referring in the present. The present tense is exactly what you think. It's speaking in the present.

"¿Cómo estás? Yo estoy bien." It means, "How are you doing? I am well."

Imperfect Tense

This tense is used to refer to actions that took place in the past, and they occurred repeatedly. It is also used to when refereeing to something that took place over a long time. But, it's used to discuss mental or emotional actions and not physical.

"Comía pan tostado todos los días," meaning, "I ate toast every day."

Past Preterite

The preterite tense speaks about particular actions that took place in the past; they are mostly one-time occurrence events. Sometimes, they have a specific time when they start and come to an end. What's more, it is used to discuss a completed event, and it's the one used when making a list of consecutive actions. For example:

"I went to the store, bought chicken, and went home." However, for you to remember preterite tense, you need to understand that this tense answers questions regarding past actions.

The Future Tense

The future tense discusses future events or things that might happen. It is used when expressing or discussing probability. Near-future is discussed using present tense, and future tense discusses a future that is far away, for example:

"Yo ganaré la medalla de oro," meaning, "I will win the gold medal."

"Yo compraré ese suéter la próxima semana," meaning "I will buy that sweater next week."

Pairing Nouns and Adjectives

Adjectives, just like in English, are describing words. Examples include small, wide, round, and white, among others. Spanish adjectives are paired with nouns, and they must match with the gender and number of the nouns.

Before you give a noun to an adjective, consider the gender and number. For example, if a noun is in singular form and feminine, your adjective should match the description. For example, using the adjective *red*:

El libro amarillo, which means the book yellow. This sentence is singular and masculine.

162

La manzana amarilla, which means the yellow apple. This sentence is feminine and singular.

Los libros Amarillo, which means the books are yellow. It is masculine and plural.

The Subjunctive

The subjunctive makes English speakers find learning Spanish extremely difficult; this tense is used to discuss future, present, and past tenses. Subjunctive reflects beyond what the speaker says and expresses uncertainty and shows how the speaker feels. When using the subjunctive, you can express your desire or will, and an indicative phrase should always follow it.

Here is an example showing how to use the indicative phrase.

"Espero que Maria **se vuelva** *professor."* This means, "I hope Mary becomes a teacher." The words "I hope that" shows the use of subjunctive and "becomes" is the subjunctive tense. This sentence presents the mood of a speaker but does not say that indeed, Mary will become a teacher. As you advance in Spanish verb tenses, learn to pay attention when a character is narrating or telling a story for you to identify the tense they are using. You can also watch Spanish movies and soaps to practice and learn more about spoken Spanish and especially the tenses.

Learning Spanish cannot happen overnight; a lot of practice is required. The more you lay a strong foundation by learning the correct grammar, basic verbs, sounds, such as reading and speaking in Spanish, the higher the chances of mastering immaculate Spanish.

Chapter 7: The Pronunciation Rules of Speaking Spanish

Phonetic guides pronunciation in Spanish, just like any other languages, such as English. However, Spanish has more character sounds than their 27 alphabets. It is not a language you can translate into based on English pronunciation rules. Actually, many rules guide your pronunciation, and a single mistake makes you sound like a foreigner trying to learn this romantic language. You will find that the intonation of different alphabetical letters is affected by their placement in a word. These are rules you have to master when reading or speaking Spanish.

Vowels in Spanish

English speakers assume that Spanish diction will be easy to grasp since the alphabets are used in the English language. It is fun to learn the little things that make Spanish intonation so different. The most notable is the vowels and the way they affect your tongue. You have to be conscious of your tongue position inside your mouth, how to twist it, or how to hold it to get the lilt right.

The most outstanding problem in vowel pronunciation is dragging the sounds, especially for new learners. This makes it wrong, and one sounds off the accent. To nail it, one should speak as if they are breathless and let the sounds come out fast and without continuous emphasis on the sound. Practicing over and over will help you get the intonation; the vowels are not meant to be pulled or pushed to the highest intonation.

In order to master the phonation, learners are advised to pay keen attention to the vowels because these are the phonetics that make up nearly the whole Spanish accent. One vowel has more than one intonation. In the beginning, the sound you will hear is your voice going off your English pronunciation. Then, with time, your tongue will learn to tilt for the Spanish language.

Key Pointers for Spanish Diction

You should learn to use your tongue around the mouth in order to say the words right by keeping the vowel intonation short. The vowels are articulated loosely on the tongue; hence, it's the reason the tongue is always moving around, searching for the right location to produce the right sound.

Vowel A

This vowel is not the easy *aah* sound in English. It is intonated correctly by placing your tongue at the far end of your mouth. The emphasis is to bring out more sharply and with deep and a little bit exaggerated accent.

This vowel is very common in the Spanish language. It is a key vowel in many words in this language. Learning the diction will not be successful if you do not get this phonetic correctly from the word. Like most tips of learning Spanish, you must take your time to master diction. There is no shortcut, and you cannot use ideas borrowed from the English language to understand Spanish dictions.

Vowel E

This sound is made with the mouth open. The sound of E is fast and brief on the tongue. This vowel does shift sounds, like in English. It remains the same, whether in past or present tense. The speakers are encouraged to say it in a sharp intonation and bring out the sound of vowel E.

Vowel I

Someone who knows English finds it easy to pronunciation vowel I in Spanish because it is basically the same. There are no tongue activities, but one has to say it fast and avoid prolonging the sound. Brevity in I intonation is what makes it Spanish. In writing, it remains as I, and learners are expected to pronounce it as written.

Vowel O

The sound O is said fast and brief. The intonation does not tone the O sound. It is said with an open mouth without prolonging the phonetic sound. The learner should not involve the lips so much. The lips should be at ease and let the O sound out, almost like a gasp, but again, it should be a short sound.

Vowel U

This sound is said fast and does not involve the lips or tongue much. It is more like pronouncing the word *two* in English, but in Spanish, the lips should not be involved. The pronunciation is precise and short. Vowel U becomes complicated in intonation as you learn the Spanish vocabularies. You will note that some of the words have a silent vowel U.

How to Handle Pronunciation Challenges

Consonant Problems

Consonants make Spanish diction very distinct from other languages. They handle the letters differently without borrowing much from other languages. Some consonants are not used at all in this language, such as the letter K, which is only present in non-native words. Consonants have their own sounds but are highly influenced by the combination with other consonants and vowels. The intonations change completely from one word to another, depending on the spelling. English learners find it easier because Spanish does not have many variations as English. A learner can master these accents very fast. Learners are advised to keep the intonation short. That's the key to learning the Spanish accent. English tends to intonate the sounds very clearly, but Spanish does not.

The Spanish Brawl

You cannot learn Spanish if you do not learn the accent, alongside the word intonation. Lack of twang will throw your words or phrases of meaning. A sentence can lack meaning if not said in the right style. Spanish accent is as outstanding as other languages. The natives may have a hard time understanding you even if you speak and pronounce the words without the twang.

Comparing Sound B and V

Spanish intonation has a special relationship for phonetic B and V. V sound tends to be pronounced as B all the time. This is a rule that learners have to observe keenly in order to master the diction correctly. Understanding the intonation of these sounds will affect not only your spoken Spanish but also written Spanish. The rules are quite simple. All the words that begin with either of these letters will be pronounced with a B sound. The sound should be said lightly on your lips. The B sound should not be pulled and emphasized.

Mastering C and L combination

C and L combination in Spanish is like a real measure of how good your pronunciation is. It is said fast without pulling the L, and it comes out as a deep yet light intonation of the phonetics. The C should not be clarified and lingered upon. The tongue should brush through the C to L intonation. This brings out the accent and gives you the sound of a true Spanish speaker.

The C and S Relationship

C and S are phonetics that has the same diction in most languages, and Spanish is no exception. Learners have a hard time mastering the pronunciation of these two sounds. As a general rule, C becomes S sound if the next letter is E or I, but when followed by other vowels, you have to pronounce it with K sound.

The D Sound

Spanish intonation tends to be sweet with a mark of softness, but letter D is different. It is pronounced with a slur, like the tongue of a dazed person not able to say it right. D pronunciation is Spanish lack elegance as if it's not there. Spanish diction does not accentuate D sound at all. It is like passing the tongue on it without willing to say it. This is a mark of the Spanish accent. Learners find this intonation weird at first, especially if they are used to high pitched D sound.

Get G and J Right

This pronunciation of these sounds can get you off guard. The rules are simple, though. For starters, J becomes are loosely pronounced H. It is pronounced as if one is running out of breath. On the other hand, letter G, when followed by vowel u, becomes *whoa* sound. But if the G is preceding other vowels, it remains as G sound that has to be pronounced sharply. The G diction has to come out clearly. Once you get these simple tips, you will handle G and J intonations effortlessly like a pro.

H Sound

H is only active in spelling, but in pronunciation, it does not exist. Any sound of H in Spanish is not an indication that the word has H but that there is G or J in the word. Learners should not attempt to intone the sound H in any word just because there is H in the spelling.

R Influence in Spanish Accent

R, especially when written as a double R, can be pretty hard on the tongue. It has to be intoned clearly, which means the tongue is twisted a lot. When it is a single R, the sound is given no emphasis. The way you handle the intonation of these two spellings can change the meaning of the word.

Handling L in Spanish Diction

It is great news for a person used to emphasizing phonation sounds. L should be pronounced with a rich tilt in Spanish. When it is a double L, the pronunciation shifts to sound like Y, orja-, and ch, depending on the region.

Letter N

All words that begin with this letter are pronounced with the N sound, but this changes if N precedes C and G. It becomes a little hushed, and the tone of N sound comes in a distant way. You will love the little difference that this intonation gives to the conversation. The meaning of the words comes out concisely and gives you a mastery edge to the Spanish language.

The diatribe aspect of the letter N gives it a little more influence on the language. These are indication marks above the letter that alludes the pronunciation to sound like the word *nay* in English.

Letter Q

Though not used frequently, it is silent only if it precedes vowel U, but in any other spelling, it should be pronounced as K.

Sound Z

Z is usually given S sound, but it can also take TH sound. Z sound is not guided by any vowels. It depends on the native region.

Tips to Help With Proper Pronunciation

Rule number is to watch intonation. As discussed throughout the article, you should know that intonation has a lot of influence on Spanish accents and, most importantly, the meaning of the words. Intonation can add an unwarranted twist to a sentence; it can make you sound rude, vague, or indecent.

As you learn the Spanish vocabularies, pay closer attention to the variation of accents that can only be accentuated through proper diction. Speaking to native Spanish people will give you the reality of the accent. It opens your mind and gives you the experience you need to differentiate the various spoken Spanish enunciation. This is the only way you can pronounce Spanish words without the influence of your first language.

Do not let your native language get in the way of pronouncing Spanish words. It will make you think in your language while saying the words in the Spanish language.

Speaking Spanish

Spanish was a once romance language, which has its initial roots from the Iberian Peninsula. Today, Spanish is a vast language with over millions of people spreading across the whole world, and the most native speakers are within Spain and some parts of America.

Right now, Spanish is the second most spoken language in the world coming right after the Chinese language that's Mandarin. The Spanish language has various ethnicities, which include but not limited, to Hispanics, Spaniards, and even Sahrawi. In Africa, the Spanish language is also used. But, it's not dominant like in other native states. These states are Germany and France. Equatorial Guinea is among other countries in Africa embracing this language.

The Spanish language is an official language used in the United Nations. In addition to that, it is also the primary language in various meetings held in the European Union.

Even though the Spanish language is significant, it is not preferred in any scientific writing. Many researchers have avoided it in their studies. However, many authors undertaking humanities have decided to use it as a primary language. According to Google, the Spanish language comes third as the primary language being used by internet lovers, where English and Chinese top the list.

It's factual that many people use the language. They are more than 470 million in the real sense. The fact mentioned above makes Spanish a native language with over 512 million people taking it as a second choice language. The Spanish language is also used as foreign by students. As mentioned earlier, many people also regard the Spanish language as the official language in many countries around the world. These countries include Spain and other nineteen countries within the Americas. In Africa, the Spanish language is also used in Equatorial Guinea. The Philippines, which used to be a Spanish colony, also practiced this language. It has been established that in European Union, it comprises of the eight percent total language being used.

The Spanish language is natural to speak and master. This will only become possible if you have the determination and an urge to understand it. There are several ways in which you can learn this language freely, without undergoing much stress or frustrations. These steps will help you to develop that confidence needed in the long process of learning the Spanish language. These steps are explained in details, as shown below.

- Taking Spanish classes is the first way of knowing and understanding the Spanish language. These courses will enable you to practice those vocabularies that are new to you. Refraining from speaking other languages during Spanish lessons will eventually boost your level of confidence and at the end of the day increases your Spanish learning. Again, you can also have extra lessons with the educator so that you have a one-on-one discussion. For this to work to your advantage, you can have some other groups of students. The sessions need to be formed to help you in learning. You can also look for more lessons by requesting to attend some through Skype. The same will even improve your skills in mastering the Spanish language. There are several online platforms where Spanish language learning can be offered without many struggles. A good example is a Verbling site. Remember to note essential things such as its availability. The same applies to where it's offered and even look at the price. These conditions will help in improving your ability to understand the Spanish language. The site has helpful features. They will guide you in the quest to learn how to speak the Spanish language. You'll also realize that it's easy to use.

- Many studies have eventually found out that watching movies can be of great help, primarily when they have been written or edited using the Spanish language. It will even improve your listening skills which will bring you great achievement toward your goals. These movies having a conversational dialogue are of a great deal. They will help you a lot in mastering the language without necessarily going for more lessons in Spanish literature. The move also works best for beginners. Beginners in learning the Spanish language can get a piece of wealthy information, especially from the body language and even visual cues. Since you are trying to learn and understand the language, work as hard as possible to watch content with subtitles. The same will assist you in understanding the Spanish language in a natural way. Practice makes perfect, and the more you get involved in watching and listening, the more you will be able to familiarize yourself with every aspect of the Spanish language. These aspects may refer to accent and voice tone used in Spanish. The same implies that you will be in a position to understand and undertake your confidence in speaking Spanish a little bit higher, especially when if you begin speaking. There are several places where you can get movies with excellent subtitles, and *Fluent* is just one of them. This site translates everything from videos to inspirational talks into Spanish. While watching your movies, you can listen to different intonations. The strategy will help you to comprehend the use of the Spanish language in different ways.

- Listen and sing in the Spanish language. It's also another step that should be taken with a lot of significance since it helps a beginner to learn and understand the Spanish language in a natural way. The reason seems to be appended to the fact that many studies have found out that the brain can easily remember something appropriately expressed in terms of song. When you listen or have a collection of songs written and composed in the Spanish language, you will be good to go. Listening to them will automatically improve your level of understanding. The same will improve your mastering skills without many issues.

  In most cases, it is better to acquire or search lyrics so that when you listen, you can also sing along. You can try as much as possible to memorize the songs and have some practice in talking and speaking. Doing this will be enjoyable, and also, it will be of great help to you in that you will be in a position of high confidence. The boost of morale will instill in you the optimism needed in learning Spanish. Just like videos, music collections are also offered in the Fluent site.

- Think in Spanish. You can start doing everything in Spanish, including having thoughts in the Spanish language. Once you are in a position to do this, your confidence will shoot tremendously. You will feel nervous at first, especially when you start fumbling with words. And having increased thoughts on what to say, you will be boosting your morale in speaking this language. It is always apparent that, at the beginning stages of understanding and learning some vocabulary, people tend to do the translation in the head before pouring out what they wanted to say. The same prevents them from having a consistent flow of conversation. That could also mean you can't keep that pace

170

required in every kind of communication. However, this will get easier with the constant exposure to the Spanish language. In the end, this becomes useful since you will be able to think without necessarily doing the translation in your head. You can also go ahead by commenting yourself in this language even when it's just a simple word. Having your journals written in this language will be of great help as well. In this situation, all thoughts will be detailed in your journal book using the Spanish language. It also automatically trains your mind and brain not to think of anything rather than the Spanish language.

- Read loudly. This is also an effective way to boost your confidence in speaking the Spanish language. You can start by reading the content very loud. This practice allows the smooth flow of words from your mouth. These words will come out naturally, thus helping you with preparation for a good flow during real conversations. You can also read books and magazines written in Spanish. Newspapers, too, contain this, and this can be a good step in learning the language. Check on the blogs and other online websites, and practice loud reading. Make yourself some challenges since they can improve your reading skills. Reading various news in Spanish is just a challenge that many people encounter. Loud reading will also assist you in understanding how to master the Spanish language. With loud reading, you'll be in a position to sharpen your mastery skills in the Spanish language. Therefore, you'll learn more about how to use the language to your advantage. Also, loud reading encourages you to take up different lessons from different packages that offer affordable units. The move is a foundation toward assisting you to become a reliable professional. In the quest to learn more about the use of verbs and adverbs, most beginners have incorporated loud reading into their programs. It's one of the ways they are learning to become pros. It's also a major strategy toward understanding the use of the Spanish language in different settings.

- Practice Spanish recordings. Take time to record yourself while having a deep conversation or just a regular reading that is done in Spanish. Play your recordings to note what you missed or where you got it wrong. By doing this, you will be able to spot the areas where you really need improvement and then work on it. Do this regularly so that you can be in a position to track yourself.

- Look for a "language friend." You can practice speaking the Spanish language with your friends. It is said to be a convenient and considerable way to learn the Spanish language. Having a partner who helps you in this kind of practice will also encourage and give you more inspiration in this process. You can practice this with a native friend who speaks Spanish. In this way, you will be in a high position to make more mistakes and get corrected. You will learn from the mistakes. The same will affect your morale, confidence, and skills required in Spanish language speaking. Having a conversation with a native speaker sometimes instills some fear in you. The best advice here is to avoid being shy for you to learn more. Speak out whether you are making mistakes or not. These mistakes are just small issues that will ease out with time.

- Know the common mistakes in the Spanish language. Common mistakes are a hindrance not only to the Spanish language when it comes to speaking but also to other words. Learning these common mistakes and understanding them will make you more comfortable in speaking the Spanish language. The same occurs because anxieties or insecurities come as a result of inadequate knowledge and lack of awareness of this language. Getting familiarized with the Spanish language common mistakes will this help you to be knowledgeable and be in a position to acquire confidence. Beginners can look at words like *por* and *para* and get their differences. Other words include *ser*, *estar*, and so on.

- Listen carefully. This is another step that a beginner should use to learn and speak the Spanish language. The same is achieved through careful listening, especially to the native group. The same will automatically increase your confidence in speaking the Spanish language. Listening to native language speakers comes handy with some benefits. These benefits include having a taste of the natural accent of the Spanish language, how to use Spanish words

- In many types of languages, there must be vocabulary that acts as a reference to new words. The latter applies to the Spanish language, too. For you to have confidence in speaking or having a conversation in Spanish, you must develop a new vocabulary every day. The result will make your contributions look strong, especially in Spanish. These new vocabulary words or rather new words can be derived from Spanish newspapers or internet content with the Spanish language. Use flashcards too. They are better sources of Spanish language phrases and other new words.

- If you have the mindset of a beginner, you'll find it challenging to learn the Spanish language. The move is a critical condition in the long run journey of knowing and understanding the Spanish language. Be ready to learn. The later will only be possible when you can have that positive attitude toward learning and understanding Spanish speaking. Have that ambitious eagerness in you, even if the process is too difficult for you. Have the faith and courage, even if you fail. What you need to know is that we learn from mistakes. These mistakes will accelerate your learning and understanding of Spanish.

- The Spanish language has additional ready-made phrases. The same refers to another step taken to learn and understand the Spanish language. Having ready-made phrases will a great deal since you are in a position to back every conversation with the correct phrases needed. To enrich yourself with this, you must consider having an interest in common Spanish phrases that are used now and then. You can also do this by buying one Spanish language phrasebook from the library.

Chapter 8: How to Read and Write in Spanish

Learning how to read and write a new language can pose a challenge to any beginner. But the good news to all beginners learning Spanish is that it is easier to understand it than any other language. The most advantageous learners are those who have English as their first language. The two languages borrow from each other so much, in such a way that the difference is minimal. With continuous practice and consistency, learning Spanish becomes more natural and funny.

Here are tips for anyone trying to read or write in Spanish.

Easy Ways on How to Read Spanish

To begin with, you need to know that each alphabet in Spanish makes a unique sound that hardly changes, regardless of the position in the word. Let us review all the basics of the language.

In learning how to spell correctly, it may seem that Spanish is rocket science to a beginner, but once you start learning, you understand it easily. You are only required to under the following.

Also, Spanish is said to be a phonetic language because the sound made by a letter is similar when pronounced as an alphabet or as a word. This may sound unbelievable, but it is the reality. As a learner, all you need to do is master every Spanish letter sound, and you will have excellent pronunciation.

a) **Vowels**

For you to spell correctly or ready smoothly in any language, you need to have a good grasp of the vowels. Understanding vowels in Spanish is an easy task as there are no rules like those applied in the English language, for instance, letter "i" should come before letter "e". A vowel in Spanish makes a similar sound when said as a vowel alone or used in a word. For example, the word "eh" is pronounced the same way as the vowel "e". The only challenging vowel is "u" as in some words is silent.

b) **Consonant**

Consonants are easy to learn in Spanish as the pronunciation is self-explanatory. However, you need to be keen when reading as some letters make similar sound and others make multiple sounds. For instance, letter "c" in some cases is read as "s", letter "b" and "v" are pronounced the same way "beh". But the two letters are sound differently when readout.

174

One of the most challenging parts of learning Spanish is the silent consonants do not make any sound. This common in the Spanish language, and you may wonder why they have them in the alphabet. It's a mystery no one can explain. But they do make written Spanish look great. Here are examples of silent consonants:

- H- This letter is not pronounced at all. For example in the word *hijo* becomes "ee-ho"
- U is combined with g and q to become silent. A good example is *guitarra*, which is read as "gee-tar-ah."
- Ps- these two letters are always silent when combined in a word. For example, pscicologia becomes "see-koh-loh-heee-ah."

c) Accents

It is essential to understand the Spanish accent to enhance your reading. Learning the accent can be hard and confusing. The best way is to find a native to get the correct accent, as some words sound the same.

d) Stressed words

When learning about stressing words in Spanish, the following tips should be put into considerations.

- If a vowel appears at the end of a word, the second last syllable is stressed out.
- When a word ends with a consonant, stress is placed on the last syllable of the word.
- Stress is placed on syllables with the accent.
- When a word ends with *"mente,"* the stress is placed on the adjective and *mente*; for example, *tristemente* is pronounced as *tris-te-men-te.*
- If your reading skills are excellent, writing in Spanish will not be hard.

e) Silent letters

To learn the sounds of the Spanish alphabets, listen to ABC songs. They will keep ringing your mind whenever you want to read a word in Spanish. Some of them are self-explanatory, but for others, you have to be keen and cram their sounds. Here are some of the letters likely to give you problems and hinder your pace in learning this new language.

B — sounds as "beh"

D — sounds as "deh"

F — sounds as "feh"

G — sounds as "geh"

H — is silent

J — sounds as "ho"

K — sounds as "kah"

L — sounds as "el"

M — sounds as "em"

N — sounds as "en"

P — sound as "peh"

Q — sounds as "coo"

R — sounds as "re"

S — sounds as "seh"

T — sounds as "te"

V — sounds as "beh"

W — doesn't exist in any original Spanish words

X — sounds as "ex"

Y — sounds as "yuh"

Z — sounds "seh"

f) **A word with any written accent ends in a vowel, N, or S**

Any word that ends with a vowel, the last syllable gets stressed on most. Some examples include:

- *Nada* goes like na-da
- *Acento* goes like a-cen-to
- And *refrigeradores* goes like re-fri-ge-ra-do-res.

g) **Tildes**

A word with a tilde means it has a written accent; the stress is on the specific syllable. Here are some examples:

- ***Biología*** sounds like bio-lo-**gí**-a
- ***Devuélvemelo*** sounds like de-**vuél**-ve-me-lo
- ***Rápido*** sounds like **rá**-pi-do

h) **Words ending with mente**

If you have any word ending mente, it means there are two stresses. One is for the solid syllable and the other one is on the "men" part.

Examples include:

- ***Rápidamente,*** which goes like, **Rá**-pi-da-**men**-te

- *Tristemente*, which goes like, Tris-te-men-te

Learning Spanish doesn't have to be the hardest thing on earth. Accept those blushing moments when you just cannot get it right. Scratch your head and sweat if you need to because this language is a whole new thing compared to English. Thank God, you can identify the alphabet letters and start learning their new meanings and sounds in Spanish.

Using video and audios can be fun. They are your best tools for daily practice, and they will dramatically change your learning journey. Reading and writing in Spanish is easy once you get to know the basics. It may be different from the language you know, but hang on, and you will master this beautiful language. Do not let your English affect you learning. Read on for more ideas on how to master Spanish despite having to deal with challenges that only a native English speaker can relate with.

Basics for Learning Spanish Pronunciation for English Natives

When learning a new language, it is hard and challenging, but if you have the interest, you can pay attention to the small details and master the latest lingo. This is the same for the Spanish language. Being used to your mother tongue, the English language does not simplify the whole process. But it is not impossible.

If you are an English speaker, be careful not to use English intonation in Spanish. This distorts the meaning of words and makes you feel left out in a conversation. Many people enroll in Spanish classes every year. Bilingual people always have an advantage not only at the workplace but also in social places.

Begin With the Vowel Sounds

Vowels A and E remain as they are in English, such as in "cat" and "red," respectively. However, I becomes like a double "ee" like the way you pronounce the word "bee" in English, while O is "o" like in "go." Vowel U changes to "oo" like in the word "loo." You can start by watching a video to learn the language. Try repeating after the tutors to see how close you can get the correct pronunciation. In the beginning, the English accent will affect your diction, but as you continue speaking, you will become better. You should remember the vowel intonation as you learn new vocabularies.

Take Note of the Accent Marks

Spanish use accent marks to emphasize the pronunciation of a word. If there is none, this means that you should not stress the first syllable. You should intonate more in the middle or last syllable. In the word like

"Amarillo," the stress is on the "ri." However, if the middle syllable has consonant N and S, then the stressing should be on the last syllable.

Pronounce T and D lightly

In English, D and T are highly emphasized. The diction has to come out clearly for every word. In Spanish, these two consonants are pronounced loosely. D sounds loosely on the tongue, like T or the sound of "th" in English. Practicing will help you learn how to place your tongue in the mouth when striving to give the correct intonation.

Get the R Intonation

Consonant R is very significant in Spanish pronunciation. But there are some words where R is pronounced gently. As you learn the accent, you should concentrate on R. Learn to roll your tongue and let it come out as the natives do. It needs a lot of practice and interaction with an actual Spanish speaker. English speakers can try to say the word "fatter." Where tongue touches the mouth when you pronounce this English word is the spot to say consonant R in Spanish. It will come out with the accent purr that original speakers use. It is funny because you have to say it like you are slurring, the same way a drunken person would say it.

Consonant Z

In English, Z is found in very few words and is hardly used. For Spanish words, Z is determined by the geographical location of the speakers. Different regions of Spanish natives have different ways of intoning it. In Latin America, Z has the same sound as S in English. In other areas, it changes to "the" like in the English language. As a learner, you can pick the one that is easier on your tongue. Z sound like in "zebra" as pronounced in English is unheard of in Spanish.

Take Note of Word Combination

Spanish speakers can easily make two words sound like one word. For a learner, this can be confusing, but you should know it happens only when the last sound of the first word is similar to the first sound of the second word. As you master the language, you will find yourself doing the same.

Another reason is when the first word ends with a consonant, and the second one begins with a vowel. These two will automatically blend and come out like one word. It can also happen if the first word ends with a vowel, and the next one starts with a vowel, too.

These little details are the one that can help you build a real Spanish accent. Copying natives helps a great deal. Listen for the various intonations and practice them when you speak to others. With time, it will become a natural accent, just like the other Spanish people.

Try Spanish Vocabularies, Too

As a learner, your tutor will begin by teaching basic Spanish. Once you have mastered this, then you can learn more on your own. Teachers cannot take you through all Spanish words. It will take you a long time to learn, just like English.

You can read, socialize in the Spanish language, and even watch movies or documentaries in Spanish. With the knowledge of how vowels and consonants interact in the Spanish intonation, you can expound your Spanish mastery by searching for Spanish literature. Learning a language is like a lifetime challenge. You will always learn something new every day.

Chapter 9: Spanish Grammar Lessons to Advance Your Language Mastery

Tips to Master Spanish Grammar

- **Practice Present Tense for Three Months**

Spend three months perfecting in the present tense. English speakers have a hard time mastering the tenses. The best way to simplify the whole Spanish learning process is to study the present tense and learn them entirely. What's more, it will help you tackle the complex Spanish tenses.

- **Engage In Private Conversations to Practice Future and Past Tenses**

Find private conversation classes where you will get extra attention to progress in the Spanish language after practicing the present tense for a long time. It will be easier to grasp the past and future tenses. Everything becomes part of you if you make it familiar through regular practice. The Spanish language will become one of your favorites if you make it so. Keep practicing without giving up.

- **Have a Notebook to Write Down Gender of Different Nouns**

Have a notebook with you all the time. It will help you note down how gender is applied in the language. This is a complex thing for English speakers. But you can simplify it by using creativity. Have two columns, one for female nouns and the other one for male nouns. A notebook will help grasp the common nouns and the general rules of using them. While the general rule is that any noun that ends with "a" is feminine, there are exceptions.

A good example is *el clima*, which means the weather. While it clearly ends with "a," this word falls under the masculine nouns. If you keep noting such points, you will eventually memorize it.

- **Write Something in Spanish Daily**

Whether it's an exercise from a book you bought online or in your local store, write something in Spanish. It helps you practice, and eventually, if writing is your thing, you can start a blog. Just like everything else that you want to perfect in Spanish, practice it daily. Or, you can write your diary in Spanish; it will help you understand the grammar tricks and work around them successfully.

• Go for a Course on How to Use the Subjunctive

Subjunctives are not common in English. But, in Spanish, they are an essential part of the language. The past and present subjunctive forms are used frequently. Being a native English speaker, you will definitely have a problem with Spanish grammar and the way to ease this is to join a program that allows professional training mainly on the subjunctive. But, nothing is impossible; just set your goals and be consistent, and the language will become your second favorite.

• Learn and Understand Connectives That Has Particular Constructions

Learning Spanish is fun if you look at it from a positive perspective. But, at times, you will feel the heat that comes with new grammar different from what you are used to. The popular Spanish connectives are *pero* for "but," *desd* meaning "from" or "since," *mientras*, which means "while," *sin embargo* meaning "however," *por lo tanto* meaning "therefore," and *de todas* maneras meaning "anyway." These are the words that enrich your language and especially any content written Spanish. They make sentences flow, and words get intertwined so beautifully. Nothing sounds terrible like content without connectives; the sentence sounds so unrelated.

• Read a Lot of Spanish Books

Reading Spanish books, especially scholarly literature, will help you perfect your grammar. Make sure the books are written in perfect Spanish so that you learn the right thing. Look for help if you do not know where to find trustworthy reading materials. Spanish newspapers are readily available online, and you will be reading news and learning Spanish at the same time.

Identify and note the differences or similarities between Spanish and English grammar

If you can identify the patterns of the Spanish language that are similar or different from the English language, you will move a level higher in learning. A good example is that a gerund always follows English prepositions, and, in Spanish, prepositions are usually followed by the verb base form.

Find the patterns and highlight the grammatical differences or similarities between the two languages. You can correctly translate grammar patterns without doing literal translations. Spanglish means poor Spanish grammar and will not help you excel, so use patterns to know the correct grammar.

- **Avoid Any Habit That Will Slow Down Your Learning**

When learning Spanish, incorporate all accents, such as tildes. Write every word as it should be, whether you are just chatting with your friend or sending a formal letter. You are a student learning a foreign language; make use of every moment to write in proper Spanish. This is the learning experience that will help you master the language like a native.

For example, when you write *hablo*, which means "I speak," it's totally different from *habló*, which means "he/she/it spoke." Show the distinction in your writing, and later on, you will not have significant grammar issues with grammar.

- **Enjoy Learning the Elements and Fundamentals of Spanish Grammar**

Spanish grammar is not a walk in the park, especially for English speakers. It is confusing and dense, but if you get the elements and the fundamentals clearly, you will be good to go. For example, if you want to use conditionals, you simply add "a" at the end of verb base form. Enjoy such moments and have fun when learning; it will not only ease the learning process but ensure you do not forget. When using conditionals, for instance, you only have to add "ía" to the end of the base form of the verb.

It's important to revel in these moments because when you're having fun with the language, you'll learn more. When Spanish grammar makes it easy for you, smile, laugh, and, most importantly, have fun chatting away in your second language.

- **Always Get Something to Enrich Your Learning Process**

If you are really looking forward to learning Spanish smartly, use apps, guides, and other materials available online. Just make sure you verify their quality before you add them to your learning arsenal. You can also watch videos on YouTube, movies, or even soccer. Combine different ways of learning Spanish, and, with time, you will be at a native level.

There is a lot to learn when taking Spanish grammar lessons. But, there are lessons that you must consider before you can confidently write or speak Spanish.

• Speak Spanish From Day One

After you have started attending class, one lesson you need to learn is speaking Spanish. Put effort and speak the few words you learn. Within a short time, you will be speaking fluently. Look for friends who speak Spanish if you are not in Spain. Burying yourself in books and audios will not give you the desired results. You must practice and talk about the language. Albeit speaking imperfectly, those who know the language will correct you, and after a few weeks, you will be conversing fluently.

• Immerse in Spanish

It's time to stop speaking English. If you keep speaking English, especially if you are in Spain, you will never break the barriers. If you have people around you, who can speak this language, immerse yourself into Spanish. You can even choose to do this at least two days a week. By practicing, you will easily remember what you learned, and living in Spain will make it easier. However, you do not have to leave your country for a Spanish speaking one. You can immerse into this language even without anyone else speaking it.

• Listen to Audios and Podcasts

You will find many audio courses and podcasts to help you practice speaking Spanish. They have features and creativity that will ease your Spanish lessons while perfecting them.

• Join a University That Teaches in Spanish

If you have been struggling with learning Spanish, join a course that is taught in Spanish. By doing this, you will be forced to study and take your language to the highest level possible. But why join the university to learn Spanish?

- o You will master Spanish excellently. Since academic papers must be written in proper grammar, you will fight with every tooth and nail to get a good grasp of the language.
- o Being in college, you will have a chance to explore Spanish literature, history, and culture.

- You will have to spend at least one year studying in a country where Spanish is the official language. That will give you an excellent chance to immerse into Spanish.

- **Take a Short Course in Summer School**

If you are not looking forward to getting a full degree, you can join a language school to learn Spanish. Look for summer school that has intensive programs that will enable you to start speaking this language from day one. And always remember that you do not have to travel or move to a Spanish-speaking country to master this language professionally.

- **Get Yourself a Tutor Online**

The worst mistake you can do is to join a class with many students. The tutor cannot concentrate on you. So, why not get yourself an online tutor? The cost maybe a little higher, but it's worth it. Look for reputable platforms and get yourself a tutor; you will not only learn the language privately but also study Spanish from the comfort of your home or office.

- **Get Yourself a Study Partner**

The study partner you find should know Spanish. It is one of the cheapest ways to get Spanish lessons. In most cases, you learn Spanish while teaching the other person English. Look for one in your city or go online. You can use Skype or any other efficient online platform to communicate and learn each other's language without spending even a dime.

- **Attend Language Meetups**

If you are not interested in a one-on-one language exchange, look for "language exchange" events in your city. It includes people from various parts of the world who come together to practice any language of their choice.

Spanish is the second language in many countries; therefore, it is possible to find Spanish meet-up groups. However, the shortcoming of taking such lessons is that you end up learning the same thing. Most people will want to know your name, where you come from, your job, and some general information. What's more, they do not have the time to teach you Spanish grammar and other rules of the language.

However, if it's useful to you, you can even create a Spanish language group. Here, you can meet other people with the same interest and learn the language together.

- **Join a Language Challenge**

If you have learned a good amount of the Spanish language, you can join a language marathon for some fun. If you meet with people who are on the same track as you, you will learn Spanish better. You will find encouragement and motivation to pursue your shared goal.

The challenge can be online or held locally. It is exciting to have one with your classmates. It will not only challenge you but will also give you support on areas where you are weak in the Spanish language.

English Problems That Will Make Your Pronunciation Sound Terrible

The Consonants Issues

The Spanish consonants make specific sounds according to the language's strict sound rules. However, there are exceptions, but the language is still completely different from English, where consonant issues are concerned. In Spanish, a consonant changes when combined with some vowels and consonants, and it's straightforward. It is more comfortable compared to the irregularities and combinations in the English sounds.

Consonants do change a lot when it comes to Spanish; most of the sounds are like in English. Nonetheless, non-natives over-enunciate them in Spanish, making them sound terrible.

Vowel issues

In general, Spanish vowels are pronounced in the same way; if you learn how to do it, you will be good to go. You need a lot of practice to get the sound right. Pay attention to the vowel sound length. The Spanish vowels tend to be pronounced quickly and shortly. A fun way to learn this is to give each vowel half a second sound. It should be brief and precise. Don't forget to pronounce the vowels strongly despite being short.

Open the mouth when pronouncing them to bring out the correct sound. For example, *a* sounds perfect with the jaw dropped, and *i* sounds well when the mouth is stretched and looks like a grin. For *u* and *o*, the mouth must open widely but with the lips rounded. Knowing how to open the mouth makes the vowels sound natural as you speak.

Accent Marks

Accent marks are significant, especially when writing in Spanish. It changes the meaning of a word if you miswrite it. When speaking, you must know the syllable to press. Check for any accent placed in a word before you read it out. The best thing is that you can find online tools to help you with Spanish pronunciation.

B/V

In English, *b* and *v* are totally different. However, in Spanish, these two letters are hardly differentiable. They sound like *b* in English, and even natives who have not had extensive education in writing and reading confuse them all the time.

For example, when a word begins with a *v* or *b*, followed by *n* or *m*, it is pronounced as b in English. In Spanish, be ready to explore strange things as you learn new pronunciations.

Cl

Cl sounds so graceful in Spanish that it makes English speakers sound off note. It is pronounced swiftly, yet softly. A good illustration is the word "clomp," where you should not be hard on the "c" sound or linger a lot in "l."

Spanish treats "*cl*" differently, for example, *aclara*r, which means clarify. Pronunciation reduces how *cl* sounds. Do it swiftly, in half a second. Let the tongue tap your mouth's roof gently and quickly, but gracefully lilt to the next letter which is *a*.

S/S

In Spanish, the letter "c" sounds like "s" when followed by "i" or "e." English speakers make the mistake of stressing it hard. English speakers take the "c" seriously, which is different from Spanish. When pronouncing this sound, the air leaves your mouth.

For example, try the word "cow," and you will feel how the air leaves the mouth. In Spanish, sound "c" does not cause the air to leave your mouth. *Acomodar,* which means accommodate, is a perfect Spanish example. The "c" sound comes out crisp, and you spend less time on it.

D

Letter d is the reason native English speakers have a problem in speaking other languages correctly. This letter is deeply pronounced in English, and it becomes a problem in Spanish where it's non-existent. It is pronounced softly and sometimes not pronounced at all. A good example is *pescado*, which is mostly read as *pescao*.

Chapter 10: Working With a Spanish Grammar Narrator to Understand the Language

Having reached this part of the book, I am sure that you have at least gotten your feet wet regarding the Spanish language. Or you just need a few adjustments to get things in line, right?

To begin, you need to first understand what roles a narrator play in your understanding and education of the Spanish language. To gain understanding, you may have to ask yourself who or what is a Spanish grammar narrator?

In brief, this is that person who talks or narrates to you about the specific grammar rules that must be observed when writing or speaking the language, and, in this context, they usually represent the grammar authors. Their role is assisting you in mastering the language. The method will enable you to grasp the proper Spanish language grammar to avoid immediate and future grammar errors.

On the other hand, a Spanish grammar narrator is an application that can be installed on your personal computer or phone. It has a pre-recorded voice that explains the different grammar rules. These apps also represent the views of the grammar authors and, in most cases, are reliable.

How a Spanish Grammar Narrator Helps You to Understand Spanish

To enable you to understand Spanish better, a capable narrator helps you in the following ways:

- A narrator makes the memorization of the grammar easy. Under normal circumstances, being talked to about something can stick longer in your memory than when reading it on paper. A narrator will help you to visualize the rules. For instance, it would be easier for you to remember the rules if you rewind a visual explaining the rules in your mind.

  On the other hand, the application narrator also makes the memorization of the grammar easy for you. For example, you can rewind what you have forgotten over and over again. The visual part of the application is also helpful as it displays to you how and where to apply the rules, which makes it hard for you to forget.

- A narrator makes the whole lesson easy to understand. A narrator will explain to you how to apply those grammar rules on your sentences and phrases. More often, they draw diagrams to explain when and how to use the different types of clauses. For instance, they would teach you in an illustrative manner where to position verbs, nouns, and quotations, among other things. The exciting thing about them is that they are real, so you can see them with your eyes and feel their emotions. You can also ask them a question if you want. Unlike other sources, such as a textbook, you do not work on your own even if you do not understand anything.

- They teach you the grammar rules that you need to learn. For you to effectively speak, listen, and read in Spanish, you have to be good in the grammar part. A narrator goes into detail to explain all the concepts concerning grammar that needs to be in place. They teach you step-by-step, explaining to you the various relations between the different parts of speech, which you could have ignored if you were left to your own devices. This makes the learning process easy, and it also reduces the time you would need to perfect your skills since you start developing them from the start.

- They inspire you to perfect your skills. Use the services of a narrator to train you to improve your work. They go into detail when explaining to you the grammar rules. That is from the simple ones to the complex ones. This kind of training makes you a better learner since you are supervised. This makes you a better learner since most new languages require such an approach to crack them. As such, they can be good aspirators and source of motivation.

Qualities of an Efficient Spanish Grammar Narrator

- They are lively. A compelling narrator needs to have a warm attitude. This will enable them to present the content effectively. Also, an energetic performer inspires their audience and makes it easy for them to ask questions in case of any need. Furthermore, they facilitate learning since the same effect passes on to the audience who appreciate having the lesson in grammar.

On the other hand, a grammar narrator application that is interactive allows more students to gain insight into the grammar rules. For it to be effective, it needs to incorporate the visual component, as well as the audio element that goes hand in hand. For instance, when a noun or verb is spelled in audio, its visual parts need to appear so that the learner can connect the two. Anything presented in audio needs to be accompanied by the corresponding visual component.

- A narrator uses body gestures and expressions to a point. An efficient narrator uses any available tool or creativity to drive their point home. Therefore, they should not shy away from expressing what they are talking about using their body language or expressions. For example, the learner can construct phrases concerning bodily actions such as hugging if the narrator uses the right gesture. They need to show the action in order to cement the idea on the learner's mind. In doing so, the learner would vividly remember their actions when they encounter structures requiring the use of the grammar rules for such actions.

- The tutor needs to have all the teaching or guiding aids. Things such as exercises, illustrations, and whiteboards, among other accessories, are a necessity for an effective grammar narrator. These enable them to offer quality explanations that can be easily remembered by the learners. For instance, they need the whiteboard to illustrate the various rules and syntaxes to follow and how they relate to each other. They would also use the pen to draw images to explain the various types of interrelations between the variables. With that said, it's vital for the tutor to have various teaching aids that will support students in their quest to learn how to speak Spanish.

How to Find a Spanish Grammar Narrator

Human Grammar Narrator

To find a human grammar narrator for your leaning needs, you can utilize two methods:

- Search for them manually. Spanish grammar narrators, in most cases, can be found in most countries across the globe. Ask around where you can find them. If there is no one who can offer such services, you may require referrals. Alternatively, you can visit different bureaus and consultants.

  If you do not find anyone around your area, you can either migrate to another location, in places where they can be found. Or migrate to any Spanish-speaking country where the probabilities of finding one are high.

- Search for them through the internet. With the availability of the World Wide Web, you can quickly get in touch with an online narrator within seconds. What you need is a high-speed internet connection, apart from a personal computer.

Google the term "online grammar narrator." You will get a lot of choices to choose from. Take a look at the interesting ones then decide. Alternatively, you can ask for referrals from your current tutor or fellow learners and then enroll with them. Some of them might require paid subscriptions, while others are for free. Choose what suits you best.

Application Grammar Narrator

To find a suitable one, you can do the following:

- Ask for referrals for a better option. You can ask your friends which applications they are using if any. If not, ask your coach or tutor the same question, and they would provide you with the appropriate answer.

- Check reviews. To get a suitable application for your narration, you can go online and check the available narrators. After noting a few that interests you, go ahead and search for a review about them. To perform this, just type the name of the application and the word "review" on a browser. Several results would appear. Go over them and see what other people talk about some of the apps that you want to install as your narrator. Go for the one that has top reviews. Remember also to check if they require some subscription fee or not.

- Take it from a friend. Alternatively, you can share one from your friend's device. Modern electronics such as smartphones, tablets, and personal computers have applications that can enable the sharing of software. Therefore, if your friend, tutor, or colleague has an app that meets your learning needs, ask them to share it with you.

Working With a Grammar Narrator to Understand Spanish

After getting your ideal grammar narrator, it's time to start working with them. Here are the different ways you can work with them.

- Face-to-face narrator

  For this kind of narrator, you need to be in the same physical environment. These could be in a hall, class, or office. Therefore, make sure that you proceed to the agreed venue equipped with the necessary learning materials. This includes things such as pens, papers, and books, among other accessories required for such type of engagements.

Listen to them keenly as they explain the various aspects of grammar. If you have any burning question within the learning session, ask them immediately to avoid any confusion since the instructions will continue to progress, which can disadvantage you. After understanding the provided explanation to your question, you can tell them to proceed with the narration. Keep repeating the same process for every presentation.

- Online narrator

  For this kind of narrator, you need to login into your device then open the internet. Such presentations could either be live or recorded sessions. For a live performance, tune in at the required time and watch as the narrator presents his or her instructions concerning grammar. Take notes concerning the essential details that you need to understand. In case it is an offline presentation, log in it to your machine at your convenient time, and start watching the performance. Do the same things as the online presentation.

- Application grammar narrator

  With this type, open the necessary application and start gaining insights concerning the grammar rules. Most of these applications allow you to navigate through them. Therefore, if you have forgotten any important lesson, you can rewind and replay the app once again.

What to Do if Spanish Feels too Hard for You to Learn

As we have discussed several times before, Spanish is one of the most spoken languages worldwide. It is used even in English-speaking countries and has numerous opportunities for people who can write and speak it correctly. It is not a simple language and has a vast difference compared to the English language. Initially, it may look like something you can never learn. If you are at the point, here is what you should do.

1. **Begin With Sounds**

   While every step of learning Spanish is essential, learning sounds should come first if you have challenges in understanding what this language is about. If you are feeling stuck and worried you might never learn Spanish, start by understanding the sounds. Their alphabet looks like English, but a closer look reveals the big difference. Practice them until you can quickly identify the letters and pronounce them correctly. Some of them are different from

English, and until you master that, you will always want to read them in English.

2. **Keep Learning Even When Moving**

Joining a Spanish language class does not relieve you with all the other tasks that you must do every day. So, incorporate your new classes at every moment where you can as you carry out your daily chores or duties at work. Every free minute can be useful, especially when you are walking. According to Alexander Arguelles, an American Professor, you can listen to Spanish all day and keep repeating what you hear. And for you to do this successfully, take note of the following:

- It is possible to feel embarrassed to listen and then repeat the Spanish words. Find a lonely path where you can walk safely and learn.

- Arguelles says that your posture contributes to how much you can understand. He recommends that you sit in an upright position and be comfortable.

- Repeat the sounds as soon as you get what the audio is saying. You should use clear and loud audios. This will help you note the rhythm, tone, and exact sound of a letter or word. Doing this does not make you look like the brightest learner, but it will bear fruits with time. It helps you develop the accent and special rhythm of the Spanish language. Just make sure you listen to the right audios that will teach native-level Spanish. Listening to the words allows you to get to know how the Spanish words are pronounced, and it helps even if you do not understand them.

3. **Start with the practical words**.

A new language comes with many new words. It can be overwhelming for you as a beginner. The best way to tackle this problem is to start with the basic words. You do not have to learn every word for you to speak a language.

The Spanish language is believed to have over 383 000 words. And even a native doesn't use more than 40,000 of the words for speaking or writing. If you can learn 20,000 words, including some vocabularies, you are good to go. The best thing is that, with 300 basic Spanish words, you can comfortably communicate in this language.

4. **Make Use of Cognates**

Almost everyone knows a Spanish word even before they step into a class. Most languages share some words, so if you check closely, you will realize that Spanish is not a strange language. English is not an exception; the majority of the words ending with "ion" have the same words in Spanish. Examples include communication, tradition, and action. These are just of the few cognates that will ease your process of learning Spanish.

5. **Get Hooked on Mnemonics**

Just keep repeating the vocabularies; it will take you to the level you want in the Spanish language. What your brain needs is something to jumpstart and to help it remember some tricky words and mnemonics to come in handy. In simple words, it involves telling yourself goofy, fun, or easy-to-remember stories, rhyme, song, or anything that can associate with a particular word. For example, you can memorize "*estas*," "*esta*," "*esas*" and "*esa*," as *these, this, that,* and *those*. You can also note that "these" and "this" have *ts*, while "that" and "those" don't.

Another mnemonic to use is learning that SOPA is soap and ROPA is not rope. *Sopa* is soup in Spanish, and *ropa* refers to clothing. By making use of such simple mnemonics, your progress in Spanish lessons will improve dramatically while reducing the struggle.

The bottom line is that you should not let any Spanish phrase, word, or even grammatical rule feel too hard to memorize. Be creative and accept going the extra mile because it will help you in the long run.

6. **Have S Note Book of Flashcard Full Of Spanish Vocabulary**

Having a journal, notebook, or a document while taking Spanish lessons is one of the best ways to help you grasp the Spanish language; this is the place where you keep vocabularies and phrases. The process of writing down ensures the words sink into you, and it becomes easy to memorize them.

Students who keep journals remember grammatical rules and vocabularies easily. The best thing is that you can turn them into flashcards and use them on your laptop or phone.

7. **Identify the Patterns**

Learning the tenses and smartly understanding them ensures you get a strong foundation in this language. What you need to master is the three main categories of verb tenses, and each is marked by one of the following ends: "ar," "er," and "ir." From here, learn how to conjugate the verbs, which means making each agree with the tense. As you are trying to identify the pattern, begin with common patterns. Take *habler* (to speak) and its different conjugations for past, simple, future, and present tenses, for example.

- *Yo trabajé*, which means I worked
- *Yo trabajo,* which means I work
- *Yo trabajaré*, which means I will work
- *Yo hablé*, which means I spoke
- *Yo hablo*, which means I speak
- *Yo hablaré*, which means I will speak

By using this method, learners can speak in various tenses from day one. By identifying the patterns, it becomes easy even for beginners and lays a solid foundation for them as they advance in learning Spanish.

Alexander Arguelles is a renowned linguist, and he has developed several techniques to improve speaking and writing in a foreign language simultaneously. His technique helps you focus on various components of the Spanish language. Here three exercises that you should practice:

- Read the sentences aloud.
- Speak out every word while writing.
- Read out the sentences after writing them.

This exercise slows you down and gives you enough time to pay attention to everything. You can absorb the spellings and sound about every word, and it will stick to your mind. What you must do is identify a high-quality source of your learning materials. Copy everything carefully while using audio to learn the sounds.

The Scriptorium Technique by Alexander offers you an easy way to learn, polish, and refine your Spanish writing and speaking skills. This is extremely important in both intermediate and advanced levels.

Listen, Watch and Read

Listen to audios and watch movies, series, soap operas, and films, and read books, newspapers, magazines, and anything that can help you increase your knowledge in the Spanish language. You have heard at least of someone who learned a foreign language without attending classes. You can also become one by making use of all materials and using them efficiently. You can fun methods, such as playing online games. While they do not teach you the grammatical rules, they familiarize you with the language. It's vital to listen to various audios. These elements help you in understanding the basics of learning how to speak Spanish. In the end, you will be able to comprehend the use of the language in many societies. You shall also garner basic knowledge based on how to apply these audios in real-life scenarios. To that end, watching Spanish movies is a way toward understanding what it takes to speak the language. Other than that, reading is also recommended to people who would like to understand the language. The latter is true for youngsters, too.

Reading or watching creates an effect on the brain, and it will stick for a long time. It is exposure to a language that you are interested in and enables you to learn without feeling like you are in class. After doing this several times, the words will become easy, and you will find yourself repeating them. You can get the accent quickly and copy from the people you listen to watch. What's more, it is a great way to pick the sound, structure, rhythm, and rules of the language without using books. However, after a while, you may have to attend lessons. This is particularly if you want to understand the grammar and perfect the language.

Interact

Most people who want to learn Spanish and interact feel the need to travel to Spain and other countries where Spanish is a first or second language. However, this is possible, regardless of your location. You can speak Spanish as much as you would like. Here are ideas on how to interact and learn more.

- Find a friend or family member who can speak Spanish. Even in your neighborhood, you are likely to find someone who knows this language. In the U.S., many people speak Spanish as their second language.

- Write a letter every day to someone or even to yourself. Then reply to it just to practice Spanish. It should be a friend or a person willing to help you learn.

- Visit areas where you know many people are speaking this language. Interact with them and have some fun while they laugh at your mistakes.

- Look for groups that meet just to share Spanish language lesson tips and ideas.

- Look for someone to chat with online. It is easy to get a person willing to have a conversation for free, especially on Skype.

- Join a forum or start contributing to a Spanish blog. But, for you to write quality content, you must master all the grammar rules of the language.

- Listen to beautiful songs in Spanish and dance as you try to sing along.

- Watch educative series and documentaries, and try to repeat what the characters say.

- Talk to yourself! You will never get bored listening to yourself, and sometimes, you can record so that you can identify mistakes when you listen later. This will help you improve and become better.

Conclusion

Thank you for making it through the end of *"Learn Spanish for Beginners the Fast Way."* Let us hope it was informative and able to provide you with all of the tools you need to achieve your objectives, whatever they may be. Going through this book up to the end does not, in a way, suggest that you have accomplished all your objectives. This is just a tiny fraction of the whole thing. There is a lot of information out there that you can read to become a master in the Spanish language.

The next step is to re-read the most critical sections of the book to get a mastery of the basics of the language. These will provide you with a robust foundation to lay on the proceeding levels, such as the intermediary level and so on. If you still find it challenging to hack the given basics, then it would be prudent that you reschedule your daily schedule so that you get more time to interact with difficult areas. Apart from that, you can create strict timelines in order to consume material for the maximum benefits. Above all, you need to incorporate strict self-discipline to go through these contents at the stipulated times. You shall also learn more about the benefits of understanding the Spanish language in running your business and becoming part of other ventures. In the end, the chapters of this book will assist you in analyzing the results of becoming a fluent Spanish speaker, not only in your jurisdiction but also in your academic endeavors. At the end of the day, the manuscript shares vital information regarding what it takes to becomes an equipped learner and tutor, as well. While at it, you will realize that there are some benefits appended to the understanding this language. As such, many colleges have resorted to working with educational centers at making sure that the employees they hire are not only learned but aware of the impact of understanding the Spanish language. To that end, you will also learn more about the actual history of Spanish speakers and their origin. The same implies that you'll get to understand the reasons behind aspiring to learn more about Spanish speaking. In different chapters, you will garner knowledge regarding the lessons to attend in order to learn how to speak Spanish. You shall also garner more knowledge based on how to utilize the chapters to your advantage. Of course, the chapters discuss what it takes to easily grasp more lessons about the language.

You can also separate the contents into smaller bits and consume each at a time since research reveals that dividing complex tasks into smaller individual ones, including time frames, is effective. You have higher chances to complete them successfully. Finally, if you found this book useful in any way, a review on Amazon is always appreciated!

One last thing to do

If you enjoyed this book or found it useful I'd be very grateful if you'd post a short review on it. Your support really does make a difference and we read all the reviews so we can get your feedback and make this book even better.

Thanks again for your support!

Learn Spanish in Your Car 1001 Common Phrases for Beginners

How to Use Words in Context. Learn Spanish Quickly, Everyday, Everywhere

[Michael Navarro]

Introduction

Congratulations on purchasing *Learn Spanish in Your Car 1001 Common Phrases for Beginners: How to Use Spanish Words in Context to Speak Spanish Quickly* and thank you for doing so.

The following chapters will provide a lot of common and not so common phrases that will teach you all of the basic and a bit of intermediate vocabularies and sentence structures.

In the six chapters of this book you will find tons (exactly 1001) of phrases from different topics, starting from greetings, meeting new people, family, relationships, preferences about music, religion, pets, sports, jobs and professions, useful phrases to apply for a job, useful sentences related to the work environment, car parts, asking for directions, and so many other topics that you will become a beginner, or maybe intermediate Spanish speaker by the end of this book.

It is recommended to, in order to practice and have a faster learning process of what you read here, use these sentences and phrases on your normal activities and then think of how it would be said on Spanish. For example, if you are going to order something to eat, you will probably say: Can I have....? Then, as soon as you finish your conversation, think about how it would have been in Spanish and I guarantee that you will find Spanish language easy.

There are plenty of books on this subject on the market, thanks again for choosing this one! Every effort was made to ensure it is full of as much useful information as possible. Please enjoy!

Chapter 1: Getting started

Hi, welcome to the first chapter of the book. If you are here it is because you are really interested in learning Spanish. Awesome! You've come to the right place.

With the short and common phrases written in this book, you will learn a lot about Spanish language. This book should be used as a guide where you will learn the structure of Spanish sentences and a lot of vocabulary. We will give you common Spanish phrases and their translation, so you can read and figure out what each word and expression mean. For a better reception and learning of the language we recommend practicing all of the given phrases in daily situations. For example, with the first one:

Hola, mucho gusto, mi nombre es Samuel / Hi, nice to meet you, my name is Samuel

So, when you get to meet someone new, introduce yourself in English, and then think about how it is said in Spanish. Also, try to translate and remember the phrases that you use daily and you will see that learning Spanish with that method is easy.

Greetings, basic information and questions

1. Un placer conocerte, yo me llamo Carlos
   Good to meet you, my name is Carlos
2. Me llamo Sebastian, tengo veintitrés años y estudio arquitectura
   My name is Sebastian, I am twenty-three years old and I am studying architecture
3. Déjame presentarme, yo soy Steven
   Let me introduce myself, I am Steven
4. Que lo disfrutes
   Hope you enjoy it
5. Espero que te guste
   Hope you like it
6. Hola, ¿Cómo estás? ¿Cómo te llamas?
   Hi, how are you? What is your name?

7. Me parece que te he visto antes, ¿Nos conocemos?

    I think I have seen you before, do we know each other?

8. Buenos días, ¿Ya está abierto?

    Good morning, is it open yet?

9. Buenas tardes, ¿A qué hora cierran?

    Good afternoon, what time do you close?

10. Saludos, ¿Cómo han estado?

    Greetings, how have you been?

11. Nos vemos luego, debo irme

    See you later, I must go.

12. Buenos días, ¿Cómo dormiste?

    Good morning, how did you sleep?

13. Bienvenido, que bueno que hayas venido

    Welcome, so nice of you to come

14. Pasa adelante, eres bienvenido aquí

    Come on in, you're welcome here

15. Buenas noches, ¿Tiene disponible mesa para cuatro?

    Good evening, do you have a table for four?

16. Me gustaría ordenar una pizza

    I would like to order a pizza

17. ¿Puede darme un vaso de agua?

    Could you give me a glass of water?

18. Tengo que irme, que tengas un buen día

    I have to go, have a good day

19. ¿Cómo has estado? No te veía desde hace bastante

    How have you been? I haven't seen you for quite a while.

20. Mi nombre es Omar y mi apellido es Rodríguez

    My first name is Alex and my last name is White

21. Yo di a luz a dos hermosos niños

    I gave birth to two beautiful kids

22. Mi hijo mayor nació en Abril, mi hija en Julio y mi hijo menor en Diciembre

    My oldest son was born in April, my daughter in July and my youngest son in December.

23. Ella es mamá de los mellizos

    She is the mother of the twins

24. Juan es mayor que Víctor por cinco años

   Juan is older than Victor for five years.

25. Leila es menor que Natalia por tres años

   Leila is younger than Natalia for three years

26. Mi mamá y mi papá tienen la misma edad pero mi mamá es mayor por tres meses y dos días

   My mom and dad are the same age but my mom is three months and two days older.

27. Nací el 25 de Octubre de 1998

   I was born on October 25th , 1998

28. Mi cumpleaños es el 16 de Abril

   My birthday is on April 16th

29. ¿Cuándo naciste?

   When where you born?

30. Mi sobrenombre es "El loco"

   My nickname is "El loco"

31. Mi nombre completo es Luis Alejandro Pérez Guzmán

   My full name is Luis Alejandro Pérez Guzmán

32. Yo soy Albert, soy de Panamá

   I am Albert, I am from Panama

33. Mi nombre es Juan y soy panameño

   My name is Juan and I am Panamanian

34. Adios, debo irme, ya se me hizo tarde

   Bye, I must go, I'm already late

35. Hasta luego, ya me tengo que ir

   See you later, I have to go.

36. Hasta pronto, que te vaya bien

   See you soon, good luck

37. Hasta la vista, un placer haberte conocido

   So long, a pleasure to have met you

38. Hasta la próxima, que tengas un buen viaje

   Until next time, have a good trip.

39. Me gustaría que nos volviéramos a ver en otra occasion

   I would like us to meet again on another occasion

40. ¿Cuando podemos vernos de nuevo?

   When can we see each other again?

41. ¿Cuando estás libre para vernos?

    When are you free to see each other?

42. Gracias por venir, lo aprecio mucho

    Thank you for coming, I appreciate it very much.

43. Estoy apurado, no puedo hablar ahora

    I'm in a hurry, I can't talk now

44. Muchas gracias por acompañarme hoy

    Thank you very much for joining me today

45. Gracias por comprar el boleto

    Thank you for purchasing the ticket.

46. No te preocupes, no fue nada

    Don't worry, it was nothing

47. Siempre a la orden

    Always at your service.

48. ¿Necesitas que te ayude con algo?

    Do you need me to help you with something?

49. ¿Quieres que te de una mano?

    Do you want me to give you a hand?

50. ¿Te importaría ayudarme un poco?

    Would you mind helping me out a little?

51. Eres muy amable, gracias por tu ayuda

    You are very kind, thank you for your help

52. El otro nieto de mi abuela es bastante educado para la edad que tiene

    My grandmother's other grandson is quite polite for his age.

53. Yo solo hablo inglés

    I only speak English

54. Yo hablo solo ingles

    I speak English only.

55. Yo no sé hablar español

    I do not know how to speak Spanish

56. Yo no hablo español todavía

    I do not speak Spanish yet

57. Yo soy bilingüe, sé hablar español e inglés

    I am bilingual, I can speak Spanish and English

The symbol that is above the letter "U" is called dieresis and it is used in gue and gui syllables when the u is not silent. For example:

Pagué – I paid. In this case it sounds Pa – Gé

Bilingüe – Bilingual. It sounds bi-lin-gue

58. ¿Qué hay de nuevo?

What is new?

59. ¿Qué tal?

What is up?

60. ¿Está todo bien?

Is everything all right?

61. ¿Cómo te sientes?

How do you feel? – How are you feeling?

62. ¿A dónde vas?

Where are you going?

63. ¿Quieres acompañarme?

Would you like to join me? – Do you want to join me?

64. ¿Dónde estas?

Where are you?

65. ¿Qué vas a hacer hoy?

What are you doing today?

66. ¿Qué harás hoy en la tarde?

What will you do this afternoon?

67. ¿Qué harás más tarde?

What will you do later?

68. ¿Estás libre? ¿Estás desocupado?

Are you free?

You may find in some places that "desocupado" means unemployed or vacant, however, in Spanish it is used as not busy. Des-Ocupado = Not busy.

69. ¿Estarás libre en un rato?

Will you be free in a while?

70. ¿Cuál es tu nombre? - ¿Cómo te llamas?

What is your name?

71. No me grites por favor

Please do not yell at me

72. ¿Cuántos años tienes? - ¿Qué edad tienes?

How old are you?

Feelings and moods

73. Estoy enojado, me fue mal en la escuela

I am angry, I did badly in school

74. Ella estaba molesta porque no consiguió su peine

She was upset because she didn't find her comb

75. Estoy triste, mi mamá me castigó

I am sad, my mother punished me

76. Estoy feliz, obtuve el nuevo trabajo

I am happy, I got the new job

In both English and Spanish, there are more than two forms to refer to happiness, in Spanish they are contento, feliz, alegre.

77. Estoy decepcionado, me engañaron de Nuevo

I am disappointed, I was fooled again

78. Estoy emocionado, hoy estrenan la nueva película

I am excited, today they're releasing the new film

79. Estoy bien

I am good – I am fine

80. Estoy mal

I am bad

81. Estoy más o menos

I am so so

82. Estoy preocupado por mi hermano, no me ha llamado

I am worried about my brother, he hasn't called me

83. Estoy hambriento, no como desde anoche

I am starving, I haven't eaten since last night.

84. Estoy molesto, me robaron el teléfono

I am angry, my phone was stolen

85. Estoy estresado, tengo muchísimo trabajo

I am stressed, I have a lot of work

86. Estoy impaciente por mi pedido

   I ca not wait for my order.

87. Estoy cansado, corrí 15 kilometros hoy

   I am tired, I ran 15 kilometers today

88. Estoy harto de estudiar tanto

   I am sick of studying so much

89. Estoy enfermo, tengo gripe

   I am sick, I have the flu

90. Estoy impactado por la noticia que dieron en la televisión esta mañana

   I am shocked by the new announced on TV this morning.

91. Estoy muy ocupado para poder ir a la fiesta de Lila

   I am too busy to go to Lila's party.

92. Estoy avergonzado por haber olvidado lo que me pediste

   I'm ashamed because I forgot what you asked for.

93. Estoy confudido, ¿La reunión es hoy o mañana?

   I am confused, is the meeting today or tomorrow?

94. Me siento mejor desde que tomé los medicamentos

   I feel better since I took my medicines

95. Me siento peor desde que me caí de la bicicleta

   I feel worse since I fell off the bike

Family

96. Ven para presentarte a mi familia

   Come to introduce you my family

97. Ella es mi mama

   She is my mom – She is my mother

98. Él es mi papá, tiene 45 años

   He is my dad – He is my father

99. Este es mi hermano menor

   This is my younger brother – This is my little brother

100.   Ésta es mi hermana mayor

   This is my older sister – This is my big sister

101.Déjame presentarte a mi tío

Let me introduce you my uncle

102. Estos son mis primos

These are my cousins (Masculine)

103. Estas son mis primas

These are my cousins (Feminine)

104. Mucho gusto, soy la tía de Bárbara

Nice to meet you. I'm Barbara's aunt.

105. Él es Steven, mi hijo

This is Steven, my son. – He is Steven, my son

106. Élla es Laura, mi hija

This is Laura, my daughter

107. Iré a visitar a mis abuelos estas vacaciones

I'm going to visit my grandparents this vacations

108. Mi abuela está bastante vieja, pronto va a cumplir los 85 años

My grandmother is quite old, she will soon turn 85.

109. Mi abuelo no es tan viejo, tiene 75 años

My grandfather is not so old, he is 75 years old

110. Él no es mi verdadero padre, es mi padrastro

He's not my real father, he's my stepfather.

111. Estos son mis hermanastros

These are my stepbrothers

112. Yo quiero mucho a mi madrina

I love my godmother very much

113. Este es mi padrino, se llama Oswaldo

This is my godfather, his name is Oswaldo

114. Lamentablemente soy huérfano

Unfortunately, I'm an orphan

115. Esta es mi familia adoptive

This is my adoptive family

116. Vengo de un orfanato

I come from an orphanage

Relationships

117. Él era mi mejor amigo hace mucho tiempo

    He was my best friend a long time ago.

118. Ella es mi mejor amiga desde hace 15 años

    She's been my best friend for 15 years.

119. Hemos sido amigos desde pequeños

    We have been friends since childhood

120. Ellos dos están comprometidos

    They are both engaged

121. Ella es mi novia

    She is my girlfriend

122. Yo soy el novio de Camila

    I am Camila's boyfriend

123. Iré a la boda de mi prima la próxima semana

    I'm going to my cousin's wedding next week.

124. Él es el futuro esposo de Amanda

    He's Amanda's future husband.

125. Esa de allá es mi esposa

    That's my wife over there.

126. Hemos estado casados desde hace 20 años

    We have been married for 20 years

127. Juan le propuso matrimonio a Diana en sus vacaciones por Europa

    John proposed to Diana on his vacation in Europe.

128. Ellos son amantes

    They are lovers

129. Te amo

    I love you

130. Te quiero

    I love you

Note that "Te amo" and "Te quiero" have the same meaning in English, however, they are not the same. "Te quiero" is something that we say to people that we appreciate, like friends. While "Te amo" is a more strong feeling, used for family and your partner.

131. Te quiero mucho, amigo mío
   I love you very much, my friend

132. Te amo, esposo mío
   I love you, my husband

133. Mi amor – Mi vida – Mi cielo
   My love

People characteristics

134. Mi amiga tiene el cabello liso
   My friend has straight hair

135. La mamá de Ana tiene el cabello ondulado
   Ana's mother has wavy hair

136. El papá de Miguel tiene el cabello negro
   Miguel's father has black hair

137. Carla tiene el pelo rojo
   Carla has red hair

138. Carla es pelirroja
   Carla is a redhead.

139. El señor que atiende en la tienda de la esquina es Moreno
   The gentleman who attends in the corner shop is dark-skinned

140. El dueño de ese libro es un muchacho alto con pecas
   The owner of that book is a tall boy with freckles

141. Él es muy bajito para pertenecer al equipo de basquetbol
   He is too short to belong to the basketball team.

142. Ella está en forma
   She is in shape

143. El novio de Alejandra tiene ojos azules
   Alejandra's boyfriend has blue eyes

144. El hermano de Carlos tiene la nariz grande
   Carlos' brother has a big nose.

145. La mamá de Britney tiene las orejas pequeñas
   Britney's mom has small ears

146. Lucía tiene las cejas gruesas
   Lucia has thick eyebrows

147. Juan tiene las manos muy grandes

Juan has very big hands

148. Sus dedos son delgados y largos

His fingers are thin and long

149. Las uñas de Vanessa son frágiles

Vanessa's nails are fragile

150. Mis uñas son duras y Fuertes

My nails are hard and strong

151. Alejandro es muy fuerte

Alejandro is very strong

152. Santiago es bastante débil porque nunca ha hecho deporte

Santiago is quite weak because it has never played sports.

153. Las pestañas de Samantha son postizas

Samantha's eyelashes are false

154. Que bonitos ojos tienes

What beautiful eyes you have

155. Me encanta tu cabello

I love your hair

156. Su hermana tiene el cabello muy largo

Her sister has very long hair

157. María tiene los cachetes bastante grandes

María has quite large cheeks

158. Lucas era gordo pero ha hecho bastante deporte y ejercicio y ahora está Delgado

Lucas was fat but has done enough sport and exercise and is now slim.

159. Las piernas de Lucía son perfectas

Lucía's legs are perfect

160. Alberto tiene muchos pelos en la espalda

Alberto has a lot of hair on his back

161. La Señora Carmen tiene muchísimas canas

Mrs. Carmen has a lot of white hair

162. Mi abuelo está tan viejo que ya está casi completamente calvo

My grandfather is so old that he is almost completely bald.

163. El Sr Pedro, el amigo de mi papá, es ciego y tiene muy buen sentido del oído

Mr. Peter, my father's friend, is blind and has a very good sense of hearing.

164. El hijo de mi amiga es sordo y está aprendiendo lenguaje de señas

My friend's son is deaf and is learning sign language.

165. Mi compañero de laboratorio es mudo, pero no sordo, él escucha todo pero no puede hablar

My lab partner is mute, but not deaf, he hears everything but cannot speak

166. Es bastante difícil ser sordo y mudo como el nieto de la vecina

It is pretty hard to be deaf and mute like the neighbor's grandson.

167. Mi primo está quedando ciego, lo mandaron a usar lentes

My cousin is going blind, he was sent to wear glasses.

168. Los ciegos y sordos desarrollan más los sentidos de olfato y tacto

The blinds and deafs develops more the senses of smell and touch.

169. Los cinco sentidos son vista, tacto, gusto, olfato y oído

The five senses are sight, touch, taste, smell, and hearing

Chapter 2: Preferences

Here you will find phrases about the preferences of the people like religion, sports, music, hobbies and colors.

Sports

170.   Mi amiga practica aerobics

   My friend practices aerobics.

171. Él practica tiro al arco

   He practices archery

172. Me encanta el béisbol

   I love baseball.

173. Mi deporte favorito es el basketball. ¿Y el tuyo?

   My favorite sport is basketball. And yours?

174. El voleibol de playa

   Beach volleyball

175.   A mi prima le encanta ir al bowling (lugar) a jugar bolos (Actividad)

   My cousin loves going to the bowling (Place) to play bowling (Activity)

176. El papá de Andrés es un profesional jugando ajedrez

   Andres' father is a professional playing chess

177. Ayer a Martín lo golpearon cuando entrenaba boxeo

   Yesterday Martin was beaten while training boxing.

178. Cristiano Ronaldo es el mejor jugador de fútbol

   Cristiano Ronaldo is the best football player

179. A la hija de mi tío la invitaron a jugar golf

   My uncle's daughter was invited to play golf

180.   Santiago y Julio practican ciclismo todos los martes

   Santiago and Julio practice cycling every Tuesday.

181. Lo mejor de ir a fiestas es bailar

   The best thing about going to parties is dancing

182.   Ayer mientras estaba en la playa me prestaron un Kayak

   Yesterday while I was on the beach I borrowed a Kayak

183.   Mira este video de mi hermano haciendo motocross

Watch this video of my brother doing motocross

184. El paracaidismo es el deporte más extremo que hay

Skydiving is the most extreme sport there is

185. Me duelen las rodillas por correr tanto

My knees hurt from running so much.

186. Mi materia favorita en la escuela es natación

My favorite subject in school is swimming.

187. En mis vacaciones en Suiza, practiqué patinaje sobre nieve y me encantó

During my vacation in Switzerland, I did snowboarding and I loved it

188. Me caí la semana pasada mientras hacía ciclismo de montaña

I fell last week while mountain biking.

189. Me gusta hacer ejercicio antes y después de trabajar, pero no sé cual disfruto más

I like to exercise before and after work, but I don't know which one I enjoy the most

190. Prefiero ver boxeo en la TV que lucha libre

I'd rather watch boxing on TV than wrestling.

191. Nunca me pierdo ningunos juegos olímpicos

I never miss any Olympic Games.

192. Todos los años mis amigos y yo nos reunímos a ver el super bowl

Every year my friends and I get together to see the super bowl.

193. Muchos preferirán el béisbol, pero yo prefiero el fútbol

Many will prefer baseball, but I prefer football.

194. El Barcelona y el Real Madrid son dos grandes equipos, nunca me decido a quién apoyar

Barcelona and Real Madrid are two great teams, I never decide who to support.

Religion

195. Hay muchas religiones en el mundo como la católica, la evangélica, la budista y la musulmana

There are many religions in the world such as Catholic, Evangelical, Buddhist and Muslim.

196. Yo soy cristiano

I am a Christian

197. La mama de Patricia es muy católica, ella es fiel creyente de la Virgen

Patricia's mother is very Catholic, she is a faithful believer of the Virgin Mary.

198. Yo voy a la iglesia bautista porque dan clases de estudio bíblico

I go to the Baptist church because they give Bible study classes.

199. ¿Sabías que la biblia es el libro que más ha sido traducido en la historia?

Did you know that the Bible is the most translated book in history?

200. Debemos confesar nuestros pecados ante Dios

We must confess our sins to God

201. En el hospital hay una capilla de oración

In the hospital there is a prayer chapel

202. Todos estamos llamados a ser discípulos de Dios

We are all called to be disciples of God

203. Los católicos ofrecen misa todos los domingos

Catholics offer Mass every Sunday.

204. Yo creo en Dios

I believe in God

205. Ellos son ateos, no creen en Dios

They are atheists, they do not believe in God

206. El sacerdote de mi ciudad es bastante creyente

The priest of my city is quite a believer

207. La biblia dice que Jesucristo murió en la cruz y resucitó al tercer día

The Bible says that Jesus Christ died on the cross and was resurrected on the third day.

208. El padre de mi amigo cree en la reencarnación

My friend's father believes in reincarnation

209. Yo creo en Dios, pero no se si es mejor ser católico o cristiano

I believe in God, but I don't know if it is better to be Catholic or Christian.

210. El budismo y el hindúismo tienen sus cosas buenas y malas, sin embargo, prefiero el budismo

Buddhism and Hinduism have their good and bad things, however, I prefer Buddhism

211. Yo leo el Corán todos los días

I read the Koran every day

212. Orar y rezar pueden parecer lo mismo, pero no lo son

Praying and Prayer may seem the same, but they are not.

213. No me gusta ninguna religión porque todas han sido modificadas a conveniencia del hombre

I do not like any religion because they have all been modified for the convenience of man.

Music

214. Me encanta la música pop, mi artista favorito es Michael Jackson

I love pop music, my favorite artist is Michael Jackson.

215. ¿Cuál es tu género musical favorito?

What is your favorite musical genre?

216. ¿Cuál es la música que no soportas?

What's the music you can't stand?

217. ¿Quieres escuchar un poco de música?

Do you want to listen to some music?

218. Bájale el volumen a la música, está muy alta

Turn down the music, it's too loud.

219. ¿Escuchaste la nueva canción que salió ayer?

Did you hear the new song that came out yesterday?

220. Odio el vallenato, esa música colombiana es terrible

I hate vallenato, that Colombian music is terrible.

221. Me encanta el nuevo álbum de 50 cent

I love the new 50-cent album

222. ¿Prefieres escuchar Rock o Metal?

Would you rather listen to Rock or Metal?

223. Estoy en una banda de música, tocamos blues.

I am in a band, we play blues.

224. ¿Qué harás el fin de semana? ¿Quieres ir a un concierto de electrónica que van a hacer en la plaza?

What are you going to do on the weekend? Do you want to go to an electronic concert they're going to do in the square?

225. ¿Descargaste el nuevo disco de Elvis? Está de moda

Did you download the new Elvis album? It's in trend

226. El remix de la canción de hace tres meses está buenísimo

The remix of the song from three months ago is very good.

227. ¿Supiste que tus artistas favoritos están planeando hacer un dueto?

Did you hear your favorite artists are planning to do a duet?

228. ¿Puedes cambiar esa canción? No me gusta para nada

Can you change that song? I don't like it at all

229. ¿Quieres poner la música que te gusta?

Do you want to play the music you like?

230. ¿Quieres que escuchemos tú música?

Do you want us to listen to your music?

231. Al vecino le encanta el hip hop, todos los días lo escucha a todo volumen

The neighbor loves hip hop, every day he listens to it at full volume.

Hobbies

232. ¿Cuál es tu pasatiempo favorito?

What is your favorite hobby?

233. ¿Cuál es tu pasatiempo preferido?

What's your favorite hobby?

234. ¿Qué es lo que más te gusta hacer?

What do you like to do the most?

235. ¿Cuáles son tus pasatiempos?

What are your hobbies?

236. Mi pasatiempo favorito es visitar el ancianato

My favorite hobby is to visit the old people's home.

237. Uno de mis pasatiempos es pasear perros

One of my hobbies is walking dogs

238. El pasatiempo del papá de Daniela es escribir

Daniela's dad's hobby is writing

239. A mi mamá le encanta ir a trotar a la montaña

My mom loves to go jogging to the mountain.

240. Tengo un vecino cuyo pasatiempo es hacer tatuajes a las personas

I have a neighbor whose hobby is tattooing people.

241. Mi amigo hace stand up como pasatiempo y además gana algo de dinero

My friend does stand up as a hobby and also earns some money

242. Desde muy pequeño el pasatiempo de mi primo era programar y ahora consiguió un trabajo haciéndolo

Since I was a child my cousin's hobby was programming and now he got a job doing it.

243. Me fascina el diseño gráfico, creo que puedo decir que es el pasatiempo que más me gusta

I love graphic design, I think I can say that is the hobby I like most

244. Ella tiene muchos pasatiempos pero el que más le gusta es entrenar en el gimnasio

She has many hobbies but the one she likes the most is training in the gym.

245. Para divertirme me gusta dibujar caricaturas

For fun I like to draw caricatures

246. A mi hermana menor le encantan los perros, está practicando para ser una entrenadora de perros

My younger sister loves dogs, she is practicing to be a dog trainer.

247. No me gusta el pasatiempo de Sebastián, la meditación me parece muy aburrida

I don't like Sebastian's hobby, meditation seems very boring to me.

248. Su tío parece un mago profesional. Seguro ha sido su pasatiempo desde hace bastante tiempo

Your-His-Her uncle looks like a professional magician. Surely it's been his hobby for quite some time.

We want to make clear that we wrote Your-His-Her because in Spanish, "Su" can be used for these three subjects, You (In a more formal way than "Tú"), He and she. So, if you see "Su" written, it could mean any of these three subjects unless other words in the phrase or the situation defines it as one of those. For example:

Su brassier le queda muy bien
Her bra fits her very good.

In this case, we know it is Her, because the bra is something that only women use

Su orden esta lista señor
Your order is ready sir.

In this case we know that it is Your, because it is referring to someone (You) in a formal way (sir)

Su cartera se le quedó en la mesa
His wallet was left on the table.

In this case, we know that it is His, because a wallet is an accessory that men use.

249. Él es una persona con bastantes conocimientos, su pasatiempo es leer libros

He is a person with quite a lot of knowledge, his hobby is to read books

250. A las cinco en punto de la tarde todos los días pasa un señor paseando perros, no sé si lo hace como pasatiempo o como empleo

At five o'clock in the afternoon every day a gentleman passes by walking dogs, I don't know if he does it as a hobby or as a job.

251. Mi hijo me pidió que lo inscribiera en artes marciales. Me dijo que era su nuevo pasatiempo favorite

My son asked me to enroll him in martial arts. He told me it was his new favorite hobby.

252. Tantos pasatiempos geniales que existen y su favorito es el origami, no lo entiendo

So many great hobbies that exist and his favorite is origami, I do not understand.

253. Mi primer pasatiempo fue hacer sudokus, el segundo fue el parkour y ahora mi tercero es aprender otros idiomas

My first hobby was sudoku, the second was parkour and now my third is to learn other languages.

254. Todos los días de la semana practico un pasatiempo diferente

Every day of the week I practice a different hobby.

255. Algunos días incluso hago dos o más pasatiempos

Some days I even do two or more hobbies

256. Los lunes me gusta salir a pasear en la moto

On Mondays I like to go for a ride on the bike

257. Los martes en la mañana voy a practicar breakdance y en la tarde voy a la biblioteca a leer

On Tuesday mornings I go to practice breakdance and in the afternoon I go to the library to read

258. Los miércoles limpio la casa

On Wednesdays I clean the house

259. Los jueves en la tarde hago senderismo y en la noche veo películas en el cine

On Thursday afternoons I go trekking and at night I watch movies in the cinema

260. Los viernes cocino algo especial para la cena

On Fridays I cook something special for dinner

261. Los sábados me voy con mi familia de camping

On Saturdays I go with my family to camp.

262. Y los domingos vamos a la iglesia

And on Sundays we go to church

263. La próxima semana tengo un torneo de tenis para el que he estado practicando durante meses

Next week I have a tennis tournament for which I have been practicing for months.

264. Durante invierno me gusta practicar snowboarding

During winter I like to practice snowboarding

265. El próximo verano alquilaré una casa en la playa y perfeccionaré mi técnica de surf

Next summer I will rent a house on the beach and perfect my surfing technique.

Colors

266. Mi color preferido es el azul

My favorite color is blue.

267. Me encantan las paredes de la casa de color rojo

I love the red walls of the house.

268. El carro de Vladimir es de su color preferido, el Amarillo

Vladimir's car is his favorite color, yellow.

269. Leila tenía el cabello marrón pero ahora se lo pintó de negro porque le gusta más

Leila had brown hair but now she painted it black because she likes it better.

270. El protector de teléfono de mi hermana es rosado porque ama ese color

My sister's phone protector is pink because she loves that color

271. No puedo creer que las personas usen ropa verde, ese color es horrible

I can't believe people wear green clothes, that color is horrible.

272. Se compró una cartera anaranjada para que combinara con el color de sus zapatos

She bought an orange handbag to match the color of her shoes.

273. Me regalaron una tarjeta de color morado, pero no me gusta para nada ese color

I was presented with a purple card, but I don't like that color at all.

274. Amo el termo de color turquesa que tiene mi prima, no me gusta mucho el color pero en el termo se ve spectacular

I love the turquoise thermos that my cousin has, I don't like the color very much but in the thermos it looks spectacular.

275. Vi una camisa de color crema que me dejó sin aliento

I saw a cream-colored shirt that took my breath away.

276. El arcoíris tiene colores hermosos como el amarillo, anaranjado, rojo y más

The rainbow has beautiful colors such as yellow, orange, red and more.

277. En clase de arte nunca me decido por cuál color usar como principal

In art class I never decide which color to use as the main one.

Pets

278. Los animales más comunes que las personas tienen como mascotas son los perros / The most common animals that people have as pets are dogs

279. Hay otros animales menos comunes que la gente tiene como mascota / There are other less common animals that people have as pets.

280. Mi vecina Linda tiene dos iguanas como mascotas / My neighbor Linda has two lizards as pets.

281. La mamá de mi amigo tiene dos loros de mascota / My friend's mom has two parrots as pets

282. En la casa de campo tenemos tres conejos como mascotas / In the country house we have three rabbits as pets

283. Mi hija quiere adoptar un gato para que sea su mascota / My daughter wants to adopt a cat to be her pet

284. Yo pienso que las aves no son animales que deban ser mascotas / I think that birds are not animals that should be pets.

285. Susan tiene una tarántula como mascota y a veces la agarra con la mano / Susan has a pet tarantula and sometimes grabs it with her hand.

286. Carl quiere comprar una anaconda bebé que vió en una tienda para tenerla de mascota / Carl wants to buy a baby anaconda he saw in a store to have it as a pet.

287. Algunas personas tienen hámsters como mascotas / Some people have hamsters as pets

288. La mascota de mi prima es un hurón / My cousin's pet is a ferret.

289. Mi otra prima tiene una pareja de conejillos de india / My other cousin has a couple of guinea pigs.

290. Están de moda los cochinos miniatura como mascotas / Miniature pigs are in fashion as pets

291. Algunos millonarios tienen mascotas exóticas como tigres y jirafas / Some millionaires have exotic pets such as tigers and giraffes.

292. En el campo es común tener otro tipo de mascotas / In the countryside it is common to have other types of pets

293. En la granja de mi tío tienen tres caballos como mascota / At my uncle's farm they have three horses as pets

294. Cuando visité a la familia de mi novia, me dijeron que tenían cuatro vacas como mascotas / When I visited my girlfriend's family, they told me they had four cows as pets.

295. Un vecino de mi padrastro tiene cinco gallos y seis gallinas de mascotas / One of my stepfather's neighbors has five roosters and six pet chickens.

296. Generalmente cuando las perras tienen cachorros, son seis o siete / Generally when dogs have puppies, they are six or seven

Politics

297. Ningún sistema político me parece adecuado / No political system seems appropriate to me

298. Los sistemas políticos dependen de muchos factores / Political systems depend on many factors

299. El comunismo es un sistema político muy corrupto / Communism is a very corrupt political system

300. Yo apoyo a los liberales por sus ideologías y propuestas / I support the liberals for their ideologies and proposals.

301. Mi abuelo toda su vida estuvo a favor de la democracia / My grandfather was all his life in favour of democracy

302. Mi abuela se inclinaba por el sistema democrático presidencialista / My grandmother was inclined towards the presidential democratic system

303. La abuela de Joe siempre prefirió el sistema democrático parlamentista / Joe's grandmother always preferred the democratic parliamentary system

304. El tió de mi novia esta muy en contra de los sistemas bipartidistas / My girlfriend's uncle is very against bipartisan systems.

305. El profesor de historia dice que el mejor sistema político es el totalitarismo / The history professor says that the best political system is totalitarianism.

306. Mientras que el profesor de economía piensa que el mejor sistema político es es liberalismo / While the economics professor thinks that the best political system is liberalism

307. Todos los expertos en política concuerdan en que el socialismo es un pésimo sistema político / All political experts agree that socialism is a very bad political system.

308. A mi me gustan algunas ideas del conservadurismo, pero no lo apoyo del todo / I like some ideas of conservatism, but I don't fully support it.

309. En mi opinión, ser de derecha es lo mas prudente, hacer una mezcla entre el conservadurismo y el liberalismo es bastante razonable / In my opinion, being right-wing political is the most prudent thing to do, making a mix between conservatism and liberalism is quite reasonable.

310. Muy pocos sistemas políticos izquierdistas funcionan realmente / Very few leftist political systems really work

311. El manifiesto comunista de Karl Marx es una gran obra / Karl Marx's communist manifesto is a great work

312. Es una gran manera de describir el sistema poliítico la manera en la que lo hace George Orwell en sus libros / It's a great way to describe the political system the way George Orwell does it in his books.

313. Los países que viven en dictadura están en crisis / Countries living under dictatorship are in crisis

314. Las dictaduras nunca terminan bien para sus políticos / Dictatorships never end well for their politicians

315. Los derechos humanos deben ser cumplidos siempre, sin importar las circunstancias / Human rights must always be respected, regardless of the circumstances.

316. El centro político me parece un sistema imposible de alcanzar / The political centre seems to me to be an impossible system to achieve

317. El comunismo y el socialismo tienen las mismas bases políticas / Communism and socialism have the same political bases

318. Estoy en total desacuerdo con los resultados de las votaciones / I totally disagree with the results of the votes.

319. Iré a votar para elegir un nuevo presidente y parlamento / I'm going to vote for a new president and parliament.

320. Ciertas personas piensan que las votaciones están compradas / Some people think that votes are bought.

321. El primo de mi primo siempre ha dicho que es mejor votar y perder que perder sin haber votado / My cousin's cousin has always said it's better to vote and lose than to lose without having voted.

322. El nuevo presidente tiene todo mi apoyo / The new president has my full support

323. Las medidas económicas tomadas por el ministro me parecen una irresponsabilidad / The economic measures taken by the minister seem to me to be irresponsible.

324. Yo creo que el alcalde está haciendo un muy buen trabajo / I think the mayor is doing a very good job.

325. El gobernador dijo que haría una reunión con su gabinete para evaluar la situación / The governor said he would meet with his cabinet to evaluate the situation.

326. El vicepresidente es un incompetente / The vice president is an incompetent

327. Habrá una reunión de emergencia del personal cercano del presidente / There will be an emergency meeting of the President's nearby staff.

328. Las monarquías me parecen sistemas políticos muy anticuados / Monarchies seem to me to be very old-fashioned political systems

329. El Rey no hace mucho por su país / The King does not do much for his country

330. Cuando el primer ministro renunció todo empeoró / When the prime minister resigned, everything got worse.

331. Mi papá trabajó en el parlamento durante cinco años / My father worked in parliament for five years

332. Me parece excelente que se permita la reelección / I think it is excellent that reelection is allowed

333. Pienso que la nueva ley no es muy prudente / I think the new law is not very prudent

334. El secretario de estado es una persona muy íntegra / The secretary of state is a very integral person

Chapter 3: Transportation

Here you will find useful common and basic phrases about things related to transportation.

Taking a bus, taking a cab

335. Buenas tardes, ¿Podría enviar un taxi a mi dirección? / Good afternoon, could you send a taxi to my address?

336. Hola, ¿Cómo esta? Me gustaría que me llevara al cine, ¿Puede? / Hello, how are you? I'd like you to take me to the movies, would you?

337. Buenos días, ¿Cuánto cuesta que me lleve hasta el centro comercial? / Good morning, how much does it cost to take me to the mall?

338. ¿Cuánto le debo? / How much do I owe you?

339. ¿Cuánto tengo que pagar? / How much do I have to pay?

340. ¿Es este el autobús de la ruta #1? / Is this the bus from route #1?

341. ¿Pasa éste autobús por la plaza? / Does this bus go through the square?

342. ¿Cuál es el horario de los autobuses? / What are the bus schedules?

343. Me gustaría saber cuál ruta de autobús me deja en la calle 5 / I'd like to know which bus route drops me off at 5th Street.

344. ¿Cuánto cuesta el ticket de autobús? / How much does a bus ticket cost?

345. Disculpe, ¿Es usted el conductor del autobús? / Excuse me, are you the bus driver?

346. Buenas noches, ¿Usted es el conductor del taxi? / Good evening, are you the taxi driver?

347. Muchas gracias por traerme, que tenga un buen día / Thank you very much for driving me, have a good day.

348. Tome, aquí esta su dinero / Take, here is your money.

349. Tome, acepte esta propina por el buen servicio / Here, accept this tip for good service

350. Buenas tardes señorita, ¿A dónde desea usted que la lleve? / Good afternoon, miss, where would you like me to take you?

351. De nada / You are welcome

352. Estamos llegando a su destino / We are arriving to your destination

353. La próxima parada es la última, por favor bájense del autobús / The next stop is the last one, please get off the bus.

354. ¿Cuánto tardaría en llegar a mi ubicación el taxi más cercano? / How long would it take for the nearest taxi to reach my location?

355. ¿Puede recogerme en la calle 23? / Can you pick me up at 23rd Street?

356. Necesito un taxi urgentemente / I need a taxi urgently.

357. Ese autobús es de 32 puestos / This bus has 32 seats

358. ¿Podría darme un aventón hasta mi casa? / Could you give me a lift home?

Asking for directions

359. ¿Cómo puedo llegar al museo? / How can I get to the museum?

360. Disculpe, ¿Podría indicarme cómo llegar a la estación de servicio más cercana? / Excuse me, could you tell me how to get to the nearest service station?

361. Siga derecho durante tres cuadras / Go straight for three blocks

362. Cruce a la izquierda después del puente / Turn left after the bridge

363. Gire a la derecha antes del túnel / Turn right before the tunnel

364. De la vuelta en la rotonda y regrésese por esta misma vía / Turn around at the roundabout and go back along the same road.

365. Continúe por la carretera por treinta y cinco kilómetros y luego entre a la autopista / Continue on the road for thirty-five kilometers and then enter the highway

366. Para llegar a esa dirección debe seguir por la avenida 23 hasta llegar a la calle 8 / To get to this address you must follow Avenue 23 until you reach 8th Street.

367. Necesito llegar para acá lo más pronto posible. ¿Qué camino debo tomar? / I need to get here as soon as possible. Which way should I go?

368. Me gustaría llegar a la playa, ¿Puede indicarme qué camino seguir? / I'd like to get to the beach; can you tell me which way to go?

369. Estoy perdido, ¿Dónde estoy? / I'm lost, where am I?

370. ¿Le importaría indicarme en que parte del mapa estamos? / Would you mind telling me where we are on the map?

371. Debo llegar a la casa de mi amigo antes de las seis y media de la tarde, ¿Conoces algún atajo? / I must get to my friend's house before half past six in the afternoon. Do you know any shortcuts?

372. ¿Hay algún camino alterno para evitar este atasco? / Is there any alternative way to avoid this traffic jam?

373. Para llegar al cine, ¿Debo girar a la izquierda o a la derecha? / To get to the cinema, do I have to turn left or right?

Car parts

374. La semana pasada llevé mi carro a que le hicieran el servicio / Last week I took my car to have the service done

375. Ya me excedí de los kilómetros sugeridos para el cambio de aceite / I have already exceeded the suggested kilometers for the oil change

376. Disculpa por llegar tarde, tuve que venir en autobús porque mi carro se averió / Sorry I'm late, I had to come by bus because my car broke down.

377. No pude llegar a tiempo porque se me espichó un caucho y tuve que poner el de repuesto / I couldn't get there in time because a tyre was punctured and I had to put in the spare tyre.

378. El carro está fallando porque se me dañó una bujía / The car is failing because a spark plug is damaged.

379. El mes pasado en la autopista una piedrita me rompió el parabrisas / Last month on the freeway a pebble broke my windshield.

380. Debo comprar los cauchos nuevos antes del invierno, estos ya no tienen adhesión / I must buy the new tyres before the winter, these no longer have adhesion

381. La esposa de Mike dañó los rines de su camioneta ayer estacionándose / Mike's wife damaged the rims of her truck yesterday parking.

382. Mi tía retrocediendo le dio un golpe al maletero del carro / My aunt reversing hit the trunk of the car.

383. Debes revisarle los frenos al carro antes de irte de viaje, ya no están muy buenos / You must check the brakes of the car before you go on a trip, they are not very good anymore.

384. Chequea el refrigerante, ayer se recalentó cuando venia para acá / Check the coolant, it reheated yesterday when I was coming here.

385. Tuve un choque con una moto y me dañó el capó / I had a collision with a motorbike and it damaged my hood.

386. Estaba llevando al bebé al doctor y vomitó en los asientos / I was taking the baby to the doctor and puked in the seats.

387. De tanto uso, el volante del carro se está desgastando, ya pronto tendremos que reemplazarlo / From so much use, the steering wheel of the car is wearing out, and soon we will have to replace it.

388. No es común que el motor esté sonando así, deberías llevar la camioneta al mecánico / It is not common for the engine to sound like this, you should take the truck to the mechanic.

389. Es bueno tener un todo terreno, pero el consumo de gasolina es muy alto / It's good to have an all-terrain vehicle, but fuel consumption is very high.

390. La transmisión esta extraña, creo que tenemos que revisarla / The transmission is weird, I think we need to check it.

391. El aire acondicionado del carro de la mamá de Isaac enfría muchísimo / The air conditioning in Isaac's mother's car is very cold.

392. La batería se daño, ya no puedo prender el carro / The battery is damaged, I can no longer start the car

393. La otra noche encontré este tornillo en el piso del garaje, se le debe haber caído al carro / The other night I found this screw on the garage floor, it must have fallen into the car.

394. Se soltó el retrovisor porque se le perdió una tuerca / The mirror came loose because it lost a nut.

395. Cuando chocó, se golpeó en la cara porque no estaba usando el cinturón de seguridad / When he crashed, he hit his face because he wasn't wearing a seat belt.

396. Si no hubiese sido por la bolsa de aire, pude haber muerto / If it hadn't been for the air bag, I could have died.

397. Las pastillas de freno ya están sonando, será mejor cambiarlas / The brake pads are already sounding, it will be better to change them

398. Revisa la liga de frenos, puede que le falte un poco / Check the brake fluid, it may be missing a bit.

399. La correa del motor está floja, por eso se siente extraño / The engine belt is loose, that' s why it feels strange.

400. Siempre he querido ponerle unos mejores bombillos al carro / I've always wanted to put better light bulbs in the car

401. El parachoque que le puse a mi minivan me ha ayudado bastante / The bumper I put on my minivan has helped me a lot.

402. Cuando caigo en un hueco suena como un golpe, deben ser los amortiguadores / When I fall into a hole sounds like a shock, must be the shock absorbers

403. Nos quedamos accidentados, prende las luces intermitentes / We got accidented, turn on the flashing lights

404. Se dañó el alternador, nos vamos a quedar sin batería pronto / Alternator damaged, we will run out of battery soon

Train

405. Me encanta viajar en tren / I love to travel by train

406. Es increíble lo rápido que avanza el tren / It's amazing how fast the train goes

407. El subterráneo es un tren que viaja por debajo de la tierra / The subway is a train that travels beneath the ground

408. La corneta del ferrocarril suena muy fuerte / The railway horn sounds very loud

409. Es más rápido viajar en tren que en taxi / It is faster to travel by train than by taxi

410. Es más económico utilizar el autobús que el tren / It is cheaper to use the bus than the train.

411. El ferrocarril y el tren significan lo mismo / The railway and the train mean the same.

412. Los trenes antes funcionaban con carbón / Trains used to run on coal

413. Los asientos del tren son bastante cómodos / The train seats are quite comfortable

414. ¿A qué hora pasa el próximo tren? / What time's the next train?

415. ¿Sabe cuánto falta para el próximo tren? / Do you know how long it is until the next train?

416. ¿A dónde se dirige este tren? / Where is this train going?

417. ¿Cuál es la próxima estación? / What's the next station?

418. ¿Cuál es la ruta de este tren? / What is the route of this train?

419. ¿Sabes si la ruta de este tren me sirve para llegar al capitolio? / Do you know if the route of this train leads me to the capitol?

420. Todos los domingos tomo el tren al salir de la iglesia / Every Sunday I take the train out of the church.

421. Ese es el tren más rápido del mundo / That's the fastest train in the world.

422. Debes esperar que el tren esté completamente detenido antes de acercarte / You must wait for the train to stop completely before approaching.

423. Por seguridad, debes siempre esperar el tren detrás de cierta línea de seguridad / For safety, you should always wait for the train behind a certain safety line.

424. Es muy importante estar sentado al momento en el que el tren arranca / It is very important to be seated at the moment the train starts.

425. Es igual de importante estar sentado cuando el tren se detiene / It is equally important to be seated when the train stops

426. ¿Hay wifi en este tren? / Is there wifi on this train?

427. ¿En qué vagón del tren estas? / What train wagon are you in?

428. ¿Cuántas estaciones faltan para poder llegar a mi destino? / How many stations are there left to get to my destination?

429. Es posible llegar a tiempo a clases si vamos en tren / It is possible to arrive on time for classes if we go by train

430. Lo mejor de usar el tren es que es bastante silencioso, por lo que puedo leer tranquilo / The best thing about using the train is that it's pretty quiet, so I can read quietly

Other transportation forms

431. Algunas veces es mas fácil pedir un Uber que un taxi / Sometimes it is easier to order a Uber than a taxi.

432. Los Uber son más económicos que los taxis / The Uber are cheaper than taxis

433. Pide un Uber usando la app para teléfonos inteligentes / Order a Uber using the app for smartphones

434. En algunas ocasiones prefiero ir a ciertos lugares en bicicleta, asi hago ejercicio / In some occasions I prefer to go to certain places in bicycle, so I do exercise

435. En algunos países como en Holanda la mayoría de las personas se translada en bicicleta / In some countries, such as the Netherlands, the majority of people travel by bicycle.

436. Al utilizar la bicicleta como método de transporte, no gasto dinero en gasolina / By using the bicycle as a form of transport, you don't spend money on gasoline.

437. Manejar bicicleta es bueno para la salud / Riding a bicycle is good for your health

438. Siempre es bueno usar casco al manejar bicicleta / It is always good to wear a helmet when riding a bicycle

439. El hermanastro de Jonah tiene una bicicleta que tiene motor eléctrico / Jonah's stepbrother has a bicycle with an electric motor.

440. Las bicicletas eléctricas tienen un pequeño motor eléctrico que funciona cuando lo deseas / Electric bicycles have a small electric motor that works when you want it.

441. Para ahorrar dinero del combustible también es bueno usar una motocicleta / To save money on fuel it is also good to use a motorcycle

442. Hay distintos estilos de motocicletas / Para ahorrar dinero en combustible también es bueno usar una motocicleta.

443. Mathias tiene una moto estilo café racer / Mathias has a cafe racer style motorcycle

444. A mi me fascinan las motocicletas estilo Touring / I am fascinated by Touring style motorcycles

445. El hermano de mi novia tiene una moto estilo chopper / My girlfriend's brother has a chopper motorcycle.

446. Las motos más veloces son las estilo racing / The fastest motorcycles are the racing ones

447. Hay que ser muy prudente al manejar moto, es muy peligroso / You have to be very careful when riding a bike, it's very dangerous.

448. Las motos que más le gustaban a mi papá eran las adventure / The bikes my dad liked the most were the adventure bikes.

449. Mi moto racing modificada alcanza los trescientos kilómetros por hora en rectas / My modified racing bike reaches three hundred kilometres per hour on straight lines.

450. Es curioso que las motos más comunes sean las motos de paseo / It is curious that the most common motorcycles are the motorcycles of tour

451. Algunas personas consideran que manejar motocicleta es un hobbie / Some people consider riding motorcycle as a hobby.

452. Otras personas lo ven más como una pasión o un estilo de vida / Other people see it more as a passion or a lifestyle

453. Mi hermano se compró una moto estilo super motard que está espectacular / My brother bought himself a super motard motorcycle that's spectacular.

454. Mi primo Eugenio va a su trabajo en patineta / My cousin Eugenio goes to work on his skateboard

455. La hermana de Fred va a su trabajo en patines / Fred's sister goes to her work on roller skates

456. Utilizar medios de transporte alternativos siempre es buena opción / Using alternative forms of transport is always a good option

457. Los medios de transporte alternativos contribuyen al cuidado del medio ambiente / Alternative forms of transport contribute to the care of the environment

458. Las motos scooter son bastante cómodas para movilizarse en la ciudad / Scooters are comfortable enough to get around the city.

459. También existen motos eléctricas que ayudan a disminuir la contaminación / There are also electric motorcycles that help to reduce pollution.

460. Es bastante entretenido manejar un segway, en algunos lugares puedes alquilar uno / It is quite entertaining to drive a segway, in some places you can rent one

461. Hace un par de años estuvieron de moda los hoverboard, todos se transportaban en uno / A couple of years ago hoverboards were trendy, everyone was transported in one.

462. Cuando mi tía era pequeña iba a todos lados en su monopatín / When my aunt was little she went everywhere on her roller skateboard

463. Muchas personas prefieren salir antes y caminar hacia sus destinos / Many people prefer to leave early and walk to their destinations

464. Es increíble lo rápido que puede ser movilizarse en bicicleta / It's amazing how fast it can be to get around on a bicycle

465. Jamás me he montado en un karting, pero me encantaría probarlo / I've never ridden a go-kart before, but I'd love to try it.

466. En el campo, muchas personas utilizan motos cuatro ruedas para movilizarse / In the countryside, many people use four-wheeled motorcycles to get around.

467. El hijo menor de mi prima va a su escuela en motocross / My cousin's youngest son goes to school in motocross

468. Cuando mi tío va a su casa de campo se suele movilizar en caballo / When my uncle goes to his country house, he usually moves on his horse.

Chapter 4: Jobs

In this chapter, we will provide you with phrases and expressions related to jobs and professions.

Jobs and professions

469. Mi mejor amigo de la infancia ahora es actor para las grandes compañías de Hollywood / My best childhood friend is now an actor for the big Hollywood companies

470. El primo de mi tía es arqueólogo en Egipto / My aunt's cousin is an archaeologist in Egypt.

471. Mi prima ha estudiado bastante y por fin se graduó de arquitecta / My cousin has studied a lot and finally graduated as an architect.

472. La vecina de mi mamá hace pan muy sabroso, ella es panadera / My mom's neighbor makes very tasty bread, she's a baker.

473. El abuelo de mi novia trabajaba como conductor de autobús cuando era joven / My girlfriend's grandfather worked as a bus driver when he was young

474. Cuando sea grande quiero ser un hombre de negocios / When I grow up I want to be a businessman

475. Me gusta comprar carne en la esquina porque el carnicero es mi amigo / I like to buy meat in the corner because the butcher is my friend.

476. Yo soy Damon, el jefe de ésta compañía / I'm Damon, the boss of this company.

477. Tú eres el nuevo asistente administrativo de finanzas / You are the new administrative finance assistant

478. Él es Peter, es el vicepresidente de ventas de la compañía / This is Peter, he's the company's vice president of sales.

479. Ella es Alice, la gerente de ventas de la región capital / This is Alice, the sales manager for the capital region.

480. Nosotros somos la parte más importante de la compañía / We are the most important part of the company

481. Ustedes son la base para el correcto funcionamiento de la empresa / You are the basis for the proper functioning of the company

482. Ellos y ellas son los empleados que día a día de esfuerzan por mejorar la empresa / They are the employees who, day by day, strive to improve the company.

483. Ese es el lema de la empresa " con esfuerzo y dedicación todo es alcanzable / It is the slogan of the company "with effort and dedication everything is achievable".

484. Ella hizo muchos cursos antes de poder ser tan buena carpintera / She did many courses before she could be such a good carpenter.

485. Leí en el periódico que en una tienda del centro comercial están buscando un cajero / I read in the newspaper that a store in the mall is looking for a cashier.

486. Los zapatos que compraste se rompieron, los llevaré al zapatero / The shoes you bought broke, I'll take them to the cobbler

487. La casa está un poco descuidada, llamaré al decorador / The house is a little careless, I'll call the decorator

488. Me está doliendo bastante una muela, creo que debo ir al dentista a hacerme un chequeo / My cheektooth is hurting quite a bit, I think I should go to the dentist for a check-up.

489. Necesito que un diseñador le haga la portada a mi libro / I need a designer to do the cover of my book

490. Ahorraré como me sugirió mi amigo el economista / I will save as my friend the economist suggested to me

491. Después de tantos años como estudiante logré convertirme en ingeniero / After so many years as a student I managed to become an engineer

492. El mecánico es un gran amigo de la familia y siempre hace un buen trabajo con nuestros carros / The mechanic is a big friend of the family and always does a good job with our cars.

493. Estas vacaciones trabajaré como niñera para ganar dinero / This holiday I will work as a nanny to earn money

494. La nueva cámara del fotógrafo de la escuela está genial / The school photographer's new camera is great

495. Un ladrón, rápido, llamen a la policía / A thief, hurry, call the police

496. El taxista está tardando mucho más de lo que dijo que tardaría / The taxi driver is taking much longer than he said it would take

497. Me encanta escribir, quizás en el futuro me convierta en escritora / I love to write, maybe in the future I will become a writer

498. Pobre Jacko, se está sintiendo mal. Llamaré al veterinario para que venga / Poor Jacko, he's feeling bad. I'll call the vet to come

499. Mi vecino cree que es cantante, canta toda la noche / My neighbor thinks he's a singer, sings all night.

500. Señorita, ¿Es usted la asistente? Necesito que organice una reunión de emergencia / Lady, are you the assistant? I need you to set up an emergency meeting

501. Mi hijo tiene miedo irracional a los perros, ¿Crees que deba llevarlo al psicólogo? / My son has an irrational fear of dogs. Do you think I should take him to a psychologist?

502. Estoy preocupada por Stan, sé que es programador, pero estar todo el día en la computadora no es algo bueno / I'm worried about Stan, I know he's a programmer, but being on the computer all day is not a good thing.

503. Buenos días, imagino que usted es la recepcionista, ¿Podría entregarle esto al Sr. Matt? / Good morning, I imagine you're the receptionist. Could you give this to Mr. Matt?

504. Buenas tardes, estoy aquí porque vi que estaban buscando un fontanero / Good afternoon, I'm here because I saw you were looking for a plumber.

505. Buenos días, vine a la entrevista de trabajo / Good morning, I'm here for the job interview.

506. Me gustaría aplicar para el trabajo de supervisor con esta empresa / I would like to apply to supervisor vacant with this company

507. A las 3:00 p.m. toca el descanso / At 3:00 p.m., it's time for the break.

508. Tengo demasiada hambre, no puedo esperar a la hora de almuerzo / I'm too hungry, I can't wait for lunch.

509. Estoy agotado, un trabajo a tiempo completo y estudiar es demasiado / I'm exhausted, a full-time job and studying is too much

510. Mamá obtuve el ascenso que tanto había estado esperando / Mom, I got the promotion I had been waiting for so long.

511. Ya quiero que llegue el día libre, hay demasiado papeleo / I want the day off to come, there's too much paperwork.

512. Cuando me despidieron de una empresa me contrataron en otra / When I was fired from one company, I was hired in another company.

513. El trabajo de Elizabeth es medio tiempo pero ella siempre trabaja horas extras / Elizabeth's job is part-time but she always works overtime.

514. Ahora que te recuperaste del accidente puedes intentar conseguir un empleo / Now that you've recovered from the accident you can try to get a job

515. Me encanta mi trabajo, el jefe es complicado, pero el salario es bastante bueno / I love my job, the boss is complicated, but the salary is quite good.

516. Soy la persona indicada para este trabajo por mis habilidades / I am the right person for this job because of my skills

517. Estoy dispuesto a aprender lo necesario para este trabajo / I am willing to learn what is necessary for this work

518. Mañana temprano hay reunión en la oficina / Tomorrow morning there is a meeting in the office

519. Me gustaría pedir un ascenso / I would like to ask for a promotion

520. Tengo las habilidades necesarias para este empleo / I have the skills necessary for this job

521. Mis cualidades son las indicadas para este puesto / My qualities are the indicated for this position

522. Estamos haciendo un presupuesto para comprar nuevos escritorios para la empresa / We are making a budget to buy new desks for the enterprise

523. Ya se están acabando las grapas que compramos, hay que buscar más / The staples that we bought are already running out, we have to look for more

524. Las computadoras son una parte fundamental para el funcionamiento de la empresa / Computers are a fundamental part for the functioning of the enterprise

525. Envíame la información por correo electrónico / Send me the information by e-mail

526. Debemos hacer una videoconferencia para aclarar las cosas sobre la tarifa de pago / We must make a videoconference to clarify things about the rate of pay rate

527. Tenemos que hablar con el personal sobre la situación de la compañía / We need to talk to the staff about the situation of the company

528. El nuevo empleado es excelente / The new employee is excellent

529. El ambiente laboral de nuestra empresa es muy agradable, hay mucho compañerismo y trabajo en equipo / The working environment of our company is very pleasant, there is a lot of companionship and teamwork.

530. Cuando termine las pasantias me darán un cargo fijo en la empresa / When I finish the internships I will be given a permanent position in the company.

531. El área de Nómina es confidencial / The Payroll area is confidential

532. Los empleados de finanzas son personal de confianza / Finance employees are trusted personnel.

533. La seguridad de la empresa está a cargo de una contratista al igual que el área de mantenimiento / The safety of the company is in charge of a contractor as well as the maintenance area.

534. La gerente de recursos humanos viene de otro país / The human resources manager comes from another country.

535. El vicepresidente de sistemas es un hombre con mucha experiencia en el área / The vice president of systems is a man with a lot of experience in the area.

536. La mayoría de los empleados de mercadeo son jóvenes recién graduados / The majority of Marketing employees are young and recently graduated.

537. Ana es la secretaria del área de ventas / Ana is the secretary of the sales area

538. La fuerza de ventas de la empresa está en entrenamiento / The company's sales force is in training.

539. La convención de ventas se realizará en República Dominicana el próximo mes / The sales convention will be held in the Dominican Republic next month.

540. Los cargos vacantes son de analista junior y analista senior / Vacant positions are junior analyst and senior analyst.

541. La empresa cuenta con 5 distribuidores a nivel nacional / The company has 5 distributors nationwide.

542. Lanzaron nuevo producto al mercado / They launched a new product on the market

543. El director de relaciones públicas está en una conferencia con su equipo / The director of public relations is at a conference with his team

544. El inventario está programado para la primera semana de Agosto / The inventory is scheduled for the first week of August.

545. El próximo mes tendremos la visita de los auditores, estarán aquí por una semana aproximadamente / Next month we will have the visit of the auditors, they will be here for about a week.

546. La visita a la planta fue suspendida por medidas de seguridad / The visit to the plant was suspended due to security measures.

547. Las órdenes de compra deben estar listas al finalizar este mes / Purchase orders should be ready by the end of this month.

548. El cierre fiscal de la empresa va desde el 1ero de julio de este año hasta el 30 de junio del próximo año / The fiscal closure of the company goes from July 1st of this year until June 30th of next year.

549. Por favor envíame el organigrama de la empresa a la brevedad posible / Please send me the organization chart of the company as soon as possible.

550. Dile al proveedor que nos envíe la cotización de las franelas / Tell the supplier to send us the quotation for the t-shirts

551. Ese material publicitario es de muy mala calidad, los colores están opacos y sin brillo / This advertising material is of very poor quality, the colours are opaque and dull.

552. Diageo se posiciona en el 1er puesto como la mejor empresa para trabajar en el mundo / Diageo ranks 1st as the best company to work for in the world.

553. Hay 5 cargos vacantes en esa empresa, voy a postularme para el de auxiliar de caja / There are 5 vacant positions in that company, I'm going to apply for the cashier's assistant

554. Todos los empleados salen de vacaciones en Navidad, solo queda el personal de seguridad cumpliendo turnos / All employees go on holiday at Christmas, only the security personnel remain in shifts.

555. Julio es el encargado de distribuir las muestras, es el mercaderista / Julio is in charge of distributing the samples, he is the merchant.

556. Las promotoras de esa marca son muy bonitas y elegantes / The promoters of that brand are very pretty and elegant.

557. La cajera del supermercado de la esquina es muy eficiente / The corner supermarket cashier is very efficient.

558. Los bomberos de mi ciudad están muy bien entrenados / The firefighters in my city are very well trained.

559. Alicia trabaja como promotora en el banco, ella me ayudó con el problema de mis tarjetas / Alicia works as a promoter in the bank, she helped me with the problem of my cards.

560. El gerente del banco autorizó mi crédito, solo falta su firma / The bank manager authorized my credit, only his signature is missing

561. Al cerrar la caja, el supervisor informó sobre el dinero faltante / At the closure of the cash register, the supervisor reported the missing money

562. Si el analista llega, le entregaré su informe / If the analyst arrives, I will give him his report.

563. En ese local hay peluqueras y un barbero / In that place there are hairdressers and a barber.

564. Prefiero arreglarme las uñas de los pies con un quiropedista, en la peluquería a veces te lastiman / I prefer to fix my toenails with a chiropedist, in the hairdresser sometimes they hurt you

565. El banco tiene 4 cajeros, 1 auxiliar contable, 1 promotora, 1 supervisor y el gerente / The bank has 4 cashiers, 1 assistant accountant, 1 promoter, 1 supervisor and the manager.

566. En la entrada de la oficina está la recepcionista, dile que te ayude / At the office entrance is the receptionist, tell her to help you.

567. Entrégale estas medicina a la enfermera de turno / Give these medicines to the nurse on duty

568. El doctor Loreto es médico pediatra y trabaja en el hospital de niños / Dr. Loreto is a pediatrician and works at the children's hospital.

569. Primero te debe atender el odontólogo y luego te refiere con el cirujano bucal / You should first be seen by your dentist and then you will be referred to the oral surgery specialist.

570. La visita al ginecólogo debe ser como mínimo una vez al año / The visit to the gynaecologist must be at least once a year.

571. El jardinero se está tardando mucho para podar ese árbol / The gardener is taking a long time to trim that tree.

572. Esos casos debe atenderlo un equipo multidisciplinario: psicólogo y psiquiatra / These cases must be treated by a multidisciplinary team: a psychologist and a psychiatrist.

573. La terapista de lenguaje lo va a ayudar para que avance en su colegio / The speech therapist will help you to progress in his school.

574. El oftalmólogo dice que debe usar lentes / The ophthalmologist says you should wear glasses

575. El niño está con una psicopedagoga y ya está nivelado con el grupo / The child is with a psychopedagogue and is already leveled with the group.

576. Entre el doctor y su asistente hicieron un buen trabajo / Between the doctor and his assistant they did a good job

577. La maestra Carmen tiene muchos años de servicio en la escuela / Teacher Carmen has many years of service in the school.

578. El profesor de física ha realizado varios trabajos de investigación / The physics professor has carried out several research projects

579. Yo trabajo como abogado en el día y en las noches doy clases de derecho en la universidad / I work as a lawyer during the day and in the evenings I teach law at the university.

580. Soy comunicadora social pero mi pasión es el ejercicio, doy clases de fit combat en varios gimnasios / I am a social communicator but my passion is exercise, I give fit combat classes in several gyms.

581. Carlos es locutor de radio y tiene un programa deportivo los fines de semana / Carlos is a radio broadcaster and has a sports program on weekends.

582. Esa farmacia no tiene medico farmaceuta en este momento, solo la atienden los vendedores / This pharmacy

does not have a pharmacist at the moment, only the salespersons attend it.

583. Dile al pasillero que te ayude a ubicar en donde están los artículos de higiene personal / Tell the attendant to help you locate where personal hygiene items are.

584. Elias y Julio son choferes privados de esa empresa / Elias and Julio are private drivers of that company.

585. El director y su esposa son los dueños de ese colegio / The principal and his wife are the owners of that school

586. Los niños le dieron un regalo al profesor de educación física por su trabajo / The children gave a gift to the physical education teacher for his work.

587. El personal de mantenimiento cumple con las labores asignadas / Maintenance personnel carry out their assigned tasks

588. La mayor parte de los ingenieros trabajan en la planta / Most of the engineers work in the plant

589. Keren está haciendo su trabajo de grado para ser licenciada en teología / Keren is doing her undergraduate work to become a licentiate in theology.

590. Si sigues las indicaciones del nutricionista podrás adelgazar / If you follow the nutritionist's instructions you can lose weight.

591. Mi abuela dice que las aeromozas son encantadoras, siempre están dispuestas a ayudarte en todo / My grandmother says that the flight attendants are charming, they are always ready to help you in everything.

592. Los martes y viernes la cocina se viste de gala con el chef Sumito Estevez / On Tuesdays and Fridays the kitchen dresses up with chef Sumito Estevez.

593. Los asesores financieros trabajan para asegurar tu inversión / Financial advisors work to secure your investment.

594. Mi maestra de primaria ha sido la mayor influencia en mi vida / My elementary school teacher has been the biggest influence in my life.

595. Voy a pedir una cita con el traumatólogo a ver si tengo alguna fractura / I'm going to make an appointment with the traumatologist to see if I have any fractures.

596. Solo faltan unos retoques del carpintero y las sillas quedan como nuevas / Only a few adjustments of the carpenter are missing and the chairs are like new.

597. Hoy comienza mi terapia con el psicólogo, definitivamente necesito ayuda profesional / Today I start my therapy with the psychologist, I definitely need professional help.

598. Ha sido un año difícil, los corredores de seguro han captado pocos clientes / It has been a difficult year, insurance brokers have attracted few customers.

599. El orfebre de esa tienda tiene piezas hermosas / The goldsmith in that shop has beautiful pieces.

600. La exposición es de dos artistas muy conocidos en el país / The exhibition is by two well-known artists in the country.

601. Carolina Herrera es una diseñadora de modas venezolana conocida mundialmente / Carolina Herrera is a worldwide known Venezuelan fashion designer.

602. Algunas costureras prefieren hacer prendas nuevas a tener que hacer arreglos / Some dressmakers prefer to make new clothes rather than have to make repairs.

603. Estoy concursando en la web por un empleo como traductor profesional / I am competing on the web for a job as a professional translator

604. Mi abuela es la mejor repostera del mundo / My grandmother is the best pastry chef in the world.

605. Alex es bailarín profesional y dirige una compañía de baile de personas discapacitadas / Alex is a professional dancer and runs a dance company for disabled people.

606. Juan es ingeniero electrónico, tiene una tienda de venta y reparación de celulares / Juan is an electronic engineer, has a store selling and repairing cell phones.

607. En mi familia hay 3 mecánicos de carros: mi papá, mi esposo y mi hijo / In my family there are 3 car mechanics: my dad, my husband and my son.

608. Ser una modelo profesional exige tener disciplina, cumplir una dieta estricta y seguir una rutina de ejercicios diaria / Being a professional model requires discipline, a strict diet, and a daily exercise routine.

609. La fiesta de mi niña estuvo animada por payasitas, cuentacuentos y malabaristas / My girl's party was animated by clowns, storytellers and jugglers.

610. La empresa de licores esta dictando cursos para bartenders / The liquor company is giving courses for bartenders.

611. Yo prefiero cortarme el cabello con un estilista / I prefer to have my hair cut by a stylist.

612. Yajaira quiere hacer un curso de maquilladora profesional para tener ingresos adicionales los fines de semana / Yajaira wants to take a professional make-up artist course to earn additional income on weekends.

613. Alejandro Sanz es mi cantante favorito / Alejandro Sanz is my favorite singer

614. Por años ha trabajado como zapatero en ese local / He has worked as cobbler for years in that place

615. En el directorio telefónico debe haber algún plomero / There must be a plumber in the phone book.

616. El trabajo de un programador es bien remunerado pero siempre debe estar capacitándose por las cosas nuevas que salen al mercado / A programmer's job is well paid but they must always be training for new things that come to market.

617. ¿Cual es la diferencia entre un psicólogo y un psiquiatra? / What is the difference between a psychologist and a psychiatrist?

618. No es lo mismo un oftalmólogo que un optometrista / An ophthalmologist is not the same as an optometrist.

619. En esa familia todos son panaderos, tienen años en el negocio / In that family they are all bakers, they have years in the business

620. En la fábrica todos los obreros trabajan por turnos / In the factory all the workers work in shifts

621. El pastor de mi iglesia ha editado algunos libros / The pastor of my church has edited some books

622. Trabajo como bombero voluntario en mi comunidad / I work as a volunteer firefighter in my community.

623. Todos los curas se reunieron con el obispo de la ciudad / All the priests met with the bishop of the city

624. Se graduó de ingeniero químico y montó una empresa de detergentes y limpiadores de carro / She graduated as a chemical engineer and set up a detergent and car washer company.

625. Entregale ese paquete al mensajero que cubre la zona / Deliver that package to the courier that covers the area

626. El repartidor de pizzas conoce todas las direcciones / The pizza delivery man knows all the addresses

627. Ser teleoperador es un poco aburrido / Being a teleoperator is a bit boring

628. En ese avión viajan puros deportistas y comentaristas deportivos / In that airplane travel only sportsmen and sports commentators.

629. Tenemos una nueva conserje en el edificio / We have a new janitor in the building

630. El oficio de albañil lo aprendió desde joven / He learned the bricklayer's profession from a young age

631. Los adolescentes de esta época solo quieren ser youtubers, influencers y jugadores de videojuegos / The teenagers of this era just want to be youtubers, influencers and video game players.

632. Siempre ha trabajado como vendedor, tiene mucha experiencia en el área / He has always worked as a salesman, he has a lot of experience in the area.

633. Se solicita cocinera con documentos en regla para trabajar en cantina escolar. Interesados dirigirse al colegio...... / It is requested cook with documents in rule to work in school canteen. Interested parties should contact the school......

634. Se ofrecen servicios de niñera con experiencia y recomendaciones comprobables. Interesados llamar al...... / Experienced nanny services with verifiable recommendations are offered. Interested call.....

635. Se informa a todos los clientes que el veterinario estará de vacaciones desde el jueves hasta el miércoles / All clients are informed that the veterinarian will be on holiday from Thursday to Wednesday.

636. El presidente y los ministros estarán reunidos todo el dia / The president and ministers will be meeting all day

637. Aprendí mucho cuando trabaje como ayudante de cocina en ese restaurante / I learned a lot when I worked as a kitchen helper in that restaurant.

638. Él gana dinero extra trabajando como cuidador de perros / He earns extra money working as a dog keeper.

639. Puedes contratar una enfermera para que te ayude con tu mamá en casa / You can hire a nurse to help you with your mom at home.

640. Pregúntale al bibliotecario, él nos puede orientar con ese libro / Ask the librarian, he can guide us with that book

641. Les presento a Leonardo, él es su guía turístico, el grupo debe seguir sus indicaciones durante el recorrido / I introduce you to Leonardo, he is your tourist guide, the group must follow his directions during the tour.

642. Te puedo recomendar a la señora Ingrid, ha sido mi empleada doméstica por años, es muy educada y responsable / I can recommend Mrs. Ingrid, she has been my maid for years, she is very polite and responsible.

643. Ese portero del hotel es muy serio, parece una estatua / That doorman at the hotel is very serious, he looks like a statue

644. En todas las entradas del museo hay un vigilante / At all museum entrances there is a security guard

645. Ese gimnasio es muy reconocido por tener buenos instructores / This gymnasium is well known for having good instructors

646. Luego de tu operación debes hacer rehabilitación con un fisioterapeuta / After your operation you should do rehabilitation with a physiotherapist.

647. La trabajadora social hizo una encuesta a todos los que asistieron para saber cual es su situación actual / The social worker surveyed all those who attended to find out their current situation.

648. Hablaba tan bonito que parecía un poeta / He spoke so beautifully that he sounded like a poet

649. Tenía los dedos largos como los pianistas / He had long fingers like pianists.

Chapter 5: Daily activities

In this chapter, we will provide tons of phrases about daily activities, daily routine, daily situation, going to the mall and more.

Daily routine

650. Buenos días, me acabo de despertar / Good morning, I just woke up

651. Ya me voy a levantar, aún tengo mucho sueño / I'm going to get up, I'm still very sleepy.

652. Debo levantarme temprano para ir a trabajar / I have to get up early to go to work

653. Todas las mañanas tan pronto me levanto voy al baño a cepillarme los dientes / Every morning as soon as I get up I go to the bathroom to brush my teeth.

654. Es parte de mi rutina diaria despertarme a las cinco de la mañana a leer y luego me levanto a las seis / It is part of my daily routine to wake up at five in the morning to read and then get up at six.

655. La alarma de mi teléfono inteligente esta puesta para que suene a las seis y media de la mañana / My smartphone alarm is set to ring at half past six in the morning.

656. En las mañanas me gusta bañarme con agua caliente / In the mornings I like to bathe with hot water

657. Mañana por la mañana estaré bastante ocupado así que dudo que pueda asistir a la reunión escolar / Tomorrow morning I will be quite busy so I doubt that I will be able to attend the school meeting.

With this sentence- phrase we want to make clear something, in Spanish, "Mañana" has two meanings; one of them is related to the early part of the day, the part of the day that we call morning. And the other meaning is related to the next day, it is what we know as tomorrow. So, in this phrase, we can see the two different meanings of the word "mañana".

658. Mi esposa se duerme temprano para poder despertarse temprano / My wife falls asleep early so she can wake up early

659. Es bueno para el cuerpo dormir mínimo ocho horas diarias / It is good for the body to sleep at least eight hours a day

660. Max se despierta temprano para ver las noticias en la televisión / Max wakes up early to watch the news on television.

661. Despierto a mis niños a las seis y cuarto de la mañana porque entran a clase a las siete en punto / I wake up my children at a quarter past six in the morning because they enter class at seven o'clock

662. Mis hijos se duchan en la mañana para ir limpios al colegios / My children shower in the morning to go clean to school.

663. Yo tomo un baño en las noches para dormir mejor / I take a bath at night to sleep better.

664. El recorrido de la casa al colegio de los niños son cinco kilómetros / The route from the house to the children's school is five kilometres

665. Llego a mi trabajo en veinte minutos si no hay tráfico / I get to work in twenty minutes if there is no traffic

666. Anoche no pude dormir bien / I couldn't sleep well last night

667. Me costó mucho dormir, aun tengo bastante sueño / It cost me a lot to sleep, I'm still quite sleepy

668. Apenas me levanto, prendo la cafetera para que haga café / As soon as I get up, I turn on the coffee maker to make coffee.

669. Mientras yo me baño, mi esposo prepara el desayuno a los niños / While I bathe, my husband prepares breakfast for the children.

670. El nieto de Edward saca a pasear al perro tres veces al día / Edward's grandson walks the dog three times a day

671. Cuando mi mamá se levanta yo la abrazo y le doy los buenos días / When my mom gets up I hug her and say good morning to her

672. Después de desayunar hay que cepillarse los dientes / After breakfast you have to brush your teeth

673. A mi novio le gusta cepillarse los dientes al despertarse y después de desayunar / My boyfriend likes to brush his teeth when he wakes up and after breakfast.

674. Siempre hago ejercicio antes de desayunar / I always exercise before breakfast

675. Todas las mañanas le reviso el refrigerante y aceite al carro antes de salir de la casa / Every morning I check the coolant and oil to the car before I leave the house.

676. Antes de llegar al trabajo me paro en la panadería a comprar un sándwich para merendar / Before I get to work I stop at the bakery to buy a sandwich for a snack.

677. Cuando llego a la oficina la recepcionista me tiene un vaso de café / When I arrive at the office, the receptionist has a glass of coffee for me.

678. Trabajo mucho durante la mañana / I work a lot in the morning.

679. Yo arreglo la casa todos los días mientras mi esposa trabaja / I do the house every day while my wife works.

680. Hay que limpiar los desechos del perro todas las mañanas / Dog waste must be cleaned up every morning.

681. Siempre la esposa de Jorge intenta levantarse temprano para hacer el desayuno y el almuerzo / Jorge's wife always tries to get up early to make breakfast and lunch.

682. Cuando no llevo almuerzo al trabajo tengo que salir a comprar / When I don't bring lunch to work I have to go out and buy

683. Mi parte favorita del día es la hora de almuerzo / My favorite part of the day is lunchtime.

684. Cuando tengo mucho trabajo y me estreso, me gusta tomar un descanso / When I have a lot of work and stress, I like to take a break.

685. Si no me da tiempo de preparar el almuerzo temprano, tengo que prepararlo después de llevar a los niños al colegio / If I don't have time to prepare lunch early, I have to prepare it after taking the children to school.

686. En las noches me gusta pensar en los errores del día para mejorarlos al día siguiente / In the evenings I like to think about the mistakes of the day to improve them the next day.

687. Mis hijas salen de la escuela a las tres y veinte de la tarde / My daughters leave school at three and twenty in the afternoon.

688. Después de recoger a los niños, los llevo al entrenamiento de tenis / After picking up the kids, I take them to tennis training

689.   Si estoy libre, en las tardes me gusta pasear en el parque / If I am free, in the afternoons I like to walk in the park

690.   Al salir del trabajo, paso por el supermercado a comprar postre para la cena / After work, I stop by the supermarket to buy dessert for dinner.

691.   Mi perro se alegra mucho todas las tardes cuando regreso del trabajo / My dog is very happy every evening when I come home from work.

692.   Algunas tardes paso por la academia de baile para practicar un poco mis movimientos / Some afternoons I go to the dance academy to practice a little my movements.

693.   Todos los sábados salimos a pasear en las mañanas y desayunamos en la calle / Every Saturday we go for a walk in the mornings and have breakfast in the street.

694.   Una vez al mes organizo un paseo en moto con mis amigos / Once a month I organize a motorcycle ride with my friends

695.   Siempre que tengo un mal día, al llegar a casa me tomo un té caliente y como galletas / Whenever I have a bad day, when I get home I have some hot tea and eat cookies.

696.   El esposo de Geraldine le da masajes en la espalda en las noches si ella tiene dolor de espalda / Geraldine's husband massages her back at night if she has back pain.

697.   Cada dos noches, vemos una película en la casa / Every two nights, we watch a movie in the house

698.   Siempre después de cenar, nos gusta conversar en familia sobre las actividades del día / Always after dinner, we like to talk as a family about the activities of the day.

699.   Antes de acostarme a dormir tomo un té relajante, para dormir mejor / Before going to bed to sleep I drink a relaxing tea, to sleep better.

700.   Mi amigo cristiano siempre ora antes de acostarse a dormir / My Christian friend always prays before going to bed.

House chores

701.   Cuando termino las tareas del hogar, me gusta hacer un poco de yoga / When I finish the household chores, I like to do a little yoga.

702.   Los martes y los jueves son los días de hacer limpieza en el hogar / Tuesdays and Thursdays are home cleaning days.

703. Me gusta barrer la casa todos los días para quitar el polvo / I like to sweep the house every day to remove dust.

704. Mi esposo y yo hicimos un horario para que nuestros hijos lavaran los platos sin pelear / My husband and I made a schedule for our children to wash the dishes without fighting.

705. Al hijo de Julia le molesta mucho sacar la basura / Julia's son finds it very annoying to take out the garbage.

706. A mi papá le fascina arreglar el jardín, siempre le queda muy bien / My dad loves to do the garden, it always suits him very well

707. Hay que trapear el piso en la casa, tenía los zapatos llenos de lodo y ensucié todo el piso / You have to mop the floor in the house, my shoes were full of mud and I dirtied the whole floor

708. Un día cocina mi hermana y otro día cocino yo y así nos turnamos / One day my sister cooks and another day I cook and so we take turns

709. Mi papá siempre hacía la cama cuando se levantaba, yo no puedo / My dad always made his bed when he got up, I can't.

710. Alexander odia cuando le dicen que tiene que cocinar / Alexander hates it when he's told he has to cook.

711. Los niños hicieron dibujos en la pared de nuevo, debemos castigarlos y pintar las paredes / The children made drawings on the wall again, we must penalize them and paint the walls

712. Todos los que vivimos en la casa somos responsables de su limpieza / All of us who live in the house are responsible for its cleanliness.

713. Cada uno tiene un día específico para poder lavar la ropa / Each one has a specific day to be able to wash clothes.

714. Desde que aumentaron la electricidad casi no usamos la secadora / Since they increased the electricity we hardly use the dryer.

715. Es necesario mantener la cocina limpia porque pueden llegar cucarachas / It is necessary to keep the kitchen clean because cockroaches can get in.

716. Cada cierto tiempo es recomendable lavar las ducha e inodoros de los baños / From time to time it is advisable to wash the showers and toilets in the bathrooms.

717. Cada vez que yo cocino me gusta dejar todo recogido, no aguanto el desorden / Every time I cook I like to leave everything tidy, I can't stand the mess

718. Las ventanas de la casa quedaron bastante sucias después de la tormenta, deberíamos limpiarlas / The windows of the house got pretty dirty after the storm, we should clean them.

719. Semanalmente es necesario cambiar las sábanas de los colchones, pues pueden tener ácaros / Weekly it is necessary to change the sheets of the mattresses, because they can have mites.

720. Hijo, limpiar lo que ensucie el perro es parte de tu responsabilidad como su dueño / Son, cleaning up the dog's mess is part of your responsibility as the dog's owner.

721. No podemos permitir que la casa esté tan descuidada y sucia, ¿Qué pasaría si viene alguien a visitar? / We cannot allow the house to be so neglected and dirty, what would happen if someone came to visit?

722. Hacerle mantenimiento a las puertas y ventanas también es parte de las tareas del hogar / Door and window maintenance is also part of household chores.

723. Debes aspirar tu cuarto, está lleno de pelos de perro y eso es lo que te está provocando la alergia / You have to vacuum your room, it's full of dog hair and that's what's causing your allergy.

724. Apúrate y mete tu plato sucio en el lavaplatos antes de que empiece a lavar / Hurry up and put your dirty dish in the dishwasher before it starts washing.

725. No es justo que yo tenga que hacer todas las tareas de la casa porque mi hermano esta paseando / It is not fair that I have to do all the chores of the house because my brother is walking.

Going to the mall

726. Mamá voy a salir al centro comercial, ¿Quieres venir conmigo? / Mom, I'm going out to the mall. Do you want to come with me?

727. Mi novio me invitó al centro comercial a cenar, ¿Puedo ir? / My boyfriend invited me to the mall for dinner. Can I go?

728. ¿Quieres ir a pasear un rato al centro comercial? / Do you want to hang out at the mall for a while?

729. Me gusta el nuevo centro comercial porque tiene un estacionamiento muy grande y siempre encuentras puesto / I like the new mall because it has a very large parking lot and you always find a parking space.

730. ¿Supiste que abrieron un nuevo restaurante en el centro comercial? / Did you hear they opened a new restaurant at the mall?

731. No tenía idea, deberíamos ir a ver cómo es / I had no idea, we should go see what it's like

732. Es una gran idea ir a visitar el nuevo restaurante del centro comercial / It's a great idea to go visit the new restaurant in the mall

733. Buenas noches, ¿Cómo esta? ¿Tiene mesa para dos? / Good evening. How are you? Do you have a table for two?

734. Este lugar está muy bonito y elegante, me gusta / This place is very nice and elegant, I like it

735. ¿Podría traerme el menú por favor? / Could you please bring me the menu?

736. Me gustaría ordenar dos especiales del día con dos jugos naturales de fresa por favor / I would like to order two specials of the day with two natural strawberry juices please

737. Buen provecho, espero que lo disfrutes / Enjoy your meal, I hope you find it enjoyable.

738. Deberíamos aprovechar que estamos aquí en el centro comercial para ver una película en el cine / We should take advantage of the fact that we are here in the mall to see a movie in the cinema.

739. Mis películas favoritas son las de terror / My favorite movies are horror movies.

740. A mí me gustan más las películas de comedia / I like comedy movies better

741. Buenas noches, dos entradas para la película de las siete y media, si es tan amable / Good evening, two tickets for the seven thirty movie, if you're so kind.

742. Me da unas palomitas extra grandes, dos gaseosas y unos nachos con extra queso / Give me some extra large popcorn, two sodas and some extra cheese nachos.

743. ¿Te parece buena idea ir a la tienda de electrodomésticos? / Do you think it's a good idea to go to the appliance store?

744. Mira todos esos electrodomésticos, hay microondas, licuadoras, hornos y refrigeradores / Look at all those appliances, there are microwaves, blenders, ovens and refrigerators.

745. Me gustaría comprar una televisión más grande pero creo que mi presupuesto no es suficiente / I would like to buy a bigger TV but I think my budget is not enough.

746. En la tienda de electrodomésticos había un equipo de sonido para la casa que estaba bastante económico / At the appliance store, there was a sound system for the house that was quite inexpensive.

747. Me encantaría poder comprar todo lo nuevo que hay en la tienda de electrodomésticos / I would love to be able to buy everything new in the appliance store.

748. Disculpe, ¿Qué precio tiene la lavadora de la esquina y la secadora que está al lado? / Excuse me, what is the price of the corner washer and dryer next to it?

749. ¿No hay alguna oferta o promoción si compro ambos artículos? / Isn't there any offer or promotion if I buy both items?

750. Hace bastante calor, ¿Dónde es que estaba la tienda de helados en este centro comercial? / It's quite hot, where was the ice cream store in this mall?

751. Buenas tardes, ¿Cómo esta? ¿Qué sabores de helado tiene? / Good afternoon. How are you? What flavors of ice cream do you have?

752. ¿Tiene alguna promoción disponible? / Do you have any promotions available?

753. ¿Cuál es tu sabor de helado favorito? / What's your favorite ice cream flavor?

754. ¿Te gustan más los helados en barquillas o en tinita? Yo prefiero las barquillas porque me la puedo comer / Do you like ice cream better in scoops or in a little jar? I prefer the scoops because I can eat it

755. Voy a querer un banana Split con mucho sirope de chocolate y cubierta extra de galletas de chocolate / I'm going to have a banana split with lots of chocolate syrup and extra chocolate cookie topping.

756. Mi sabor favorito de helado es el de galletas con crema, aunque también me gusta mucho el de torta suiza / My favourite ice-cream flavour is cookies and cream, although I also like Swiss cake.

757. A mi mamá le encanta el helado sabor ron con pasas, yo lo detesto / My mom loves rum and raisin ice cream, I hate it.

758. La novia de mi amigo siempre pide helado sabor a arequipe / My friend's girlfriend always asks for ice cream caramelised milk flavor

759. El helado preferido de mi hermanita es el de chocolate blanco con trozos de chocolate por encima / My little sister's favourite ice cream is white chocolate with pieces of chocolate on top.

760. El helado sabor a mantecado es el más común y vendido en todo el mundo / Vanila-flavored ice cream is the most common and sold worldwide.

761. Vayamos a la tienda de electrónicos para ver qué nuevos lanzamientos hay / Let's go to the electronics store to see what new releases there are.

762. El nuevo televisor táctil es lo máximo, además es 4k HD / The new touchscreen TV is the best, plus it's 4k HD

763. Yo quiero comprarme esa estación de juego / I want to buy that gaming station.

764. ¿Esta es la nueva laptop para jugadores? Son asombrosas todas las características que tiene / Is this the new laptop for gamers? All the features it has are amazing

765. Mira este conjunto que venden de la consola última generación con 20 juegos / Look at this bundle for sale of the latest generation console with 20 games

766. Ya tienen disponibles los teléfonos inteligentes que anunciaron la semana pasada / They have available the smartphones announced last week.

767. ¿En cuánto quedarían las cuotas para pagarlo en un plazo de dos años? / How much would the rates be to pay within two years?

768. ¿De cuánto serían los intereses? / How much would the interest be?

769. ¿Qué computadora me recomienda para poder trabajar cómodamente como diseñador gráfico? / What computer do

you recommend for me to work comfortably as a graphic designer?

770. ¿Cuál es el precio del reloj inteligente más barato? / What is the price of the cheapest smart watch?

771. Entremos al supermercado, debemos comprar varias cosas antes de regresar a casa / Let's go into the supermarket, we must buy several things before returning home

772. Este supermercado es inmenso, el que queda del otro lado de la calle es pequeñísimo / This supermarket is huge, the one on the other side of the street is tiny.

773. Compremos pan, jamón y queso para preparar unos sanduches para el desayuno de mañana / Let's buy bread, ham and cheese to prepare some sandwiches for tomorrow's breakfast.

774. Hay que comprar arroz y pasta porque ya se están acabando / We have to buy rice and pasta because they are already running out.

775. Mi tipo de pasta preferida son los fideos / My favorite type of pasta are noodles.

776. Compremos milanesas de pollo para hacerlas fritas / Let's buy chicken milaneses to make them fried

777. Mira todos esos tomates, están muy frescos / Look at all those tomatoes, they're very fresh.

778. ¿Te parece si compramos costillas de cerdo para hacerlas bbq? / How about we buy pork ribs to make them bbq?

779. Deberiamos comprar lechuga y mayonesa para hacer una ensalada César / We should buy lettuce and mayonnaise to make a Caesar salad.

780. Iré al pasillo de artículos de limpieza para el hogar / I'll go to the housecleaning hall.

781. Voy a ir a la sección de artículos de higiene personal / I'm going to the personal hygiene items section.

782. Los niños aman la sección de chucherías, hay cientos de dulces diferentes / Children love the candy section, there are hundreds of different candies

783. La parte de frutas y verduras me gusta bastante, tienen buenos precios y buenos productos / I like the fruits and vegetables part quite a lot, they have good prices and good products.

784. La calidad de los productos es inigualable / The quality of the products is unbeatable

785. Es impactante la variedad de marcas de productos que tienen / It is shocking the variety of brands of products that they have

786. Busca unas salchichas para preparar perros calientes / Look for some sausages to prepare hot dogs

787. Sal y azúcar son dos ingredientes esenciales en la cocina / Salt and sugar are two essential ingredients in the kitchen

788. Compra carbón para hacer una parrilla / Buy charcoal to make a grill

789. Quiero hacer pan, para hacerlo solo necesito harina, huevo, azúcar, levadura y sal ¿Verdad? / I want to make bread, to do it I only need flour, egg, sugar, yeast and salt, right?

790. ¿Qué opinas de comprar los ingredientes para hacer una pizza de pepperoni? / What do you think about buying the ingredients to make a pepperoni pizza?

791. Mi comida favorita son las hamburguesas, hagamos una reunión este fin de semana y preparamos unas / My favorite food are hamburgers, let's have a meeting this weekend and make some

792. Las papas fritas son lo mejor que hay en el mundo / French fries are the best thing in the world

793. ¿Te fijaste en la nevera de bebidas? Tienen bebidas de todos los sabores / Did you notice the drinks fridge? They have drinks of all flavours

794. ¿Sabes en que pasillo esta el papel higiénico? / Do you know what hallway the toilet paper is in?

795. Hay demasiadas marcas distintas de champú, ¿Cuál debería llevarle a mi mamá? / There are too many different brands of shampoo, which one should I take to my mom?

796. Para hacer una fiesta en la casa debo comprar un montón de cosas aquí en el supermercado / To have a party at home I must buy a lot of things here at the supermarket

Clothing

797. Veamos que ropa bonita hay en las tiendas de ropa / Let's see what nice clothes are in the clothing stores

798. Me encanta visitar la tienda de ropa del segundo piso, siempre hay descuentos y tienen la ropa que está de moda / I

love to visit the clothing store on the second floor, there are always discounts and they have clothes that are trending

799. Me fascina comprar bufandas, en esta época de invierno siempre hace un montón de frio / I love to buy scarves, in this time of winter it is always a really cold

800. La tienda de trajes de baño del sótano tiene los trajes de baño que siempre me compro para verano / The swimsuit shop in the basement has the swimsuits I always buy for summer.

801. En la tienda de descuentos encuentro camisas y suéteres a muy buen precio / In the discount store I find shirts and sweaters at very good prices.

802. El año pasado me compré tres faldas preciosas en la misma tienda / Last year I bought three beautiful skirts in the same store

803. Quiero una camisa de botones bonita para la fiesta de promoción de este año / I want a nice button-down shirt for this year's promotional party.

804. Soy talla M en camisas deportivas / I am size M in sports shirts

805. A mi tía le encanta que le regalen medias de distintos colores / My aunt loves to be given socks of different colors.

806. Necesito comprarme un vestido formal para ir a la boda de mi prima / I need to buy a formal dress to go to my cousin's wedding.

807. Hay ofertas en ropa deportiva en aquella tienda de allá / There are offers on sportswear in that store over there

808. Mis pantalones ya están bastante desgastados, es hora de comprarme unos nuevos / My pants are worn out enough, it's time to buy new ones.

809. Yo suelo ir a trotar cuando tengo tiempo libre, veamos si hay zapatos para correr aquí / I usually go jogging when I have free time, let's see if there are shoes to run here.

810. He escuchado que la joyería que está en planta baja tiene cosas preciosas. ¿Vamos? / I've heard that the jewelry on the main floor has beautiful things. Shall we go?

811. Mira que zarcillos tan perfectos, me encantaría que me regalaran unos así / Look at that perfect earrings, I would love to be given ones like this

812. Buenas tardes, estoy buscando un anillo de compromiso para mi novia, ¿Puede mostrarme cuáles tiene? / Good afternoon, I'm looking for an engagement ring for my girlfriend, can you show me which ones you have?

813. Para poder inscribirme en natación me pidieron un traje de baño de una pieza, no puede ser bikini / In order to sign up for swimming I was asked for a one-piece swimsuit, it can't be a bikini.

814. Vamos a la tienda de ropa interior, ya tengo que comprarme nuevas pantaletas y un brassier / Let's go to the underwear store, I already have to buy new panties and a bra.

815. Está inmensa esta tienda de ropa, tienen distintas secciones / This clothing store is immense, they have different sections

816. Tienen sección de niños, de niñas, de jóvenes, de hombres, de mujeres y de ancianos / They have a section for boys, girls, young people, men, women and the elderly.

817. Iré a ver si consigo una falda que combine con la blusa que tengo en la casa / I'll go see if I can get a skirt that matches the blouse I have at home.

818. ¿Crees que estos tacones se vean bien con el vestido que vimos en la otra tienda? / Do you think these heels look good with the dress we saw in the other store?

819. Tu también deberías comprarte un traje nuevo para la boda de mi prima, el que tienes en casa ya te queda pequeño / You should buy a new suit for my cousin's wedding too, the one you have at home is already small.

820. Aprovecha y te compras una también una corbata que combine / Make the most of it and buy yourself a tie that combines

821. Amé las pijamas que vi en la primera tienda que entramos, las quiero todas / I loved the pajamas I saw in the first store we came in, I want them all.

822. Para nuestro viaje necesitaremos un abrigo / For our trip we will need a coat

823. Yo pienso que es mejor llevar una chaqueta, ocupa menos espacio en la maleta / I think it's better to wear a jacket, it takes up less space in the suitcase.

824. Quisiera poder usar este pantalón sin correa, pero se me caen / I wish I could wear these pants without a belt, but they fall off.

825. Yo siempre trato de comprar ropa hecha de algodón, dura más y es mas cómoda / I always try to buy clothes made of cotton, it lasts longer and is more comfortable.

826. ¿Sabes dónde puedo comprar un collar que combine con estos zarcillos? / Do you know where I can buy a necklace that matches these earrings?

Chapter 6: Vacations

This chapter includes useful phrases for going on vacations.

Vacations

827. Nos iremos de vacaciones a España la próxima semana / We're going on vacation to Spain next week.

828. Hay que comenzar a empacar las cosas / We have to start packing things up

829. Debemos preparar el equipaje para el viaje / We must prepare the luggage for the trip

830. ¿A qué parte del mundo nos vamos? /Which part of the world are we going to?

831. ¿Iremos a Europa o a Asia? / Are we going to Europe or Asia?

832. Podemos intentar ir a centroamerica / We can try to go to Central America

833. Yo quería ir a África, por una película que vi / I wanted to go to Africa, because of a movie I saw.

834. Sur América me parece muy genial, tienen muchísimos destinos turísticos allá / South America seems to me very cool, they have many tourist destinations there

835. La Antártida es un continente del que no mucha gente tiene conocimiento / Antarctica is a continent of which not many people are aware.

836. ¿A qué país iremos de viaje? / What country are we going to travel to?

837. Mi agente de viajes sugirió que visitaramos Italia / My travel agent suggested that we visit Italy

838. Francia es el país ideal para ir con una pareja / France is the ideal country to go with a partner

839. Australia es el país con mayor cantidad de animales peligrosos / Australia is the country with the highest number of dangerous animals

840. En España se pueden visitar las Islas Canarias / In Spain you can visit the Canary Islands

841. En China se encuentra la famosísima muralla china / In China you will find the very famous Chinese wall

842. El Taj Majal se encuentra ubicado en la India / The Taj Majal is located in India.

843. Mi nieto visitó la catedral de Notre Dame hace dos años / My grandson visited Notre Dame Cathedral two years ago.

844. Cada país tiene sus monumentos famosos y por eso deberíamos visitarlos todos / Every country has its famous monuments and that's why we should visit them all.

845. ¿Cuál es el gentilicio de la gente de ese país? / What is the name of the people of that country?

846. ¿Cuál es la nacionalidad de esa persona? / What is that person's nationality?

847. ¿De qué país eres? / What country are you from?

848. Si naces en España, eres entonces un Español / If you are born in Spain, then you are a Spanish

849. Mi tía es alemana, ella nació en Alemania / My aunt is German, she was born in Germany

850. Fred es estadounidense, aunque él se haga llamar americano / Fred is an US citizen, even though he calls himself an American.

851. Puedes decir que eres Argentino, o que eres de Argentina / You can say that you are Argentine, or that you are from Argentina

852. Si naciste en cualquier país de europa, perteneces a la unión europea / If you were born in any European country, you belong to the European Union.

853. El presidente de Rusia es Ruso / The President of Russia is Russian

854. ¿Qué idioma hablan a donde vamos? / What language is spoken where are we going?

855. Hay muchísimos idiomas en el mundo / There are many languages in the world

856. El Español es el segundo idioma más hablado en el mundo / Spanish is the second most spoken language in the world

857. ¿Sabías que hay veinte países en los cuales se habla español? / Did you know that there are twenty countries in which Spanish is spoken?

858. Es complicado que no haya un idioma universal / It is difficult that there is no a universal language

859. Para ir a China es necesario saber hablar chino / To go to China it is necessary to know how to speak Chinese

860. Hay algunos países en donde se hablan dos idiomas, como en Canadá / There are some countries where two languages are spoken, such as Canada

861. No puedo esperar a que llegue el día del viaje / I can't wait for the day of the trip to come

862. Estoy muy impaciente por el viaje / I am very impatient for the trip

863. ¿Vamos a viajar en avión? / Are we going to travel by plane?

864. ¿Será un vuelo directo o vamos a tener escalas? / Will it be a direct flight or are we going to have stopovers?

865. Hay que estar en en aeropuerto antes de las once de la mañana / We have to be at the airport before eleven o'clock in the morning.

866. Tenemos que hacer el check-in una hora antes del vuelo / We have to do the check-in one hour before the flight

867. El vuelo sale a las dos y media de la tarde / The flight departs at two thirty in the afternoon

868. Primero iremos hacia Valencia, donde haremos escala / First we will go to Valencia, where we will make a stopover

869. La duración del vuelo será de cuatro horas y quince minutos / The duration of the flight will be four hours and fifteen minutes.

870. Debemos acercarnos a la puerta numero 8 para abordar el avión / We must approach gate number 8 to board the plane.

871. El vuelo que íbamos a tomar está retrasado, tendremos que esperar un poco más / The flight that we were going to take is delayed, we will have to wait a little more

872. ¿Todos tienen sus boletos a la mano? / Do you all have your tickets at hand?

873. Tengan sus pasaportes preparados para mostrar en el aeropuerto / Have your passports ready to show at the airport

874. Para el próximo año tendremos que renovar el pasaporte, ya se va a vencer / For next year we will have to renew the passport, it will expire soon

875. La seguridad del aeropuerto es bastante estricta, me gusta / The airport security is quite strict, I like it

876. Tengo miedo de viajar en avión / I'm afraid to travel by plane

877. Estamos en la feria de comida del aeropuerto / We are at the airport food fair

878. Hay muchos kioskos con variedad de comidas / There are many kiosks with a variety of foods

879. Las tiendas de recuerdos estan abarrotadas de gente / The souvenir shops are crowded with people

880. ¿Iremos en taxi al aeropuerto o dejaremos el carro allá? / Shall we take a taxi to the airport or leave the car there?

881. Debemos contactar a un taxista para que nos busque en el aeropuerto al llegar / We must contact a taxi driver to meet us at the airport upon arrival.

882. ¿Crees que sea necesario contratar un traductor? / Do you think it is necessary to hire a translator?

883. La nieta de Julia es guía turístico allá, deberíamos llamarla / Julia's granddaughter is a tour guide there, we should call her

884. Deberíamos alquilar un carro para movilizarnos mientras estamos de vacaciones / We should rent a car to get around while we're on vacation.

885. Soy turista / I am a tourist

886. Yo no soy de aquí, vine de vacaciones / I'm not from here, I came on vacation

887. ¿Cuánto cuestan los pasajes? / How much are the tickets?

888. ¿Contactaste a la agencia de viajes? / Did you contact the travel agency?

889. ¿Le dijiste a tu tía que iremos a visitarla? / Did you tell your aunt we're going to visit her?

890. Sería buena idea traer varios recuerdos de nuestro viaje / It would be a good idea to bring several souvenirs of our trip

891. Tenemos que hacer un itinerario para el viaje / We have to make an itinerary for the trip

892. Debemos llevar ropa para el frío, allá en invierno hace bastante frío / We must bring clothes for the cold, there in winter it is quite cold

893. Empaquen sus trajes de baño que iremos al parque acuático / Pack your bathing suits and we'll go to the water park.

894. No olviden traer sus artículos de higiene personal / Don't forget to bring your personal hygiene items.

895. Creo que tendré que llevar la laptop para trabajar a distancia / I think I'll have to take the laptop to work remotely.

896. Debemos llevarnos nuestro libro de 1001 frases en español / We must take our book of 1001 phrases in Spanish

897. El plan que me ofreció la agencia de viaje era todo incluido / The plan offered to me by the travel agency was all-inclusive

898. ¿Podría llevarnos al hotel? / Could you take us to the hotel?

899. El hotel incluye desayuno, almuerzo y cena / The hotel includes breakfast, lunch and dinner

900. Escuché que en el hotel hay excelente servicio a la habitación / I heard there's excellent room service at the hotel.

901. Buenos dáas, para ordenar servicio a la habitación a la número 123 / Good morning, to order room service at 123.

902. Me fascina el hotel / I love the hotel

903. Quiero una habitación para tres personas con una cama matrimonial y una individual / I want a room for three people with a double bed and a single bed.

904. Me gustaría reservar la habitación de lujo / I would like to reserve the luxury room

905. Me hospedaré acá por tres noches, ¿Tiene disponibilidad? / I'll stay here for three nights. Do you have availability?

906. ¿Sería tan amable de darme una habitación con tres cuartos separados? / Would you be so kind as to give me a room with three separate rooms?

907. ¿Tiene vacantes en habitaciones individuales? / Do you have vacancies in single rooms?

908. Escuché que el hotel tenía un comedor, ¿Puede decirme dónde está? / I heard the hotel had a dining room, can you tell me where it is?

909. Quedémonos hoy aquí en el hotel y vayamos a la piscina a hacer las actividades que hay / Let's stay here today in the hotel and go to the pool to do the activities that there are

910. Mañana levántense temprano que compré un full day para una playa / Tomorrow wake up early that I bought a full day for a beach

911. Recuerden guardar en el bolso su protector solar, gorra, traje de baño y toalla / Remember to pack your sunscreen, hat, bathing suit and towel in your bag.

912. Haremos un paseo en lancha / We'll take a boat ride

913. La hermana de Carlos nos invitó a una isla muy bonita / Carlos' sister invited us to a very beautiful island

914. En la playa habían muchas palmeras de cocos / On the beach there were many coconut palms

915. En el restaurante de la playa servían todo tipo de pescados / In the restaurant on the beach they served all kinds of fish

916. Mi hija pidió unos camarones al ajillo que estaban buenísimos / My daughter asked for some garlic shrimp that were very good

917. Tomar una cerveza fría en la playa es súper refrescante / Having a cold beer on the beach is super refreshing.

918. El agua de esta playa es azul verdoso, está espectacular / The water of this beach is greenish blue, it is spectacular

919. Quiero broncearme bastante el día que vayamos a la playa / I want to get a good tan the day we go to the beach

920. Tomemos bastantes fotos para recordar estos momentos / Let's take enough photos to remember these moments

921. ¿Alguien vio mis lentes de Sol? / Has anyone seen my sunglasses?

922. A las doce en punto es cuando el sol está más fuerte / Twelve o'clock is when the sun is strongest

923. La arena está muy caliente, cuidado se queman los pies / The sand is very hot, be careful you burn your feet

924. No puedo esperar a llegar al yate que alquilamos / I can't wait to get to the yacht we rented

925. Que excelente día tuvimos en la playa. Ya es hora de regresar al hotel / What an excellent day we had on the beach. It's time to go back to the hotel.

926. Mañana iremos al parque acuático / Tomorrow we'll go to the water park

927. Es increíble la cantidad de piscinas que hay en este parque acuático / It is incredible the amount of pools that there are in this aquatic park

928. Mira todos los geniales toboganes que hay aquí / See all the great water slides you can find here

929. Quiero surfear en la piscina oleada / I want to surf in the waved pool

930. El Insano es el tobogán más alto del mundo y está en Brasil / El Insano is the highest slide in the world and it is in Brazil.

931. Me dijeron que en el parque acuático hay motos de agua (jetski) / I was told that in the water park there are jetski motorcycles.

932. Hay un paseo suave que se hace sobre un flotador muy grande, es relajante / There is a soft ride that is made on a very large float, it is relaxing

933. Hay un tobogán del parque acuático que pasa a través de una pecera y puedes ver todos los peces, es algo increíble / There's a water park slide that goes through a fish tank and you can see all the fish, it's something incredible.

934. Es genial que la habitación del hotel tenga una bañera / It's great that the hotel room has a bathtub

935. Mañana iremos al parque de atracciones que queda al sur / Tomorrow we will go to the amusement park to the south

936. Debemos ir temprano porque hay muchas atracciones y quiero que probemos todas / We must go early because there are many attractions and I want us to try them all.

937. Mira esa montaña rusa, se ve genial / Look at that roller coaster, it looks great.

938. Hay también dos pistas de kartings, una para adultos y una para niños / There are also two go-kart tracks, one for adults and one for children.

939. Prueba la tirolina que hay, pasa sobre un lago / Try the zip line there, pass over a lake

940. Quiero que vayamos a la casa del terror, he escuchado que es de las mejores / I want us to go to the haunted house, I've heard it's one of the best.

941. Dicen que desde la cima de la rueda de la fortuna se ve todo el parque / It is said that from the top of the wheel of fortune you can see the whole park

942. A los niños pequeños les fascina montarse en el carrusel / Young children love to ride the carousel

943. Yo me quiero montar en el Slingshot, siempre he querido hacerlo / I want to ride the Slingshot, I've always wanted to do it

944. Amo los parques temáticos / I love theme parks

945. La próxima semana iremos al museo de historia / Next week we will go to the history museum

946. Esta semana iremos al museo de arte / This week we will go to the art museum

947. En el museo de historia hay objetos antiguos con gran importancia histórica / In the history museum there are ancient objects of great historical importance

948. Los objetos son obras invaluables / The objects are invaluable works

949. Es increíble toda la historia que puede haber en un simple objeto / It is incredible all the history that can be in a simple object

950. Hay que caminar con cuidado en los museos / It is necessary to walk carefully in the museums

951. No hay que hacer mucho ruido ni tampoco correr / Don't make too much noise and don't run either

952. En los museos de arte hay obras de arte / In art museums there are pieces of art

953. Pueden ser pinturas, esculturas o estructuras / They can be paintings, sculptures or structures

954. La mona lisa o la Gioconda es una obra de arte muy conocida / La mona lisa or La Gioconda is a well-known piece of art.

955. El grito es una pintura de Edvard Munch / The scream is a painting by Edward Munch

956. El pensador es una escultura que también es muy conocida / The thinker is a sculpture that is also well known

957. Los museos son lugares interesantes de visitar para aprender sobre distintos temas / Museums are interesting places to visit to learn about different topics

958. Escuché que hay un zoológico cerca de aquí, ¿Quieren ir a visitarlo? / I heard that there is a zoo near here, do you want to go visit it?

959. Me encantan los zoológicos porque puedes ver muchas especies distintas de animales / I love zoos because you can see many different species of animals

960. Los reptilarios no son de mi agrado, me dan escalofrío las serpientes y reptiles / The reptiles houses are not to my liking, I shudder at snakes and reptiles

961. La cascabel es increíble por el sonido característico que hace   The rattlesnake is incredible for the characteristic sound it makes

962. Los lagartos son generalmente de sangre fría / Lizards are generally cold-blooded

963. Dicen que los cocodrilos son los únicos dinosaurios que aún existen / It is said that crocodiles are the only dinosaurs that still exist.

964. Los aviarios me gustan bastante, escuchar a todas las aves es algo increíble / I like aviaries quite a lot, listening to all the birds is something incredible

965. Los búhos son capaces de voltear su cuello más de ciento ochenta grados / Owls are able to turn their necks more than one hundred and eighty degrees.

966. Las águilas tienen la mejor vista del reino animal / Eagles have the best sight of the animal kingdom

967. Los buitres se alimentan de animales muertos o moribundos / Vultures feed on dead or dying animals

968. Las gaviotas son animales que se pueden observar en la playa / The seagulls are animals that can be observed on the beach

969. Los acuarios le encantan a mis hijos porque son muy coloridos y llamativos / My children love aquariums because they are very colourful and striking.

970. Hay miles de distintas especies de peces / There are thousands of different species of fish

971. Encuentro bastante interesante al pez globo / I find the pufferfish quite interesting

972. El pez dorado es muy común en las peceras de los hogares / The goldfish is very common in home fish tanks.

973. Nemo, el de la película, es un pez payaso / Nemo, the one of the film, is a clown fish.

974. Este acuario es muy pequeño para albergar una ballena azul / This aquarium is too small to hold a blue whale.

975. Tienen tiburones pequeños en los estanques / They have small sharks in the tanks

976. En esa pecera tienen a la medusa más venenosa del planeta / In that fishbowl they have the most poisonous jellyfish on the planet

977. Algunas especies de pulpos tienen la habilidad de camuflajearse cuando están en peligro / Some species of octopus have the ability to camouflage themselves when endangered.

978. El tiburón martillo y el tiburón gato son los menos agresivos / The hammerhead shark and the cat shark are the least aggressive.

979. Las arañas no nos llaman la atención, entonces no iremos a verlas / Spiders don't catch our attention, so we're not going to see them.

980. Soy fan de los tigres, me parecen unos animales majestuosos / I'm a fan of tigers, they seem to me to be majestic animals

981. Es curiosa la diferencia entre el león macho y la hembra / It is curious the difference between the male and female lion

982. Los pumas son animales increíblemente fuertes / Cougars are incredibly strong animals

983. El oso pardo es mi favorito, aunque también me gusta bastante el oso panda / The grizzly bear is my favorite, although I also like the panda bear quite a lot.

984. El jaguar tiene unos ojos espectaculares / The jaguar has spectacular eyes

985. En este zoológico tienen una sección de animales de la Antártida / In this zoo there is a section of Antarctic animals

986. No sabía que existían distintos tipos de pingüinos / I did not know that there were different types of penguins

987. Estoy anonadada por la belleza de el oso polar / I am stunned by the beauty of the polar bear

988. Los leones marinos son unas bestias enormes / Sea lions are enormous beasts

989. Hay una sección de aquí del zoológico en donde podemos encontrar distintos tipos de monos / There is a section here of the zoo where we can find different types of monkeys

990. Mañana es el día de regresarnos a nuestro hogar / Tomorrow is the day to return to our home

991. Espero que no se nos olvide nada de lo que compramos / I hope we don't forget anything we bought.

992. Hay que empezar a empacar apenas lleguemos al hotel / We have to start packing as soon as we get to the hotel.

993. Estas fueron las mejores vacaciones que hemos tenido hasta ahora / This was the best vacation we have had so far

994. Amé haber venido a este país / I loved coming to this country

995. La recomendación de mi amiga fue acertada / My friend's recommendation was correct

996. Debemos agradecerle también al guía turístico que nos acompañó / We must also thank the tourist guide who accompanied us

997. El vuelo de regreso será directo, a diferencia del de ida / The return flight will be direct, unlike the outward flight.

998. Es increíble lo relajante que pueden ser unas vacaciones / It's amazing how relaxing a vacation can be.

999. Vacacionar es lo mejor que se puede hacer para conocer otros países, culturas e idiomas / Vacationing is the best thing you can do to get to know other countries, cultures, and languages.

1000. Se me hizo muy fácil hablar español en el viaje gracias a mi libro de 1001 frases en español / It was very easy for me to speak Spanish on the trip thanks to my 1001 phrases book in Spanish.

Es importante mencionar que en español, hay algo que se llama polisema, lo que consiste en que una palabra, escrita de cierta manera, puede tener más de un significado, por lo que es realmente importante fijarse en el contexto de la palabra para poder descifrar a cuál de los distintos significados se está haciendo referencia en la oración, acá le pondremos algunos ejemplos / It is important to mention that in Spanish, there is something called polysemy, which is that a word, written in a certain way, can have more than one meaning, so it is really important to look at the context of the word to be able to figure out which of the different meanings is being referred to in the sentence, here are some examples:

- **Banco**: Esta palabra se utiliza para hablar de los bancos de dinero y finanzas y de los bancos en los que las personas se sientan / This word is used to speak of money and finance banks and of benches on which people sit.

  Yo estaba en el banco depositando / I was in the bank depositing

  Yo estaba sentado en el banco cuando me llamaste / I was sitting on the bench when you called me

- **Carta**: Esta palabra se utiliza para hablar de las cartas enviadas por correo y las cartas que se utilizan en juegos de cartas / This word is used to speak of letters sent by mail and cards that are used in card games.
  Le envié una carta hace meses y aún no me responde / I sent him a letter months ago and he still does not reply

  Estaba jugando cartas con mis amigos cuando sentimos el terremoto / I was playing cards with my friends when we felt the earthquake

- **Nada**: Esta palabra se utiliza para describir la acción de nadar y también para decir que algo está vacio o que no hay nada / This word is used to describe the action of swimming and also to say that something is empty or that there is nothing
  Stefan nada todas las mañanas antes de estudiar / Stefan swims every morning before studying

  Nada es más importante que amar a los que te aman / Nothing is more important than loving those who love you

- **Ven:** Esta palabra se refiere a dos verbos diferentes, el primero está relacionado con el verbo venir, mientras el segundo se refiere a la acción de ver algo / This word refers to two different verbs, the first is related to the verb come, while the second refers to the action of seeing or watching something

Ven conmigo mañana al estreno de la película / Come with me tomorrow to the movie premiere

Ellos siempre ven la película el dia del estreno / They always watch the movie the day of the premiere.

Éstas son solo algunas de las muchísimas palabras polisémicas que existen en el idioma español. Como pudiste ver, el significado de la palabra vendrá dado por el contexto de la misma, por eso siempre es prudente leer completamente la oración antes de intentar buscarle sentido. Si realizar la traducción palabra por palabra como método de estudio, puedes encontrarte con casos como éstos, donde te encontrarás con una complicación / These are just a few of the many polysemous words that exist in the Spanish language. As you could see, the meaning of the word will come from the context of the word, so it is always wise to read the sentence completely before trying to make sense of it. If you do word by word translation as a method of study, you may come across cases like these, where you will find yourself with a complication.

Y eso es todo; has llegado a la frase #1001, felicitaciones, ahora tienes un conocimiento básico del idioma español. Para ver que has leído todo el libro y que no te has saltado frases hasta que llegaste aquí, añadiremos una breve sección en la que nosotros (pero sobre todo tú) comprobaremos que has aprendido las cosas escritas en este libro /And that is all; you have made it to the #1001 phrase, congratulations, now you have a basic knowledge of the Spanish language. In order to see that you have read all the book and that you have not just skipped phrases until you got here, we will add a short sections where we (but mostly you) will check that you have learned the things written in this book

Traduce las siguientes frases / translate the following phrases:

- El hermano de Carlos tiene la nariz grande
- Estoy preocupada por Stan, sé que es programador, pero estar todo el día en la computadora no es algo bueno
- Tu también deberías comprarte un traje nuevo para la boda de mi prima, el que tienes en casa ya te queda pequeño

- Ellos y ellas son los empleados que día a día de esfuerzan por mejorar la empresa

- Se informa a todos los clientes que el veterinario estará de vacaciones desde el jueves hasta el miércoles

- Ser una modelo profesional exige tener disciplina, cumplir una dieta estricta y seguir una rutina de ejercicios diaria

- ¿Sabías que la biblia es el libro que más ha sido traducido en la historia?

- Desde muy pequeño el pasatiempo de mi primo era programar y ahora consiguió un trabajo haciéndolo

- Hasta la próxima, que tengas un buen viaje

- Todos los empleados salen de vacaciones en Navidad, solo queda el personal de seguridad cumpliendo turnos

- These cases must be treated by a multidisciplinary team: a psychologist and a psychiatrist

- You must check the brakes of the car before you go on a trip, they are not very good anymore.

- Carl wants to buy a baby anaconda he saw in a store to have it as a pet.

- Did you hear the new song that came out yesterday?

- Scooters are comfortable enough to get around the city

- For safety, you should always wait for the train behind a certain safety line.

- My cousin's cousin has always said it's better to vote and lose than to lose without having voted.

Si fuiste capaz de traducir todas esas frases sin necesidad de regresar a leerlas y buscar los significados, felicitaciones, haz hecho un gran trabajo / If you were able to translate all those phrases without having to go back and read them and look for the meanings, congratulations, you have done a great job.

Conclusion

Thank you for making it through to the end of *Learn Spanish in Your Car 1001 Common Phrases for Beginners: How to Use Spanish Words in Context to Speak Spanish Quickly*. We really hope that you found it informative and that you were able to, with all the tools that we provided here, achieve your goal of being capable of reading, writing, listening and speaking the Spanish language with the short but really useful phrases.

It is highly recommended for first-time readers and for people that have any knowledge about Spanish language to read this book a couple times, in order to become familiar with the words, symbols and structures of the phrases of the book. We also suggest you to, in order to keep improving the things that you learned here, speak in Spanish with someone whose native language is the Spanish, in order to practice your pronunciation; watch TV shows or listen to radio in Spanish, in order to improve your listening; write the phrases here written for some others that are look alike. For example, in the phrase #158: "María tiene los cachetes bastante grandes", you could rewrite it like "María tenía los cachetes bastante grandes, ahora son pequeños" or "María no tiene los cachetes bastante grandes" or "María tiene los cachetes muy pequeños". Do you see? Create similar phrases that help you to analyze and understand better the language.

We also recommend you to look for more vocabulary and more words so that you can broaden and improve the usage of the phrases that you found here.

Finally, if you found this book useful in any way, a review on Amazon is always appreciated!

One last thing to do

If you enjoyed this book or found it useful I'd be very grateful if you'd post a short review on it. Your support really does make a difference and we read all the reviews so we can get your feedback and make this book even better.

Thanks again for your support!

Spanish Short Stories for Intermediate Level

Improve your Spanish Reading Comprehension Skills with 7 Captivating Stories. Learn Fluent Conversation Whenever You Want

[Michael Navarro]

Introduction

Congratulations on purchasing *Spanish Short Stories for Intermediate Level: Improve your Spanish Listening Comprehension Skills with 7 Captivating Stories. Learn Fluent Conversation in your Car. Audiobook with Spanish Narrator* and thank you for doing so.

The following chapters have seven captivating stories which are going to guide you through the Spanish language so that you can build up the vocabulary you already know. You are going to be able to decipher unknown words because they are used in context and also have the English translation.

These short stories are meant to elevate the current Spanish student into learning more words in an engaging and fun way.   When you take an active part to incorporate a foreign language into your life, you will find that this book is an excellent tool for building your vocabulary quickly outside of the classroom.

There are plenty of books on this subject on the market, thanks again for choosing this one! Every effort was made to ensure it is full of as much useful information as possible, please enjoy!

Chapter 1: Using This Book to Learn Spanish Efficiently

The format of this book has been thoughtfully set up with the intermediate Spanish student in mind. It does not matter how young or old you are. There are always benefits to expanding your mind by broadening your experiences. While you are reading and listening to the stories in this book, use the tips which are found in this chapter to help you to solidify the vocabulary so you can efficiently learn Spanish.

Firstly, you made the right choice in learning Spanish through reading short stories, as it is proven to help you understand a new language more quickly as you are learning about words within context. Many make the mistake of simply learning grammar and vocabulary solely which leads the student to not be able to hold an engaging conversation fully.

When you are reading the stories, you will be able to memorize and learn different phrases in which you can use in conversations. In fact, there are phrases in the vocabulary at the end of each story to help you learn the most important phrases. As mentioned in each chapter, it is extremely helpful to focus on the vocabulary and repeat the words and phrases until they are imprinted in your memory.

Another helpful tip is to focus on the main concepts of the stories which will help you to learn the rest of the vocabulary due to context. This is also a great way to learn new words as you continue to read other Spanish books which may be more advanced. If it helps you out, underline phrases and sentences which you have issues with so you can focus on these until you become more comfortable. Be sure to read when you are able to concentrate and not be interrupted.

As you are reading through the story in Spanish, you will see that there are several words which have been bolded. This is a sign that this word or phrase is found below the English translation in the *Vocabulario* section. If you do not understand the bolded word, you can easily look it up as they are in alphabetical order. There is also an easy English-Spanish Dictionary at the end which will also aid you.

For each of the words in the *Vocabulario* section, there is a pronunciation guide for each word and phrase, and it will indicate what type of word it is such as Masculine or Feminine noun or Intransitive verb. It will then give you the English translation for that word. There are words which have several meanings within Spanish, so pay attention to the surrounding words to ensure you are using the word in the correct context.

Afterward, you can test your comprehension of the story by referring to the *Preguentas* section found at the end of each story. These are written fully in Spanish. After you have answered the questions, check your understanding of the story by reading fully through the English translation. The answers to all of the questions are found together in the *Conclusion* of the book.

Now that you have an understanding, let's get to the short stories. Enjoy!

Chapter 2: La Vieja Biblioteca - The Old Library

La vieja **biblioteca** había cerrado hace un año pero todos los **libros** siguen ahí. Era un pueblo **pequeño**, muy pequeño. Los niños **solían** jugar libres por las plazas y parques. Jugaban a la **pelota**, paseaban en bicicleta y jugaban a las **escondidas** como todos los niños. Lo que más les gustaba era imaginar si la biblioteca estaba **embrujada** o no. Pasaban **al frente** de la biblioteca y se **quedaban** un rato largo mirando sus ventanas, las **paredes** y el techo. Amanda, una de las niñas, de nueve años, fue la primera en hablar:

Amanda: Yo quiero entrar! Como vamos a saber si hay fantasmas o dragones o **duendes** si no entramos?

Apenas Amanda dijo esto, todos los niños - seis en total - se miraron, **permanecieron** en silencio. Le **brillaron** los ojos. Ese aire de **travesura** se les notaba en los **rostros**. Dejaron sus bicicletas, **patinetas** y **patines**. Soltaron los balones y se sentaron a planear debajo de un árbol del parque.

Habían llegado a un **acuerdo**. Tenían un plan. Montaron un puesto de venta de limonadas y galletas al frente de la biblioteca con una mesita y un **toldo**. Usaban sus uniformes de Boys Scout, todos los días. Mientras tres de ellos vendían limonada, los otros tres **averiguaban** cómo entrar a la biblioteca. Se **turnaban**: el primer turno lo tenían las niñas, Amanda, Amaya y Anyara. El segundo turno era de los chicos, Quique, Nicolás y Santiago. Pasó una semana entre limonadas galletas y planes, hasta que **encontraron** la manera perfecta de entrar a la vieja biblioteca.

La biblioteca tenía una amplia **terraza** donde antes **proyectaban** películas y hacían recitales de poesía. Sería fácil **trepar** las paredes y ventanas al más puro **estilo** hombre araña y una vez arriba intentar entrar a **algunos** de los pasillos que daban a las **salas** de lecturas. Esta vez se **mezclaron** - Amanda y Santiago **pertenecían** al equipo que escalaría los **muros** de la biblioteca. Anyara y Quique debían distraer a las personas **vendiendo** limonada. Amaya y Nicolás tendrían que **vigilar** la entrada.

Habían hecho hasta unos **dibujos**, una especie de historieta donde **representaban** todo el plan. Todo eso solo porque querían entrar a la biblioteca - solo entrar - a la espera de algún indicio de la existencia de **monstruos**, duendes, **fantasmas,** o vida **extraterrestre**.

Lejos estaba el grupo de amigos de saber cuál era la verdad con la que se **conseguirían** ahí adentro. Una vez que **lograron** entrar los niños se dedicaron a **recorrer** todos y cada uno de los **rincones** de la biblioteca: sus **pasillos**, los **salones**, el café y la sala de conferencias. Lo hacían en silencio, un poco por prudencia y otro poco por miedo. No sabían lo que que podían encontrar. Una vez más fue Amanda la que rompió el silencio,

Amanda: Creo que escuché algo raro - un **sonido** como de un silbato o algo así, en el **piso de abajo**.

Quique: A mi también me pareció escuchar un ruido. No estoy muy seguro, pero era como el canto de un **búho**.

Anyara: Entonces que estamos esperando? **Vamos a ver!**

Amaya: Todos juntos, sin hacer mucho ruido. Tenemos que **quitarnos** los zapatos.

Nicolás: Es mejor **dividirnos** en grupos.

Santiago: Así **cubriremos** todos los espacios.

De esta manera se dividieron en parejas y recorrieron todo el lugar. A medida que caminaban por los distintos lugares de la biblioteca. Los sonidos raros y los ruidos **tenebrosos aumentaban considerablemente**. Era una verdadera **escena** de suspenso. A veces se encontraban todos, coincidían en un rincón o en alguna otra parte de esos largos pasillos llenos de libros.

De pronto, así como si nada, todo se calmó. Ya no habían sonidos ni ruidos ni **susurros** ni nada. Se encontraron los seis en un mismo lugar, permanecieron **callados**. Amanda se le **ocurrió** agarrar un libro. Era *Los Viajes de Gulliver* del escritor **irlandés** Jonathan Swift y lo abrió al

azar. Al abrirlo salieron dos **mariposas** y unos **pétalos de la flor** de diente de león **caían** flotando. Cuando los pétalos tocaron el **suelo** y las mariposas **alzaron** vuelo se escuchó una voz que decía:

Que están haciendo aquí niños?

Era una voz amable y **sabia**, como de un abuelo. Miraron en todas las direcciones y no **vieron** a nadie. La voz volvió a hablar:

Quizas deberias tomar otro libro! Amanda **cogió** otro libro - *Alicia en el País de las Maravillas* de Lewis Carroll. Había tres **plumas** de **ganso** como **marcalibros**. En ese momento la voz tuvo rostro, un señor de unos 75 años. Entró **silenciosamente** y se presentó:

Me llamo Anastasio Córdoba y soy el guardián de los libros. Vivo aquí entre todas estas historias. Ustedes en este mismo instante también están **siendo** parte de una historia, que aún no se ha contado. Pero que será contada en su debido momento.

Los niños escuchaban **asombrados**.

Anyara: Tu no eres un fantasma, verdad?

Quique: Y eres muy alto, así que **tampoco** eres un duende.

Santiago: Puedes ser un extraterrestre que adoptó una forma humana.

Niños, niños....tranquilos! Que imaginación tan grande y imaginan muchas cosas como los **autores** de todos estos libros. Soy una persona normal y un viejo de 75 años. **Trabajé** en esta biblioteca toda mi vida. Cuando cerró, simplemente no **quise** irme. **Pertenezco** a este lugar y he leído todos estos libros más de tres veces cada uno. Recuerdo también a las miles de cientos de personas que pasaban por aquí cada día: lectores **apasionados**, niños como ustedes, viejos como yo, jóvenes y adolescentes. Hice muchas **amistades**. Venía gente importante - muy cultos, inteligentes, poetas, **filósofos** y escritores, profesores y conferencistas. Una vez nos visitaron niños de otros países , de todas partes del mundo. Esta biblioteca es mi hogar y aquí me quedo. Este es mi Titanic. Pero ustedes niños, tienen un **abanico** enorme de historias que contar y universos que descubrir. **Vengan conmigo**! Quiero **mostrarles** algo.

El bibliotecario los llevó a una parte de la biblioteca que no habían visto nunca. Era un pasillo por el que ya habían pasado varias veces pero no se dieron cuenta de que había una puerta secreta en el piso, **oculta** con un **tapete**, **bajaron** por unas escaleras pequeñas, todo estaba muy oscuro. El bibliotecario los guiaba y llevaba un **candelabro**. La luz de la vela iluminaba los **escalones**. Poco a poco se podían ver objetos extraños y muy antiguos: **máscaras**, **espadas**, **arcos** y **flechas**, **cuadros** y **retratos** y sobre todo muchos libros, muy distintos a los de la biblioteca. Eran grandes, de piel, de **cuero**, con un **olor** extraño, escritos en otras **lenguas**, idiomas ancestrales que ya no existen.

Los niños observaban maravillados. El bibliotecario les iba narrando historias y cuentos extraordinarios y fantásticos sobre la **procedencia** y el origen de cada objeto. Luego les **pidió** que se sentaran en el suelo alrededor de un antiguo mapa que había sido utilizado por piratas legendarios y les entregó a cada uno un objeto diferente. Para Amanda una **brújula** china, para Quique una **cerbatana** indígena, a Nicolás un reloj de arena, para Anyara una **cítara**, una **lámpara** persa para Amaya y a Santiago una katana. Luego los acompañó hasta un túnel que los llevaba afuera, hacia la calle, justo a su puesto de limonadas y galletas.

Preguntas - Questions

Que hacían para distraer a las personas y entrar a la biblioteca?

Cuántos niños hay en esta historia?

A quien se encontraron en adentro de la biblioteca?

Resumen en Ingles - English Summary

The old library had closed a year ago, but all the books are still there. It was a small town, very small. Children used to play free in the squares and parks. They played ball, rode bicycles, and played hide and seek like all children. What they liked most was to imagine if the library was haunted or not. They passed the front of the library and stayed a long time looking at their windows, walls, and the ceiling. Amanda, one of the nine-year-old girls, was the first to speak.

Amanda: "I want to enter! How are we going to know if there are ghosts, dragons, or goblins if we don't enter?"

As soon as Amanda said this, all the children - six in all - looked at each other and remained silent. Her eyes shone. That air of mischief could be seen on their faces. They left their bicycles, skateboards, and skates. They released the balls and sat down to plan under a park tree.

They had reached an agreement. They had a plan. They set up a stall selling lemonade and cookies in front of the library with a small table and an awning. They wore their Boys Scout uniforms every day. While three of them were selling lemonade, the other three found out how to enter the library. They took turns; the first turn was the girls, Amanda, Amaya, and Anyara. The second turn was from the boys, Quique, Nicolás, and Santiago. A week passed between lemonade cookies and plans until they found the perfect way to enter the old library.

The library had a large terrace where they previously projected films and conducted poetry recitals. It would be easy to climb the walls and windows in the purest spider style, and once upstairs, try to enter some of the corridors that led to the reading rooms. This time, they mixed; Amanda and Santiago belonged to the team that would climb the walls of the library. Anyara and Quique should distract people from selling lemonade. Amaya and Nicolás would have to watch the entrance.

They had even made some drawings, a kind of cartoon where they represented the whole plan. All this just because they wanted to enter the library - just enter - waiting for some indication of the existence of monsters, goblins, ghosts, or extraterrestrial life.

Once the children were able to enter, they dedicated themselves to touring each and every corner of the library: its corridors, classrooms, coffee, and the conference room. They did it in silence; a little for prudence and a little out of fear. They did not know what they would find. Once again, it was Amanda who broke the silence.

Amanda: "I think I heard something weird, a sound like a whistle or something downstairs."

Quique: "I also thought I heard a noise. I'm not sure, but it was like the song of an owl."

Anyara: "So, what are we waiting for? Let us see!"

Amaya: "Altogether, without making much noise. We have to take off our shoes."

Nicolás: "It is better to divide into groups."

Santiago: "This way, we will cover all the spaces."

In this way, they divided into pairs and toured the whole place. As they walked through the different places in the library, the strange sounds and the dark noises increased considerably. It was a true suspense scene. Sometimes, they all met, coincided in a corner or somewhere else in those long corridors full of books.

Suddenly, as if nothing, everything calmed down. There were no sounds, noises, whispers, or anything. The six were in one place, remained silent. Amanda came up with a book. It was *Gulliver's Travels* by Irish writer Jonathan Swift and he opened it at random. When he opened it, two butterflies came out and some petals of the dandelion flower were floating. When the petals touched the ground and the butterflies took flight, a voice was heard saying:

"What are children doing here?"

He was a kind and wise voice, like a grandfather's. They looked in all directions and saw no one. The voice spoke again:

"Maybe you should take another book!" Amanda picked up another book - *Alice in Wonderland* by Lewis Carroll. There were three goose feathers like bookmarks. At that moment, the voice had a face, a man of about 75 years. He entered silently and introduced himself:

293

"My name is Anastasio Córdoba and I am the guardian of the books. I live here among all these stories. You, at this very moment, are also being part of a story, which has not yet been told. But that will be told in due course."

The children listened in amazement.

Anyara: "You're not a ghost, right?"

Quique: "And you're very tall, so you're not an elf either."

Santiago: "You can be an alien who adopted a human form."

"Children, children... calm! What a great imagination and imagine many things as the authors of all these books. I am a normal person and an old man of 75 years. I worked in this library all my life. When it closed, I just didn't want to leave. I belong to this place and I have read all these books more than three times each. I also remember the thousands of hundreds of people who passed by here every day: passionate readers, children like you, old people like me, young people, and teenagers. I made many friendships. Important people came - very educated, intelligent, poets, philosophers and writers, professors, and speakers. Once we were visited by children from other countries from all over the world. This library is my home and here I stay. This is my Titanic. But you children have a huge range of stories to tell and universes to discover. Come with me! I want to show you something."

The librarian took them to a part of the library they had never seen. It was a corridor through which they had already passed several times, but they did not realize that there was a secret door on the floor, hidden with a mat. They went down some small stairs. Everything was very dark. The librarian guided them and carried a candlestick. Candlelight illuminated the steps. Little by little, you could see strange and very old objects: masks, swords, bows and arrows, pictures and portraits, and especially many books, very different from those in the library. They were large, leather, with a strange smell, written in other languages, ancestral languages that no longer exist.

The children watched in wonder. The librarian was telling them extraordinary and fantastic stories and stories about the origin and origin

294

of each object. He then asked them to sit on the ground around an ancient map that had been used by legendary pirates and handed each of them a different object. For Amanda, a Chinese compass; for Quique, an indigenous blowgun; for Nicolás, an hourglass; for Anyara, a zither; a Persian lamp for Amaya, and Santiago for a katana. Then, he accompanied them to a tunnel that led them outside, towards the street, right to their lemonade and biscuit stand.

Vocabulario - Vocabulary

abanico (ah-bah-nee-koh) Masculine noun - fan, ventilator

acuerdo (ah-kwehr-doh) Masculine noun - agreement

al frente (ahl frehn-teh) Phrase - in front

algunos (ahl-goo-nohs) Adjective - some

alzaron (ahl-sah-rohn) Transitive verb - they lifted

amistades (ah-mees-tah-dehs) Plural noun - friends

apasionados (ah-pah-syoh-nahr) Transitive verb - to be passionate about

apenas (ah-peh-nahs) Adverb - hardly

arco (ahr-koh) Masculine noun - arch

asombrados (ah-sohm-brah-dohs) Transitive verb - to amaze

aumentaban (ow-mehn-tahr) Transitive verb - they increased

autores (ow-tohr) Masculine or Feminine noun - authors

averiguaban (ah-beh-ree-gwahr) Transitive verb - they found out

azar (ah-sahr) Masculine noun - chance

bajaron (bah-hah-rohn) Intransitive verb - they went down

biblioteca (bee-blyoh-teh-kah) Feminine noun - library

brillaron (bree-yah-rohn) Intransitive verb - they shone

brújula (broo-hoo-lah) Feminine noun - compass

búho (boo-oh) Masculine noun - owl

caían (ka-ee-ahn) Intransitive verb - they fell

callados (kah-yah-dohs) Intransitive verb - to keep quiet

candelabro (kahn-deh-lah-broh) Masculine noun - candelabra

cerbatana (sehr-bah-tah-nah) Feminine noun - blowpipe

cítara (cee-tah-rah) Feminine noun - zither

cogió (koh-heh-oh) Transitive verb - he or she grabbed

conseguirían (kohn-seh-gee-ree-ahn) Transitive verb - they would get considerablemente (kohn-see-deh-rah-bleh-mehn-teh) Adverb - considerably

cuadros (kwah-drohs) Masculine noun - painting

cubriremos (koo-bree-reh-mohs) Transitive verb - we will cover

cuero (kweh-roh) Masculine noun - leather

dibujos (dee-boo-hoh) Masculine noun - drawing

dividirnos (dee-bee-deer-nohs) Transitive verb - to divide

duende (dwehn-deh) Masculine noun - elf

embrujada (ehm-broo-ha-dah) Adjective - haunted

encontraron (ehn-kohn-trah-rohn) Transitive verb - they found

escalones (ehs-kah-loh-nahr) Transitive - you stagger

escena (eh-seh-nah) Feminine noun - scene

escondidas escondidas Plural noun - hide and seek

espadas (ehs-pah-dah) Feminine noun - sword

estilo (ehs-tee-loh) Masculine noun - style

extraterrestre (ehks-trah-teh-rrehs-treh) Masculine or Feminine noun - extraterrestrial

fantasma (fahn-tahs-mah) Masculine noun - ghost

filósofo (fee-loh-soh-foh) Masculine or Feminine noun - philosopher

flechas (fleh-chahr) Transitive verb - to hit with an arrow

ganso (gahn-soh) Masculine or Feminine noun - goose

irlandés (eer-lahn-dehs) Masculine noun - Irish

lámpara (lahm-pah-rah) Feminine noun - lamp

lenguas (lehng-gwah) Feminine noun - tongue, language

libro (lee-broh) Masculine noun - book

lograron (loh-grah-rohn) Transitive verb - they reached

marcalibro (mahr-kah lee-broh) Feminine noun - bookmark

mariposa (mah-ree-poh-sah) Feminine noun - butterfly

máscaras (mahs-kah-rahs) Transitive verb - you will chew

mezclaron (mehs-klah-rohn) Transitive verb - they mixed

monstruos (mohns-trwoh) Masculine noun - monster

mostrarles (mohs-trahr-lehs) Transitive verb - to show

muro (moo-roh) Masculine noun - wall

oculta (oh-kool-tah) Transitive verb - he or she hides

ocurrió (oh-koo-rreer) Intransitive verb - he or she happened

olor (oh-lohr) Masculine noun - smell

pared (pah-rehd) Feminine noun - wall

pasillo (pah-see-yoh) Masculine noun - hallway

patines (pah-tee-nehs) Transitive verb - you skate

patineta (pah-tee-neh-tah) Feminine noun - skateboard

pelota (peh-loh-tah) Feminine noun - ball

pequeño (peh-keh-nyoh) Adjective - small, little

permanecieron (pehr-mah-neh-sehr) Intransitive verb - they stayed

pertenecían (pehr-teh-neh-sehr) Intransitive verb - you belong to

Pertenezco (pehr-teh-neh-sehr) Intransitive verb - I belong to

pétalos de la flor (peh-tah-loh deh lah flowr) Feminine noun - flower petals

pidió (peh-deer) Transitive verb - he or she asks for

piso de abajo (pee-soh deh ah-bah-ho) Feminine noun - downstairs

pluma (ploo-mah) Feminine noun - feather

procedencia (proh-seh-dehn-syah) Feminine noun - origin

proyectaban (proh-yehk-tah-bahn) Transitive verb - they planned

quedaban (keh-dahr) Intransitive verb - they stayed

quise (keh-rehr) Transitive verb - I wanted

quitarnos (kee-tahr-nohs) Transitive verb - I removed

recorrer (rreh-koh-rrehr) Transitive verb - to travel around

representaban (rreh-preh-sehn-tahr) Transitive verb - they represented

retrato (rreh-trah-toh) Masculine noun - portrait

rincones (rreeng-kohn) Masculine noun - corner

rostros (rrohs-troh) Masculine noun - face

sabia (sah-bee-ah) Transitive verb - I knew

salas (sah-lahr) Transitive verb - you salt

salones (sah-lohn) Masculine noun - living room

siendo (see-ehno-doh) Copular verb - to be

silenciosamente (see-lehn-syoh-sah-mehn-teh) Adverb - silently

solían (soh-lehr) Intransitive verb - you used to

sonido (soh-nee-doh) Masculine noun - sound

suelo (sweh-loh) Masculine noun - floor, ground

susurros(soo-soo-rroh) Masculine noun - whisper

tampoco (tahm-poh-koh) Adverb - neither

tapete (tah-peh-teh) Masculine noun - rug

tenebrosos (teh-neh-broh-soh) Adjective - sinister, gloomy

terraza (teh-rrah-sah) Feminine noun - roof, terrace

toldo (tohl-doh) Masculine noun - awning

Trabajé (trah-bah-hey) Intransitive verb - I worked

travesura (trah-beh-soo-rah) Feminine noun - prank

trepar (treh-pahr) Intransitive verb - to climb

turnaban (toor-nahr) Transitive - you take turns

Vamos a ver (bah-mohs ah behr) Phrase - let us see

vendiendo (behn-dehr) Transitive verb - to sell

Vengan conmigo (beh-neer cohn-mee-goh) Phrase - (they) come with me

vieron (behr-ohn) Transitive verb - they saw

vigilar (bee-hee-lahr) Transitive verb - to watch, to guard

Chapter 3: El Restaurante de Los Sueños - The Restaurant of Dreams

Dos **arquitectos** locos tenían un **proyecto** crear el restaurante de los sueños. Un sitio donde la gente pueda ir a comer y a **soñar** con **recetas** de la **gastronomía** de todo el planeta. Las más extrañas y exóticas combinaciones de alimentos, preparados y cocinados por los mejores chef de todo el mundo. Cada plato es presentado por un poeta un pintor un **cineasta** un comediante y un filósofo. El arte de la cocina presentado con arte: soñar y comer, comer y soñar. Se llamaría el Restaurante de Los Sueños. Los arquitectos querían que el restaurante **tuviera** forma de tren porque *El tren del sabor y el saber* era su slogan.

El sábado a las a las doce del mediodía ya estaba listo todo para la **inauguración** y **apertura** del restaurante de los sueños después de tres meses de duro trabajo. Poco a poco fueron llegando los clientes, en su mayoría artistas y bohemios. El acto de bienvenida fue todo un espectáculo y un verdadero show de **altura**.

Primero entraron **malabaristas** acompañados por una banda de jazz, mientras una bailarina hacía una coreografía y un poeta **recitaba** versos **entregando** las cartas del menú. Un cineasta proyectó un documental sobre la historia de la cocina y historias de los primeros restaurantes y comedores populares del mundo. Un **mimo regalaba** rosas mientras un pintor pintaba un **cuadro** de todas las personas que se encontraban ahí. Un **caricaturista** hacía **dibujos** animados cómicos de los **comensales** y al final un comediante daba un show de un monólogo humorístico. La **tertulia** artística terminó para darle paso a los exquisitos platos presentados con originalidad talento y vocación gastronómica que la gente fue **degustando** y disfrutando con mucho placer.

Durante todo el día recibieron más y más clientes que se iban **complacidos**, **maravillados** y **satisfechos** con ganas de volver, el negocio **empezaba** a marchar sobre **ruedas** - las ruedas del tren del sabor y el saber.

Al día siguiente abrieron más **temprano**. Cambiaron el menú y los espectáculos de arte y todo funcionaba de la mejor manera hasta que llegaron cuatro tipos muy extraños todos **vestidos** de negro.

Preguntaron por el **dueño** del restaurante y querían hablar con el **jefe**. Los atendió a un mimo que **rompió** su carácter y habló:

Aquí no hay jefes. Todos tenemos los mismos **derechos**. En este restaurante los dueños somos todos.

Tipo de negro: No te creo ni una palabra.

mimo: Por qué no me cree, señor?

Tipo de negro: Porque eres un mimo y se **supone** que los mimos no hablan! Ni **siquiera** puedo creer que te estoy escuchando!

Mimo: **Calmese**, señor. Tiene talento para la comedia, no lo sabía? ahora por favor, ¿dígame, que quiere?

Tipo de negro: Queremos **proponerle** un negocio muy **ambicioso** a los dueños de este lugar. Abrir **sucursales** en todo el mundo. Una enorme **franquicia**!

Mimo: Lo siento, señor. El restaurante de los sueños es el tren del sabor y el saber y una peña de artistas que **aman** la buena comida y el buen arte. No somos una fábrica de **salchichas**. No estamos en venta y no queremos ser un McDonald's.

Tipo de negro: Un tren que no va a ninguna parte? Un tren que se queda **estacionado**?

Mimo: El movimiento es relativo, señor. La gente se **mueve** hacia nosotros. Vienen de todas partes del mundo! Cuando eres bueno en lo - que haces porque amas lo que haces - la gente viene a tí, donde sea que estés. No necesitas **moverte**.

El tipo de negro y el mimo siguieron **discutiendo** un rato más que se extendió como unos quince minutos. Luego empezó a llegar la gente, todos **entusiasmados**. Durante el show y la comida pasaron muchas cosas:

Una niña que se paró a bailar en la mesa mientras los **mesoneros** la aplaudían y la felicitaban.

Un abuelo que se puso a imitar Charles Chaplin.

Una **pareja** de enamorados que no paraban de **besarse** mientras le **arrojaban** rosas a la mesa.

Un joven que inspirado por los artistas del restaurante **sacó** de su mochila un violín y se puso a tocar música **balcánica**.

Todas las personas que se reunían en El Restaurante de Los Sueños no iban solo a comer, había otra clase de alimento - el alimento del espíritu. Se nutrían el alma y eso los hacía felices. Por eso el restaurante estaba siempre lleno y cada día se hacen eventos extraordinarios que logran inspirar y emocionar a la gente.

Estaba saliendo todo de una manera tan perfecta que organizaron una gran fiesta. Una especie de varieté cómo se hacían en los años 20 para celebrar el éxito que estaban **teniendo**. Llamaron a todos los artistas que trabajaron en la inauguración y además mandaron invitaciones a los artistas más **consagrados** y **reconocidos** de todos los **géneros** del arte y esto. Fue lo que pasó:

Un día antes del evento, ya habían llegado todos los artistas y los recibieron con un gran **banquete**. Estaban sentados a la mesa:

El famoso cantante de opera, Loretto Cantattuti

El poeta, Laureano Lira

El **escultor**, Faravelo Domínico

El humorista, Lebi Cekado

El jazzista, Mel Braund

La bailadora de flamenco, Rebeca Malaga

y la pintora, Fabiola Muñoz

El espectáculo de varieté se llamó Universo Gastroart y comenzó con una opereta para piano y orquesta de Loretto Cantattuti. Mientras el gran tenor cantaba **sucedió** algo extraño. Fue llegando gente de afuera, de la calle, a pesar de que ya el restaurante estaba **repleto**. Seguía entrando gente pero lo curioso era que no iban a comer ni a escuchar y aplaudir al cantante.

Sino que se **dirigieron** a las mesas, a la barra y a la cocina. Tomaron cada uno una copa de **vidrio** vacía se la **colocaron** en la oreja. Una copa en cada oreja **sostenida** con sus manos como si escucharan música con unos audifonos de cristal. Se sentaron en el suelo en **posiciones** de yoga y se movían al **ritmo** de una melodía ajena a la música de la ópera. El restaurante de los sueños causaba esos efectos en las personas y los **conectaba** con algo que estaba más allá de este mundo.

Preguntas - Questions

¿Como es el slogan del restaurante de los sueños?

¿Qué día de la semana se inauguró el restaurante?

¿Con quien habló el tipo de negro que quería una franquicia?

Resumen en Ingles - English Summary

Two crazy architects had a project to create the Restaurant of Dreams, a place where people can go to eat and dream of recipes from the gastronomy of the entire planet. The strangest and most exotic combinations of food prepared and cooked by the best chefs in the world. Each dish is presented by a poet, a painter, a filmmaker, a comedian, and a philosopher. The art of cooking presented with art: dream and eat, eat and dream. It would be called Los Sueños Restaurant. The architects wanted the restaurant to be shaped like a train because The Train of Taste and Knowledge was its slogan.

On Saturday, at twelve noon, everything was ready for the opening of the Restaurant of Dreams after three months of hard work. Little by little, customers were arriving, mostly artists and bohemians. The welcome act was a show and a true show of height.

First jugglers entered accompanied by a jazz band, while a dancer did choreography and a poet recited verses delivering the menus. A filmmaker screened a documentary about the history of cooking and stories of the world's first popular restaurants and dining rooms. A mime gave roses while a painter painted a picture of all the people who were there. A cartoonist made comic cartoons of diners, and in the end, a comedian gave a show of a humorous monologue. The artistic gathering ended to give way to the exquisite dishes presented with original talent and gastronomic vocation that people were tasting and enjoying with pleasure.

Throughout the day, they received more and more customers who were pleased, amazed, and satisfied with the desire to return. The business began to run on wheels, the wheels of the train of flavor and knowledge.

The next day, they opened earlier. The menu and art show changed and everything worked in the best way until four very strange guys, all dressed in black, arrived. They asked about the restaurant owner and wanted to talk to the boss. He attended a mime who broke his character and spoke, "There are no bosses here. We all have the same rights. In this restaurant, the owners are all."

Man in Black: "I don't believe a word you say."

Mime: "Why don't you believe me, sir?"

Man in Black: "Because you're a mime and mimes aren't supposed to speak! I can't even believe that I'm listening to you!"

Mime: "Calm down, sir. He has a talent for comedy, didn't he know? Now please, tell me, what do you want?"

Man in Black: "We want to propose a very ambitious business to the owners of this place. Open branches worldwide. A huge franchise!"

Mime: "I'm sorry, sir. The Restaurant of Dreams is the train of taste and knowledge and a rock of artists who love good food and good art. We are not a sausage factory. We are not for sale, and we do not want to be a McDonald's."

Man in Black: "A train that is not going anywhere? A train that stays parked?"

Mime: "The movement is relative, sir. People move towards us. They come from all over the world! When you are good at what you do because you love what you do, people come to you wherever you are. You do not need to move."

The guy in black and the mime continued to argue for a while that lasted about fifteen minutes. Then people began to arrive, all excited. Many things happened during the show and the meal:

A girl who stopped dancing at the table while the waiters applauded and congratulated her.

A grandfather who began to imitate Charles Chaplin.

A couple in love who did not stop kissing while they threw roses at the table.

A young man who, inspired by the artists of the restaurant, took a violin out of his backpack and began to play Balkan music.

All the people who gathered at Los Sueños Restaurant were not just going to eat, there was another kind of food - the food of the spirit. They nourished the soul and that made them happy. That is why the restaurant was always full, and every day, there are extraordinary events that inspire and excite people.

Everything was going so perfectly that they organized a big party. A kind of variety similar to ones made in the 20s to celebrate the success they were having. They called all the artists who worked at the inauguration and also sent invitations to the most established and recognized artists of all genres of art and this. This is what happened:

One day, before the event, all the artists had arrived and received them with a great banquet. They were sitting at the table:

The famous opera singer, Loretto Cantattuti

The poet, Laureano Lira

The sculptor, Faravelo Domínico

The humorist, Lebi Cekado

The jazz player, Mel Braund

The flamenco dancer, Rebeca Malaga

and the painter, Fabiola Muñoz

The variety show was called Universal Gastroart and began with an operetta for piano and orchestra by Loretto Cantattuti. While the great tenor sang, something strange happened. People were coming from outside, from the street, even though the restaurant was already full. People were still entering but the funny thing was that they were not going to eat or listen and applaud the singer.

But they went to the tables, the bar, and the kitchen. They each took an empty glass cup and placed it on their ear, a cup in each ear held with their hands as if listening to music with crystal headphones. They sat on the floor in yoga positions and moved to the rhythm of a tune in alignment to opera music. The Restaurant of Dreams caused those effects on people and connected them with something that was beyond this world.

Vocabulario - Vocabulary

altura (ahl-too-rah) Feminine noun - height

aman (ah-mahn) Transitive verb - they love

ambicioso (ahm-bee-syoh-soh) Adjective - ambitious

apertura (ah-pehr-too-rah) Feminine noun - opening

arquitectos (ahr-kee-tehk-toh) Masculine or Feminine noun - architect

arrojaban (ah-rroh-hah-bahn) Transitive verb - they threw

balcánica (bahl-cahn-ee-ko) Adjective - Balkin

banquete (bahng-keh-teh) Masculine noun - banquet

besarse (beh-sahr-seh) Reciprocal verb - to kiss each other

Calmese (kahl-mah-sey) Transitive verb - to calm

caricaturista (ka-ree-ka-too-ree-stah) Masculine or Feminine noun - caricaturist

cineasta (see-neh-ahs-tah) Masculine or Feminine noun - filmmaker

colocaron (koh-loh-kah-rohn) Transitive verb - they placed

comensales (koh-mehn-sahl) Masculine or Feminine noun - dinner guest

complacido (kohm-plah-see-doh) Adjective - pleased

conectaba (koh-nehk-tah-bah) Transitive verb - I connected

consagrados (kohn-sah-grah-dohs) Transitive verb - to consecrate

cuadro (kwah-droh) Masculine noun - painting

degustando (deh-goos-tahn-doh) Transitive verb - to taste

derechos (deh-reh-chohs) Plural noun - duties

dibujo (dee-boo-hoh) Masculine noun - drawing

dirigieron (dee-ree-hee-rohn) Transitive verb - they managed

discutiendo (dees-koo-teer) Transitive verb - they argued

dueño (dweh-nyoh) Masculine or Feminine noun - owner

empezaba (ehm-peh-sah-bah) Intransitive verb - I began

entregando (ehn-treh-gahr) Transitive verb - to deliver

entusiasmados (ehn-too-syahs-mah-dohs) Transitive verb - to fill with excitement

escultor (ehs-kool-tohr) Masculine or Feminine noun - sculptor

estacionado (ehs-tah-syoh-nah-doh) Transitive verb - to park

franquicia (frahng-kee-syah) Feminine noun - franchise

gastronomía (gahs-troh-noh-mee-ah) Feminine noun - gastronomy

género (heh-neh-roh) Masculine noun - kind

inauguración (ee-now-goo-rah-syohn) Feminine noun - inauguration

jefe (heh-feh) Masculine or Feminine noun - boss

malabarista (mah-lah-bah-rees-tah) Masculine or Feminine noun - juggler

maravillados (mah-rah-bee-ah-dohs) Transitive verb - to amaze

mesonero (meh-soh-neh-roh) Masculine or Feminine noun - waiter

mimo (mee-moh) Masculine noun - mime

moverte (moh-behr) Transitive verb - to move

mueve (moh-beh-hey) Transitive verb - he or she moves

pareja (pah-reh-hah) Feminine noun - couple

posiciones (poh-sih-cee-ohn-ehs) Transitive verb - you position

proponerle (proh-poh-nehr) Transitive verb - to propose

proyecto (proh-yehk-toh) Masculine noun - project

recetas (rreh-seh-tahs) Transitive verb - you prescribe

recitaba (rreh-see-tah-bah) Transitive verb - I prescribe

reconocidos (rreh-koh-noh-seh-dohs) Transitive verb - to recite

regalaba (rreh-gah-lah-bah) Transitive verb - I gave

repleto (rreh-pleh-toh) Adjective - full

ritmo (rreet-moh) Masculine noun - rhythm

rompió (rrohm-peh-oh) Transitive verb - he or she broke

ruedas (rroh-dahs) Intransitive verb - you roll

sacó (sah-koh) Transitive verb - he or she takes out

salchicha (sahl-chee-chah) Feminine noun - sausage

satisfecho (sah-tees-feh-cho) Transitive verb - to satisfy

siquiera (see-kyeh-rah) Conjunction - at least

soñar (soh-nyahr) Transitive verb - to dream

sostenida (sohs-teh-nee-doh) Masculine noun - sharp

sucedió (soo-seh-deh-oh) Intransitive verb - he or she happened

sucursales (soo-koor-sahl-ehs) Feminine noun - branch

supone (soo-poh-neh) Transitive verb - he or she supposes

temprano (tehm-prah-noh) Adverb - early

teniendo (teh-neh-doh) Transitive verb - to have

tertulia (tehr-too-lyah) Feminine noun - gathering

tuviera (too-beh-rah) Transitive verb - I had

vestidos (behs-tee-dohs) Transitive verb - to wear

vidrio (bee-dryoh) Masculine noun - glass, cup

Chapter 4: La Historia del Teniente Guitarra - The Lieutenant Guitar Story

El Teniente Guitarra era un ex **combatiente** de la **guerra** civil española, que había **peleado** del lado de los **anarquistas**. Durante los años 1936 a 1939 que fue el periodo que duró esa guerra en España. Eran pocos los momentos de paz y tranquilidad en **aquellos** tiempos. Pero en los extraños ratos donde **reinaba** una **sospechosa** calma, Ventura Durrell, tocaba la guitarra. A su espalda, **al lado** de su **fusil**, siempre llevaba **colgada** su guitarra. Tocaba canciones que daban **esperanzas** a los **oprimidos**, **devastados**, **desplazados** y **perseguidos** por la guerra. Por eso le decían El Teniente Guitarra.

Estaba lloviendo mucho la noche del 7 de abril. Las personas corrían **desesperadas** a sus casas - no por la lluvia - sino porque había **toque de queda**. Eran días difíciles. El ambiente era **triste, desolado** y **gris**. Bombas explotando en cada esquina. **Trincheras** y barricadas en las calles. Camiones que se llevaban a la gente a refugios, los hospitales repletos, **tanques** y **ametralladoras**. Civiles, militares, republicanos, **fascistas, comunistas** y anarquistas por las calles, **heridos** y **perseguidos**. Cientos de muertos. En medio de toda esa angustia y dolor pasaba, el Teniente Guitarra cantando sus canciones de esperanza. Una de esas canciones decía así:

Mi gente querida esta **herida**
es valiente y **aguerrida**
vamos mi pueblo **oprimido**
no te des por **vencido**
levanta tu **puño** y tu cara
lleva siempre puesta la **esperanza**
es el arma que más desarma
salgan todos a la calle
que la libertad no se calle
levanta tu puño y tu cara
que las injusticias le salgan caras.
vamos mi gente querida
la libertad y el amor es la única salida.

La gente lo **veía** pasar y escuchaba sus canciones, le aplaudían y les daban las gracias. Era medicina para sus almas porque los llenaba de **fuerzas** y **ánimos** para seguir **resistiendo**. Las canciones del Teniente Guitarra era el único **albergue** para los espíritus tristes. Sus letras y melodías eran el **combustible** de toda una nación devastada por la guerra. Los niños cantaban sus canciones con alegría. Hasta jugaban a ser el Teniente Guitarra usando **escobas** como si fueran guitarras y repitiendo sus canciones de memoria. Así **transcurrían** los días en medio de la guerra.

Pero un día el Teniente Guitarra **desapareció**. No se le volvió a ver por ningún lado. Había desaparecido de las calles, de las trincheras, de los refugios y de los hospitales. Nadie sabía nada - ni una noticia, señales de vida. Nada. Los rumores de que lo habían **matado** o de que estuviera **preso** eran frecuentes. En España no se hablaba de otra cosa que no fuera la repentina **desaparición** del Teniente Guitarra. Las personas más cercanas a él tampoco tenían ninguna información. Familiares y amigos, hasta sus enemigos estaban **desconcertados**. Simplemente se volvió invisible y el pueblo entero lo buscaba.

Republicano: Qué crees que le pasó al Teniente Guitarra?

Anarquista: Al teniente junto a sus seis cuerdas lo **metieron** al **calabozo**!

Socialista: Y lo deben estar **torturando** en este preciso momento!

Un niño: Yo creo que esta dando un concierto muy bonito en un lugar sin guerra!

Soldado: Todo el **endemoniado** mundo está en guerra!

Las personas que se al azar por las calles se hacían la misma pregunta a **manera** de saludo...¿sabes algo del Teniente Guitarra? A pesar de que la gente conocía de **antemano** la respuesta negativa seguían preguntando porque no perdían la esperanza de **encontrarlo** con vida.

Hasta que una tarde alguien **cruzó** las calles corriendo como un loco y **gritando**,

Lo ví! Lo ví! Yo lo ví! Oh claro, que lo ví....yo sí lo ví!

Era un joven como de 18 años con una **boina** marrón y unos **tirantes** negros que llevaba los zapatos **rotos** y la camisa llena de **huecos**. Se le notaba un hambre como de cuatro días pero el **rostro** le **brillaba** de felicidad y no paraba de gritar,

Yo lo ví! Yo sí lo ví!

La gente que lo veía y escuchaba corrió a su encuentro. Una multitud como de ochenta personas rodeó al joven y casi lo **aplasta**. Todos hablaban al mismo tiempo y sin respirar:

¿Dónde está? ¿Qué le pasó? ¿**Estuvo preso**? Se escapó? Lo torturaron? ¿Está bien? ¿Tiene su guitarra? **Está herido**? Lo viste muy **lejos** de aquí?

El joven intentó responder las preguntas de todas las personas pero él mismo estaba muy cansado. Se sentó sobre los restos de un automóvil que se había **quemado** en una de las tantas explosiones. Ya un poco más calmado, comenzó a explicar lo que había **sucedido**:

El joven salía de una **fábrica** en la que se encontraba escondido durante las **redadas** fascistas. Había **permanecido** escondido por nueve horas. No salió hasta que se **aseguró** que ya todas las **tropas** se habían ido. Empezó a caminar con mucha atención, alerta de cualquier movimiento o ruido extraño viendo a todos lados para que no lo fueran a capturar.

Cuando de pronto escuchó el ruido de un auto que se **acercaba**. Se escondió detrás de un **camión** de verduras y pudo ver que pasaba otro camión. De la guardia y entre varios prisioneros llevaban a el Teniente Guitarra. Estaba muy seguro. Lo reconoció **enseguida**. Incluso tenía su guitarra encima. El camión de la guardia se **dirigía** hacia las **cárceles** y **calabozos**. Después lo perdí de vista.

Cuando las personas terminaron de escuchar el relato del joven decidieron hacer algo. Se dirigieron en marcha al lugar donde el joven había visto el camión. Tenía prisionero al Teniente Guitarra y lo hicieron cantando las canciones que él siempre les había cantado:

No pierdes fuerzas ni valor
juntos somos una **batalla**
que **genera** lucha y amor
vamos todos arriba
levanta tu espíritu hasta la **cima**
seamos una sola voz

Cantaban todos juntos y hasta **improvisaban** canciones ellos mismos para cantarselas al teniente guitarra. Una de esas canciones decía así:

Tu que de tanto **coraje** y esperanza nos armaste
aquí estamos contigo teniente
te defenderemos hasta con los dientes
sacaremos nuestras **garras** y espadas
te **apoyamos** Teniente Guitarra

Las canciones se escucharon por todo el pueblo y se fueron **transmitiendo** de ciudad en ciudad. Toda España las cantaba con valor y humildad. Un día un niño **emocionado** y a lo loco pegaba **brincos** de alegría y decía,

Es él! Es él! **Ha vuelto**! Ya está aquí!

Entonces vieron una **silueta** con su sombra y una guitarra a **cuestas** por el camino.

Preguntas - Questions

Como es el nombre de verdad del teniente guitarra..... respuesta: Ventura Durrell

cuánto tiempo duró la guerra civil española........ respuesta: de 1936 a 1939

dónde estaba escondido el joven que vio al teniente guitarra....respuesta:en una fábrica

Resumen en Ingles - English Summary

Lieutenant Guitar was a former Spanish Civil War fighter who had fought on the side of the anarchists during the years 1936 to 1939, that was the period that the war lasted in Spain. There were few moments of peace and tranquility in those times. But in the strange moments where a suspicious calm reigned, Ventura Durrell played the guitar. At his back, next to his rifle, he always had his guitar hanging. He played songs that gave hope to the oppressed, devastated, displaced, and persecuted by war. That's why they called him Lieutenant Guitar.

It was raining heavily on the night of April 7. People ran desperately to their homes, not because of the rain, but because there was a curfew. It was a difficult time. The atmosphere was sad, desolate, and gray. Bombs were exploding in every corner. Trenches and barricades were in the streets. Trucks took people to shelters, full hospitals, tanks, and machine guns. Civilians, military, republicans, fascists, communists, and anarchists are in the streets, injured and persecuted. Hundreds dead. In the midst of all that anguish and pain passed was Lieutenant Guitar singing his songs of hope. One of those songs read like this:

My dear people are hurt

She is brave and hardened

Let's go, my oppressed people,

Do not give up

Raise your fist and your face

Always wear hope

It is the weapon that most disarms

Everyone goes out

That freedom does not stop

Raise your fist and your face

May injustices come out expensive costs

Come on my dear people

Freedom and love is the only way out.

People watched him go by and listened to his songs, applauded him, and thanked them. It was medicine for their souls because it filled them with strength and courage to continue resisting. The Lieutenant Guitar's songs were the only shelter for sad spirits. His lyrics and melodies were the fuel of an entire war-torn nation. The children sang his songs with joy. They even mimicked Lieutenant Guitar using brooms as if they were guitars and repeated his songs by heart. Thus, the days passed in the middle of the war.

But one day, the Lieutenant Guitar disappeared. He was never seen again. He had disappeared from the streets, trenches, shelters, and hospitals. No one knew anything - no news or signs of life. Nothing. Rumors that he had been killed or that he was in prison were frequent. In Spain, there was no talk of anything other than the sudden disappearance of Lieutenant Guitar. The people closest to him didn't have any information either. Family and friends, even his enemies were baffled. He simply became invisible and the entire town was looking for him.

Republican: "What do you think happened to Lieutenant Guitar?"
Anarchist: "The lieutenant was put in the dungeon!
Socialist: "And they must be torturing him right now!"
A child: "I think he is giving a very nice concert in a place without war!"
Soldier: "The whole demonized world is at war!"

The people who are randomly in the streets asked the same question by way of greeting ... "Do you know anything about Lieutenant Guitar?" Although people knew the negative answer beforehand, they kept asking and they didn't lose hope of finding him alive.

Until one afternoon, someone crossed the streets running like crazy and screaming,

"I saw him! I saw him! I saw him! Oh sure, I saw him... I saw him!"

He was an 18-year-old young man with a brown beret and black suspenders wearing broken shoes and a shirt full of holes. He was hungry for about four days, but his face shone with happiness and he kept screaming, "I saw him! I did see him!"

People who saw and heard ran to meet him. A crowd of about eighty people surrounded the young man and almost crushed him. Everyone spoke at the same time and without breathing: "Where is he? What happened? Was he in prison? Did he escape? Did they torture him? Is he okay? Did he have his guitar? Is he hurt? Did you see him far from here?"

313

The young man tried to answer all the people's questions, but he himself was very tired. He sat on the remains of a car that had been burned in one of the many explosions. Already a little calmer, he began to explain what had happened:

The young man left a factory where he was hiding during the fascist raids. He had been hiding for nine hours. He did not leave until he made sure that all the troops had already left. He began to walk with great attention, alert of any strange movement or noise, and looking everywhere so that they would not capture him.

When suddenly he heard the noise of a car approaching. He hid behind a vegetable truck and could see another truck passing by. From the guard and among several prisoners, they took Lieutenant Guitar. He was very sure. He recognized it right away. He even had his guitar on top. The guard truck was heading towards prisons and dungeons, then lost sight of him.

When people finished listening to the young man's story, they decided to do something. They made their way to the place where the young man had seen the truck who had the Lieutenant Guitar prisoner and they did it by singing the songs he had always sung to them.

You don't lose strength or courage
Together we are a battle
That generates struggle and love
Let's all go up
Lift your spirit to the top
Let's be one voice

They all sang together and even improvised songs themselves to sing to the Guitar Lieutenant. One of those songs read like this:

You of so much courage and hope you armed us
Here we are with you lieutenant
We will defend you even with your teeth
We will take out our claws and swords
We support you Lieutenant Guitar

The songs were heard throughout the town and were transmitted from city to city. All of Spain sang them with courage and humility. One day, an excited and crazy boy was jumping with joy and saying, "It's him! It's him! He's back! He's here!" Then they saw a silhouette with its shadow and a guitar in tow along the way.

Vocabulario - Vocabulary

acercaba (ah-sehr-kah-bah) Transitive verb - I move closer

aguerrida (ah-goo-rree-dah) Adjective - hardened, veteran

al lado (ahl lah-doh) Adverb - nearby

albergue (ahl-behr-geh) Masculine noun - shelter

ametralladoras (ah-meh-trah-yah-doh-rah) Feminine noun - machine gun

anarquista (ah-nahr-kees-tah) Masculine or Feminine noun - anarchist

ánimo (ah-nee-moh) Masculine noun - mood

antemano (ahn-teh-mah-noh) Adverb - beforehand

aplasta (ah-plahs-tahr) Transitive verb - he or she crushes

apoyamos (ah-poh-yah-mohs) Transitive verb - we support

aquellos (ah-keh-yohs) Adjective - those

aseguró (ah-seh-goo-roh) Transitive verb - he or she assured

batalla (bah-tah-yah) Feminine noun - battle

boina (boy-nah) Feminine noun - beret

brillaba (bree-yah-bah) Intransitive verb - I shone

brinco (breeng-koh) Masculine noun - jump

calabozo (kah-lah-boh-soh) Masculine noun - dungeon

camión (kah-myohn) Masculine noun - truck

cárcel (kahr-sehl) Feminin noun - prison

cima (see-mah) Feminine noun - top

colgada (kohl-gah-dah) Adjective- hanging

combatiente (kohm-bah-tyehn-teh) Adjective - fighter

combustible (kohm-boos-tee-bleh) Masculine noun - combustible

comunista (koh-moo-nees-tah) Adjective - Communist

coraje (koh-rah-heh) Masculine noun - courage

cruzó (kroo-soh) Transitive verb - he or she crossed

cuestas (kohs-tahs) Transitive verb - you cost

desapareció (dehs-ah-pah-reh-seh-oh) Intransitive verb - he or she disappeared desaparición (dehs-ah-pah-ree-syohn) Feminine noun - disappearance

desconcertados (dehs-kohn-sehr-tah-dohs) Pronominal verb - to be disconcerted

desesperadas (dehs-ehs-por-ah-dahs) Pronominal verb - to be desperate

desolado (deh-soh-lah-doh) Adjective - desolate

desplazados (dehs-plah-sahr) Transitive verb - to displace

devastados (deh-bahs-tahr) Transitive verb - to devastate

dirigía (dee-ree-hee-ah) Transitive verb - I managed

emocionado (eh-moh-syoh-nah-doh) Adjective - excited

endemoniado (ehn-deh-moh-nyah-doh) Adjective - wicked

enseguida (ehn-seh-gee-dah) Adverb - immediately

escobas (ehs-koh-bahs) Transitive verb - you sweep

esperanza (ehs-peh-rahn-sah) Feminine noun - hope

Está herido (ess-tah eh-ree-doh) Phrase - Is he hurt?

Estuvo preso (ehs-too-voh preh-soh) Phrase - Is he imprisoned?

fábrica (fah-bree-kah) Feminine noun - factory

fascista (fah-sees-tah) Adjective - Fascist

fuerzas (fohr-sahs) Transitive verb - you force

fusil (foo-seel) Masculine noun - rifle

garras (gah-rrahs) Plural noun - clutches

genera (heh-neh-rah) Transitive verb - he or she generates

gris (grees) Adjective - grey

gritando (gree-tahn-doh) Intransitive verb - to yell

guerra (geh-rrah) Feminine noun - war

Ha vuelto (ah bwehl-toh) Phrase - He has returned!

herida (eh-ree-dah) Feminine noun - wound

heridos (eh-ree-dohs) Transitive verb - to wound

huecos (weh-koh) Masculine noun - hole

improvisaban (eem-proh-bee-sah-bahn) Transitive verb - they improvised

lejos (leh-hohs) Adverb - far away

levanta (leh-bahn-tah) Transitive verb - he or she raises

Lo ví (loh bee) Phrase - I saw him

manera (mah-neh-rah) Feminine noun - way

matado (mah-tah-doh) Transitive verb - to kill

metieron (meh-teh-rohn) Transitive verb - they put

oprimido (oh-pree-mee-doh) Adjective - oppressed

peleado (peh-leh-ah-doh) Adjective - hard-fought

permanecido (pehr-mah-neh-seh-doh) Intransitive verb - to stay

perseguidos (pehr-seh-gee-dohs) Transitive verb - to pursue

preso (preh-soh) Masculine or Feminine noun - prisoner

puño (poo-nyoh) Masculine noun - fist

quemado (keh-mah-doh) Adjective - burnt

redada (rreh-dah-dah) Feminine noun - raid

reinaba (rrey-nah-bah) Intransitive verb - to prevail

resistiendo (rreh-sees-teer) Transitive verb - to withstand

rostro (rrohs-troh) Masculine noun - face

rotos (row-tohs) Adjective - broken

sacaremos (sah-kah-reh-mohs) Transitive verb - to take out

salgan (sahl-hahn) Transitive verb - you go out

seamos (say-ah-mohs) Copular verb - we are

silueta (see-lweh-tah) Feminine noun - silhouette

sospechosa (sohs-peh-choh-sah) Adjective - suspicious

sucedido (soo-seh-deh-doh) Intransitive verb - to happen

tanque (tahng-keh) Masculine noun - tank

tirantes (tee-rahn-tehs) Plural noun - suspenders

toque de queda (toh-keh deh keh-dah) Masculine noun - curfew

torturando (tohr-too-rahn-doh) Transitive verb - to torture

transcurrían (trahns-koo-rree-ahn) Intransitive verb - they passed

transmitiendo (trahns-mee-tee-in-doh) Transitive verb - to transmit

Trinchera (treen-cheh-rah) Feminine noun - trench

triste (trees-teh) Adjective - sad

tropas (troh-pahs) Plural noun - army

veía (beh-ee-ah) Transitive verb - I saw

vencido (behn-see-doh) Adjective - defeated

Chapter 5: Los Secretos del Escorpión - The Secrets of the Scorpion

El Escorpión era un club de comedia donde se reunían los mejores **comediantes** del **país**. Todos los martes, se **realizaban** verdaderos de humor. El resto de los días de la semana los humoristas se reunían en **interminables tertulias** de café y cervezas, compartían ideas y proyectos para sus shows y **sobretodo** hablaban mucho y hacían **bastantes chistes** de humor negro. Como se conocían tanto y eran tan amigos se gastan bromas, **pesadas** y **crueles**. Muchas risas **garantizadas**, un **agudo** sentido crítico, un toque de cinismo y una buena dosis de sarcasmo eran los ingredientes que se cocinaban cada noche en El Escorpión.

Los humoristas que se daban cita cada día en este templo de la comedia eran Luis Martelli, Roberto Fontana, Sebastian Lupus, Diana Solís y Emilia González. Esta noche estaban todos juntos en la misma mesa. Los meseros no paraban de traer café, vasos con agua, **ceniceros**, mucho café y cigarrillos para conversaciones satíricas y **burlescas**.

Luis Martelli: Miren quien llegó el gran Sebastian Lupus! Estás más **gordo**! **Cambiaste** a tu esposa por otra que si sabe cocinar?

Sebastian Lupus: Yo no, pero me enteré que tu si cambiaste a tu esposa por un **marinero** musculoso!

Roberto Fontana: Niños, dejen de **pelear**! Que si no se quedan sin postre.

Diana Solís: Miren, **cuerda** de insensibles! No me han dicho nada. Fuí al salón de belleza.

Luis Martelli: ¿Qué pasó? Estaba cerrado?

Emilia Gonzalez: Si, querida! Odio decirlo pero Luis tiene razón. Te ves terrible!

Diana Solís: Tu no digas nada, Emilia! Cada día tienes más **bigote**! Ya te pareces a Emiliano Zapata!

Mesero: Aquí está la ronda de café, señores cómicos.

Y en ese delirio de diálogos **vertiginosos**, se pasaban toda la noche. A veces hacían una pausa de tanta y se ponían a jugar poker o **ajedrez**. Eran unos bastardos estos comediantes. Una noche dos **borrachos** se agarraron a **puños** y **patadas** y casi **destrozan** el bar. Pero los comediantes en vez de separarlos acabar con la **pelea** y evitar que siguieran **rompiendo** botellas y sillas, estos **cabrones** se pusieron a narrar la pelea como si fueran **comentaristas** deportivos en un ring de boxeo:

"Tremendo **gancho** derecho le conectó el borracho de la camisa de cuadros al **pugilista** de los bermudas de colores! **Salpicaron** de sangre las mesas y el público **enloquece**! Que suban las **apuestas**, señoras y señores! Esta es la pelea del siglo no se había visto algo así desde que Mike Tyson le **mordió** la oreja a Holyfield! Es una verdadera **locura**, damas y caballeros! Hagan sus apuestas!"
Todo esto lo decían entre risas **carcajadas** y aplausos. Los meseros no podían creer esta **insólita** conducta por parte de los comediantes.

Mesero: **Oigan** mucho descaro el de ustedes **pandilla** de desadaptados! Qué conducta es esa?

Roberto: Esta es mala conducta...ja ja ja ja!

Francisco, el dueño del Bar el Escorpión, también le **cuestionaba** el **comportamiento** inapropiado a sus mejores clientes pero a la vez eran los más desordenados y **fiesteros**.

Francisco: Muchachos, por favor, **pórtense** bien!

Sebastian Lupus: Portarse bien? Qué es eso?

Roberto: De qué habla?

Luis: Portese bien usted, don Francisco! Que para eso tiene nombre de Papa **vaticano**.

Entre comentarios sarcásticos **bromas** y cantidades industriales de café los comediantes del Escorpión, sus empleados socios y dueños pasaban una agradable y **jocosa** velada humorística. Todas estas bromas eran apenas un pre **calentamiento** para entrenar para el próximo martes que es el día del maratón semanal de humor. Faltaba una semana exactamente para el gran show, se **relajaron** un poco más de lo que ya estaban. **Colocaron** buena música: *Simpatía por el Diablo* de los Rolling Stones. Muy **adecuada** para el espíritu de estos eternos incorregibles **amantes** de la desobediencia amos y señores de las risas y los **espasmos**.

Después de cinco rondas más de café y cervezas con las infaltables, papas fritas y **bocados** de queso, los comediantes del Escorpión se despiden entre abrazos y últimos chistes antes de perderse en las **incierta** noche. Bajo una luna cómplice de robos, **asesinatos** y largas **cortinas** que tapan la corrupción y otros demonios **cotidianos**, de una ciudad que hace rato largo ya se la llevó el tedio la indiferencia y la inseguridad.

El tan esperado día martes había llegado. La gente iba llegando al El Escorpión poco a poco: solos, en **parejas** y en grupos. Una banda de rock alternativo llamada No tengo Saldo ambientaba la noche con su rock and roll **desgarrante**. Meanwhile, los comediantes calentaban sus gargantas con ron y cerveza antes de subirse a la **tarima** y agarrar el micrófono como un revolver. La noche prometía ser cómica y salvaje, como suelen ser las noches de humor. Los comediantes estaban listos y los reflectores y el sonido ya instalados era la hora del show. El primero en subirse al **escenario** fue Luis Martelli.

Luis Martelli: Buenas noches, tribu **trasnochada** del Escorpión! Hoy les hablaré del **matrimonio**. Creo que la gente se casa porque se **cansa** de ser feliz. Un día te despiertas y dices he tengo 35 años y estoy soltero! 35 años de fiestas, **rumbas**, aventuras irresponsabilidad y **despreocupación**. ¿Qué es esto? Ya me canse de tanta felicidad voy a probar ese holocausto nazi que dicen que es el matrimonio. Me voy a suicidar; digo me voy a **casar**. Bueno prácticamente es lo mismo. El matrimonio es la única guerra en la que se duerme con el **enemigo**.

Así siguió su **rutina** Luis entre risas y aplausos y le tocó el turno a Diana:

Diana Solís: No entiendo a los hombres que te quieren llevar a la cama solo porque te invitan un trago. Qué te pasa, enfermo **engreído**? Me estás comprando una piña colada. No me estás donando un **riñon**!

Y así se despidió Diana: Señoras y señores! Reciban con un fuerte aplauso al siguiente comediante de la noche! El caballero Roberto Fontana!

Roberto Fontana: Ayer me ladró un perro **enfurecido** y **rabioso** que estaba arriba de un techo! Esa bola de pelos con **pulgas** y dientes me ladraba y me **ladraba** desde el techo! Hay algo más **inútil** que un perro en un techo? Yo le gritaba, baja! Que espera? **Ven**! Me vas a morder? Vente que pasa? No tengo todo el día! Llega, que te llegues te digo, perro no come perro!

Y así uno a uno los comediantes del Escorpión fueron contando sus secretos más íntimos while **exponiendo** la realidad de sus **grandezas** y **debilidades enfrentados** al amor la política el sexo y la vida **cotidiana**.

Preguntas - Questions

¿Cuántos eran los comediantes habituales al escorpión?

¿Como se llama la banda de rock alternativo que tocó en El Scorpion?

¿Cual es la canción que pusieron la primera noche una semana antes del show?

Resumen en Ingles - English Summary

The Scorpio was a comedy club where the best comedians in the country met. Every Tuesday, true humor was performed. The rest of the days of the week, the comedians met in endless coffee and beer gatherings, shared ideas and projects for their shows and, above all, talked a lot and made many jokes of black humor. Since they knew each other so well and were friends, they played jokes, heavy and cruel. Many guaranteed laughs. A sharp critical sense, a touch of cynicism, and a good dose of sarcasm were the ingredients that were cooked every night at El Scorpión.

The comedians who met every day in this temple of comedy were Luis Martelli, Roberto Fontana, Sebastian Lupus, Diana Solís, and Emilia González. Tonight, they were all together at the same table. The waiters kept bringing coffee, glasses of water, ashtrays, lots of coffee, and cigarettes for satirical and burlesque conversations.

Luis Martelli: "Look who arrived - the great Sebastian Lupus! You are fatter! Did you change your wife for another one who knows how to cook?"

Sebastian Lupus: "I didn't, but I found out that you did trade your wife for a muscular sailor!"

Roberto Fontana: "Children, stop fighting!"

Diana Solís: "Look, insensitive fool! They haven't told me anything. I went to the beauty salon."

Luis Martelli: "What happened? Was it closed?"

Emilia Gonzalez: "Yes, mistress! I hate to say it, but Luis is right. You look terrible!"

Diana Solís: "Don't say anything, Emilia! Every day, you have more mustache! You look like Emiliano Zapata!"

Waiter: "Here is the round of coffee, comic gentlemen."

And in that delirium of dizzying dialogues, they spent the whole night. Sometimes, they paused and started playing poker or chess. These comedians were bastards. One night, two drunks got into a brawl with fists and kicks and almost destroyed the bar. But the comedians, instead of separating them, to prevent them from continuing to break bottles and chairs put an end to the fight, these bastards began to narrate the fight, as if they were sports commentators in a boxing ring:

"Tremendous right hook connected the drunk of the plaid shirt to the boxer in the colored Bermuda shirt! The tables splashed with blood and the public goes wild! Let the bets rise, ladies and gentlemen! This is the fight of the century. There has not been anything seen like that since Mike Tyson bit Holyfield's ear! It's real madness, ladies and gentlemen! Place your bets!"

All this was said between laughter and applause. The waiters could not believe this unusual behavior on the part of the comedians.

Waiter: "Hear me you lot of cheeky men from your gang of misfits! What behavior is that?"
Roberto: "This is bad behavior ... ha ha ha ha!"

Francisco, the owner of the Scorpion Bar, also questioned the inappropriate behavior of his best clients, but at the same time, they were the messiest and partying.

Francisco: "Boys, please, behave well!"

Sebastian Lupus: "Behaving well? What is that?"

Roberto: "What are you talking about?"

Luis: "Be good, Don Francisco! That is the name of the Vatican Pope."

Among sarcastic comments, jokes, and industrial quantities of coffee, the Scorpion comedians, their partners, and owners spent a pleasant and humorous evening. All these jokes were just a warm-up to train for next Tuesday, which is the day of the weekly humor marathon. Missing a week exactly for the big show, they relaxed a little more than they already were. They played good music: Sympathy for the Devil by the Rolling Stones. Very suitable for the spirit of these eternal incorrigible lovers of disobedience masters and lords of laughter and spasms.

After five more rounds of coffee and beers with the inevitable fries and cheese bites, the Scorpion comedians say goodbye between hugs and last jokes before getting lost in the uncertain night. Under an accomplice moon of robberies, murders, and long curtains that cover corruption and other everyday demons, it was a city that long ago was already bored by indifference and insecurity.

The long-awaited day, Tuesday had arrived. People were arriving at El Scorpión little by little: alone, in pairs, and in groups. An alternative rock band called "I Have No Balance" set the night with its tearing rock and roll. Meanwhile, comedians warmed their throats with rum and beer before stepping on the stage and grabbing the microphone. The night promised to be funny and wild, as are usually the nights of humor. The comedians were ready and the reflectors and sound already installed by the time of the show. The first to get on stage was Luis Martelli.

Luis Martelli: "Good evening, outdated Scorpion tribe! Today, I will talk about marriage. I think people get married because they get tired of being happy. One day, you wake up and say I'm 35 years old and single! 35 years of parties, rumbas, irresponsibility, and carefree adventures. What is this? I'm tired of so much happiness, I'm going to try that Nazi holocaust that they call marriage. I'm going to kill myself. I say I'm going to get married. Well, it's practically the same. Marriage is the only war in which one sleeps with the enemy."

This is how Luis followed his routine with laughter and applause, and then it was Diana's turn:

Diana Solís: "I don't understand the men who want to take you to bed just because they invite you for a drink. What's wrong with you, sick cocky man? You are buying me a pina colada. You are not giving me a kidney!"

And so Diana said goodbye: "Ladies and gentlemen! Receive with loud applause the next comedian of the night! The gentleman, Roberto Fontana!"

Roberto Fontana: "Yesterday, I was barked at by an angry and rabid dog that was on top of a roof! That ball of hair with fleas and teeth barked at me from the terrace! Is there anything more useless than a dog on a roof? I yelled at him, come down! What are you waiting for? Come! Are you going to bite me? Come on! What's taking you so long? I do not have all day! It comes, and I can tell you, dog does not eat dog!"

And so, one by one, the Scorpion comedians were telling their most intimate secrets while exposing the reality of their greatness and weaknesses faced with love, politics, sex, and everyday life.

Vocabulario - Vocabulary

adecuada (ah-deh-kwah-doh) Adjective - appropriate

agudo (ah-goo-doh) Adjective - sharp

ajedrez (ah-heh-drehs) Masculine noun - chess

amante (ah-mahn-teh) Masculine or Feminine noun - lover

apuestas (ah-pohs-tahs) Transitive verb - you bet

asesinato (ah-seh-see-nah-toh) Masculine noun - murder

bastante (bahs-tahn-teh) Adjective - quite a lot of

bigote (bee-goh-teh) Masculine noun - mustache

bocado (boh-kah-doh) Masculine noun - bite

borracho (boh-rrah-choh) Adjective - drunk

broma (broh-mah) Feminine noun - joke

burlesca (boor-leh-ska) Masculine or Feminine noun - joker, comic

cabrone (kah-brohn) Masculine or Feminine noun - bastard

calentamiento (kah-lehn-tah-myehn-toh) Masculine noun - warm-up

Cambiaste (kahm-byah-stey) Transitive verb - you changed

cansa (kahn-sah) Transitive verb - he or she tires

carcajada (kahr-kah-hah-dah) Feminine noun - loud laugh

casar (kah-sahr) Transitive verb - to marry

cenicero (seh-nee-seh-roh) Masculine noun - ashtray

chiste (chees-teh) Masculine noun - joke

Colocaron (koh-loh-kah-rohn) Transitive verb - they placed

comediante (koh-meh-dyahn-teh) Masculine or Feminine noun - comedian

comentarista (koh-mehn-tah-rees-tah) Masculine or Feminine noun - commentator

comportamiento (kohm-pohr-tah-myehn-toh) Masculine noun - behavior

cortina (kohr-tee-nah) Feminine noun - curtain

cotidiana (koh-tee-dyah-nah) Adjective - daily

crueles (krwehl-ehs) Adjective - cruel

cuerda (kwehr-dah) Feminine noun - rope

cuestionaba (kwehs-tyoh-nah-bah) Transitive verb - I questioned

debilidades (deh-bee-lee-dahd) Feminine noun - weakness

desgarrante (dehs-gah-rrahr) Transitive verb - to tear

despreocupación (dehs-prey-ocoo-pay-see-ohn) noun - lack of worry or concern

destrozan (dehs-troh-sah-ahn) Transitive verb - they destroy

enemigo (eh-neh-mee-goh) Masculine or Feminine noun - enemy

enfrentados (ehm-frehn-tah-dohs) Transitive verb - to confront

enfurecido (ehm-foo-reh-see-doh) Adjective - furious

engreído (ehng-greh-ee-doh) Adjective - conceited

enloquece (ehn-loh-keh-sehr) Transitive verb - to drive crazy

escenario (eh-seh-nah-ryoh) Masculine noun - stage

espasmo (ehs-pahs-moh) Feminine noun - spasm

exponiendo (ehks-poh-nehn-doh) Transitive verb - to expose

fiestero (fyehs-teh-roh) Adjective - party animals

gancho (gahn-choh) Masculine noun - hook

garantizadas (gah-rahn-tee-sah-dahs) Adjective - guaranteed

gordo (gohr-doh) Adjective - fat

grandeza (grahn-deh-sah) Feminine noun - nobility

incierta (een-syehr-toh) Adjective - uncertain

insólita (een-soh-lee-toh) Adjective - unusual

interminables (een-tehr-mee-nah-bleh) Adjective - endless

inútil (een-oo-teel) Adjective - useless

jocosa (ho-koh-sah) Adjective - funny

ladraba (lah-drah-bra) Intransitive verb - I barked

locura (loh-koo-rah) Feminine noun - madness

marinero (mah-ree-neh-roh) Masculine or Feminine noun - sailor

matrimonio (mah-tree-moh-nyoh) Masculine noun - marriage

mordió (mohr-dee-oh) Transitive verb - he or she bites

Oigan (oh-ee-hahn) Transitive verb - they hear

país (pah-ees) Masculine noun - country

pandilla (pahn-dee-yah) Feminine noun - gang

pareja (pah-reh-hah) Feminine noun - partners

patada (pah-tah-dah) Feminine noun - kick

pelea (peh-leh-ah) Feminine noun - fight

pelear (peh-leh-ahr) Intransitive verb - to fight

pesadas (peh-sahr) Intransitive verb - to be heavy

pórtense (pohr-tin-sah) Transitive verb - to carry

pugilista (poo-hill-ees-tah) Masculine or Feminine noun - boxer pulga (pool-gah) Feminine noun - flea

puños (poo-nyoh) Masculine noun - fist

rabioso (rrah-byoh-soh) Adjective - rabid

realizaban (rreh-ah-lee-sah-bahn) Transitive verb - to carry out

relajaron (rreh-lah-hah-rohn) Transitive verb - they relaxed

riñon (rree-nyohn) Masculine noun - kidney

rompiendo (rrohm-pehn-doh) Transitive verb - to break

rumba (rum-buh) Feminine noun - dance

rutina (rroo-tee-nah) Feminine noun - routine

Salpicaron (sahl-pee-kah-rohn) Transitive verb - they splashed

sobretodo (soh-breh-toh-doh) Masculine noun - raincoat

tarima (tah-ree-mah) Feminine noun - platform

tertulia (teh-too-lee-ah) Masculine noun - reunion, to get together

trasnochada (trahs-noh-chah-dah) Masculine noun - sleepless night

vaticano (bah-tee-cah-noh) Masculine noun - Vatican

Ven (behn) Phrase - come

vertiginosos (behr-tee-hee-noh-sohs) Adjective - fast, dizzy

Chapter 6: Señor que Camina -
The Man who Walks

Dicen que caminaba sin **rumbo** desde los 11 años y **aquel** niño **huérfano** se **convirtió** en el Señor que Camina. Su historia comienza en las remotas esquinas de las calles más peligrosas de la ciudad. Su padre lo abandonó al nacer y la madre murió cuando tenía 10 años. No tenía hermanos y nunca conoció otro familiar. Nadie se **encargó** de él. Una sóla vez lo **detuvieron** unos policías porque se estaba **robando** unas manzanas y lo **metieron** en un **orfanato** del que se escapó rápidamente.

Sin embargo ahí en ese albergue de niños abandonados pasaron una serie de eventos asombrosos que permitieron formar su carácter y su criterio. El hogar se llamaba La Casa de las Nubes. Pero podía haberse llamado Casa Tormenta ya que la horrible **matrona** Doña Gertrudis era una **déspota** con los niños. Los **maltrataba** en todas las formas de maltrato existentes. Niños de tres a diez años que los obligaba a lavar baños, **destapar cañerías**, **fregar** platos, barrer, **trapear**, hacer **mandados** al supermercado y sacar la basura. La falta o **incumplimiento** de cualquiera de estos oficios se **castigaba** dejando a los niños sin comer y sin salir de sus habitaciones a no ser que sea para más trabajos **forzosos**.

Los **azotaban** con **látigos** como si fueran **esclavos** en los tiempos de la esclavitud, los insultaba hasta **quebrarlos** y los **humillaba** hasta exprimir sus almas.

Un día dejó a un niño de 4 años sin comer y **encerrado** todo el día porque trajo seis panes en vez de ocho. Así que la vida de estos niños en ese orfanato era cualquier cosa menos vida. Ese niño llamado Joaquín se escapó del orfanato y años después sería conocido en todo el mundo como el Señor que Camina.

El Señor que Camina había recorrido a pie más de 26 países, ayudando a los niños maltratados de todo el mundo, decidido a hacer justicia por la infancia **explotada**. **Rescató** a 40 niños que trabajan esclavizados en una fábrica de **ensamblaje** de celulares en china, a 15 niños obligados a vender flores en Brasil, 8 niñas de Nepal explotadas sexualmente y el resto de niños maltratados que el Caminante salvó eran de Bolivia, Colombia, Perú, El Salvador, Venezuela, Ecuador y Haití.

El Señor que Camina se encontraba ahora llegando a la frontera de Palestina. Lo detuvieron ocho militares fuertemente armados sin explicarle nada. Lo **empujaron** le dieron patadas y un **puñetazo** pero el caminante les dió **pelea** también. Le **apuntaron** con un arma en la cabeza y le dijeron que era mejor que se **devolviera** o lo **mataban**.

El Señor que Camina solo los miraba con una sonrisa sarcástica en su **rostro**. Con toda la calma del mundo solo les decía,

Lo siento, caballeros, pero debo seguir caminando. No puedo parar y no lo voy a hacer.

Al Caminante lo **protegían** ángeles y demonios. En ese momento, apareció un Jeep de guerra con mercenarios del **ejército** de israel y comenzó una **balacera** - una verdadera masacre entre israelíes y palestinos. En medio de toda esa **sangrienta** batalla, el Señor que Camina simplemente siguió caminando **lenta** y **pausadamente** mientras dejaba atrás una estela de sangre, **balas** y muerte. De esa manera cruzaba tranquilamente a Palestina donde encontró a un niño de 10 años que limpiaba un **fusil**.

Señor que Camina: Por qué limpias un fusil?

Niño de Palestina: Porque las armas deben estar bien presentadas.

Señor que Camina: Bien, presentadas para que?

Niño de Palestina: Para **matar**.

Señor que Camina: Las armas deben estar limpias para matar? Presentar armas?

Presentarselas a quien?

Niño de Palestina: Al jefe.

Señor que Camina: ¿Cual jefe?

Niño de Palestina: Al jefe de la guerra.

Señor que Camina: El jefe de la que...un je...¿que dices niño? Dónde está ese jefe ahora? Por qué el jefe no limpia el mismo sus armas?

Niño de Palestina: El jefe no limpia las armas por eso es el jefe. Y esta no es su arma. Es mi arma.

Señor que Camina: Como que es tu arma? Cuantos años tienes?

Niño de Palestina: Diez años.

Señor que camina: ¿Cuantos niños como tú trabajan para el jefe?

Niño de Palestina: **No los he contado**, señor - pero creo que somos más o menos unos 400 niños.

El Señor que Camina guardó silencio por un rato. Sacó un **billete** de veinte dólares de su **bolsillo** y le preguntó al niño, ¿Qué te parece si te doy estos veinte dólares y además te invito a comer?

Niño de Palestina: ¿A quién tengo que matar?

Señor que Camina: No tienes que matar a nadie. Solo acompañarme a caminar.

El niño y el Caminante caminaron como caminan los piratas buscando su **tesoro**. Caminaron con la **prisa** del fugitivo y la **paciencia** de los elefantes. Caminaron por la arena entre campos **minados** y miradas desoladas. Caminaron sin la ley de **gravedad** como los astronautas. Caminaron y caminaron con esa esperanza de los que no tienen nada que perder. Pasaron pueblos y refugios, tanquetas y trincheras. Caminaron bajo el **inquietante** ruido de los helicópteros y los **disparos**. Mientras más caminaban más paz iba sintiendo el niño. Se **alejaron** lo suficiente de la zona del conflicto hasta que el señor que camina decidió que debían descansar, recuperar **fuerzas** y comenzar su plan para rescatar a los otros niños que seguían bajo la **tiranía** del jefe.

Pero primero se tenían que alimentar. El Caminante sacó de su **mochila** un bolsa con un pan de centeno y una libra de queso de **cabra**. Se escondieron en una **cueva** por las laderas de las montañas y no hicieron ninguna **fogata** porque el humo del fuego sería una señal muy evidente y revelaría su ubicación. Debían ser **cautelosos** y prudentes.

Mientras comían en silencio y recuperaban su energía ahora ya más tranquilos, el niño y el caminante conversaron por un largo rato.

Caminante: Dónde están tus padres?

Niño Palestino: A diez metros bajo tierra.

Caminante: Están presos en un **calabozo**?

Niño Palestino: Están muertos.

Caminante: ¿Tienes hermanos o hermanas?

Niño Palestino: Cada uno **huyó** de los ataques como pudo cuando los soldados entraron a la casa. Tengo una hermana pequeña de seis años y un hermano mayor de doce años, pero no tengo ni idea de donde estarán. Nunca más los volví a ver.

Caminante: Los vamos a encontrar, **ya verás**. Los vamos a encontrar.
El niño y el Caminante siguieron conversando, **ideando** una estrategia para rescatar a los hermanos del niño y a los 400 niños que están bajo el despotismo del jefe.

Caminante: **Por cierto**, aún no sé cual es tu nombre.

Niño Palestino: Me llamo Ibrhaím.

Caminante: Mi nombre es Joaquín pero todos me dicen El Señor que Camina.
Salieron de las montañas y siguieron caminando kilómetros y kilómetros. En una parte del camino, tuvieron que esconderse de nuevo. Estaba pasando una caravana de camiones y tanques repleta de soldados y levantaban mucho polvo y arena. El niño y el caminante se

camuflajearon en unos **matorrales**, sin moverse, aguantando hasta la respiración porque esos soldados están muy bien **entrenados**.

Apenas pasó la caravana de la muerte, el niño y el caminante **retomaron** su caminata. Tuvieron que esquivar minas explosivas y campos con trampas de arena. Fue necesario esconderse unas cuatro veces más hasta que llegaron al pueblo más cercano. El Señor que Camina compró más provisiones y salieron de la tienda.

Se encontraron con una **anciana** que pedía a gritos que la ayudaran. Le habían **quitado** a sus nietos - una niña de cinco años y un niño de nueve años habían sido **secuestrados** por las fuerzas militares israelíes. El niño y el Caminante buscaron los rastros y las pistas que le **proporcionó** la abuela. Buscaron por todas partes y todas las **pistas** llevaban al mismo sitio: el centro de operaciones de El Jefe donde estaban los hermanos de Ibrahim, los 400 niños de todas partes de Palestina y seguramente los **nietos** de la abuela.

Después de caminar dos horas, llegaron al ghetto, fuertemente custodiado por soldados mercenarios y asesinos a **sueldo**. Pero ya tenían un plan. El Caminante buscaría ayuda en los colectivos clandestinos de la resistencia, Ibrahim llamaría a todos los niños que aún no habían sido atrapados por El Jefe, los que estaban escondidos en los bunkers y los que **vagaban** a su suerte. Ibrahim llegaría con cuántos niños le fuera posible conseguir y le diría al jefe que los había **reclutado** y que por eso se había perdido todo un día. Mientras le **lanzaba** ese **anzuelo** al jefe, el Caminante trataría de armar un escuadrón de civiles y planificar una **emboscada** para desmantelar la banda de El Jefe.

En una sincronía y conexión perfectas el Caminante y el niño llegaron al mismo tiempo al punto de **encuentro** a una cuadra del ghetto. El caminante con doce hombres y el niño con once niños. Primero se adelantó Ibrahim con los otros niños.

Cuando los **matones** del el jefe les abrieron la puerta, el Señor que Camina entró a toda furia con los 12 hombres que le dieron una gran batalla a los mercenarios mientras el Caminante y el niño rescataban a los 400 niños y buscaban a los nietos de la abuela.

Han pasado dos años desde ese día y el Señor que Camina sigue caminando.

Preguntas - Questions

¿A qué edad empezó a caminar el Señor que Camina?

Cómo es el nombre del Señor que Camina?

¿De qué país eran las 8 niñas explotadas sexualmente?

Resumen en Ingles - English Summary

They say that he walked aimlessly since he was 11 years old, and that orphan child became the Lord who Walks. His history begins in the remote corners of the most dangerous streets of the city. His father abandoned him at birth and his mother died when he was 10 years old. He had no brothers and never met another relative. No one took care of him. Only once did some police officers stop him because he was stealing some apples and put him in an orphanage from which he quickly escaped.

However, there in that shelter of abandoned children passed a series of amazing events that allowed to form his character and criteria. The home was called The House of Clouds. But it could have been called Storm House since the horrible mistress Doña Gertrudis was a terror with the children. She mistreated them in all existing forms of abuse. Children from three to ten years were forced to wash bathrooms, uncover pipes, wash dishes, sweep, mop, run errands, and take out the trash. The lack or breach of any of these trades was punished by leaving children without food and without leaving their rooms unless it is for more forced labor.

They whipped them with whips, as if they were slaves in the times of slavery, insulted them until they broke them, and humiliated them to squeeze their souls.

One day, she left a 4-year-old boy without eating and locked up all day because he brought six loaves instead of eight. So, the life of these children in that orphanage was anything but life. That boy named Joaquin escaped from the orphanage, and years later, he would be known throughout the world as the Man who Walks.

The Walking Man had traveled more than 26 countries on foot, helping abused children around the world, and determined to do justice for exploited children. He rescued 40 children who worked enslaved in a cell phone assembly factory in China, 15 children forced to sell flowers in Brazil, 8 girls from Nepal who were sexually exploited, and the rest of the battered children that the Walker saved were from Bolivia, Colombia, Peru, El Salvador, Venezuela, Ecuador, and Haiti.

The Man who Walks was now reaching the border of Palestine. He was arrested by eight heavily armed soldiers without explaining anything. They pushed him, kicked, and punched him but the Walker fought them, too. They pointed a gun at his head and told him it was better to be returned or killed.

The Walking Man only looked at them with a sarcastic smile on his face. With all the calm in the world, he told them, "I'm sorry, gentlemen, but I must keep walking. I can't stop and I won't do it."

The Walker was protected by angels and demons. At that time, a war Jeep appeared with Israeli army mercenaries and shooting began - a real massacre between Israelis and Palestinians. In the midst of that bloody battle, the Walking Man simply kept walking slowly while leaving behind a trail of blood, bullets, and death. In that fashion, he crossed quietly to Palestine where he found a 10-year-old boy cleaning a rifle.

Man who Walks: "Why are you cleaning a rifle?"

Child of Palestine: "Because the weapons must be well presented."

Man Who Walks: "Well, presented for what?"

Child of Palestine: "To kill."

Man Who Walks: "Should weapons be clean to kill? Present arms? Present them to who?"

Child of Palestine: "To the boss."

Man who Walks: "Which boss?"

Child of Palestine: "To the war chief."

Man who Walks: "The war chief ...the war ... what do you say, boy? Where is that boss now? Why doesn't the boss clean his weapons himself?"

Child of Palestine: "The boss does not clean the weapons so he is the boss. And this is not his weapon. It is my weapon."

Man who Walks: "That is your weapon? How old are you?"

Child of Palestine: "Ten years old."

Man who Walks: "How many children like you work for the boss?"

Child of Palestine: "I have not told you, sir - but I think we are about 400 children."

The Man who Walks was silent for a while. He took a twenty-dollar bill from his pocket and asked the boy, "What do you think if I give you these twenty dollars, and I also invite you to eat?"

Child of Palestine: "Who do I have to kill?"

Man who Walks: "You don't have to kill anyone. Just join me for a walk."

The boy and the Walker walked as the pirates walk looking for their treasure.

They walked in the hurry of the fugitive and the patience of the elephants. They walked through the sand between minefields and desolate gazes. They walked without the law of gravity like astronauts. They walked and walked with that hope of those who have nothing to lose. Villages and shelters, tanks, and trenches they passed. They walked under the disturbing noise of helicopters and gunfire. The more they walked, the more peace the child felt. They moved far enough away from the conflict zone until the walking man decided they should rest, regain strength, and begin their plan to rescue the other children who were still under the tyranny of the boss.

But first, they had to eat. The Walker took a bag of rye bread and a pound of goat cheese from his backpack. They hid in a cave on the slopes of the mountains and made no campfire because the smoke from the fire would be a very obvious sign and would reveal their location. They must be cautious and prudent.

While they were eating in silence and recovering their energy, now calmer, the boy and the Walker talked for a long time.

Walker: "Where are your parents?"

Palestinian Child: "Ten meters underground."

Walker: "Are they in a dungeon?"

Palestinian Child: "They are dead."

Walker: "Do you have any brothers or sisters?"

Palestinian Child: "Each one fled the attacks as he could when the soldiers entered the house. I have a six-year-old little sister and an older brother of twelve, but I have no idea where they will be. I never saw them again."

Walker: "We will find them, you'll see. We will find them."

The boy and the Walker continued talking, devising a strategy to rescue the boy's brothers and the 400 children who are under the chief's despotism.

Walker: "By the way, I still don't know what your name is."

Palestinian Child: "My name is Ibrhaim."

Walker: "My name is Joaquin, but everyone calls me The Man who Walks."

They left the mountains and continued walking kilometers and kilometers. In one part of the road, they had to hide again. A caravan of trucks and tanks full of soldiers was passing, and they raised a lot of dust and sand. The boy and the walker camouflaged themselves in some bushes, without moving, holding their breath until those soldiers, who were very well trained, left.

As soon as the caravan of death passed, the boy and the walker resumed their walk. They had to dodge explosive mines and fields with sand traps. It was necessary to hide about four more times until they reached the nearest town. The Man who Walks bought more supplies and left the store.

They met an old woman who was screaming for help. They had taken their grandchildren, a five-year-old girl and a nine-year-old boy had been kidnapped by Israeli military forces. The boy and the Walker looked for the traces and clues provided by the grandmother. They searched everywhere and all the clues led to the same place: the chief operating center where Ibrahim's brothers, the 400 children from all over Palestine, and surely the grandmother's grandchildren were.

After walking two hours, they arrived at the ghetto, heavily guarded by mercenary soldiers and hired assassins. But they already had a plan. The Walker would seek help in the clandestine resistance groups. Ibrahim would call all the children who had not yet been caught by the war chief, those who were hidden in the bunkers and those who wandered to their fate. Ibrahim would arrive with how many children he could get and tell the boss that he had recruited them and that was why he had been lost a whole day. While throwing that hook to the boss, the Walker would try to build a squad of civilians and plan an ambush to dismantle the band of the boss.

In perfect synchrony and connection, the Walker and the child arrived at the same time at the meeting point one block from the ghetto. The Walker with twelve men and the boy with eleven children. First, Ibrahim came forward with the other children.

When the chief's thugs opened the door for them, the Man who Walks in full rage gave a great battle with the 12 men to the mercenaries while the Walker and the boy rescued the 400 children and looked for the grandma's grandchildren. Two years have passed since that day and the Man who Walks is still walking.

Vocabulario - Vocabulary

alejaron (ah-leh-hah-rohn) Transitive verb - to move away from

anciana (ahn-syah-noh) Adjective - elderly

anzuelo (ahn-sweh-loh) Masculine noun - hook

apuntaron (ah-poon-tah-rohn) Transitive verb - they aimed

aquel (ah-kehl) Adjective - that one

azotaban (ah-soh-tahr) Transitive verb - they whipped

balacera (bah-lah-seh-rah) Feminine noun - shooting

bala (bah-lah) Feminine noun - bullet

billete (bee-yeh-teh) Masculine noun - bill (money)

bolsillo (bohl-see-yoh) Masculine noun - pocket

cabra (kah-brah) Feminine noun - goat

calabozo (kah-lah-boh-soh) Masculine noun - jail

camuflajearon (camoo-flah-hee-air-ohn) Adjective - camouflaged

cañería (kah-nyeh-ree-ah) Feminine noun - pipe

castigaba (kahs-tee-gah-bah) Transitive verb - to punish

cautelosos (kow-teh-loh-soh) Adjective - cautious

convirtió (kohm-behr-teer) Transitive verb - to turn into

cueva (kweh-bah) Feminine noun - cave

déspota (dehs-poh-tah) Masculine or Feminine noun - tyrant

destapar (dehs-tah-pahr) Transitive verb - to open

detuvieron (deh-teh-neh-rohn) Transitive verb - they stopped

devolviera (deh-bohl-beh-rah) Transitive verb - to give back

disparo (dees-pah-roh) Masculine noun - shot

ejército (eh-hehr-see-toh) Masculine noun - army

emboscada (ehm-bohs-kah-dah) Feminine noun - ambush

empujaron (ehm-poo-hah-rohn) Transitive verb - they pushed

encargó (ehng-kahr-gahr) Transitive verb - he or she ordered

encerrado (ehn-seh-rrah-doh) Adjective - shut-in

encuentro (ehng-kwehn-troh) Masculine noun - meeting

ensamblaje (ehn-sahm-blah-heh) Masculine noun - assembly

entrenados (ehn-treh-nah-dohs) Transitive verb - to train

esclavo (ehs-klah-boh) Masculine or Feminine noun - slave

explotada (ehks-ploh-tahr) Transitive verb - to exploit

fogata (foh-gah-tah) Feminine noun - bonfire

forzoso (fohr-soh-soh) Adjective - obligatory

fregar (freh-gahr) Transitive verb - to clean

fuerzas (fohr-sahs) Transitive verb - you force

fusil (foo-seel) Masculine noun - rifle

gravedad (grah-beh-dahd) Feminine noun - seriousness

huérfano (wehr-fah-noh) Masculine or Feminine noun - orphan

humillaba (oo-mee-yah-bah) Transitive verb - to humiliate

huyó (weer) Intransitive verb - he or she escaped

ideando (ee-deh-ahr) Transitive verb - to devise

incumplimiento (eeng-koom-plee-myehn-toh) Masculine noun - breach

inquietante (eeng-kyeh-tahn-teh) Adjective - disturbing

lanzaba (lahn-sah-bah) Transitive verb - I throw

látigo (lah-tee-goh) Masculine noun - whip

lenta (lehn-tah) Adjective - slow

maltrataba (mahl-trah-tah-bah) Transitive verb - I mistreat

mandados (mahn-dah-dos) Transitive verb - to order

mataban (mah-tah-bahn) Transitive verb - they killed

matar (mah-tahr) Transitive verb - to kill

matone (mah-tohn-ehs) Masculine or Feminine noun - thugs

matorral (mah-toh-rrahl) Masculine noun - undergrowth, thicket

matrona (mah-troh-nah) Feminine noun - matron

metieron (meh-teh-rohn) Transitive verb - they put

minados (mee-nah-dos) Transitive verb - to undermine

mochila (moh-chee-lah) Feminine noun - backpack

nieto (nyeh-toh) Plural noun - grandchildren

No los he contado (noh lohs hey kohn-tah-doh) Phrase - You did not hear it from me

orfanato (ohr-fah-nah-toh) Masculine noun - orphanage

paciencia (pah-syehn-syah) Feminine noun - patience

pausadamente (paw-sah-dah-mehn-tey) Adverb - slowly

pelea (peh-leh-ah) Feminine noun - quarrel

pista (pees-tah) Feminine noun - trail

Por cierto (pohr syehr-toh) Phrase - by the way

prisa (pree-sah) Feminine noun - hurry

proporcionó (proh-pohr-syoh-nahr) Transitive verb - he or she provided

protegían (proh-teh-heh-ahn) Transitive verb - they protected

puñetazo (poo-nyeh-tah-soh) Masculine noun - punch

quebrarlos (keh-brahr-lohs) Transitive verb - to break

quitado (kee-tah-doh) Transitive verb - to take away

reclutado (rreh-kloo-tah-doh) Transitive verb - to take on

Rescató (rrehs-kah-toh) Transitive verb - he or she rescued

retomaron (rreh-toh-mah-rohn) Transitive verb - they resumed

robando (rroh-bahn-doh) Transitive verb - to steal

rostro (rrohs-troh) Masculine noun - face

rumbo (rroom-boh) Masculine noun - course, direction

sangrienta (sahng-gryehn-tah) Adjective - bloody

secuestrados (seh-kwehs-trahr) Transitive verb - to kidnap

sueldo (swehl-doh) Masculine noun - wage

tesoro (teh-soh-roh) Masculine noun - treasure

tiranía (tee-rah-nee-ah) Feminine noun - tyranny

trapear (trah-peh-ahr) Transitive verb - to mop

vagaban (bah-gah-bahn) Intransitive verb - they wandered

ya verás (yah beh-rahs) Phrase - you will see

Chapter 7: El Club de Jazz - The Jazz Club

Se reunían a escuchar Jazz y Blues en el bar de Natalia, jóvenes músicos con ganas de hacer y crear nuevos ritmos y melodías para darle un **aporte** nuevo al jazz y al blues. Escuchaban a Miles Davis, Charlie Parker, Louis Armstrong, Chick Corea, Paquito D´Rivera y Frank Sinatra. Noches **alocadas** de buena música y mucho vino.

El bar de Natalia era un verdadero templo de la música pero sobre todo era un lugar para crear. En las mesas había más clarinetes, saxofones, guitarras y **armónicas** que botellas de vino y cerveza. Se tocaba mucho, se bebía bastante y se hablaba mucho más todavía.

Larry Newman, Beto Lennys, Marcos Flaman y Nina Londera eran los jóvenes jazzistas que armaban las tertulias musicales en el bar de Natalia. Natalia es la hija de un famoso músico de Jazz que llegó a compartir **tarima** con Frank Sinatra. Se llamaba Santi Gorrión y **fundó** el bar de Jazz con el nombre de su hija que en ese entonces tenía 4 años. Así que el Bar de Natalia se convirtió el el mejor club de Jazz del país. Hoy Natalia tiene 25 años y **dirige** el club. Todos aman a Natalia. **Heredó** de su padre el buen gusto y la pasión por el jazz y el blues y de su mamá heredó otro tipo de cosas como la cocina de alta gastronomía gourmet y la práctica del yoga. Aunque como toda joven de 25 años amaba también el Rock, la pizza las hamburguesas y la cerveza, pero todos iban al bar por el jazz.

Se hacían unas apuestas muy locas que consistían en que debían beber grandes cantidades de vino y brandy. Entonces al estar completamente **ebrios** debían interpretar una pieza de jazz famosa con intervenciones improvisadas y **ejecutarla** a la perfección. Era la actividad preferida del club además de las veladas de jam session en vivo con jazzistas invitados que daban recitales **inolvidables**. Las conversaciones también eran memorables.

Larry: Quien se acuerda de cómo murió Charlie Parker?

Beto: Murió **riendo** y **tosiendo**.

Marcos: No fué de una **sobredosis**.

Nina: De una sobredosis de exceso de vida!

Natalia: Nadie muere de eso!

Beto: Sus biógrafos y amigos aseguran que fué en un bar como este, que simplemente se bebió no un buen **ron** sino un **inofensivo** vaso de agua fría que resultó no ser tan inofensivo. Inmediatamente comenzó a vomitar sangre, los médicos dando uno que otro diagnóstico dicen que era una **úlcera gástrica**. Los amigos que estaban con Parker esa noche en el bar intentan llevarlo al hospital pero Charlie se **negó**. Con las fuerzas que le quedaban pidió que lo llevaran a su departamento donde dos días después cuando **supuestamente** ya estaba más estable cayó **fulminado** en una silla tras el ataque de risa que le **provocó** un programa cómico de televisión.

Larry: Así que Charlie Parker murió entre la risa, la úlcera, una **neumonía** y un fallo **cardiaco** a los 34 años.

Marcos: Por tomar un vaso con agua fría? Por eso prefiero el whisky!

Natalia: Vamos, Marcos! Tu te bebes hasta el agua de los **floreros**.

Marcos: Tu no te quedas atrás, Natalia. Eres dueña de un Bar de jazz y bebes más que todos nosotros juntos!

Natalia: Solo que yo sí sé beber, cariño. No como ustedes que se vuelven bebés de **pañales** o **cavernícolas trogloditas**.

Larry: Somos músicos de jazz. Tenemos un lado **salvaje** y peligroso! Que querías?

Marcos: A propósito de borracheras esta noche, es el maratón de Ebrios Jazz verdad? Va a estar genial!

Natalia: Sí. y el invitado especial es una sorpresa que los hará caer de **espaldas** sobre sus propios **traseros**.

Nani: No me digas que invitaste al saxofonista Argentino! Es super guapo!

Beto: Tranquila, **fiera**.

Natalia: No, ese galán está fuera del país y además tiene **novia**. Invité al cineasta de **Rumanía**, Mihai Vasile, quiere **grabar** el show de Ebrios Jazz esta noche y hará un **documental**.

Natalia y los jazzistas se prepararon para la **velada** del Ebrios Jazz y **afinaron** sus instrumentos pero lo más importante del **entrenamiento**. Lo más fundamental del **ensayo** para el ebrios jazz era beber y beber y Natalia no paraba de traerles vino, brandy, whisky, cerveza y ron. Después de cuatro horas **ininterrumpidas** de **ingerir** grandes cantidades de alcohol Larry, Nina, Marcos y Beto estaban completamente borrachos.

Cada uno con sus instrumentos y probando sonido en el **escenario**, empezaron a tocar **notas** y **acordes** locos al azar para ir **calentando** mientras esperaban al público y al invitado especial de Rumania. La música ya estaba **inundando** el bar - todas sus paredes respiraban jazz. Natalia les **sirvió** un par de **tragos** más y las últimas botellas rodaron al ritmo de la batería de Beto el saxofón de Larry la guitarra de Marcos y el bajo de Nani. El padre de Natalia estaría **orgulloso** al ver a su hija creando toda una **vanguardia** con la nueva generación de músicos y convirtiendo su bar en un templo del jazz.

Fueron llegando los **melómanos entusiasmados** y curiosos porque todas las noches eran diferentes en el Bar de Natalia. En las veladas del Ebrios jazz sucedía de todo. El famoso y **polémico** director de cine Mihai Vasile ya estaba presente con sus cámara y su equipo de técnicos todo listo para el **espectáculo**. Los jazzistas y bien borrachos fueron presentados por la hermosa Natalia.

Natalia: Damas y caballeros, amantes **enloquecidos** del jazz, músicos **empedernidos**, artistas y bohemios, recibamos con un fuerte **aplauso** al cuarteto de Jazz El Sombrero de Louis Jammin Band!

Los chicos de la banda **intentaron** decir algunas palabras pero estaban tan borrachos que solo decían **incoherencias** como estas.

Larry: Es para un placer yo y mi **paraguas**! Gracias de nada hoy. Yo allá los quiero!

Beto: Sin zapatos es mejor pero me **pica** la cabeza. Daré un salto con ustedes!

Nina: Estoy enamorada de...lo que y ustedes quiénes son? Que lindos!

Marcos: En este pantalon, tengo **azúcar** pero no importa!

Natalia tuvo que intervenir debido al grado de **embriaguez** de los jazzistas y lo **explicó** de esta manera.

Natalia: Respetable público, estos caballeros cuando están ebrios no son capaces de hablar correctamente y dicen solo puras incoherencias. Pero lo que sí hacen perfectamente en ese estado etílico es tocar las mejores piezas del mejor jazz del mundo! Así que a continuación **comprobarán** que lo que digo es completamente cierto. Dicho esto solo queda decir - música señores y que viva el jazz!

Al pronunciar estas palabras El Sombrero de Louis Jammin Band comenzó a tocar. Se escucharon los aplausos y los jazzistas **desbordaron** su talento y su **virtuosismo**. La primera pieza que **interpretaron** fue *Bird of Paradise* de Charlie Parker que interpretaron **magistralmente** seguida de la hermosa *What a Wonderful World* de Louis Armstrong para seguir con el clásico *Summertime* de Ella Fitzgerald y terminar con *All Blues* de Miles Davis.

El público ovacionó, a la banda **aplaudiendo** de pie con **silbidos** y gritos de emoción, increíblemente a pesar de la borrachera. Tan grande que **cargaban** los músicos el concierto fue uno de los más asombrosos y extraordinarios de la historia del jazz. La gente de verdad se transportó por un momento a la **época dorada** del jazz como si fueran los verdaderos intérpretes de **aquellos** años.

Natalia se emocionó tanto que cerró los ojos llenos de **lágrimas**, evocó la imagen de su padre, respiró y dijo, Gracias Papá! Este es tu **legado**!

Los músicos bajaron de la **tarima** y compartieron más tragos con el público. Que estaban tan maravillados con los artistas que no paraban de invitarlos a sus mesas para conversar y compartir sus gustos por el jazz.

Natalia no paraba de tomar fotos para inmortalizar este legendario momento.

Pero lo mejor de todo fué que el cineasta de Rumania había grabado usando cuatro cámaras. Cada uno de los miembros de su equipo cinematográfico grabó desde un **ángulo** diferente del bar así pudo **captar** cada uno de los **movimientos** de los jazzistas para **inmortalizar** los mejores momentos de ese gran concierto.

La noche no terminó ahí. La fiesta del jazz siguió ya que en un **arrebato** de felicidad improvisaron un viaje a la montaña, a una cabaña de un amigo de Natalia. Por supuesto se llevaron todos sus instrumentos y buena parte de la reserva más antigua del bar - los mejores licores, vinos y whiskys, **cosecha añeja** del 1800 - para celebrar la gran noche.

Una vez ya instalados en la cabaña lo primero que hicieron fue acomodar un sitio para proyectar el documental y volver a revivir. Entre risas con buen vino y excelentes amigos, ese mágico concierto que había terminado hace apenas unas horas atrás. El video - aún así sin editar, **masterizar** y **montar** - era una verdadera obra de arte. Así que cuando el documental estuviera listo estaría en las mejores salas de cine del mundo y el Bar de Natalia y el Sombrero de Louis Jammin Band se harían famosos en todos los países del planeta tierra.

Destaparon las botellas de vino y una cosecha de la mejor Champaña. Casi al mismo tiempo, los jazzistas se **pusieron** a tocar y dejaron a todos **atónitos** al dar un concierto completamente diferente al que tocaron en el bar, con piezas aún más complejas y **consagradas dándole** a la noche un aire de festival interminable.

Preguntas - Questions

¿Como se llamaba el papá de Natalia?

¿Que instrumento toca Beto?

¿Como se llama el grupo de jazz?

Resumen en Ingles - English Summary

They met to listen to Jazz and Blues at Natalia's bar, young musicians wanting to make and create new rhythms and melodies to give a new contribution to jazz and blues. They listened to Miles Davis, Charlie

Parker, Louis Armstrong, Chick Corea, Paquito D´Rivera, and Frank Sinatra. Crazy nights of good music and lots of wine.

Natalia's bar was a true temple of music, but above all, it was a place to create. At the tables, there were more clarinets, saxophones, guitars, and harmonics than bottles of wine and beer. They played a lot, drank a lot, and talked a lot more.

Larry Newman, Beto Lennys, Marcos Flaman, and Nina Londera were the young jazz players who put together the music gatherings at Natalia's bar. Natalia is the daughter of a famous Jazz musician who came to share the stage with Frank Sinatra. His name was Santi Gorrión and he founded the Jazz bar with the name of his daughter who was 4 years old at the time. So Natalia's Bar became the best Jazz club in the country. Today, Natalia is 25 years old and runs the club. Everyone loves Natalia. She created good taste and passion for jazz and blues from her father, and from her mother, she inherited other kinds of things such as gourmet cuisine and yoga. Although like every 25-year-old, she loved rock, pizza, hamburgers, and beer, everyone went to the bar for jazz.

There were very crazy bets that consisted of drinking large quantities of wine and brandy. Then being completely drunk, they had to perform a famous jazz piece with improvised interventions and perform it perfectly. It was the club's favorite activity in addition to the live jam session evenings with guest jazz players who gave unforgettable recitals. The conversations were also memorable.

Larry: "Who remembers how Charlie Parker died?"

Beto: "He died laughing and coughing."

Marcos: "It was not an overdose."

Nina: "From an overdose of excess life!"

Natalia: "Nobody dies of that!"

Beto: "His biographers and friends say it was in a bar like this, that he simply drank not a good rum but a harmless glass of cold water that turned out not to be so harmless. Immediately began to vomit blood, doctors giving, one or another, diagnosis says it was a gastric ulcer. The friends who were with Parker that night at the bar try to take him to the hospital, but Charlie refused. With the remaining forces, he asked to be taken to his apartment where two days later, when he was supposedly more stable, he fell fulminated in a chair after the attack of laughter caused by a comedy television program."

Larry: "So, Charlie Parker died between laughter, ulcer, pneumonia, and heart failure at age 34."

Marcos: "For a glass of cold water? That's why I prefer whiskey!"

Natalia: "Come on, Marcos! You drink water from vases."

Marcos: "You don't fall far behind, Natalia. You own a jazz bar and drink more than all of us together!"

Natalia: "Only I do know how to drink, honey. Not like you who become babies of
diapers or caveman troglodytes."

Larry: "We are jazz musicians. We have a wild and dangerous side! What did you want?"

Marcos: "By the way of drunkenness tonight, it's the Jazz Drunk marathon, right? It will be great!"

Natalia: "Yes. And the special guest is a surprise that will make them fall on their backs on their own butts."

Nani: "Don't tell me you invited the Argentine saxophonist! He is super handsome!"

Beto: "Quiet, beast."

Natalia: "No, that man is out of the country and also has a girlfriend. I invited Romania's filmmaker Mihai Vasile. She wants to record the Ebrios Jazz show tonight and will make a documentary."

Natalia and the jazz players prepared for the Ebrios Jazz evening and tuned their instruments but the most important part of the training. The most fundamental part of the rehearsal for drunken jazz was drinking and drinking and Natalia kept bringing them wine, brandy, whiskey, beer, and rum. After four uninterrupted hours of ingesting large amounts of alcohol, Larry, Nina, Marcos, and Beto were completely drunk.

Each with their instruments and testing sound on stage, they began to play random crazy notes and chords to warm up while waiting for the public and the special guest of Romania. Music was already flooding the bar - all its walls breathed jazz. Natalia served them a couple more drinks and the last bottles to the rhythm of Beto's drums, Larry's saxophone, Marcos' guitar, and Nani's bass. Natalia's father would be proud to see his daughter creating a whole vanguard with the new generation of musicians and turning his bar into a jazz temple.

The enthusiastic and curious music lovers arrived, because every night, they were different at Natalia's Bar. In the evenings of Drunk jazz, everything happened. The famous and controversial film director Mihai Vasile was already present with his camera and his team of technicians all ready for the show. The jazz and well drunk were presented by the beautiful Natalia.

Natalia: Ladies and gentlemen, crazed lovers of jazz, inveterate musicians, artists, and bohemians, we welcome with loud applause the Jazz Quartet, The Hat of Louis Jammin Band!

The guys in the band tried to say a few words but they were so drunk that they only said inconsistencies like these:

Larry: "It's a pleasure for me and my umbrella! Thanks, you're welcome today. I love you right there!"

Beto: "Without shoes, it's better, but my head itches. I will take a leap with you!"

Nina: "I'm in love with...what and who are you? How cute!"

Marcos: "In these pants, I have sugar, but it doesn't matter!"

Natalia had to intervene due to the degree of drunkenness of jazz players and explained it this way:

Natalia: Respected patrons, these gentlemen, when they are drunk are not able to speak correctly and say only pure inconsistencies. But what they do perfectly in that ethyl state is to play the best pieces of the best jazz in the world! So, then you will verify that what I say is completely true. That said, it only remains to say - music gentlemen and long live jazz!

When she pronounced these words, The Hat of Louis Jammin Band began to play. The applause was heard and the jazz players overflowed their talent and virtuosity. The first piece they performed was Charlie Parker's *Bird of Paradise* that they masterfully performed followed by Louis Armstrong's beautiful *What a Wonderful World* to continue with Ella Fitzgerald's classic *Summertime* and ended with Miles Davis's *All Blues*.

The audience cheered, the band clapping their feet with whistles and shouts of emotion, incredibly, despite the drunkenness. The musicians loaded the concert greatly and were one of the most amazing and extraordinary in the history of jazz. Real people were transported for a moment to the golden age of jazz as if they were the true performers of those years.

Natalia was so excited that she closed her eyes full of tears, evoked her father's image, breathed and said, "Thank you, Dad! This is your legacy!"

The musicians got off the stage and shared more drinks with the audience. They were so amazed by the artists that they kept inviting them to their tables to talk and share their tastes for jazz. Natalia did not stop taking photos to immortalize this legendary moment.

But best of all was that the Romanian filmmaker had recorded using four cameras. Each member of his film team recorded from a different angle of the bar, so he could capture each of the movements of the jazz players to immortalize the best moments of that great concert. The night did not end there. The jazz party continued because, in an outburst of happiness, they improvised a trip to the mountain, to a cabin of a friend of Natalia. Of course, they took all their instruments and a good part of the oldest reserve in the bar - the best wine and whiskey spirits, vintage harvest from 1800 - to celebrate the great night.

Once they got everything set up in the cabin, the first thing they did was to arrange a site to screen the documentary and relive it. Amidst the laughter with good wine and excellent friends, that magical concert that had ended just a few hours ago was enjoyed. The video - still unedited, mastered, and assembled - was a true work of art. So, when the documentary was ready, it would be in the best movie theaters in the world, and the Natalia Bar and the Hat of Louis Jammin Band would become famous in every country on planet Earth.

They opened the wine bottles and harvest of the best Champagne. Almost at the same time, the jazz players began to play and left everyone stunned by giving a completely different concert than they played in the bar, with even more complex and consecrated pieces, giving the night an endless festival air.

Vocabulario - Vocabulary

acordes (ah-kohr-dehs) Transitive verb - to agree

afinaron (ah-fee-nah-rohn) Transitive verb - they tuned

alocadas (ah-loh-kah-dahs) Transitive verb - to drive crazy

añeja (ahn-yah-hah) Transitive verb - to age

ángulo (ahng-goo-loh) Masculinine noun - angle

aplaudiendo (ah-plow-dee-en-doh) Intransitive verb - to applaud

aplauso (ah-plow-soh) Masculine noun - applause

aporte (ah-pohr-teh) Masculine noun - contribution

aquellos (ah-keh-yohs) Adjective - those

armónica (ahr-moh-nee-kah) Feminine noun - harmonica

arrebato (ah-rreh-bah-toh) Masculine noun - outburst

atónito (ah-toh-nee-toh) Adjective - astonished

azúcar (ah-soo-kahr) Masculine or Feminine noun - sugar

calentando (kah-lehn-tahn-doh) Transitive verb - to heat

captar (kahp-tahr) Transitive verb - to capture

cardiaco (kahr-dee-ah-koh) Adjective - person with a heart condition

cargaban (kahr-gah-bahn) Transitive verb - loaded

cavernícola (kah-behr-nee-koh-lah) Masculine or Feminine noun - cavemen

comprobarán (kohm-proh-bahr) Transitive verb - they will check

consagradas (kohn-sah-grahs) Transitive verb - to consecrate

cosecha (koh-seh-chah) Feminine noun - harvest

dándole (dahn-doh-leh) Phrase - handing over

desbordaron (dehs-bohr-dahr) Transitive verb - they overflowed

Destaparon (dehs-tah-pah-rohn) Transitive verb - they opened

dirige (dee-ree-heer) Transitive verb - he or she manages

documental (doh-koo-mehn-tahl) Masculine noun - documentary

dorada (doh-rah-doh) Adjective - golden

ebrio (eh-bryoh) Adjective - drunk

ejecutarla (eh-heh-koo-tahr-lah) Transitive verb - to execute

embriaguez (ehm-bryah-gehs) Feminine noun - drunkenness

empedernidos (ehm-pehd-ehr-nee-dohs) Transitive verb - to harden

enloquecido (ehn-loh-keh-see-doh) Adjective - crazed

ensayo (ehn-sah-yoh) Masculine noun - rehearsal

entrenamiento (ehn-treh-nah-myehn-toh) Masculine noun - training

entusiasmados (ehn-too-syahs-mah-dohs) Transitive verb - to fill with excitement

época (eh-poh-kah) Feminine noun - period of time

escenario (eh-seh-nah-ryoh) Masculine noun - stage

espalda (ehs-pahl-dah) Feminine noun - back

espectáculo (ehs-pehk-tah-koo-loh) Masculine noun - show

explicó (ehks-plee-koh) Transitive verb - he or she explained

fiera (fyeh-rah) Feminine noun - wild beast

florero (floh-reh-roh) Masculine noun - vase

fulminado (fool-mee-nah-doh) Adjective - dead

fundó (foon-doh) Transitive verb - he or she found

gástrica (gahs-tree-kah) Adjective - gastric

grabar (grah-bahr) Transitive verb - to record

heredó (eh-reh-doh) Transitive verb - he or she inherited

incoherencia (en-coh-ree-en-cee-ah) Masculine noun - incoherent ingerir (eeng-heh-reer) Transitive verb - to ingest

ininterrumpidas (een-een-teh-rroom-pee-dahs) Adjective - uninterrupted

inmortalizar (en-mohr-tahl-ee-zahr) Adjective - to immortalize

inofensivo (een-oh-fehn-see-boh) Adjective - harmless

inolvidable (een-ohl-bee-dah-bleh) Adjective - unforgettable

intentaron (een-tehn-tah-rohn) Transitive verb - they tried

interpretaron (een-tehr-preh-tah-rohn) Transitive verb - to perform

inundando (ee-noon-dahn-doh) Transitive verb - to flood

lágrima (lah-gree-mah) Feminine noun - tear

legado (leh-gah-doh) Masculine noun - legacy

magistralmente (mah-hees-trahl-mehn-tey) Adverb - masterly

masterizar (mahs-tehr-ee-sahr) Masculine noun - master

melómano (meh-low-mah-noh) Masculine or Feminine noun - music lover

montar (mohn-tahr) Transitive verb - to put together

movimiento (moh-bee-myehn-toh) Masculine noun - movement

negó (neh-goh) Transitive verb - he or she denies

neumonía (neyoo-moh-nee-ah) Feminine noun - pneumonia

nota (noh-tah) Feminine noun - musical note

novia (noh-bee-ah) Feminine noun - girlfriend

orgulloso (ohr-goo-yoh-soh) Adjective - proud

pañales (pah-nyah-lehs) Masculine noun - diaper

paraguas (pah-rah-gwahs) Masculine noun - umbrella

polémico (poh-leh-mee-koh) Adjective - controversial

provocó (proh-boh-koh) Transitive verb - he or she caused

pusieron (poh-neh-rohn) Transitive verb - they put

riendo (rreh-eehn-doh) Intransitive verb - to laugh

ron (rrohn) Masculine noun - rum

Rumanía (rroo-mahn-ee-ah) Proper noun - Romanian

salvaje (sahl-bah-heh) Adjective - wild

silbido (seel-bee-doh) Masculine noun - whistle

sirvió (sehr-bee-oh) Transitive verb - he or she served

sobredosis (soh-breh-doh-sees) Feminine noun - overdose

supuestamente (soo-pwehs-tah-mehn-teh) Adverb - supposedly

tarima (tah-ree-mah) Feminine noun - platform

tosiendo (toh-sehn-doh) Intransitive verb - to cough

trago (trah-goh) Masculine noun - drink

traseros (trah-seh-roh) Adjective - backside, rear

troglodita (trow-low-dee-tah) Adjective - cave-dwelling

úlcera (ool-seh-rah) Feminine noun - ulcer

vanguardia (bahng-gwahr-dyah) Feminine noun - avant-garde

velada (beh-lah-dah) Feminine noun - evening

virtuosismo (veet-too-oh-sees-moh) Noun - virtuosity

Chapter 8: Los Papeles Perdidos del Poeta Maldito - The Lost Papers of the Cursed Poet

Cinco **historiadores** de **renombre** mundial fueron seleccionados por el instituto, de investigaciones literarias La Pluma de Cervantes, para encontrar los papeles perdidos de la última novela que estaba escribiendo Belso Bú el último. Escritor **maldito**, Belso Bú se encontraba trabajando en un nuevo libro sobre la **peste** medieval cuando de pronto decidió que llevaba bastante **adelantada** la novela. Se tomó una pausa para ir a comprar cigarros y cervezas, pero fue interceptado por un cadillacs negro, en el que iban tres de sus mejores amigos, el poeta Bernardo Simer, la periodista Dayana Esther y el filosófo Ateneo Gracián. Nunca más se supo nada de ellos. Los cuatro desaparecieron sin dejar **rastro**.

Cuentan que Belso Bú era muy obsesivo con sus manuscritos originales y que nunca los **dejaba** solos en ningún sitio ni por un minuto. Si tenía que salir - así sea para la esquina - **agarraba** todos sus papeles, los **metia** en una mochila y los llevaba encima. Debe ser cierto porque aquella tarde en la que salió a comprar cervezas y desapareció. También desaparecieron todos los nuevos escritos apuntes y notas en las que estaba trabajando.

El instituto La Pluma de Cervantes le encargó la importante labor de seguir el rastro de esos manuscritos a Silvana Noguera, Renzo Perdomo, Elías Cano, Belinda Verona y Eric Palmer. Los mejores investigadores literarios a nivel internacional comenzaron con una inspección en la casa del escritor.

Silvana: Aquí hay más botellas de cerveza que en la **cervecería** y el Hard Rock Café! **Que barbaridad**! Yo sería feliz con esta dosis diaria!

Renzo: Venimos por los papeles, no por las botellas. Buscamos un libro; no una **cirrosis**.

Elias: Tiene sentido si lo analizas bien. Las botellas y latas de cerveza pueden ser la **huellas** que nos **guíen** a un punto de partida. Algo por donde comenzar.

Belinda: Belso bebía con la misma rapidez con la que escribía.

Erick: Y creo que haciendo un calculo asi por encima el promedio era de cuatro botellas por página.

Silvana: A eso le llamo beber y escribir!

Erick: Bueno, por donde **empezamos**?

Belinda: Quienes eran esos amigos que lo convencieron de **montarse** en el carro?

Elias: Eran sus mejores amigo. Pero lo que hay que **averiguar** es si había alguien más en ese auto.

Silvana: Todos los **testigos** coinciden en que solo estaban tres personas en el auto. Era un cadillacs **descapotable**, se podía ver perfectamente cuántas personas habían. Creo que hay que buscar por otro sitio. En los bares por **ejemplo**.

Los investigadores literarios pasaron unas dos horas **revolviendo** toda la casa del escritor y después fueron a buscar información en los bares que frecuentaba el poeta. En los bares le dijeron que a veces él **solía** ir mucho a los **burdeles** a escribir entre prostitutas porque decía que esos **antros** eran verdaderos refugios para la calma del espíritu. El reposo del escritor - el **albergue** de sus demonios. Al menos esa era la filosofía de vida de Belso Bú. Así que fueron a los **prostíbulos** y **entrevistaron** a varias **cortesanas**.

Betsy la Calentona: Belso era un hombre muy extraño. Venía todos los días y era nuestro mejor cliente. Pero muy pocas veces solicitaba los servicios sexuales. Solo querían que le trajeran una botella tras otra y lo dejaran tranquilo escribiendo. No sé cómo se **concentraba**.

Lola la Loba: Conmigo sí se **acostó** al menos una docena de veces, pero era obsesivo con sus papeles. Me gustaba ese hombre. Muchas noches me le **entregaba** gratis. Es decente. Un buen hombre.

Cada una de las prostitutas colaboraron dando datos, pistas y **anécdotas** de gran ayuda para seguir su **búsqueda**. Lo extraño es que parecía haber más intriga y preocupación por encontrar los manuscritos del escritor y no al escritor. Los historiadores literarios se **cuestionaban** todo. ¿Ya lo dieron por muerto? Saben algo y están escondiendo información? Porque están tan **apurados** en encontrar esos papeles?

Era en realidad una novela sobre las pestes en la **Edad Media** o era un libro que escondía algún tipo de denuncia? Tendría ese libro **criptogramas** o mensajes ocultos que revelaban casos de corrupción y asesinatos por parte de los políticos o las mafias del crimen organizado. Aquí pasaba algo raro, pero al fin y al cabo a ellos los habían contratado única y exclusivamente para encontrar los papeles y no al escritor. Pero decidieron hacer su tarea para mantener tranquilas a las **autoridades** del instituto La Pluma de Cervantes y a la par iniciar una segunda investigación secreta para saber qué había pasado con Belso Bú.

Ya habían ido a su casa, a los bares y a los burdeles. Habían entrevistado a las prostitutas a los vecinos al señor del kiosko donde compraba todas las mañanas el periódico. Hablaron con las tiendas donde compraba sus cigarrillos y se reunieron con su ex novias. Tenían casi toda la ciudad **cubierta** y no habían **logrado** encontrar ni una sola pista, ni un solo indicio de donde estaban el poeta y sus papeles.

Después de mucho pensar y recorrer las calles, llegaron a la conclusión de que tenían que salir de la ciudad y seguir la investigación en otros estados. Viajar a otras ciudades o pueblos donde el poeta haya dado recitales o conferencias o simplemente se haya ido de **farra** con sus amigos. **Recorrieron** siete pueblos, cuatro casas culturales, nueve teatros y pasaban un día en cada ciudad. Una verdadera gira literaria donde conocieron una **fauna** de personajes excéntricos:

Un indigente que se sabía de memoria las **obras** de Shakespeare y una abuela de noventa años que decía que era Shirley Temple. Un ex boxeador que quería ser científico de la NASA y una **monja** que vendía marihuana. Un obeso que se hizo fakir un loco que decía que tenía pruebas de que Jim Morrison y John F Kennedy estaban vivos y vendían empanadas en una playa del caribe. Un niño que había **descifrado** la teoría de las cuerdas de los **agujeros** negros. Además **encontraron** toda clase de hojas sueltas con poemas de Belso Bú pero nada de los papeles de la novela del poeta. Uno de los poemas lo encontraron en una cafetería era una hoja pegada en el baño que decía así:

´¨El **Alacrán** de tus Sentidos¨¨

Tus sentidos **retorcidos** son un alacrán que habita mi piel

Desgarrado como una serpiente abierta por la mitad

Me pierdo en tus tormentas de noches venenosas

Y grito tu nombre con un **cuchillo** de campamento

Después de romper las paredes que sudan tu recuerdo.

Poemas como ese los encontraban en los lugares más insólitos - en los techos de los terminales de autobuses, en las ventanas de los trenes, en las mesas de los restaurantes y en algunas cervecerías.

Había algo que no **cuadraba** en todo esta historia. Ni los amigos más íntimos del poeta sabían de la desaparición de Belso Bú. Muchos hasta **aseguran** haberlo visto hace pocos días, bebiendo cerveza o en peleas de bares donde los puños, las patadas y los **botellazos** eran frecuentes, lo que quiere decir que en todo este caso alguien no estaba diciendo la verdad. Pocas personas sabían de la última novela que estaba escribiendo ni de los manuscritos perdidos. Alguien estaba ocultando algo y estos investigadores literarios estaban en medio del **huracán** de teorías y conspiraciones y cada vez estaban más cerca de encontrar la pista definitiva que los llevaría a **descifrar** el enigma de todo este misterio literario.

Silvana, Renzo, Belinda y Erick se reunieron en un apartamento que convirtieron en oficina para estudiar comparar y analizar todas las pistas que habían recolectado hasta este momento.

Perdieron la noción del tiempo y pasaron toda la noche revisando las entrevistas, las notas, los periódicos, el itinerario de todos los viajes del poeta, las distintas versiones de los amigos, los lugares a los que iba, los testimonios de sus editores y **productores**. Toda absolutamente toda la información que tenían la estaban **corroborando**. Llevaban apenas un día en ese apartamento y parecía que habían pasado meses por todo el desorden de libros cuadernos libretas periódicos notas sueltas fotos y videos.

Estaban tan concentrados que ninguno había escuchado el timbre de la puerta que ya había sonado unas tres veces seguidas fuertemente. A la cuarta campanada todos escucharon al mismo tiempo el timbre y algunos golpes en la puerta. Era como haber salido de un trance hipnótico que los tenía **sumergidos** en un laberinto de poemas versos y prosas. Silvana abrió la puerta y vió a un extraño señor todo vestido de negro con una boina como la que usan los pintores Franceses. Tenía aspecto de **Marroquí** pero hablaba un perfecto español. **Traía** consigo un amarillo

sobre en la mano. A pesar de que hablaba bien no dijo mucho. Se limitó a saludar a presentarse, dijo su nombre, Rupert Fabián. Le entregó el sobre a Silvana. No aceptó la invitación a entrar por una taza de café, ni respondió las preguntas que le hacían todos casi al mismo tiempo. Solo entregó el sobre y se fue.

Apenas Silvana cerró la puerta y abrió el sobre los demás se abrió sobre ella para ver cual era el contenido del sobre. Pero lo que había adentro era otro sobre. ¿Un sobre dentro de un sobre? *Eso es muy raro*, pensó Belinda, pero abrieron el segundo sobre tan rápido como el primero y se quedaron **estupefactos** al ver que lo que contenía el segundo sobre era solo una hoja que tenía un solo mensaje que decía:

"Están cerca. No se **desanimen**. Tomen el tren de las cinco."

Leyeron esta nota unas catorce veces hasta que salieron del asombro y de la **perplejidad** y se dieron cuenta que alguien los estaba guiando hacia alguna parte donde seguro encontrarán un **desenlace** más claro en todo ese asunto. Vieron el reloj. Eran las las 4 y 15 de la tarde. Debían **apurarse** si querían llegar a la estación de tren antes de las cinco. Dejaron todo desordenado en el apartamento y salieron corriendo a buscar un taxi. Perdieron los primeros dos y a la tercera si lograron parar uno. Le dijeron al taxista que era urgente llegar antes de las cinco a la estación. Que le pagarían el doble o el triple si **manejaba** rápido y se evitaba los **trancones de tráfico**. El taxista voló por ese dinero extra y como si fuera un corredor profesional.

Llegó a la estación de trenes sin **contratiempos** y los historiadores le pagaron tres veces más de lo que marcaba el **taxímetro**. Corrieron a tomar el tren de las cinco que ya estaba por salir. Mientras Silvana compraba los boletos los demás hacían la fila para **abordar** el vagón.

El viaje duró una hora en la que ninguno dijo nada. **Permanecieron** en silencio, cada uno sumergido en sus **pensamientos**. Cuando el tren se detuvo en la última estación y llegaron a su destino, los nervios empezaron a subir **aceleradamente**, pero trataron de mantener la calma. Cuando se **bajaron** del tren no podían creer lo que estaban viendo - era el **mismísimo** escritor, Belso Bú, vivo y en persona con su mochila de siempre en la que guardaba su manuscrito y todos sus papeles. Prendió un cigarrillo y les dijo a los investigadores, **¿Por qué tardaron tanto?**

Ninguno entendía nada.

Belso Bú: Se que les debo una explicación pero no la hay. Estaba **aburrido** y a la vez **estresado** porque no podía encontrar un final para mi novela. Así que para divertirme, inventé todo este plan.

Silvana: Eres un maldito, Belso Bú.

Preguntas - Questions

Sobre que era la novela que estaba escribiendo Belso Bú?

¿Como se llamaba el instituto que contrató a los historiadores?

Cual es el título del primer poema que encontraron?

Resumen en Ingles - English Summary

Five world-renowned historians were selected by the institute of literary research, La Penma de Cervantes, to find the lost papers of the last novel that Belso Bú was writing. Cursed writer, Belso Bú, was working on a new book about the medieval plague when he suddenly decided that he was quite ahead of schedule for the novel. He took a break to buy cigarettes and beers but was intercepted by a black Cadillac which three of his best friends, the poet Bernardo Simer, the journalist Dayana Esther, and the philosopher Athenaeum Gracian were in the car. Nothing was ever heard of them. The four disappeared without a trace.

They say that Belso Bú was very obsessive with his original manuscripts and that he never left them alone anywhere for a minute. If he had to leave - even for the corner - he grabbed all his papers, put them in a backpack, and carried them. It must be true, because that afternoon when he went out to buy beers and disappeared, the papers disappeared as well including the newly written notes that he was working on.

The La Penma de Cervantes institute entrusted the important work of following up those manuscripts to Silvana Noguera, Renzo Perdomo, Elías Cano, Belinda Verona, and Eric Palmer. The best international literary researchers began with an inspection in the writer's house.

Silvana: "Here are more beer bottles than in the brewery and Hard Rock Café! That awful! I would not be happy with this daily dose!"

Renzo: "We come for the papers, not for the bottles. We look for the book, not for cirrhosis."

Elias: "It makes sense if you analyze it well. Bottles and cans of beer can be the footprints that lead us to a starting point. Something to start with."

Belinda: "Belso drank as quickly as he wrote."

Erick: "And I think that making a calculation like that, the average was four bottles per page."

Silvana: "That's what I call drinking and writing!"

Erick: "Well, where do we start?"

Belinda: "Who were those friends who convinced him to get in the car?"

Elias: "They were his best friends. But the thing to find out is if there was anyone else in that car."

Silvana: "All witnesses agree that there were only three people in the car. It was a convertible Cadillac. You could see perfectly how many people there were. I think you have to look elsewhere. In bars, for example."

The literary researchers spent about two hours stirring the writer's house and then went to look for information in the bars frequented by the poet. In the bars, they were told that, sometimes, he used to go to brothels a lot to write among prostitutes, because he said that those clubs were true shelters for the calm of the spirit. The writer's rest - the shelter of his demons. At least, that was Belso Bu's life philosophy. So, they went to the brothels and interviewed several courtesans.

Betsy la Calentona: "Belso was a very strange man. He came every day and was our best customer. But very rarely requested sexual services. He just wanted them to bring him one bottle after another and leave him alone writing. I don't know how he concentrated."

Lola la Loba: "With me, he did go to bed at least a dozen times, but he was obsessive with his papers. I liked that man. He's decent. A good man.

Each of the prostitutes collaborated giving clues and anecdotes of great help to continue their search. The strange thing is that there seemed to be more intrigue and concern about finding the writer's manuscripts and not the writer. Literary historians questioned everything. Is he already dead? Did he know something and was hiding information? Why are you in such a hurry to find those papers? Was it really a novel about plagues in the Middle Ages or was it a book that hid some kind of complaint? That book would have cryptograms or hidden messages that revealed cases of corruption and murders by politicians or organized crime mafias.

Something strange was happening here, but after all, they had been hired only and exclusively to find the papers and not the writer. But they decided to do their homework to keep the authorities of the La Pluma de Cervantes Institute calm and, at the same time, initiate a second secret investigation to find out what had happened to Belso Bú.

They had already gone to his home, to bars, and brothels. They had interviewed the prostitutes, the neighbors, and the man of the kiosk where he bought the newspaper every morning. They talked to the stores where he bought his cigarettes and met his ex-girlfriends. They had almost the entire city covered and had failed to find a single clue, not a single hint of where the poet and his papers were.

After much thought and travel in the streets, they concluded that they had to leave the city and continue research in other states. They had to travel to other cities or towns where the poet had given recitals, conferences, or has simply gone to parties with his friends. They toured seven villages, four cultural houses, nine theaters, and spent a day in each city. A true literary tour where they met a group of eccentric characters:

A homeless man who knew Shakespeare's works by heart and a ninety-year-old grandmother who said it was Shirley Temple. A former boxer who wanted to be a NASA scientist and a nun selling marijuana. An obese man who became a madman who said he had evidence that Jim Morrison and John F. Kennedy were alive and sold empanadas on a Caribbean beach. A boy who had deciphered the String Theory of Black Holes. They also found all kinds of loose sheets with poems by Belso Bú but nothing of the poet's novel papers. One of the poems found in a cafeteria was a sheet stuck in the bathroom that read:

"The Scorpion of your Senses"

Your twisted senses are a scorpion that inhabits my skin
Torn like a snake open in half
I get lost in your storms of poisonous nights
And I shout your name with a camping knife
After breaking the walls that sweat your memory.

Poems like that were found in the most unusual places - on the roofs of bus terminals, on train windows, at restaurant tables, and in some breweries. There was something that didn't fit in this whole story. Not even the poet's closest friends knew about Belso Bú's disappearance. Many even claim to have seen it a few days ago, drinking beer or in bar fights where fists, kicks, and fights with bottles were frequent, which means that, in this case, someone was not telling the truth. Few people knew about the last novel he was writing or the lost manuscripts. Someone was hiding something and these literary researchers were in the middle of the hurricane of theories and conspiracies and were getting closer to finding the definitive clue that would lead them to decipher the enigma of all this literary mystery.

Silvana, Renzo, Belinda, and Erick met in an apartment that they turned into an office to study, compare, and analyze all the clues they had collected so far. They lost track of time and spent the whole night reviewing the interviews, the notes, the newspapers, the itinerary of all the poet's trips, the different versions of stories from his friends, the places he went to, and the testimonies of his editors and producers. Absolutely everything. All the information they had was corroborating it. They had been in that apartment for just one day, and it seemed that months had passed through the whole mess of books, notebooks, loose notes, photos, and videos.

They were so focused that none had heard the doorbell that had already rung three times in a row. At the fourth bell, everyone heard the bell at the same time and some knocks on the door. It was like coming out of a hypnotic trance that had them immersed in a maze of poems verses and prose. Silvana opened the door and saw a strange man all dressed in black with a beret like the one used by French painters. He looked like a Moroccan but spoke perfect Spanish. He had a yellow envelope in his hand. Although he spoke well, he didn't say much. He just said hello to introduce himself, and said his name, Rupert Fabian. He handed the envelope to Silvana. He did not accept the invitation to enter for a cup of coffee, nor did he answer the questions they all asked almost at the same time. He just handed over the envelope and left.

As soon as Silvana closed the door and opened the envelope, the others rushed over it to see what the contents of the envelope were. But what was inside was another envelope. An envelope inside an envelope? That is very rare, Belinda thought, but they opened the second envelope as fast as the first and were stunned to see that what contained on the second envelope was just a sheet that had a single message that said:

"They're close. Don't be discouraged. Take the five o'clock train."

They read this note fourteen times until they came out of amazement and perplexity and realized that someone was leading them somewhere where they will surely find a clearer outcome in that whole affair. They saw the clock. It was 4:15 in the afternoon. They had to hurry if they wanted to get to the train station before five. They left everything messy in the apartment and ran to get a taxi. They missed the first two, and the third one, they managed to stop. They told the taxi driver that it was urgent to arrive before five at the station. That he would be paid double or triple if he drove fast and avoided traffic jams. The taxi driver flew for that extra money and as if he were a professional broker.

He arrived at the train station smoothly and historians paid him three times more than what the meter indicated. They ran to take the five o'clock train that was about to leave. While Silvana bought the tickets, the others lined up to board the train car.

The trip lasted an hour in which no one said anything. They remained silent, each immersed in their thoughts. When the train stopped at the last station and reached their destination, the nerves began to rise rapidly, but they tried to remain calm. When they got off the train, they could not believe what they were seeing - it was the writer himself, Belso Bú, alive and in person with his usual backpack in which he kept his manuscript and all his papers. He lit a cigarette and told investigators, "Why did it take so long?"

None understood anything.

Belso Bú: "I know I owe you an explanation, but there is none. I was bored and stressed at the same time because I couldn't find an end to my novel. So to have fun, I invented this whole plan.

Silvana: You're a curse, Belso Bú.

Vocabulario - Vocabulary

abordar (ah-bohr-dahr) Transitive verb - to board

aburrido (ah-boo-rree-doh) Adjective - bored

aceleradamente (ah-cehl-ehr-ah-dah-mehn-tey) Adverb - rapidly

acostó (ah-kohs-toh) Transitive verb - to put to bed

adelantada (ah-deh-lahn-tah-dah) Adjective - advanced

agarraba (ah-gah-rrah-bah) Transitive verb - I grabbed

agujero (ah-goo-heh-roh) Masculine noun - hole

Alacrán (ah-lah-krahn) Masculine noun - scorpion

albergue (ahl-behr-geh) Masculine noun - shelter

anécdotas (ah-nehg-doh-tah) Feminine noun - anecdote

antro (ahn-troh) Masculine noun - club

apurados (ah-poo-rah-dohs) Transitive verb - to finish

apurarse (ah-poo-rahr-seh) Pronominal verb - to hurry

aseguran (ah-seh-goo-rahn) Transitive verb - they assure

autoridad (ow-toh-ree-dahd) Feminine noun - authority

averiguar (ah-beh-ree-gwahr) Transitive verb - to find out

bajaron (bah-hah-rohn) Intransitive verb - to go down

botellazo (boh-teh-yah-soh) Noun - blow with a bottle

burdel (boor-dehl) Masculine noun - brothel

búsqueda (boos-keh-dah) Feminine noun - search

cervecería (sehr-beh-seh-ree-ah) Feminine noun - brewery

cirrosis (see-rroh-sees) Feminine noun - cirrhosis

concentraba (kohn-sehn-trah-bah) Transitive verb - I concentrated

contratiempo (kohn-trah-tyehm-poh) Masculine noun - setback

corroborando (koh-rroh-boh-rahr) Transitive verb - to corroborate

cortesana (kohr-teh-sah-nah) Feminine noun - courtesan

criptogramas (cry-toh-grah-mah) Noun - cryptogram

cuadraba (kwah-drah-bah) Intransitive verb - I tallied

cubierta (koo-byehr-tah) Feminine noun - cover

cuchillo (koo-chee-yoh) Masculine noun - knife

cuestionaban (kwehs-tyoh-nah-bahn) Transitive verb - they questioned

dejaba (deh-hah-bah) Transitive verb - I left

desanimen (dehs-ah-nee-mehn) Transitive verb - they discourage

descapotable (dehs-kah-poh-tah-bleh) Adjective - convertible

descifrado (deh-see-frah-doh) Transitive verb - to decipher

desenlace (dehs-ehn-lah-seh) Masculine noun - ending

Desgarrado (dehs-gah-rrah-doh) Adjective - torn

Edad Media (eh-dahd meh-dyah) Feminine noun - Middle Ages

ejemplo   (eh-hehm-ploh)   Masculine   noun   -   example

empezamos (ehm-peh-sah-mohs) Intransitive verb - we begin

encontraron (ehn-kohn-trah-rohn) Transitive verb - they found

entregaba (ehn-treh-gahr) Transitive verb - to turn in

entrevistaron   (ehn-treh-bees-tah-rohn)   Transitive   verb   -   they interviewed

estresado (ehs-treh-sah-doh) Adjective - stressed

estupefacto (ehs-too-peh-fahk-toh) Adjective - astonished

farra (fah-rrah) Feminine noun - party

fauna (fow-nah) Feminine noun - group of people

guíen (gee-ehn) Transitive verb - they guide

historiador (ees-toh-ryah-dohr) Masculine or Feminine noun - historian

huellas (oh-yeh-ahs) Transitive verb - they tread

huracán (oo-rah-kahn) Masculine noun - hurricane

Leyeron (leh-eh-rohn) Transitive verb - they read

logrado (loh-grah-doh) Adjective - successful

maldito (mahl-dee-toh) Adjective - cursed

manejaba (mah-neh-hah-bah) Transitive verb - I handled

Marroquí (mah-rroh-kee) Adjective - Moroccan

metia (meh-tee-ah) Transitive verb - I put

mismísimo (mees-mee-see-moh) Adjective - very

monja (mohng-hah) Feminine noun - nun

montarse (mohn-tahr-seh) Pronominal verb - to mount

obras (oh-brahs) Plural noun - work

pensamiento (pehn-sah-myehn-toh) Masculine noun - thought

Permanecieron (pehr-mah-neh-seh-rohn) Intransitive verb - they stayed

perplejidad (pear-plea-he-dahd) Feminine noun - perplexity

peste (pehs-teh) Feminine noun - plague

Por qué tardaron tanto (pohr keh kay tahr-dah-rohn tahn-toe) Phrase - What took you so long?

productor (proh-dook-tohr) Adjective - producing

prostíbulos (prohs-tee-boo-loh) Masculine noun - brothel

Que barbaridad (kay bahr-bah-ree-dahd) Phrase - what nonsense

rastro (rrahs-troh) Masculine noun - trace

Recorrieron (rreh-koh-rreh-rohn) Transitive verb - to travel around

renombre (rreh-nohm-breh) Masculine noun - renown

retorcido (rreh-tohr-see-doh) Adjective - twisted

revolviendo (rreh-bohl-behn-doh) Transitive verb - to stir

sobre (soh-breh) Masculine noun - envelope

solía (soh-lehr) Intransitive verb - to use to

sumergidos (soo-mehr-hee-dohs) Transitive verb - to submerge

taxímetro (tah-cee-meh-troh) Masculine noun - taxi meter

testigo (tehs-tee-goh) Masculine or Feminine noun - witness

Traía (trah-ee-ah) Transitive verb - I brought

trancones (trahn-cohn-ehs) Masculine noun - traffic jam

English-Spanish Dictionary

advanced   -   adelantada   (ah-deh-lahn-tah-dah)

agreement   -   acuerdo(ah-kwehr-doh)

ambitious   -   ambicioso   (ahm-bee-syoh-soh)

ambush   -   emboscada   (ehm-bohs-kah-dah)

anarchist   -   anarquista   (ah-nahr-kees-tah)

anecdote   -   anécdotas   (ah-nehg-doh-tah)

angle   -   ángulo   (ahng-goo-loh)

applause   -   aplauso (ah-plow-soh)

appropriate   -   adecuada   (ah-deh-kwah-doh)

arch   -   arco   (ahr-koh)

architect   -   arquitectos   (ahr-kee-tehk-toh)

army   -   ejército (eh-hehr-see-toh)

ashtray   -   cenicero   (seh-nee-seh-roh)

assembly   -   ensamblaje   (ehn-sahm-blah-heh)

astonished   -   atónito (ah-toh-nee-toh)

at least   -   siquiera(see-kyeh-rah)

authority   -   autoridad   (ow-toh-ree-dahd)

authors   -   autores (ow-tohr)

avant-garde   -   vanguardia   (bahng-gwahr-dyah)

awning   -   toldo   (tohl-doh)

back   -   espalda (ehs-pahl-dah)

backpack   -   mochila(moh-chee-lah)

backside, rear   -   traseros(trah-seh-roh)

Balkin   -   balcánica   (bahl-cahn-ee-ko)

ball   -   pelota   (peh-loh-tah)

banquet   -   banquete   (bahng-keh-teh)

bastard   -   cabrone(kah-brohn)

battle   -   batalla (bah-tah-yah)

beforehand   -   antemano   ahn-teh-mah-noh)

behavior   -   comportamiento   (kohm-pohr-tah-myehn-toh)

beret   -   boina   (boy-nah)

bill (money)   -   billete   (bee-yeh-teh)

bite - bocado (boh-kah-doh)

bloody - sangrienta (sahng-gryehn-tah)

blow with a bottle - botellazo (boh-teh-yah-soh)

blowpipe - cerbatana (sehr-bah-tah-nah)

bonfire - fogata (foh-gah-tah)

book - libro (lee-broh)

bookmark - marcalibro (mahr-kah-lee-broh)

bored - aburrido (ah-boo-rree-doh)

boss - jefe (heh-feh)

boxer - pugilista (poo-hill-ees-tah)

branch - sucursales (soo-koor-sahl-ehs)

breach - incumplimiento (eeng-koom-plee-myehn-toh)

brewery - cervecería (sehr-beh-seh-ree-ah)

broken - rotos (row-tohs)

brothel - burdel (boor-dehl)

bullet - bala (bah-lah)

burnt - quemado (keh-mah-doh)

butterfly - mariposa (mah-ree-poh-sah)

camouflaged - camuflajearon (camoo-flah-hee-air-ohn)

candelabra - candelabro (kahn-deh-lah-broh)

caricaturist - caricaturista (ka-ree-ka-too-ree-stah)

cautious - cautelosos (kow-teh-loh-soh)

cave - cueva (kweh-bah)

cave-dwelling - troglodita (trow-low-dee-tah)

cavemen - cavernícola (kah-behr-nee-koh-lah)

chance - azar (ah-sahr)

chess - ajedrez (ah-heh-drehs)

cirrhosis - cirrosis (see-rroh-sees)

club - antro (ahn-troh)

clutches - garras (gah-rrahs)

combustible - combustible (kohm-boos-tee-bleh)

comedian - comediante (koh-meh-dyahn-teh)

commentator - comentarista (koh-mehn-tah-rees-tah)

368

Communist	-	comunista	(koh-moo-nees-tah)
compass	-	brújula (broo-hoo-lah)	
conceited	-	engreído	(ehng-greh-ee-doh)
considerably	-	considerablemente	(kohn-see-deh-
rah-bleh-mehn-teh)			
contribution	-	aporte (ah-pohr-teh)	
controversial	-	polémico	(poh-leh-mee-koh)
convertible	-	descapotable	(dehs-kah-poh-tah-
bleh)			
corner	-	rincones	(rreeng-kohn)
country	-	país	(pah-ees)
couple	-	pareja (pah-reh-hah)	
courage	-	coraje	(koh-rah-heh)
course, direction	-	rumbo (rroom-boh)	
courtesan	-	cortesana	(kohr-teh-sah-nah)
cover	-	cubierta	(koo-byehr-tah)
crazed	-	enloquecido	(ehn-loh-keh-see-doh)
cruel	-	crueles (krwehl-ehs)	
cryptogram	-	criptogramas	(cry-toh-grah-mah)
curfew	-	toque de queda (toh-keh deh keh-dah)	
cursed	-	maldito (mahl-dee-toh)	
curtain	-	cortina	(kohr-tee-nah)
daily	-	cotidiana	(koh-tee-dyah-nah)
dance	-	rumba (rum-buh)	
dead	-	fulminado	(fool-mee-nah-doh)
defeated	-	vencido (behn-see-doh)	
desolate	-	desolado	(deh-soh-lah-doh)
diaper	-	pañales (pah-nyah-lehs)	
dinner guest	-	comensales	(koh-mehn-sahl)
disappearance	-	desaparición	(dehs-ah-pah-ree-syohn)
disturbing	-	inquietante	(eeng-kyeh-tahn-teh)
documentary	-	documental	(doh-koo-mehn-tahl)
downstairs	-	piso de abajo	(pee-soh deh ah-bah-
ho)			
drawing	-	dibujos (dee-boo-hoh)	
drink	-	trago	(trah-goh)

369

drunk	-	borracho	(boh-rrah-choh)
drunkenness	-	embriaguez	(ehm-bryah-gehs)
dungeon	-	calabozo	(kah-lah-boh-soh)
duties	-	derechos	(deh-reh-chohs)
early	-	temprano	(tehm-prah-noh)
elderly	-	anciana (ahn-syah-noh)	
elf	-	duende (dwehn-deh)	
ending	-	desenlace	(dehs-ehn-lah-seh)
endless	-	interminables	(een-tehr-mee-nah-bleh)
enemy	-	enemigo	(eh-neh-mee-goh)
envelope	-	sobre	(soh-breh)
evening	-	velada (beh-lah-dah)	
example	-	ejemplo(eh-hehm-ploh)	
excited	-	emocionado	(eh-moh-syoh-nah-doh)
extraterrestrial	-	extraterrestre	(ehks-trah-teh-rrehs-treh)
face	-	rostros (rrohs-troh)	
factory	-	fábrica (fah-bree-kah)	
fan, ventilator	-	abanico (ah-bah-nee-koh)	
far away	-	lejos	(leh-hohs)
Fascist	-	fascista (fah-sees-tah)	
fast, dizzy	-	vertiginosos	(behr-tee-hee-noh-
sohs)			
fat	-	gordo	(gohr-doh)
feather	-	pluma (ploo-mah)	
fight	-	pelea	(peh-leh-ah)
fighter	-	combatiente	(kohm-bah-tyehn-teh)
filmmaker	-	cineasta	(see-neh-ahs-tah)
fist	-	puño	(poo-nyoh)
flea	-	pulga	(pool-gah)
floor, ground	-	suelo	(sweh-loh)
flower petels	-	pétalos de la flor	(peh-tah-loh
deh lah flowr)			
franchise	-	franquicia	(frahng-kee-syah)
friends	-	amistades	(ah-mees-tah-dehs)
full	-	repleto (rreh-pleh-toh)	
funny	-	jocosa (ho-koh-sah)	

furious	-	enfurecido	(ehm-foo-reh-see-doh)
gang	-	pandilla	(pahn-dee-yah)
gastric	-	gástrica	(gahs-tree-kah)
gastronomy	-	gastronomía	(gahs-troh-noh-mee-ah)
gathering	-	tertulia	(tehr-too-lyah)
ghost	-	fantasma	(fahn-tahs-mah)
girlfriend	-	novia	(noh-bee-ah)
glass, cup	-	vidrio	(bee-dryoh)
goat	-	cabra	(kah-brah)
golden	-	dorada	(doh-rah-doh)
goose	-	ganso	(gahn-soh)
grandchildren	-	nieto	(nyeh-toh)
grey	-	gris	(grees)
group of people	-	fauna	(fow-nah)
guaranteed	-	garantizadas	(gah-rahn-tee-sah-dahs)
hallway	-	pasillo	(pah-see-yoh)
hanging	-	colgada	(kohl-gah-dah)
hard-fought	-	peleado	(peh-leh-ah-doh)
hardened, veteran	-	aguerrida	(ah-goo-rree-dah)
hardly	-	apenas	(ah-peh-nahs)
harmless	-	inofensivo	(een-oh-fehn-see-boh)
harmonica	-	armónica	(ahr-moh-nee-kah)
harvest	-	cosecha	(koh-seh-chah)
haunted	-	embrujada	(ehm-broo-ha-dah)
he or she ask for	-	pidió	(peh-deer)
he or she assured	-	aseguró	(ah-seh-goo-roh)
he or she bite	-	mordió	(mohr-dee-oh)
he or she broke	-	rompió	(rrohm-peh-oh)
he or she caused	-	provocó	(proh-boh-koh)
he or she crossed	-	cruzó	(kroo-soh)
he or she crushes	-	aplasta	(ah-plahs-tahr)
he or she denies	-	negó	(neh-goh)
he or she disappeared	-	desapareció	(dehs-ah-pah-reh-seh-oh)
he or she escaped	-	huyó	(weer)

371

he or she explained	-	explicó (ehks-plee-koh)
he or she found	-	fundó (foon-doh)
he or she generates	-	genera (heh-neh-rah)
he or she grabbed	-	cogió (koh-heh-oh)
he or she happened	-	ocurrió (oh-koo-rreer)
he or she hides	-	oculta (oh-kool-tah)
he or she inherited	-	heredó (eh-reh-doh)
he or she manages	-	dirige (dee-ree-heer)
he or she moves	-	mueve (moh-beh-hey)
he or she ordered	-	encargó (ehng-kahr-gahr)
he or she provided	-	proporcionó (proh-pohr-syoh-nahr)
he or she raises	-	levanta (leh-bahn-tah)
he or she rescued	-	Rescató (rrehs-kah-toh)
he or she served	-	sirvió (sehr-bee-oh)
he or she supposes	-	supone (soo-poh-neh)
he or she take out	-	sacó (sah-koh)
he or she tires	-	cansa (kahn-sah)
height	-	altura (ahl-too-rah)
hide and seek	-	escondidas escondidas
historian	-	historiador (ees-toh-ryah-dohr)
hole	-	huecos (weh-koh)
hook	-	gancho (gahn-choh)
hope	-	esperanza (ehs-peh-rahn-sah)
hurricane	-	huracán (oo-rah-kahn)
hurry	-	prisa (pree-sah)
I barked	-	ladraba (lah-drah-bra)
I began	-	empezaba (ehm-peh-sah-bah)
I belong to	-	Pertenezco (pehr-teh-neh-sehr)
I brought	-	Traía (trah-ee-ah)
I concentrated	-	concentraba (kohn-sehn-trah-bah)
I connected	-	conectaba (koh-nehk-tah-bah)
I gave	-	regalaba (rreh-gah-lah-bah)
I grabbed	-	agarraba (ah-gah-rrah-bah)
I had	-	tuviera (too-beh-rah)
I handled	-	manejaba (mah-neh-hah-bah)

I knew	-	sabia (sah-bee-ah)
I left	-	dejaba (deh-hah-bah)
I managed	-	dirigía (dee-ree-hee-ah)
I mistreat	-	maltrataba (mahl-trah-tah-bah)
I move closer	-	acercaba (ah-sehr-kah-bah)
I prescribe	-	recitaba(rreh-see-tah-bah)
I put	-	metia (meh-tee-ah)
I questioned	-	cuestionaba (kwehs-tyoh-nah-bah)
I removed	-	quitarnos (kee-tahr-nohs)
I saw	-	veía (beh-ee-ah)
I shone	-	brillaba (bree-yah-bah)
I tallied	-	cuadraba (kwah-drah-bah)
I throw	-	lanzaba (lahn-sah-bah)
I wanted	-	quise (keh-rehr)
I worked	-	Trabajé (trah-bah-hey)
immediately	-	enseguida (ehn-seh-gee-dah)
inauguration	-	inauguración (ee-now-goo-rah-syohn)
incoherent	-	incoherencia (en-coh-ree-en-cee-ah)
Irish	-	irlandés(eer-lahn-dehs)
jail	-	calabozo (kah-lah-boh-soh)
joke	-	broma (broh-mah)
joker, comic	-	burlesca (boor-leh-ska)
juggler	-	malabarista (mah-lah-bah-rees-tah)
jump	-	brinco (breeng-koh)
kick	-	patada (pah-tah-dah)
kidney	-	riñon (rree-nyohn)
kind	-	género (heh-neh-roh)
knife	-	cuchillo (koo-chee-yoh)
lack of worry or concern	-	despreocupación (dehs-prey-ocoo-pay-see-ohn)
lamp	-	lámpara (lahm-pah-rah)
leather	-	cuero (kweh-roh)
legacy	-	legado (leh-gah-doh)
library	-	biblioteca (bee-blyoh-teh-kah)
living room	-	salones (sah-lohn)
loaded	-	cargaban (kahr-gah-bahn)

loud laugh	-	carcajada	(kahr-kah-hah-dah)
lover	-	amante (ah-mahn-teh)	
machine gun	-	ametralladoras (ah-meh-trah-yah-doh-rah)	
madness	-	locura (loh-koo-rah)	
marriage	-	matrimonio	(mah-tree-moh-nyoh)
master	-	masterizar	(mahs-tehr-ee-sahr)
masterly	-	magistralmente (mah-hees-trahl-mehn-tey)	
matron	-	matrona	(mah-troh-nah)
meeting	-	encuentro	(ehng-kwehn-troh)
Middle Ages	-	Edad Media	(eh-dahd meh-dyah)
mime	-	mimo (mee-moh)	
monster	-	monstruos	(mohns-trwoh)
mood	-	ánimo (ah-nee-moh)	
Moroccan	-	Marroquí	(mah-rroh-kee)
moustache	-	bigote (bee-goh-teh)	
movement	-	movimiento	(moh-bee-myehn-toh)
murder	-	asesinato	(ah-seh-see-nah-toh)
music lover	-	melómano	(meh-low-mah-noh)
musical note	-	nota (noh-tah)	
nearby	-	al lado (ahl lah-doh)	
neither	-	tampoco	(tahm-poh-koh)
nobility	-	grandeza	(grahn-deh-sah)
nun	-	monja (mohng-hah)	
obligatory	-	forzoso (fohr-soh-soh)	
opening	-	apertura	(ah-pehr-too-rah)
oppressed	-	oprimido	(oh-pree-mee-doh)
origin	-	procedencia	(proh-seh-dehn-syah)
orphan	-	huérfano	(wehr-fah-noh)
orphanage	-	orfanato	(ohr-fah-nah-toh)
outburst	-	arrebato	(ah-rreh-bah-toh)
overdose	-	sobredosis	(soh-breh-doh-sees)
owl	-	búho (boo-oh)	
owner	-	dueño (dweh-nyoh)	
painting	-	cuadros (kwah-drohs)	

374

partners	-	pareja (pah-reh-hah)
party	-	farra (fah-rrah)
party animals	-	fiestero (fyehs-teh-roh)
patience	-	paciencia (pah-syehn-syah)
period of time	-	época (eh-poh-kah)
perplexity	-	perplejidad (pear-plea-he-dahd)
person with a heart condition	-	cardiaco (kahr-dee-ah-koh)
philospher	-	filósofo (fee-loh-soh-foh)
pipe	-	cañería (kah-nyeh-ree-ah)
plague	-	peste (pehs-teh)
platform	-	tarima (tah-ree-mah)
pleased	-	complacido (kohm-plah-see-doh)
pneumonia	-	neumonía (neyoo-moh-nee-ah)
pocket	-	bolsillo (bohl-see-yoh)
portrait	-	retrato (rreh-trah-toh)
prank	-	travesura (trah-beh-soo-rah)
prison	-	cárcel (kahr-sehl)
prisoner	-	preso (preh-soh)
producing	-	productor (proh-dook-tohr)
project	-	proyecto (proh-yehk-toh)
proud	-	orgulloso (ohr-goo-yoh-soh)
punch	-	puñetazo (poo-nyeh-tah-soh)
quarrel	-	pelea (peh-leh-ah)
quite a lot of	-	bastante (bahs-tahn-teh)
rabid	-	rabioso (rrah-byoh-soh)
raid	-	redada (rreh-dah-dah)
raincoat	-	sobretodo (soh-breh-toh-doh)
rapidly	-	aceleradamente (ah-cehl-ehr-ah-dah-mehn-tey)
rehearsal	-	ensayo (ehn-sah-yoh)
renown	-	renombre (rreh-nohm-breh)
reunion, to get together	-	tertulia (teh-too-lee-ah)
rhythm	-	ritmo (rreet-moh)
rifle	-	fusil (foo-seel)
Romanian	-	Rumanía (rroo-mahn-ee-ah)
roof, terrace	-	terraza (teh-rrah-sah)

rope	-	cuerda (kwehr-dah)
routine	-	rutina (rroo-tee-nah)
rug	-	tapete (tah-peh-teh)
rum	-	ron (rrohn)
sad	-	triste (trees-teh)
sailor	-	marinero (mah-ree-neh-roh)
sausage	-	salchicha (sahl-chee-chah)
scene	-	escena (eh-seh-nah)
scorpion	-	Alacrán (ah-lah-krahn)
sculptor	-	escultor(ehs-kool-tohr)
search	-	búsqueda (boos-keh-dah)
seriousness	-	gravedad (grah-beh-dahd)
setback	-	contratiempo (kohn-trah-tyehm-poh)
sharp	-	agudo (ah-goo-doh)
shelter	-	albergue (ahl-behr-geh)
shooting	-	balacera (bah-lah-seh-rah)
shot	-	disparo (dees-pah-roh)
show	-	espectáculo (ehs-pehk-tah-koo-loh)
shut in	-	encerrado (ehn-seh-rrah-doh)
silently	-	silenciosamente(see-lehn-syoh-sah-mehn-teh)
silhouette	-	silueta (see-lweh-tah)
sinister, gloomy	-	tenebrosos (teh-neh-broh-soh)
skateboard	-	patineta (pah-tee-neh-tah)
slave	-	esclavo (ehs-klah-boh)
sleepless night	-	trasnochada (trahs-noh-chah-dah)
slow	-	lenta (lehn-tah)
slowly	-	pausadamente (paw-sah-dah-mehn-tey)
small, little	-	pequeño (peh-keh-nyoh)
smell	-	olor (oh-lohr)
some	-	algunos (ahl-goo-nohs)
sound	-	sonido (soh-nee-doh)
spasm	-	espasmo (ehs-pahs-moh)
stage	-	escenario (eh-seh-nah-ryoh)
stressed	-	estresado (ehs-treh-sah-doh)
style	-	estilo (ehs-tee-loh)

successful	-	logrado (loh-grah-doh)
sugar	-	azúcar (ah-soo-kahr)
supposedly	-	supuestamente (soo-pwehs-tah-mehn-teh)
suspenders	-	tirantes (tee-rahn-tehs)
suspicious	-	sospechosa (sohs-peh-choh-sah)
sword	-	espadas (ehs-pah-dah)
tank	-	tanque (tahng-keh)
taxi meter	-	taxímetro (tah-cee-meh-troh)
tear	-	lágrima (lah-gree-mah)
that one	-	aquel (ah-kehl)
they aimed	-	apuntaron (ah-poon-tah-rohn)
they argued	-	discutiendo (dees-koo-teer)
they assure	-	aseguran (ah-seh-goo-rahn)
they destroy	-	destrozan (dehs-troh-sah-ahn)
they discourage	-	desanimen (dehs-ah-nee-mehn)
they fell	-	caían (ka-ee-ahn)
they found	-	encontraron (ehn-kohn-trah-rohn)
they found out	-	averiguaban (ah-beh-ree-gwahr)
they guide	-	guíen (gee-ehn)
they hear	-	Oigan (oh-ee-hahn)
they improvised	-	improvisaban (eem-proh-bee-sah-bahn)
they increased	-	aumentaban (ow-mehn-tahr)
they interviewed	-	entrevistaron (ehn-treh-bees-tah-rohn)
they killed	-	mataban (mah-tah-bahn)
they lifted	-	alzaron (ahl-sah-rohn)
they love	-	aman (ah-mahn)
they managed	-	dirigieron (dee-ree-hee-rohn)
they mixed	-	mezclaron (mehs-klah-rohn)
they opened	-	Destaparon (dehs-tah-pah-rohn)
they overflowed	-	desbordaron (dehs-bohr-dahr)
they passed	-	transcurrían (trahns-koo-rree-ahn)
they placed	-	colocaron (koh-loh-kah-rohn)
they planned	-	proyectaban (proh-yehk-tah-bahn)
they protected	-	protegían (proh-teh-heh-ahn)

they pushed	-	empujaron	(ehm-poo-hah-rohn)
they put	-	metieron	(meh-teh-rohn)
they questioned	-	cuestionaban	(kwehs-tyoh-nah-bahn)
they reached	-	lograron	(loh-grah-rohn)
they read	-	Leyeron	(leh-eh-rohn)
they relaxed	-	relajaron	(rreh-lah-hah-rohn)
they represented	-	representaban	(rreh-preh-sehn-tahr)
they resumed	-	retomaron	(rreh-toh-mah-rohn)
they saw	-	vieron	(behr-ohn)
they shone	-	brillaron	(bree-yah-rohn)
they splashed	-	Salpicaron	(sahl-pee-kah-rohn)
they stayed	-	permanecieron	(pehr-mah-neh-sehr)
they stopped	-	detuvieron	(deh-teh-neh-rohn)
they threw	-	arrojaban	(ah-rroh-hah-bahn)
they tread	-	huellas	(oh-yeh-ahs)
they tried	-	intentaron	(een-tehn-tah-rohn)
they tuned	-	afinaron	(ah-fee-nah-rohn)
they wandered	-	vagaban	(bah-gah-bahn)
they went down	-	bajaron	(bah-hah-rohn)
they whipped	-	azotaban	(ah-soh-tahr)
they will check	-	comprobarán	(kohm-proh-bahr)
they would get	-	conseguirían	(kohn-seh-gee-ree-ahn)
those	-	aquellos	(ah-keh-yohs)
thought	-	pensamiento	(pehn-sah-myehn-toh)
thugs	-	matone	(mah-tohn-ehs)
to age	-	añeja	(ahn-yah-hah)
to agree	-	acordes	(ah-kohr-dehs)
to amaze	-	asombrados	(ah-sohm-brah-dohs)
to applaud	-	aplaudiendo	(ah-plow-dee-en-doh)
to be	-	siendo	(see-ehno-doh)
to be desperate	-	desesperadas	(dehs-ehs-por-ah-dahs)
to be disconcerted	-	desconcertados	(dehs-kohn-sehr-tah-dohs)
to be heavy	-	pesadas	(peh-sahr)
to be passionate about	-	apasionados	(ah-pah-syoh-nahr)
to board	-	abordar	(ah-bohr-dahr)

to break	-	rompiendo	(rrohm-pehn-doh)
to calm	-	Calmese	(kahl-mah-sey)
to capture	-	captar	(kahp-tahr)
to carry	-	pórtense	(pohr-tin-sah)
to carry out	-	realizaban	(rreh-ah-lee-sah-bahn)
to clean	-	fregar	(freh-gahr)
to climb	-	trepar	(treh-pahr)
to confront	-	enfrentados	(ehm-frehn-tah-dohs)
to consecrate	-	consagrados	(kohn-sah-grah-dohs)
to corroborate	-	corroborando	(koh-rroh-boh-rahr)
to cough	-	tosiendo	(toh-sehn-doh)
to decipher	-	descifrado	(deh-see-frah-doh)
to deliver	-	entregando	(ehn-treh-gahr)
to devastate	-	devastados	(deh-bahs-tahr)
to devise	-	ideando	(ee-deh-ahr)
to displace	-	desplazados	(dehs-plah-sahr)
to divide	-	dividirnos	(dee-bee-deer-nohs)
to dream	-	soñar	(soh-nyahr)
to drive crazy	-	enloquece	(ehn-loh-keh-sehr)
to execute	-	ejecutarla	(eh-heh-koo-tahr-lah)
to exploit	-	explotada	(ehks-ploh-tahr)
to expose	-	exponiendo	(ehks-poh-nehn-doh)
to fight	-	pelear	(peh-leh-ahr)
to fill with excitement	-	entusiasmados	(ehn-too-syahs-mah-dohs)
to find out	-	averiguar	(ah-beh-ree-gwahr)
to finish	-	apurados	(ah-poo-rah-dohs)
to flood	-	inundando	(ee-noon-dahn-doh)
to give back	-	devolviera	(deh-bohl-beh-rah)
to go down	-	bajaron	(bah-hah-rohn)
to happen	-	sucedido	(soo-seh-deh-doh)
to harden	-	empedernidos	(ehm-pehd-ehr-nee-dohs)
to have	-	teniendo	(teh-neh-doh)
to heat	-	calentando	(kah-lehn-tahn-doh)
to hit with an arrow	-	flechas	(fleh-chahr)

to humiliate	- humillaba	(oo-mee-yah-bah)
to hurry	- apurarse	(ah-poo-rahr-seh)
to immortalize	- inmortalizar	(en-mohr-tahl-ee-zahr)
to ingest	- ingerir	(eeng-heh-reer)
to keep quiet	- callados	(kah-yah-dohs)
to kidnap	- secuestrados	(seh-kwehs-trahr)
to kill	- matado	(mah-tah-doh)
to kiss each other	- besarse	(beh-sahr-seh)
to laugh	- riendo	(rreh-eehn-doh)
to marry	- casar	(kah-sahr)
to mop	- trapear	(trah-peh-ahr)
to mount	- montarse	(mohn-tahr-seh)
to move	- moverte	(moh-behr)
to move away from	- alejaron	(ah-leh-hah-rohn)
to open	- destapar	(dehs-tah-pahr)
to order	- mandados	(mahn-dah-dos)
to park	- estacionado	(ehs-tah-syoh-nah-doh)
to perform	- interpretaron	(een-tehr-preh-tah-rohn)
to prevail	- reinaba	(rrey-nah-bah)
to propose	- proponerle	(proh-poh-nehr)
to punish	- castigaba	(kahs-tee-gah-bah)
to pursue	- perseguidos	(pehr-seh-gee-dohs)
to put to bed	- acostó	(ah-kohs-toh)
to put together	- montar	(mohn-tahr)
to recite	- reconocidos	(rreh-koh-noh-seh-dohs)
to record	- grabar	(grah-bahr)
to satisfy	- satisfecho	(sah-tees-feh-cho)
to sell	- vendiendo	(behn-dehr)
to show	- mostrarles	(mohs-trahr-lehs)
to stay	- permanecido	(pehr-mah-neh-seh-doh)
to steal	- robando	(rroh-bahn-doh)
to stir	- revolviendo	(rreh-bohl-behn-doh)
to submerge	- sumergidos	(soo-mehr-hee-dohs)
to take away	- quitado	(kee-tah-doh)

to take on	-	reclutado	(rreh-kloo-tah-doh)
to take out	-	sacaremos	(sah-kah-reh-mohs)
to taste	-	degustando	(deh-goos-tahn-doh)
to tear	-	desgarrante	(dehs-gah-rrahr)
to torture	-	torturando	(tohr-too-rahn-doh)
to train	-	entrenados	(ehn-treh-nah-dohs)
to transmit	-	transmitiendo	(trahns-mee-tee-in-doh)
to travel around	-	recorrer	(rreh-koh-rrehr)
to turn in	-	entregaba	(ehn-treh-gahr)
to turn into	-	convirtió	(kohm-behr-teer)
to undermine	-	minados	(mee-nah-dos)
to use to	-	solía	(soh-lehr)
to watch, to guard	-	vigilar	(bee-hee-lahr)
to wear	-	vestidos	(behs-tee-dohs)
to withstand	-	resistiendo	(rreh-sees-teer)
to wound	-	heridos	(eh-ree-dohs)
to yell	-	gritando	(gree-tahn-doh)
tongue, language	-	lenguas	(lehng-gwah)
top	-	cima	(see-mah)
torn	-	Desgarrado	(dehs-gah-rrah-doh)
trace	-	rastro	(rrahs-troh)
traffic jam	-	trancones	(trahn-cohn-ehs)
trail	-	pista	(pees-tah)
training	-	entrenamiento	(ehn-treh-nah-myehn-toh)
treasure	-	tesoro	(teh-soh-roh)
trench	-	Trinchera	(treen-cheh-rah)
truck	-	camión	(kah-myohn)
twisted	-	retorcido	(rreh-tohr-see-doh)
tyranny	-	tiranía	(tee-rah-nee-ah)
tyrant	-	déspota	(dehs-poh-tah)
ulcer	-	úlcera	(ool-seh-rah)
umbrella	-	paraguas	(pah-rah-gwahs)
uncertain	-	incierta	(een-syehr-toh)
undergrowth, thicket	-	matorral	(mah-toh-rrahl)
unforgettable	-	inolvidable	(een-ohl-bee-dah-bleh)

uninterrupted - ininterrumpidas (een-een-teh-rroom-pee-dahs)

unusual - insólita (een-soh-lee-toh)

useless - inútil (een-oo-teel)

vase - florero (floh-reh-roh)

Vatican - vaticano (bah-tee-cah-noh)

very - mismísimo (mees-mee-see-moh)

virtuosity - virtuosismo (veet-too-oh-sees-moh)

wage - sueldo (swehl-doh)

waiter - mesonero (meh-soh-neh-roh)

wall - pared (pah-rehd)

war - guerra (geh-rrah)

warm-up - calentamiento (kah-lehn-tah-myehn-toh)

way - manera (mah-neh-rah)

we are - seamos (say-ah-mohs)

we begin - empezamos (ehm-peh-sah-mohs)

we support - apoyamos (ah-poh-yah-mohs)

we will cover - cubriremos (koo-bree-reh-mohs)

weakness - debilidades (deh-bee-lee-dahd)

whip - látigo (lah-tee-goh)

whisper - susurros(soo-soo-rroh) Masculine

whistle - silbido (seel-bee-doh)

wicked - endemoniado (ehn-deh-moh-nyah-doh)

wild - salvaje (sahl-bah-heh)

wild beast - fiera (fyeh-rah)

witness - testigo (tehs-tee-goh)

work - obras (oh-brahs)

wound - herida (eh-ree-dah)

you belong to - pertenecían (pehr-teh-neh-sehr)

you bet - apuestas (ah-pohs-tahs)

you changed - Cambiaste (kahm-byah-stey)

you cost - cuestas (kohs-tahs)

you force - fuerzas (fohr-sahs)

you go out - salgan (sahl-hahn)

you position - posiciones (poh-sih-cee-ohn-ehs)

you prescribe	-	recetas	(rreh-seh-tahs)
you roll	-	ruedas	(rroh-dahs)
you salt	-	salas	(sah-lahr)
you skate	-	patines	(pah-tee-nehs)
you stagger	-	escalones	(ehs-kah-loh-nahr)
you sweep	-	escobas	(ehs-koh-bahs)
you take turns	-	turnaban	(toor-nahr)
you used to	-	solían	(soh-lehr)
you will chew	-	máscaras	(mahs-kah-rahs)
zither	-	cítara	(cee-tah-rah)

Conclusion

Thank you for making it through to the end of *Spanish Short Stories for Intermediate Level: Improve your Spanish Listening Comprehension Skills with 7 Captivating Stories. Learn Fluent Conversation in your Car. Audiobook with Spanish Narrator.* Let's hope it was informative and able to provide you with all of the tools you need to achieve your goals whatever they may be.

The next step is to continue to practice Spanish. It is helpful to speak the language with another person, but you can also do this on your own. The more you fortify your understanding of Spanish, the more you are going to use it. When you do this, it creates a cycle which will only propel you to solidifying your knowledge of Spanish and continue to push you to learn more.

If there were any short stories you had a difficult time understanding, take time to go over those stories specifically. Again, the more you practice, the more you will learn and keep in your memory banks.

With that said, here are the answers to the questions for each of the stories:

La Vieja Biblioteca - vender limonadas y galletas; seis niños; al antiguo bibliotecario

El Restaurante de Los Sueños - El tren del sabor y el saber; el sabado; con un mimo

La Historia del Teniente Guitarra - Ventura Durrell; de 1936 a 1939; en una fábrica

Los Secretos del Escorpión - cinco comediantes; No tengo saldo; Simpatía por el Diablo de Los Rolling Stones.

Señor que Camina - A los 11 años; Joaquín; de Nepal

384

El Club de Jazz - Santi Gorrión; la bateria; El sombrero de Louis Jammin Band.

Los Papeles Perdidos del Poeta Maldito - sobre las pestes en la Edad Media; la pluma de Cervantes; el alacrán de tus sentidos

Did you get them all right? Congratulations! If you missed some, you know which stories you need to go back and practice again. Keep up the great work!

I hope you had fun while you were reading these engaging stories. Finally, if you found this book useful in any way, a review on Amazon is always appreciated!

Learn Spanish for Intermediate Level the Fast Way

Learn New Vocabulary Words and Phrases for Fluent Conversation While Killing Time in Your Car.

[Michael Navarro]

Introduction

Learn Spanish for Intermediate Level the Fast Way is a progressive language-learning program that has been produced with the needs of the intermediate learner in mind. This book expands on the previously acquired knowledge of the Spanish language and takes it to another level where the reader will be able to easily identify, practice and continue to grow his Spanish vocabulary. And he will be doing so in a way that's not only highly instructive but also entertaining, fast and easy-to-understand.

Learn Spanish for Intermediate Level the Fast Way is divided into 5 main chapters, each one dealing with a specific lesson that will invaluable in the process toward fluency. In turn, each chapter is further divided into many smaller and easily digestible lessons that will help the reader develop his language skills. You're encouraged to study this book in order, following the gradual development of the lessons and the tips that are provided throughout the book.

It's understandable that at first, you might come to the conclusion that learning Spanish is a very hard goal to achieve. But in reality, while it still calls for effort on your part, the goal of reaching fluency can be achieved if you keep practicing with the tools at your disposal and continue learning more. *Learn Spanish for Intermediate Level the Fast Way* is one of those tools that you'll come to need to achieve such a goal and improve your language skills.

To that end, *Learn Spanish for Intermediate Level the Fast Way* includes exercises at the end of each lesson to assist you solidify that freshly acquired knowledge. A simple and useful piece of text will also be a great aide in understanding how certain phrases, terms, and vocabulary are used in a casual, yet useful context. You can rest assured that all the vocabulary you'll come to see in this book, including the exercises and texts, is useful thanks in part to being up-to-date and tested by native Spanish speakers.

With *Learn Spanish for Intermediate Level the Fast Way* you'll come to enjoy and ultimately love the Spanish language! What might seem to be difficult concepts at first are explained in such a way that you'll surely appreciate, making accessible to everyone reading this book. Don't forget to practice and have fun while you embark on the amazing journey that is learning the Spanish language!

Chapter 1: *Presente Continuo:* Present Tense in Spanish; Negative Sentences; Interrogative Sentences and Uses

Part 1: Present Tense in Spanish

The Verbs *Ser* and *Estar*

Among all the verbs in Spanish, one stands out for its usefulness. You may have already learned about them previously. This are the verbs *ser* and *estar*, which is the English equivalent of the verb *to be*. These two verbs can convey the idea of location, state, and existence. Since they are very important, let's see how they are used in Spanish. Like any other verb in Spanish, they need to be conjugated in order to function properly:

I am	Yo soy
You are	Tú eres
He is	Él es
She is	Ella es
It is	Eso es
We are	Nosotros somos
You are	Ustedes son
They are	Ellos son

All of these verb conjugations don't need the personal pronoun when in a sentence. Why is that? Because the conjugation carries the information needed to establish the personal pronoun that's using it. The verb *ser* is used to describe the person or object that's using it and it also conveys the ideas of **existence, profession, nationality, materials, and possessions and to indicate where something is taking place.**

Yo soy un doctor	I am a doctor
Él es mi mejor amigo	He's my best friends
Somos del sur España	We are from southern Spain
Son mis padres	They're my parents

The verb *estar* follows a similar rule. The way it is conjugated is as follows:

Yo estoy	I am
Tú estás	You are
Él está	He is
Ella está	She is
Eso está	It is
Nosotros estamos	We are
Ustedes están	You are
Ellos están	They are

The verb *estar* conveys the basic ideas of **location, appearance, and health**

Estoy con mis padres en casa	I am with my parents at home
Estamos en la escuela	We're at school
Están muy deliciosos	They are very delicious
Este pastel está horrible	This cake is horrible
La casa está muy bonita	The house is very pretty
Está loco	He's crazy
¿Cómo está tu mamá?	How's your mother?

In order to learn the use of these verbs, some vocabulary is needed:

Professions and Occupations:

Doctor Doctora	Doctor
Profesor Profesora	Teacher
Electricista	Electrician
Carpintero Carpintera	Carpenter
Escritor Escritora	Writer
Cantante	Singer
Conductor de taxi	Taxi driver

Conductor de taxi	
Guardia de seguridad	Security guard
Presidente Presidenta	President
Bombero Bombera	Fireman
Abogado Abogada	Lawyer
Mesero Mesera	Waiter Waitress
Dentista	Dentist
Peluquero Peluquera	Hairdresser
Actor Actora	Actor Actress
Bailarín Bailarina	Dancer
Ingeniero Ingeniera	Engineer
Granjero Granjera	Farmer
Pintor Pintor	Painter
Veterinario Veterinaria	Vet

As you may have noticed, some names of occupations have a distinctive form in Spanish. This is done to have the right concordance between gender and noun. Most professions and occupations that end with −*o* only need to replace it with the letter −*a*. In most cases, when the profession already ends with an −*a*, as in the case of *dentista* and *guardia*, there's no need to change the last letter to conform it to the feminine gender.

Adjectives:

Triste	Sad
Hermoso Hermosa	Beautiful
Feo Fea	Ugly
Feliz	Happy
Cansado Cansada	Tired
Alto Alta	Tall
Enojado Enojada	Angry
Rápido Rápida	Fast
Amigable	Friendly
Amable	Kind
Paciente	Patient
Ruidoso Ruidosa	Noisy
Delicioso Deliciosa	Delicious
Inteligente	Smart

Exercise 1.1

*Fill in the following sentences with the correct form of the verb **ser**.*

Example: Ellos *están* en la iglesia

1. Nosotros _____ en el campo deportivo
2. Ellas _____ mis mejores amigas.
3. Yo _____ un profesor
4. Tú _____ un muy buen arquitecto
5. Ella _____ muy bonita
6. ¿_____ ustedes jugadores de fútbol?
7. ¿_____ usted el profesor de matemáticas?

8. Él _____ el conductor de taxi

9. Mi perrito _____ pequeño

10. Mi computadora _____ nueva.

Exercise 1.2

Interpret the following phrases into English.

1. *We are firemen*

_____

2. *I'm at home right now*

_____

3. *How are you?*

____

4. *Your sister is very smart*

____

5. *My parents are on vacation*

____

6. *The cake is delicious*

____

7. *My friend is very sad.*

____

8. *The cellphone is broken*

____

9. *The teacher is very tired.*

____

10. *People are very kind in this city*

____

The verb *estar* is also a very important verb since it's needed to form the present tense in Spanish.

Gerund Formation:

The common structure of the gerund is as follows:

Subject	Verb to be	Verb in gerund form	Complement
Sujeto	Verbo *estar*	Verbo en *gerundio*	Complemento

In order to form the present tense, regular and irregular verbs need to have certain terminations. The terminations used for the gerund are –**ando** and –**iendo.** Let's see how to form the gerund in Spanish:

Verb	Root form	Gerund form of the verb	English translation
Caminar	Camin-	Caminando	Walking
Jugar	Jug-	Jugando	Playing
Escribir	Escrib-	Escribiendo	Writing
Leer	Ley-	Leyendo	Reading
Saludar	Salud-	Saludando	Greeting
Hablar	Habl-	Hablando	Speaking
Escuchar	Escuch-	Escuchando	Hearing
Conversar	Convers-	Conversando	Talking
Saber	Sab-	Sabiendo	Knowing
Mirar	Mir-	Mirando	Seeing
Pensar	Pens-	Pensando	Thinking
Correr	Corr-	Corriendo	Running
Subir	Sub-	Subiendo	Going up
Ayudar	Ayud-	Ayudando	Helping
Cocinar	Cocin-	Cocinando	Cooking
Dibujar	Dibuj-	Dibujando	Draw
Limpiar	Limpi-	Limpiando	Clean
Hacer	Hac-	Haciendo	Doing
Estudiar	Estudi-	Estudiando	Study

As you can see, all these verbs change, and the terminations are added to convey the present tense. So, how do these verbs really look in sentences?

Yo estoy ayudando a mis padres	I'm helping my parents

Estoy conversando con mis amigos	I'm talking with my friends
Él está corriendo para atrapar el bus	He's running to catch the bus
María está escribiendo en su cuaderno	Maria is writing in her notebook.
Juan está mirando televisión.	Juan is watching TV.
Nosotros estamos esperando a nuestros padres.	We're waiting for our parents
Estamos hacienda nuestra tarea ahora mismo.	We're doing our homework right now.
Estamos jugando fútbol.	We're playing soccer.

Vocabulary:

Like in English, the present tense in Spanish is used to convey an action that is being done at the moment of speaking. Some expressions in Spanish that might appear alongside the present tense are:

Ahora mismo	Right now
En estos instantes	In this moment
Ahorita	Right now
En estos momentos	In this moment
Actualmente	Currently

Let's see some examples:

Estamos jugando tenis ahora mismo.	We're playing tennis right now.
Estamos llamando por teléfono en estos momentos.	We're calling (by phone) in this moment.
En estos instantes, el presidente está dando un discurso	In this moment, the president is giving a speech
Actualmente, estamos haciendo lo mejor que podemos.	We're currently doing the best we can.
Ahorita estoy yendo de compras con mi madre.	Right now, I'm going shopping with my mother.
No estoy trabajando en estos momentos.	I'm not working right now.

Vocabulary:

Sports:

Hago	Karate	Karate
	Ejercicio	
Juego	Fútbol	Soccer
	Tenis	Tennis
	Vóleibol	Volleyball
	Ajedrez	Chess
	Básquetbol	Basketball
	Beisbol	Baseball
	A los bolos	Bowling

Some sports don't need to have the verb *hacer* or *jugar* preceded before them. Rather, they become the verbs or use other verbs:

	Boxeo	To Box
Manejar	Bicicleta	Ride bicycle

You can also employ the verb *practicar* to indicate that you're more than just an occasional player. Depending on the context, it could mean that you're training or on your way to becoming a professional athlete.

Practico fútbol los fines de semana	I practice soccer on weekends
Ella está en su práctica de voleibol.	She's is in her volleyball training.
Estamos practicando tenis.	We're practicing tennis.
Ellos practican beisbol en la escuela	They practice baseball at school.

Exercise 1.3

Fill in the following sentences with the correct form of the verb estar and the correct form of the gerund

1. Mi papa ____ (jugar) tenis con sus amigos.

2. Mi hermana ____ (conversar) con sus amigas por teléfono

3. Yo ____ (comer) en estos momentos.

4. Mi perrito ____ (crecer) muy rápido.

5. Ellos ____ (pensar) qué van a hacer después de la escuela.

6. Nosotros ____ (hacer) la tarea que nos dejó el profesor de matemáticas.

7. Lucia y yo ____ (escuchar) música pop.

8. Ramón ____ (ayudar) a su mamá a hacer el almuerzo.

9. Mi hermano y mi papá ____ (comprar) los ingredientes para el almuerzo.

10. Mis amigos ____ (llamar) para ir a jugar fútbol.

Reading Comprehension

Fulbito

Soccer

Es un lunes como cualquier otro. Mi papá está limpiando su auto. A él le gusta mucho limpiar su auto. Él se lo compró hace muchos años. Mi mamá está haciendo el almuerzo, y no sólo eso, ella también está horneando un delicioso pastel. Lo sé porque puedo olerlo desde mi habitación. Mi hermana menor está dibujando un paisaje. Ella siempre viene a mi habitación y me muestra sus dibujos. Pienso que ella tiene mucho talento y que ella podría convertirse en una gran artista. De repente, mi mamá empieza a llamarme:

"Hijo, tus amigos te están buscando" – dice mi mamá

No esperaba a mis amigos esta tarde. De seguro están buscándome para ir a jugar fútbol. Cuando voy a la puerta de mi casa, mis amigos me dicen que ellos están llamando a todos los vecinos y amigos para jugar fútbol esta tarde.

"Esperen aquí mientras voy a cambiarme" – les digo

"No hay problema. Te esperamos." – ellos responden

No me toma mucho tiempo cambiarme de ropa. Después de solo unos minutos, pido permiso a mi mamá, salgo de mi casa y voy a jugar fútbol con todos mis amigos.

Verbos

Limpiar	To clean
Gusta	To like
Horneando	Baking
Oler	To smell
Convertirse	To become
Buscando	Searching
Esperen	To wait
Cambiar	To change
Pedir	To ask
Salgo	To go out

Nouns

Auto	Car

Pastel	Cake
Habitación	Bedroom
Dibujos	Drawings
Talento	Talento
Artista	Artist
Vecinos	Neighbors

Expresiones:

Es un lunes como cualquier otro any other	It's Monday like
De repente	All of a sudden
No me toma mucho tiempo long	It doesn't take me too
Pido permiso permission	Ask for

Preguntas

After reading this short text, try to answer the following questions:

1. ¿Qué está haciendo el papá del protagonista?
2. ¿Qué le gusta hacer al papá del protagonista?
3. ¿Qué está haciendo la mamá del protagonista?
4. ¿Qué está haciendo la hermana del protagonista?
5. ¿Quiénes vienen a buscar al protagonista, y para qué?
6. ¿Qué le dice el protagonista a sus amigos?
7. ¿Podrías decir que al protagonista le gusta jugar fútbol con sus amigos? ¿Por qué?

Part 2: Present Tense: Negative Form

Now that you know how to form the present tense in Spanish, it will come in handy to also know how to use the negative form. It's actually very simple. The structure is as follows:

Subject	No	Verb to be	Verb in present tense	Complement
Sujeto	No	Verbo *estar*	Verbo en presente continuo	Complemento
José	No	Está	Haciendo	Su tarea

Use the negative form of the present tense to negate any sentence that expresses an action that's happening at the moment of speaking.

Yo no estoy paseando a mi perro	I'm not walking my dog
Ellos no están jugando béisbol en estos momentos	They're not playing baseball at the moment.
Actualmente, no estamos dando información a ningún cliente	Currently, we're not giving information to any client
Creo que no me estás escuchando	I think you're not listening to me.
No deberías ver televisión si estás haciendo tarea.	You shouldn't watch TV if you're doing homework
No estoy escuchando música, estoy prestando atención al pronóstico.	I am not listening to music, I am paying attention to the forecast.
Creo que tu hermano te está llamando	I think your brother is calling you.
Ella está yéndose de compras con sus amigas	She's going shopping with her friends.

Vocabulary

Pasear	To walk
Información	Information
No deberías	You shouldn't
Creo que...	I think (that)...

Exercise 2.1

Fill in the following sentences with the correct form of the tense.

1. Yo ____ (no/comer) porque el almuerzo aún no está listo.
2. Ellos ____ (no/bailar) porque no saben bailar salsa.
3. Julio y yo ____ (no/presentar) nuestra tarea porque nos olvidamos de hacerla.
4. Mi prima ____ (no/ir) a su trabajo porque hoy día es feriado.
5. Mi mamá ____ (no/cocinar) en estos momentos porque ella ____ (comprar) los ingredientes en el mercado
6. Mis amigos ____ (llamar) a mi mamá para decirle que tuve un accidente.
7. Yo ____ (no/jugar) con mi gato porque él ____ (dormir).
8. Los profesores ____ (participar) en el simulacro.
9. La caja ____ (ser) llevada a la basura.
10. Mi computadora ____ (no/funcionar) ahora mismo y no sé por qué.

Vocabulary:

Salsa	Salsa dance (a style of dance common in Latin America)
Olvidar	To forget
Feriado	Holyday
Mercado	Market
Simulacro	Drill
Caja	Box
Basura	Trash/ garbage
Funcionar	To work

Exercise 2.2

Interpret the following sentences

1. Yo no estoy manejando bicicleta.
2. Mis amigos no me están buscando ahorita.
3. No sé por qué la lavadora no está funcionando.
4. Mis manos están temblando
5. Veo que estás sudando mucho.

Vocabulary:

Lavadora — Washing machine

Temblando — Trembling

Sudando — Sweating

Reading Comprehension

La Cena

Dinner

Después de que mis amigos y yo acabáramos de jugar fútbol, nos sentamos a conversar sobre la escuela y otras cosas más. Creo que nos quedamos conversando hasta las 8 de la noche. Mi mamá me había dicho que yo tenía que volver a la casa temprano, así que me despedí de mis amigos. Ellos me dijeron para jugar mañana también:

"¿Puedes venir a jugar mañana? Jugaremos fútbol y también conversaremos así como lo estamos haciendo ahorita"

Yo les respondí:

"Voy a pedir permiso a mi mamá. Ella siempre está diciéndome que yo debo hacer mis tareas primero para luego salir a jugar"

"Ok, nos avisas."

"Vale"

Cuando llegué a casa me di con la sorpresa de que mi madre había hecho la cena. Normalmente yo le ayudo a hacer la cena.

"Estoy sirviendo un plato para tu papá y para tu hermana, ¿tú también quieres un poco?" – me preguntó mi mamá.

"Quisiera cambiarme de ropa primero" – respondí

"No demores mucho"

Subí las escaleras lo más rápido que pude y me preparé para entrar a la ducha. Pero para mi sorpresa, la ducha estaba ocupada

"Juana, ¿estás tomando una ducha?" – pregunté

"Sí, estoy tomando una ducha." – respondió mi hermana

"Yo también quiero entrar. No demores mucho" – le dije

Puedo escuchar la voz de mi hermana. A ella siempre le ha gustado cantar en la ducha, y hoy día no es la excepción. El agua caliente en nuestra casa es un poco costoso, pero parece que eso no le importa mucho a mi hermana. Creo que tendré que sentarme y esperar a que ella salga. No creo que demore mucho, ¿Cuánto tiempo más se podría ella demorar?

Y así me quedé. Hasta ahorita estoy esperando a que salga mi hermana menor de la ducha. Al menos estoy descansando un poco.

Verbs

Acabáramos   Finish

Sentamos	Sit down
Me despedí	I said goodbye
Venir	To come
Diciéndome	Telling me
Avisas	Tell
Sirviendo	Serving
Quieres	Want
Tomando	Taking
Descansando	Resting
Demorar	To delay
Entrar	Enter
Quiero	To want
Esperando	Waiting

Nouns

Escuela	School
Sorpresa	Surprise
Plato	Dish (Portion of food in
a dish)	
Ropa	Clothes
Escaleras	Stairs
Ducha	Shower

Expresiones

Me di con la sorpresa	I was surprised

Preguntas

1. ¿Sobre qué estaban conversando el protagonista y sus amigos?
2. ¿Hasta qué hora se quedaron conversando?
3. ¿Qué es lo que la mamá del protagonista siempre le está diciendo?
4. ¿Qué está haciendo la mamá del protagonista cuando él llega a casa?
5. ¿Qué está haciendo la hermana del protagonista?
6. ¿Qué termina haciendo el protagonista?

Part 3: Present Tense: Interrogative Form

So far, you've been able to see how the affirmative and negative form of the present tense is formed. Now you'll see how the interrogative form of the present tense.

To form the interrogative form of the present tense, you just need to add the questions mark to the affirmative sentence.

Remember: Unlike English, Spanish needs two questions marks: "¿" at the beginning of the question, and "?" at the end.

¿	Subject	Verb to be	Verb in present tense	Complement	?
¿	María	Está	Comiendo	Con su mamá	?

How can you identify that a sentence is interrogative and not affirmative? If you're speaking, you won't be able to see the question marks, but the intonation at the end of the question is enough to tell whether the person is asking or not. You should also follow the same rule when asking. Raise your voice at the end of the question and try to give the right interrogative intonation.

Remember: Spanish also allows for "inversion." Just like in English, the verb and subject can switch places to form a question. This rule doesn't apply only to the present tense; it applies to all tenses. This is a more natural way of asking, but both ways are widely acceptable.

¿	Verb to be	Subject	Verb in present tense	Complement	?
¿	Está	María	Comiendo	Con su mama	?

How to Answer Questions in Present Tense:

Depending on the question, you can answer with a yes or no answer:

¿Está Michael haciendo su tarea?	Is Michael doing his homework?
Sí, (él) está haciendo su tarea	Yes, he's doing his homework

Have in mind that the personal pronoun "*él*" is in brackets since it can be deleted and the sentence would still be understandable.

¿Estás jugando videojuegos con tu hermano?	Are you playing videogames with your brother?
No, no estoy jugando videojuegos con mi hermano.	No, I'm not playing videogames with my brother.

If the person is asking for more information, then you'll have to give a larger answer.

Remember:

- *¿Qué?*

Use this when you want to know what the person is doing.

¿Qué estás haciendo?	What are you doing?
Estoy mirando televisión	I'm watching TV

- *¿Quién?*

Use this when you want to know about the person who's doing the action.

¿Quién está tocando la puerta?	Who is knocking at the gate?
El cartero está tocando la puerta	The mailman is knocking on the door.

¿Quién está llorando?	Who's crying?
El bebé está llorando.	The baby's crying.

- *¿Cómo?*

Use this when you want to ask about the way something's being done.

¿Cómo lo estoy haciendo?	How am I doing it?
Lo estás haciendo genial.	You're doing it great.

- *¿Cuándo?*

Use this to know about the time something's happening. It wouldn't make much sense to use it in the present tense since it's obvious the action is happening at the moment of speaking. Still, there are some phrases in present tense that can convey the idea of future tense, though this an exception rather than a rule.

¿Cuándo está partiendo el avión?	When's the plane leaving?
El avión está partiendo esta noche.	The plane is leaving tonight.

¿Cuándo están comenzando las clases?	When are the classes beginning?
Las clases están comenzando el 3 de abril.	Classes are beginning on April 3.

- *¿Dónde?*

Use this to ask about the location of the action that's taking place at the moment.

¿Dónde estás jugando con tus amigos?	Where are you playing with your friends?
Estoy jugando con mis amigos en mi casa.	I'm playing with my friends in my house.

¿Dónde está María haciendo su tarea?	Where's Maria doing her homework?
Ella está haciendo su tarea en su dormitorio.	She's doing her homework in her bedroom.

- *¿Por qué?*

Use this to ask about the reason why the action's taking place.

¿Por qué lloras?	Why are you weeping?
Porque me golpeé la pierna.	Because I hit my leg.

¿Por qué estamos viendo este programa de televisión?	Why are we watching this TV show?
Porque es mi turno de escoger qué ver en la televisión.	Because it's my turn to choose what to see on TV.

To have in mind: In Spanish, the word that's used to introduce the answer to the question *"¿Por qué...? (Why)"* might look similar but if you look closer, you'll see some important differences:

¿Por qué...?	Why...?
Porque	Because

"Porque" doesn't have a written accent and it's written altogether.

Some variations of the questions here mentioned are:

¿Con quién...? / ¿Con quiénes...?	Who with...?
¿A quién...?	Whom...?
Used to ask about the person who's with you when the action took place	
¿Con quién...? is singular	
¿Con quiénes...? is plural	
¿Con qué...?	In what
Used to ask about the instrument the person used	
¿Cuál...? / ¿Cuáles...?	Which...?
Used to ask about two or more options	
¿Qué tan (adjetivo)...?	How (adjective)...?
Used to ask about the extent to which the adjective affected the action or person.	
¿Cuál es la razón...?	What's the reason...?

¿Cuál es el motivo...?	What's the motive...?
These two expressions carry the same meaning as "¿Por qué?"	

Let's see some examples of these questions:

¿Con quién estás conversando?	Who are you talking with?
Estoy conversando con el vecino	I'm talking with the neighbor

¿A quién estás viendo?	Whom are you seeing?
Estoy viendo al professor.	I'm seeing the teacher.

¿Cuál es la ruta que debemos tomar?	What's the route we should take?
Es la ruta que aparece aquí en el mapa.	It's the route that appears here on the map.

¿Qué tan rápido está Juan corriendo?	How fast is Juan running?
Juan está corriendo rapidísimo.	Juan is running very fast.

Exercises:

Fill in the following sentences with the correct form of the present tense:

1. ¿Qué _____ (hacer/tú) afuera tan tarde?
2. ¿Dónde _____ (ustedes/practicar)?
3. ¿Con quiénes _____ (Juana/jugar) voleibol?
4. ¿Qué _____ (tú/leer)?
5. ¿Por qué _____ (tú/llorar)?
6. ¿Qué _____ (personas/hacer) afuera?
7. ¿Quién _____ (cuidar) al bebé?
8. ¿_____ (tu mamá/hacer) la cena?
9. ¿Qué _____ (tú/pensar)?
10. ¿_____ (tu/planear) en ir a la fiesta?

Reading Comprehension

Curiosidad

Curiosity

Elsa está ayudando a su mamá a cocinar. Ella no sabe mucho sobre cocina, pero su mamá está contenta de tenerla en la cocina para poder enseñarle a cocinar. La mamá de Elsa siempre cocina temprano, y hoy día no es la excepción. El único problema es que, en esta ocasión, la preparación está tomando más tiempo de lo esperado.

Elsa empieza a preguntar su mamá:

"¿Qué estamos esperando, mamá?"

"Estamos esperando a que el horno se caliente lo suficiente" – responde su mamá

"¿Hay algo más que nos falta hacer?" – pregunta Elsa

"Tenemos que limpiar los instrumentos de cocina para seguir con la preparación"

Elsa obedece a su mamá e inmediatamente va a limpiar los instrumentos de cocina Mientras ella está limpiando, ella observa a su mamá haciendo otras cosas en la cocina, así que ella le pregunta:

"¿Qué estás haciendo, mamá?"

"Estoy pelando las papas y cortando los tomates" – responde la mamá de Elsa

"¿Y qué es lo que está sonando?"

"El agua está hirviendo"

La mamá de Elsa le pide que le ayude a encender la licuadora. Elsa la trae con mucho cuidado y la conecta. Al principio, la licuadora no enciende.

"¿Qué pasa, mamá? ¿Por qué no está la licuadora funcionando?"

"No lo sé"

La mamá de Elsa empieza a buscar una solución. Después de unos minutos, ella se da cuenta que la licuadora no está bien conectada.

"Hija, no puedes conectar la licuadora de esta manera."

"Ok, mamá"

Hay que tener cuidado cuando se usan artefactos eléctricos. Tal parece que ahora Elsa ha aprendido la lección.

"¿Y para qué necesitamos la licuadora? ¿Para qué la estamos usando?" – pregunta Elsa

"Veo que tienes muchas preguntas hija, déjame responder"

La mamá de Elsa saca un libro muy grande. Es obvio que es un libro de cocina, ya que este libro tiene bastantes fotos de comida en la portada.

"Este libro me lo regaló mi mamá cuando yo era pequeña. Ella quería que yo aprendiera a preparar ricos postres tal como ella lo hacía"

"¿Qué hay en este libro?"

"En este libro encontrarás la descripción de muchas recetas y también de muchos platillos. No importa si son postres o platillos principales, lo encontrarás todo aquí. También hay una lista de todos los instrumentos que necesitarás usar."

"Muchas gracias, mamá"

"Trátalo con cuidado, por favor"

"Lo haré"

Verbs

Ayudando	Helping
Cocinar	Cook
Caliente	To heat
Limpiar	To clean
Observa	To watch
Pregunta	To ask
Encender	To turn on
Conectar	Connect
Buscar	To search
Hirviendo	Boiling
Necesitamos	To need
Usando	Using

Nouns

Excepción	Exception
Horno	Oven
Instrumentos de cocina	Cleaning tolos
Papas	Potatoes
Tomates	Tomatoes
Agua	Water
Licuadora	Blender

Expressions

Hoy día no es la excepción	Today is not the exception
Mientras	While
Tal parece que	It seems that

Preguntas:

1. ¿Qué están haciendo Elsa y su mamá?
2. ¿Cuál es el problema con la preparación?
3. ¿Qué están esperando Elsa y su mamá?
4. ¿Qué es lo que Elsa ve hacer a su mamá?
5. ¿Qué causa el sonido que Elsa escucha?
6. ¿Está funcionando la licuadora? ¿Por qué no?
7. ¿Responde la mamá de Elsa todas sus preguntas?

Chapter 2: El Imperativo: The Imperative Form in Spanish

Part 1: Affirmative Sentences

Formation of the Imperative

Like in any other language, you'll find the Spanish also has an imperative form. The imperative form in Spanish is used to direct and give commands and orders. To form the imperative form, you only need the right conjugation of the verb you want to use.

In Spanish, orders and commands can only be given to the second person, either in singular or plural; and the first person but only in its plural form.

Let's begin with the formation of the imperative having in mind the singular form of the second person, *tú*.

Imperative with *Tú*

To form the imperative, use the conjugation used for the third person in the present simple tense

- Verb: *Comer*

Verb	Third-person form	Sentence	Translation
Comer	Él come	¡Come tu almuerzo!	Eat your lunch!

- Verb *Escribir*

Verb	Third-person form	Sentence	Translation
Escribir	Él escribe	¡Escribe aquí!	Write here!

- Verb *Obedecer*

Verb	Third-person form	Sentence	Translation
Obedecer	Él obedece	¡Obedece a tus padres!	Obey your parents!

Irregular Verbs:

Some irregular verbs do not follow the same rules as regular verbs do. Some of them are

- Verb *ser*

Verb	Imperative form	Sentence	Translation
Ser	Sé	¡Sé tú mismo!	Be yourself!

Remember: Don't confuse the imperative form of the verb *ser* (to be) and the first-person conjugation of the verb *saber* (to know), even though both of them have the similar spelling and have the same pronunciation. Context is key in determining when it's either verb.

- *Yo sé la respuesta.* I know the answer.

- *¡Sé fuerte!* Be strong!

- Verb *ir*

Verb	Imperative form	Sentence	Translation
Ir	Ve	¡Ve a tu casa!	Go home!

Remember: Don't confuse the imperative form of the verb *ir* (to go) and the third-person conjugation of the verb *ver* (to see), even though both of them have the similar spelling and have the same pronunciation. Context is key in determining when it's either verb.

- *Él ve una película con su hermana.* He sees a movie with her sister.

- ¡Ve a ayudar a tu mamá! Go help your mother!

- Verb *tener*

Verb	Imperative form	Sentence	Translation
Tener	Ten	¡Ten tu dinero!	Have your money!

Also have in mind that, unlike English. Spanish uses an additional exclamation mark at the beginning of the sentence to indicate surprise, give commands or show more emotion than usual.

Imperative with *Ustedes* and *Nosotros*

To form the imperative form of regular verbs with *ustedes* and *nosotros* you first need to know about the subjunctive form in Spanish. The subjunctive form in Spanish is used to express desires, possibilities, and doubts. Even though you don't need right now to learn all the verbs in their subjunctive forms, some of them might prove to be very useful.

The imperative form of the verbs that are used with *ustedes and nosotros* have the same spelling as the verbs used in the subjunctive form:

- Verb *comer*

	Verb	Imperative form	Sentence	Translation
(Ustedes)	Comer	Coman	¡Coman su almuerzo!	Eat your lunch!
(Nosotros)	Comer	Comamos	¡Comamos ya!	Let's eat now!

- Verb *escribir*

	Verb	Imperative form	Sentence	Translation
(Ustedes)	Escribir	Escriban	¡Escriban sus nombres!	Write your names!
(Nosotros)	Escribir	Escribamos	¡Escribamos nuestros números!	Let's write our numbers!

- Verb *obedecer*

	Verb	Imperative form	Sentence	Translation
(Ustedes)	Obedecer	Obedezcan	¡Obedezcan a sus maestros!	Obey your teachers!
(Nosotros)	Obedecer	Obedezcamos	¡Obedezcamos lo que dice el capitán!	Let's obey what the captain says!

Irregular Verbs:

- The verb *ser*

(Ustedes)	Ser	Sean	¡Sean bienvenidos!	(Be) welcome!
(Nosotros)	Ser	Seamos	¡Seamos amigos!	Let's be friends!

- The verb *ir*

(Ustedes)	Ir	Vayan	¡Vayan al colegio!	Go to school!
(Nosotros)	Ir	Vamos	¡Vamos a la casa!	Let's go home!

- Verb *tener*

(Ustedes)	Tener	Tengan	¡Tengan su cambio!	Have your change!
(Nosotros)	Tener	Tengamos	¡Tengamos nuestra revancha!	Let's have our revenge!

As you have seen, the translation of the first person in the plural form (*nosotros*) begins with *Let's*.

Imperative with *Usted*

The personal pronoun *usted* is a special case. As you know, *usted* is the singular, second-person pronoun that is used to address someone with a greater level of politeness and respect. *Usted* is mostly used when talking to a teacher, older people, people you meet for the first time, authorities, and everyone you feel should be treated with respect and politeness. After a while, you might be able to address them with *tú*.

Even though *usted* carries the sense of politeness, it's not immune to receiving orders, commands, or advice. To form the imperative form with *usted*, you also need to know the subjunctive form of the verbs.

	Verb	Imperative form	Sentence	Translation
(Usted)	Hablar	Hable	¡Hable ahora!	Speak now!

The imperative is used for commands so you'll mostly see it in these cases:

- Suggestions: some suggestions are phrased in an imperative way to add strength and the need for the person to do it if he wants to reach an outcome.
  - *Agradezcamos al profesor por su ayuda.*
  - Let's thank the teacher for his help.
- Advice: the imperative form is also used to add strength to the advice
  - *Haz tu tarea antes de salir a jugar con tus amigos.*
  - Do your homework before going out to play with your friends
- Instructions: You'll note that the instructions that most instructions are in imperative mode, such as a recipe, a manual, repair instructions and more:
  - *Añada 3 tazas de agua.*
  - Add three cups of water

Let's see some of the most popular verb in their imperative form:

Verb	Usted	Ustedes	Nosotros	Translation
Hablar	*Hable*	*Hablen*	*Hablemos*	Speak
Ayudar	*Ayude*	*Ayuden*	*Ayudemos*	Help
Tocar	*Toque*	*Toquen*	*Toquemos*	Touch

Mirar	Mire	Miren	Miremos	See
Sonríe	Sonría	Sonrían	Sonriemos	Smile
Decir	Diga	Idgan	Digamos	Say
Apagar	Apague	Apaguen	Apaguemos	Turn off
Firmar	Firme	Firmen	Firmemos	Sign
Seguir	Siga	Sigan	Sigamos	Follow
Escuchar	Escuche	Escuchen	Eschemos	Listen
Entrar	Entre	Entren	Entremos	Enter
Salir	Salga	Salgan	Salgamos	Exit
Poner	Ponga	Pongan	Pongamos	Put
Hacer	Haga	Hagan	Hagamos	Do
Mover	Mueva	Muevan	Movamos	Move
Comprar	Compre	Compren	Compremos	Buy

Exercise 1.1

Fill in the following sentences with the correct form of the imperative

1. ____ (hacer/tú) toda tu tarea.
2. ____ (comer/tú) todo tu comida.
3. ¡____ (ayudar/tú) a tu papá a reparar el auto!
4. ¡____ (entra/usted) a la clase!
5. La receta dice: "____ (añadir/usted) 3 tazas de agua"
6. ¡____ (jugar/tú) con tu hermano!
7. ¡____ (respetar/ustedes) a tus mayores!
8. ¡____ (hablar/ustedes) más fuerte!

Exercise 1.2

Interpret the following sentences

1. Speak louder!
2. Do your homework!
3. Study harder!
4. Wash your clothes!
5. Tell me now!
6. Let's ask the teacher!
7. Let's play a game!
8. Use your head!
9. Think about it!
10. Do what you want!
11. ¡Mírame!
12. ¡Ven aquí!
13. ¡Vete lejos!
14. ¡Estudia para el examen!
15. ¡Olvídate de mí!

Reading Comprehension:

Mi madre

My mother

¡Mi mama es la mejor mamá del mundo! La quiero mucho, pero a veces ella me saca de quicio con tantas órdenes que me da. Ella siempre me está diciendo:

"Hijo, haz esto; hijo haz lo otro"

A veces es un poco insoportable tener que escuchar tantas órdenes en un día. Ni bien me levanto, ella ya me está mandando a hacer mis quehaceres. Todos los días que estoy de vacaciones ella siempre me dice:

"Lava los platos, haz tu cama, limpia tu cuarto, ponte a estudiar..."

No tengo problema en hacer ninguna de esas cosas, pero a veces quisiera que mi mamá no me esté recordando todo lo que tengo que hacer. Una de las cosas que más me desagradan es que cuando mi mamá me ordena:

"Cuida a tu hermanito mientras yo voy de compras"

¡Es lo peor! Mi hermano menor siempre está rompiendo todo lo que hay en la casa y nunca está tranquilo. No me deja jugar mis videojuegos ni tampoco puedo encender la televisión porque si no, él empieza a hacer berrinche para que yo le dé el control remoto:

"¡Dame el control! O si no, voy a llorar"

Al menos mi mamá me deja salir a jugar con mis amigos en la tarde después de hacer todos mis quehaceres. Mi mamá a veces me da un poco de dinero para poder salir con mis amigos. También ella cocina riquísimo, aunque a veces ella me manda a comprar a la bodega cada vez que le falta algún ingrediente.

"Anda a comprar, por favor. Compra 1 kilo de sal y trae el cambio"

¡Vaya! Espero que la tienda esté abierta. A veces, la bodega está cerrada sin ninguna razón. En ocasiones he tenido que irme muy lejos para poder comprar simples ingredientes. A veces quisiera que mi mamá no se olvide de lo que tiene que comprar. Es tan frustrante tener que ir cada vez que a ella se le olvida algo.

Al menos ya llegué a la tienda. ¡Y enhorabuena! Está abierta. El vendedor me conoce muy bien ya que yo he estado yendo a la misma bodega por bastantes años. Después de comprar todos los ingredientes necesarios, regreso a casa. No necesito tomar un bus porque mi casa está cerca de la bodega. Pero creo que me tomaré mi tiempo caminando.

Al menos la comida siempre sale deliciosa, eso es algo de lo que no me puedo quejar.

Verbs

Quiero	To love
Da	To give
Haz	To do
Levanto	To get up
Lava	to wash

Limpia	To clean
Estudiar	To study
Recordando	Remembering
Gusta	To like
Cuida	To take care of
Rompiendo	To break
Encender	To turn on
Llorar	To cry
Quejar	Complain

Nouns

Mundo	World
Órdenes	Orders
Vacaciones	Vacation
Quehaceres	House Chores
Platos	Dishes
Cama	Bed
Videojuegos	Videogames
Control Remoto	Remote Control
Dinero	Money
Bodega	Bodega (A Little Convenience Store)
Ingrediente	Ingredient

Expressions

Me saca de quicio	It makes me mad
Ni bien me levanto	As soon as I get up
Hacer berrinche	To make a tantrum

Preguntas

1. ¿Qué es lo que siempre está diciendo la mamá del protagonista?
2. ¿Por qué el protagonista dice que su mamá lo saca de quicio?
3. ¿Qué es lo que la mamá le ordena al protagonista?
4. ¿Qué es lo que no le gusta al protagonista?
5. ¿Cuál es la orden que más desagrada al protagonista?

6. Según el protagonista, ¿qué es lo que siempre está haciendo su hermano menor?

7. ¿Qué es lo que no puede hacer el protagonista cada vez que él cuida a su hermano menor?

8. ¿A dónde le manda su mamá cada vez que necesita comprar un ingrediente que se olvida?

9. ¿De qué no se puede quejar el protagonista?

Part 2: Negative Imperative Sentences

How to Form the Negative Form of the Imperative

To structure of the negative form of the imperative is the same for all personal pronouns. You just need to know the conjugation of the verbs in their subjunctive form. This applies even to *tú*.

Previously, you learned that in order to form the imperative form with the pronoun *tú*, you had to conjugate the verb as a third-person singular. Now, in negative, you only need the subjunctive form of said verb. Let's see some examples.

Pronoun	Verb	Imperative form	Translation
(Tú)	Comer	Come!	Eat
(Ustedes)	Comer	Coman	Eat
(Nosotros)	Comer	Comamos	Eat

Now, let's see these conjugation in the negative form:

Pronoun	Verb	Imperative form	Translation
(Tú)	Comer	No comas	Do not eat
(Ustedes)	Comer	No coman	Do not eat
(Nosotros)	Comer	No comamos	Do not eat

To form negative imperative sentences, just write *no* before the command.

Let's see other verbs of how negative imperative sentences can be formed with *tú*.

	Tú	Usted	Ustedes	Nosotros	Translation
Ser	No seas	No sea	No sean	No seamos	Don't be
Decir	No digas	No diga	No digan	No digamos	Don't say
Ver	No veas	No vea	No vean	No veamos	Don't see
Dar	No des	No de	No den	No demos	Don't give
Llegar	No llegues	No llegue	No lleguen	No lleguemos	Don't arrive
Llamar	No llames	No llame	No llamen	No llamemos	Don't call

425

Volver	No vuelvas	No vuelva	No vuelvan	No volvamos	Don't come back
Mirar	No mires	No mire	No miren	No miremos	Don't watch
Empezar	No empieces	No empiece	No empiecen	No empecemos	Don't begin
Buscar	No busques	No busque	No busquen	No busquemos	Don't search
Perder	No pierdas	No pierda	No pierdan	No perdamos	Don't lose
Recibir	No recibas	No reciba	No reciban	No recibamos	Don't receive
Hacer	No hagas	No haga	No hagan	No hagan	Don't do
Añadir	No añadas	No añada	No añadan	No añadamos	Don't add
Cambiar	No cambies	No cambie	No cambien	No cambien	Don't change
Suponer	No supongas	No suponga	No supongan	No supongamos	Don't suppose
Preguntar	No preguntes	No pregunte	No pregunten	No preguntemos	Don't ask
Correr	No corras	No corra	No corran	No corramos	Don't run

- ¡No corras en el pasillo!
- Don't run in the hallway!

- ¡No fume en espacio público!
- Don't smoke in public spaces!
- ¡No me llames mientras estoy trabajando!
- Don't call me while I'm at work!

- ¡No te quejes!
- Don't complain!

- ¡No me digas lo que tengo que hacer!
- Don't tell me what I have to do!

- ¡No me hables de esa manera!
- Don't talk to me like that!

- No te olvides de sacar la basura
- Don't forget to take the garbage out.

- ¡No te vayas tan lejos!
- Don't go far away!

Exercise 2.1

Fill in the following sentences with the correct negative form of the verbs

1. No te ____ (ir/tú) aún.
2. ¡No me ____ (mirar/usted) de esa manera!
3. ¡No ____ (jugar/tú) con mis sentimientos!
4. ¡No le ____ (decir/tú) al profesor!
5. ¡No ____ (hablar/tú)!
6. ¡No te ____ (perder/tú)!
7. ¡No me ____ (buscar/ustedes) cuando estoy ocupado!

Exercise 2.2

Interpret the following sentences

1. No llegues tarde, por favor
2. No seas irresponsable
3. No golpees a tu hermano
4. No hablemos mal del profesor
5. No escribas muy rápido
6. No nos digas lo que tenemos que hacer
7. No coman comida chatarra
8. No fumen
9. No compren alimentos echados a perder

Reading Comprehension

El policía

The police officer

Juan, Rodrigo y Alberto estaban caminando tranquilamente en una calle en Madrid. Ellos no sabían qué hora era pero era ya muy oscuro, así que pensaban que era un poco tarde.

"Juan, mira en tu celular qué hora es" – dice Rodrigo

"Son las 9 de la noche" – responde Juan

"Mi mamá me dijo que tengo que llegar antes de las 10 a mi casa" – añade Rodrigo

"No te preocupes, vamos a llegar a tiempo. Confía en mí" – dice Juan

Ellos siguen caminando hasta llegar a la estación de tren. Pero antes de poder entrar, ellos se dan con una sorpresa, ¡el tren está cerrado! O al menos eso es lo que parece. Ellos llegan a la entrada del terminal pero un policía los detiene:

"¡Esperen! ¡Quédense quietos! ¡No entren a la estación de tren!"

"¿Por qué no podemos entrar, oficial?"

"Ha habido un accidente hace unas horas y estamos asegurándonos de que no haya heridos. Por su seguridad, diríjanse a la siguiente estación o tomen un taxi."

"¿Hasta cuándo no podremos entrar?"

"Nadie puede entrar hasta mañana. Tienen que tomar un taxi o irse a la siguiente estación. Si no conocen donde tomar un taxi, yo los puedo guiar."

"Gracias, oficial"

Los muchachos caminan junto al oficial y llegan a un paradero de taxi. En el paradero de taxi hay bastantes personas. Muchas personas tampoco pudieron tomar el tren en la estación de tren debido al accidente. El policía los lleva hasta el paradero de taxi y les dice:

"Esperen aquí por un taxi. No suban a un taxi que está muy viejo y siempre tengan mucho cuidado. No se distraigan mucho. Estén siempre atentos a dónde el taxi los está llevando, ¿entendido?"

"Entendido, oficial. Muchas gracias"

El policía los deja en el paradero de taxi y regresa a la estación de tren. Los muchachos pueden finalmente tomar un taxi y éste los lleva a sus respectivas casas.

Verbs:

Caminando	Walking
Preocupes	To Worry
Confía	To Trust
Esperen	Wait
Entren	Enter
Podemos	Can
Tomen	Take
Conocen	Know
Guiar	Guide
Hay	There Are
Suban	Get On (According To Context)
Entendido	Understood
Asegurandonos	Making Sure

Nouns

Calle	Street
Hora	Hour
Celular	Cellphone
Casa	House
Estación De Tren	Train Station
Sorpresa	Surprise
Entrada	Entrance
Policía	Police Officer
Oficial	Another way to say Police Officer
Accidente	Accident
Seguridad	Safety/Security
Personas	People

Adjectives

Oscuro	Dark
Cerrado	Closed
Viejo	Old

Expressions

No te preocupes	Don't worry
Vamos a llegar a tiempo	We're going to arrive on time
Confía en mi	Trust in me
Quédense quietos	Stay quiet/ Stand still
Tengan mucho cuidado	Be very careful
No se distraigan	Don't get distracted

Preguntas

1. ¿Dónde estaban Juan, Rodrigo y Alberto, y qué estaban haciendo?
2. ¿Qué pregunta Rodrigo a Juan?
3. ¿Qué dice Juan a Rodrigo para que no se preocupe?
4. ¿A dónde se dirigen los tres muchachos, y a quién encuentran ahí?
5. ¿Qué les dice el policía a los tres muchachos?
6. ¿Qué pasó en la estación de tren?
7. ¿A dónde los lleva el policía?
8. ¿Qué último consejo les da el policía?

Part 3: When to Use the Imperative

As you have seen, the imperative form is widely used in a number of cases and circumstances. In this section, you'll see more details on how to use the imperative the right way and the most common scenarios where you'll see the imperative being used.

Common Cases Where the Imperative Form Is Used

There are many cases where the imperative form is used, such as

Manual

Why would you see the imperative being used in a manual? Well, a manual provides instruction and direction on how to do certain things. Usually, you will have to follow all the instructions if you want to have the outcome described in the manual. To put more emphasis and to highlight the need to follow all the instructions, these commands are presented in an imperative way. Let's see some examples:

In a Repair Manual:

- Inserte este objeto aquí.
- Insert this object here

- Abra con mucho cuidado
- Open very carefully

- Retire el plástico
- Take the plastic off

- Conecte el aparato
- Connect/Plug the device

- Desconecte el aparato
- Disconnect/Unplug the device
- Encienda/Apague el aparato
- Turn on/Turn off the device

- Llame al servicio tecnico
- Call technical service

As you can see, many of the instructions are directed to the personal pronoun *usted*, which is the formal second personal pronoun. This is to show respect to the reader.

1. A recipe

Many instructions can be found inside a cookbook. The most common of all are:

- Hierva el agua
- Boil the water

- Añada más sal/azúcar
- Add more salt/sugar

- Caliente el horno
- Heat the oven

- Espere a que esté listo
- Wait until it is ready

- Bata la crema
- Whip the cream

- Pese los ingredientes en la balanza
- Weigh the ingredients in the scales

- Saqué/retire el pastel del horno
- Take the cake out of the oven

- Corte las frutas en pequeñas piezas
- Cut the fruits into small pieces

- Limpie bien el pollo
- Clean the chicken well

2. Some Documents

Some government or formal documents need you to give certain personal information such as:

- Escriba su nombre y apellidos
- Write your name and last name

- Reponda todas las preguntas
- Answer all the questions

- Adjunte todos los documentos
- Attach all documents

- Escriba solo con lapicero azul
- Write only with a blue pen

3. Advice

Some advice might come in the form of a command, such as:

- Recuerda ir al supermercado
- Remember to go to the supermarket

- No te vayas tan lejos
- Don't go very far

- Haz todos tus quehaceres
- Do all your chores

- Estudia para el examen
- Study for the exam

- No fumes en frente de los niños

- Don't smoke in front of the kids

- Baja el volume del televisor
- Turn down the volume of the TV

- No te duermas tan tarde
- Don't go to sleep so late

- Despiértate más temprano
- Wake up earlier

Reading Comprehension

La tarea

Homework

Fabricio llega de la escuela todos los días a las 2 de la tarde. A él le gusta mucho estudian en su nueva escuela. Así es, es su nueva escuela ya que él se acaba de mudar a Málaga hace sólo 1 mes. Fabricio es el chico nuevo en su escuela secundaria. Él pensaba que iba a estar muy sólo y que nadie quería ser su amigo, pero su temor no era necesario; después de tan sólo un mes, Fabricio ha hecho muchísimos amigos.

Sus amigos lo tratan muy bien. Él se divierte con ellos en la escuela y él los ayuda con algunas tareas ya que Fabricio es un muchacho muy inteligente. Lo único que no le gusta a Fabricio sobre su nueva escuela es que los profesores siempre dejan mucha tarea. Es verdad que Fabricio es un muchacho muy inteligente, pero a él no le gusta pasarse bastantes horas haciendo tarea.

Él se acuerda que en una ocasión el profesor de matemáticas le dejo una tarea muy complicada. Y el profesor de ciencia también le deja bastante tarea.

"Resuelve estos problemas, suma, resta y divide el resultado" – murmura Fabricio

"Escribe en una hoja lo que has entendido del tema y preséntalo a la clase" – continua pensando Fabricio

A pesar de que no le gusta hacer tanta tarea, su mamá le ha dicho varias veces que él no tendrá permiso para jugar a menos que él haga termine toda la tarea del día. Cada vez que su mamá le dice eso, Fabricio siempre responde:

"Pero mamá, el profesor deja demasiada tarea, además en su clase él siempre da demasiadas órdenes. El profesor no nos deja ni siquiera conversar."

"¿En serio? ¿Y qué les dice?" – dice la mamá de Fabricio

"No hagan ruido, siéntense, no interrumpan la clase, no corran, pidan permiso para ir al baño, no se rían..."

"Pero hijo, todas esas órdenes son necesarias para que la clase funcione muy bien. Tiene que haber un orden" – responde la mamá de Fabricio

Fabricio sabe que no importa cuánto se queje, él igual tendrá que hacer la tarea que él profesor ha dejado a la clase. Fabricio se va a su habitación, abre su libro y empieza a escribir.

"Suma los siguientes número, resuelve estas ecuaciones, presenta evidencia de tu resultado..."

Verbs

Mudar	To Move
Pensaba	Think
Quería	Wanted
Ha Hecho	Has Done
Tratan	Treat
Divierte	Has Fun
Ayuda	Help
Dejan	Leave
Pasarse	Spend Time
Se Acuerda	Remember
Resuelve	Solve
Suma	Add
Resta	Take Away/Substract
Divide	Divide
Presenta	Presents
Sientense	Sit Down
Interrumpan	Interrupt
Corran	Run
Rían	Laugh
Quejar	Complain
Abrir	Open

Nouns

Escuela	School
Secundaria	High School
Chico	Guy
Amigos	Friends
Tareas	Tasks/Homework
Profesor	Teacher
Matemáticas	Math
Ciencia	Science
Clase	Class
Baño	Bathroom

Habitación	Bedroom
Libro	Book
Resultado	Result

Expresssions

Acaba De Mudar	Has Moved Recently
Ni Siquiera	Not Even
Pidan Permiso	Ask For Permission

Preguntas

1. ¿A qué hora llega Fabricio de la escuela?
2. ¿Qué le gusta a Fabricio sobre su nueva escuela?
3. ¿Qué es lo que no le gusta sobre su nueva escuela?
4. ¿Qué profesores le dejaron bastante tarea?
5. ¿Qué es lo que le ha dicho su mamá?
6. ¿Qué órdenes no le gusta a Fabricio?
7. ¿Qué le dice su mamá sobre esas órdenes?
8. ¿Qué termina haciendo Fabricio?

Chapter 3: El Futuro: Future Tense in Spanish

Part 1: How the Future Is Formed

The future does what it's supposed to do: talk about the actions that haven't happened yet. How can you form future sentences in Spanish? Before seeing how other verbs are formed, let's see how the future form of the verbs *ser* and *estar* are formed, respectively.

Conjugations of the Verbs *Ser* and *Estar*

- Verb *ser*

To form the future form of the verb *ser*, you required to have the base form. In this case, the base form is *ser*, this is usually called *infinitivo,* or *infinitive.*

Personal pronoun	Verb	Translation
Yo	Ser-é Sere	I will be
Tú	Ser-ás Serás	You will be
Usted	Ser-á Será	You will be
Él/ella	Ser-á Será	He/she will be
Nosotros	Ser-emos Seremos	We will be
Ustedes	Ser-án Serán	You will be
Ellos	Ser-án Serán	They will be

- Yo seré astronauta cuando crezca
- I will be an astronaut when I grow up

- Ellos serán mis compañeros de clase
- They will be my classmates

- María será una muy buena cantante
- Maria will be a very good Singer

- Seremos voluntarios.
- We'll be volunteers

- Verb *estar*

The same rule follows the verb *estar*. Its infinitive form plus the right terminations.

Personal pronoun	Verb	Translation
Yo	Estar-é Estaré	I will be
Tú	Estar-ás Estarás	You will be
Usted	Estar-á Estará	You will be
Él/ella	Estar-á Estará	He/she will be
Nosotros	Estar-emos Estaremos	We will be
Ustedes	Estar-án Estarán	You will be
Ellos	Estar-án Estarán	They will be

- Estaremos en el parque esperando por ti.
- We'll be in the park waiting for you.

- Estaré ocupado el martes por la tarde.
- I'll be busy Tuesday afternoon

- Estaré con mi mamá en el hospital
- I'll be with my mom at the hospital

- Juana estará con sus amigos.

- Juana will be with her friends

Other Verbs

As you may have been able to see, the key to forming the future is very simple: the infinitive form and the right termination. This formula is repeated throughout most Spanish verbs. Let's see some examples.

	Yo	Tú	Él/ella	Nosotros	Ellos
Comer	Comeré	Comerás	Comerán	Comeremos	Comerán
Cantar	Cantaré	Cantarás	Cantará	Cantaremos	Cantarán
Decir	Diré	Dirás	Dirá	Diremos	Dirán
Despertar	Despertaré	Despertarás	Despertará	Despertaremos	Despertarán
Beber	Beberé	Beberás	Beberá	Beberemos	Beberán
Mirar	Miraré	Mirarás	Mirará	Miraremos	Mirarán
Escribir	Escribiré	Escribirás	Escribirá	Escribiremos	Escribirán
Pagar	Pagaré	Pagarás	Pagará	Pagaremos	Pagarán
Leer	Leeré	Leerás	Leerá	Leeremos	Leerán
Terminación	-é	-ás	-á	-emos	-án

In this chart, the personal pronouns *usted* and *ustedes* are not present since they have the same conjugations as *él* and *ellos,* respectively.

- Comeré cuando tenga hambre.
- I'll eat when I'm hungry

- Cantaré esta canción en un show de la escuela
- I'll sing this sing in a school performance

- Tendrás que leer todo el libro si quieres saber el final de la historia
- You will have to read all the book if you want to know the end of the story

- Pagaré la cuenta
- I'll pay the bill

- Buscaré mi pasaporte
- I'll search my passport

- Haré toda mi tarea después de ver televisión por un rato
- I'll do all my homework after watching TV for a while.

Exercise 1.1

Fill in the following sentences with the correct form of the verb

1. Yo ____ (ir) a comprar al supermercado. ¿Quieres venir conmigo?
2. María ____ (limpiar) la mesa mientras nosotros lavamos los platos.
3. Fabián ____ (correr) en la maratón que habrá en la siguiente semana.
4. El profesor me dijo que él ____ (dejar) bastante tarea.
5. Yo te ____ (ayudar) con el proyecto
6. Ellos ____ (escribir) sus nombres.
7. Juan y yo ____ (comer) cualquier cosa. Tenemos mucha hambre.
8. Yo ____ (manejar) mi bicicleta mañana para ir a trabajar.
9. El profesor ____ (tomar) el bus después que acaben las clases.
10. Monica ____ (presentar) el proyecto en frente de la clase.

Exercise 1.2

Interpret the following sentences

1. Iremos al parque esta noche.
2. Comeremos hamburguesas e pasearemos con nuestros amigos.
3. Ellos traerán dinero.
4. Pasearemos al perro y jugaremos con él.
5. Mis amigos traerán a sus mascotas.
6. Las personas creerán que somos turistas.
7. No hablaremos en español.
8. Ellos nos escucharán hablar sólo en inglés.
9. They won't need a dictionary
10. My friend will be the interpreter.
11. They will realize that we are playing.

The verbs you have seen so far in this lesson have been solely from one group: the regular verb groups. There are some irregular verbs that pretty much defy the conjugation rules, but nonetheless are important to learn:

- Some verbs that ends with –er:

Verbs like *haber, poder, saber and querer* are all irregular.

	Yo	Tú	Él/ella	Nosotros	Ellos	
Haber	Habré	Habrás	Habrá	Habremos	Habrán	Have
Poder	Podré	Podrás	Podrá	Podremos	Podrán	Can
Querer	Querré	Querrás	Querrá	Querremos	Querrán	Want
Saber	Sabré	Sabrás	Sabrá	Sabremos	Sabrán	Know
Caber	Cabré	Cabrás	Cabrá	Cabremos	cabrán	Fit

- Yo podré hacer mi tarea más tarde.
- I'll be able to do my homework later.

- Los invitados querrán sentarse
- The guests will want to sit.

One rule of thumb is that these verbs drop the −er and replace it with the right termination.

- Some verbs that ends with −er or −ir and need to add another letter

The only letter that's added is just the letter *d*. Some verbs in this list include *poner, salir* and *tener*.

	Yo	Tú	Él/ella	Nosotros	Ellos	
Poner	Pondré	Pondrás	Pondrá	Pondremos	Pondrán	Put
Salir	Saldré	Saldrás	Saldrá	Saldremos	Saldrán	Go out/exit
Venir	Vendré	Vendrás	Vendrá	Vendremos	Vendrán	Come
Tener	Tendré	Tendrás	Tendrá	Tendremos	Tendrán	Have

- Graciela saldrá a las 5 de su trabajo
- Graciela will get out of work at 5

- Tendrás tu dinero mañana
- You'll have your money tomorrow

One rule of thumb is that these verbs drop the −er and −ir and you need to add the letter *d*.

- Other verbs

They are called here like that because that's just what they are, they don't really belong to any group. If it's of any comfort, they are few, so you won't deal with them all the time. Some of these verbs include *hacer* and *decir*

	Yo	Tú	Él/ella	Nosotros	Ellos	
Hacer	Hare	Harás	Harán	Haremos	Harán	Do
Decir	Dire	Dirás	Dirá	Diremos	Dirán	Say/tell

- María me dirá sobre el proyecto mañana.
- Maria will tell me about the project tomorrow

- Ellos harán toda la presentación.
- They will do all the presentation.

Have in mind that not all verbs that ends with −er or −ir have to behave like this. There are many verbs that ends with −er and −ir that are regular.

Exercise 1.3

Fill in the following sentences with the right form of the verbs in brackets

1. María me dijo que ella ____ (poder) venir a la fiesta.
2. Él me ____ (decir) lo que pasó.
3. Nosotros ____ (hacer) todo el proyecto.
4. Ellos ____(tener) una sorpresa.
5. Juan ____ (salir) de la clase
6. Él ____ (saber) lo que tiene que hacer
7. Ellos ____ (querer) ir a la fiesta.
8. María ____ (salir) de la fiesta porque se está aburriendo.

Exercise 1.4

Interpret the following sentences

1. They will tell me what to do.
2. She will do her homework tomorrow.
3. I don't think you will finish your presentation on time.
4. I will go out of my house at 5 p.m.
5. Yo ____ (poder) ir a tu casa esta noche.

Negative sentences

All the verbs follow the same structure when forming negative sentences in the future.

Subject	No	Verb	complement
María	No	Sabra	Lo que pasó.
María	Will not	Know	What happened

You only need to add *no* before the verb. This applies to both regular and irregular verbs in the future.

Exercise 1.5

Fill in the following sentences with the right form of the verb in brackets

1. Yo ____ (no hacer) lo que tú me digas.
2. Yo ____ (no poder) llevarte a tu casa.
3. Él ____ (no poder) ayudarte.

4. Ella ____ (no saber) lo que estamos haciendo.

5. Nosotros ____ (no ir) a la fiesta de promoción.

Exercise 1.6

Change the verb tense in every sentence so that they now refer to the future.

1. Yo como con mi mamá.
2. Él canta en el show de su escuela.
3. Estoy aquí con mis padres.
4. Jugamos fútbol con mis amigos.
5. Estamos cansados por haber jugado tanto.
6. La planta crece muy rápido.
7. No siento ningún dolor.
8. Ella no me envía mensajes de texto.
9. Nosotros caímos en una trampa.
10. No te digo lo que pasará porque es una sorpresa.

Interrogative Sentences

To form the interrogative form of the future tense, you don't need any special knowledge, you already know how to do it! How so? Well, interrogative sentences in the future tense follow the same rules as the simple tense form. You can either:

- Write it as an affirmative sentence but adding both questions mark at the beginning and at the end of the question.

¿	Subject	Verb	Complement	?
¿	Juan	Hará	La tarea	?

- "Invert it"

¿	Verb	Subject	Complement	?
¿	Hará	María	La tarea	?

How can you answer these questions? Let's see some examples:

¿Irás a la fiesta esta noche?	Will you go to the party tonight?
No, estaré ocupado.	No, I'll be busy.

¿Cantarás en el show de la escuela?	Will you sing in the school performance?
Sí, cantaré con todos mis compañeros de clase.	Yes, I'll sing with all my classmates.

¿Vendrás temprano a la reunión?	Will you come early to the meeting?
Sí, no lo dudes.	Yes, don't doubt it.

Remember that there are questions that ask for more than a yes-or-no answer:

¿Cuándo será la fiesta?	When will the party be?
Será el siguiente sábado.	It will be next Saturday

¿Dónde será la fiesta?	Where will the party be?
Será en la casa de Miguel	It will be in Miguel's house

¿Quiénes irán a la fiesta?	Who will go to the party?
Todos nuestros compañeros de clase.	All our classmates.

¿Por qué no podrás venir a la fiesta?	Why won't you be able to come to the party?
Porque tendré que cuidar a mi hermano pequeño.	Because I will have to take care of my little brother.

Exercise 1.7

Fill in the following sentences

1. ¿Dónde ____ (ser) la fiesta?
2. La fiesta ____ (ser) en la casa de Martín
3. ¿ (tener) ____ María hambre?
4. María ____ (comer) en su casa
5. ¿(venir) ____ tú a la siguiente a la clase?
6. Yo ____ (venir) un poco tarde.
7. ¿Por qué ____ (venir) tarde a la siguiente clase?
8. Porque ____ (ir) al banco a pagar una deuda.
9. Nosotros ____ (necesitar) tu ayuda para la siguiente obra de teatro.
10. ¿Qué ____ (querer) comprar ustedes?

Exercise 1.8

Answer the following questions as you see fit.

1. ¿Qué harás mañana?
2. ¿Viajarás el siguiente año?
3. ¿Comerás con tus amigos este fin de semana?
4. ¿Aprenderás otro idioma?
5. ¿Harás deporte hoy día?

Reading Comprehension

Mis siguientes vacaciones

My next vacation

Mis padres y yo estamos planeando nuestras siguientes vacaciones. Dentro de poco, mis clases terminarán y mi hermana y yo tendremos 2 meses para poder descansar y estar con nuestros padres. Mis padres también tendrán vacaciones.

Lo mejor de todo es que nosotros tendremos nuestras vacaciones en los meses de verano. Me encanta el verano. En el verano puedo ir a la playa y puedo jugar con mis amigos casi todo el día.

Mis padres ya me dijeron que iremos en un crucero estas vacaciones. ¡Qué nervios! Yo nunca he estado en un crucero. Será la primera vez en mi vida en que me suba a uno de esos. Mis padres harán las reservaciones y comprarán los boletos la siguiente semana. Como mi hermana es menor de edad, mis padres no pagarán el precio completo; ellos tendrán un descuento.

Mis padres me dijeron que tengo que empacar todo lo que necesito. Honestamente, no sé qué llevaré. ¿Estará bien si llevo mi balón de fútbol? ¿Habrá otros muchachos con los que podré jugar fútbol? Sé que tengo que llevar sólo lo que necesito pero espero no aburrirme en el crucero.

Sé que habrá una piscina enorme. ¡Ya vi en las fotos del crucero que la piscina es tan grande como mi casa! Creo que tendré que llevar mi ropa de baño. También vi en la página web del crucero que habrá mucha comida deliciosa y también vendrán muchas personas de todo el mundo. El crucero visitará bastantes ciudades en Europa y se quedará 3 horas en cada una. Estoy muy emocionado porque el crucero irá a Venecia. Pondré mi cámara dentro de mi maleta para poder tomar muchísimas fotos cuando llegue a Venecia.

Bueno, seguiré alistándome para el crucero. Espero que mis padres también estén listo para cuando el crucero tenga que partir.

Verbs

Planeando	Planning
Terminarán	Finish
Tendremos	Have
Descansar	Rest/Have Some Time Off
Encanta	Love
Jugar	Play

Pagarán	Pay
Llevo	Bring
Aburrirme	Get Bored
Habrá	There Will Be
Pondré	Put
Seguiré	Continue
Alistándome	Getting Ready
Partir	Leave

Nouns

Vacaciones	Vacation
Clases	Classes
Meses	Months
Verano	Summer
Playa	Beach
Crucero	Cruise Ship
Reservaciones	Reservations
Boletos	Tickets
Precio	Price
Descuento	Discount
Balón De Fútbol	Soccer Ball
Piscina	Swimming Pool
Fotos	Pictures
Ropa De Baño	Swimwear
Página Web	Web Page
Comida	Food
Ciudades	Cities
Cámara	Camera
Maleta	Suitcase/Baggage

Adjctives

Enorme   Huge

Expressions

Menor de edad   Underage
Primera vez en mi vida   First time in my life

Preguntas

1. ¿Qué están planeando el protagonista y sus padres?
2. ¿Cuántos meses de vacaciones tendrán el protagonista y su hermana?
3. ¿Le gusta el verano al protagonista? ¿Por qué?
4. ¿Qué es lo que el protagonista hará por primera vez en su vida?
5. ¿Por qué sus padres no pagarán el precio completo para su hermana?
6. ¿Sabe que llevar el protagonista al crucero?
7. ¿Qué habrá en el crucero?
8. ¿A qué lugar planea ir el protagonista?

Part 2: Structures That Convey the Idea of Future

Just like English, some sentence structures can convey the idea of future. The only way to identify clearly if they are referring to a future event or not is to get the context.

Present

The present tense in Spanish can refer to the future, given the right context.

¿A qué hora estarás en casa?	What time will you be at home?
Llego a las 8 de la noche.	I'll arrive at 8 p.m.

This is used when it's sure that the action will happen in the future.

A verb that is used to express the future is the verb **pensar**.

Don't confuse the structure **pensar + infinitive,** which is used to indicate future, and **pensar en + infinitive,** which could be translated just as **thinking about.**

Pienso comprar un nuevo videojuego	I think I'll buy a new videogame.
Pienso en comprar un nuevo videojuego.	I'm thinking about buying a new videogame.

Verb ir + a + Infinitive

The verb *ir* can help us form a structure that will convey the idea of the future, this structure is called *future inmediato*.

Yo	Voy a comer con mis amigos.	I'm going to eat with my friends.
Tú	Vas a salir con tus padres.	You are going to go out with your parents.
Usted	Va a traer a sus hijos.	You are going to bring your kids.
Él	Va a pasar las vacaciones en Málaga	He's going to spend his holidays in Malaga
Ella	Va a comprar ropa para sus hijos	She's going to but clothes for her children

Nosotros	Vamos a tener una fiesta esta noche	We are going to have a party tonight
Ustedes	Van a estudiar en la Universidad	You are going to study in college.
Ellos	Van a salir otra vez.	They are going to go out again

Expressions That Accompany the Future Tense

There are many expressions that used alongside the future tense so that it has more sense and added meaning. These are the most used of all such expressions.

El Próximo / La Próxima

El próximo verano	Next summer
Iremos de vacaciones el próximo verano.	We'll go on vacation next summer.

El próximo jueves	Next Thursday
Te visitaré el siguiente jueves.	I'll visit you next Thursday

El próximo año	Next year
Viajaré el próximo año	I'll travel next year

La próxima visita	Next visit
Traeré algo en mi próxima visita.	I will bring something on my next visit.

La proxima fiesta	Next party
Vendrán muchas personas a la próxima fiesta	Many people will come to the next party

La próxima semana	Next week
No estaremos en casa la próxima semana	We will not be home next week.

La próxima vez	Next time
Llamaremos a más personas la siguiente vez.	We will call more people next time.

El Siguiente / La Siguiente

El siguiente is basically just another way of saying *el próximo*. Let's see some examples:

El siguiente mes	Next month
Vendré a casa el siguiente mes	I'll come home next month

El siguiente marzo	Next March
El siguiente marzo iré a Italia	Next March, I'll go to Italy

La siguiente ocasión	Next occasion/ next time
¿Debemos venir más temprano la siguiente ocasión?	Should we come earlier next time?

El siguiente lunes	Next Monday
Faltaré a clases el siguiente lunes.	I'll miss classes next Monday

Time Indicators

Mañana	Tomorrow
Iré a clases mañana	I'll go to classes tomorrow
Mañana, mis abuelos vendrán a visitarme.	Tomorrow, my grandparents will come to visit me.
En una hora	In an hour
Acabaré mi tarea en una hora	I'll finish my homework in an hour
El avión llegará en una hora	The plane will arrive in an hour

En media hora	In half an hour
Mis padres vendrán a recogerme en media hora	My parents will come to pick me up in half an hour
Él llegará a casa en media hora.	He will come home in half an

	hour.

Luego	Afterward/then
Lo haré luego	I will do it later.
Luego iremos a comer.	Then we will go to eat.

Have in mind that *luego* is not exclusively used for the future tense since it also means *then*.

Mañana por la tarde	Tomorrow afternoon
Comeré con mis amigos mañana por la tarde.	I'll eat with my friends tomorrow afternoon.

Más tarde	Later
Ellos me llamarán más tarde.	They will call me later
Mi mama irá al mercado más tarde	My mom will go to the market later.

Esta noche	Tonight
Iré a tu casa esta noche.	I'll go to your house tonight.
Te llamaré esta noche	I'll call you tonight

Mañana por la mañana	Tomorrow morning
Vendré mañana por la mañana	I'll visit you tomorrow morning.

Pasado mañana	The day after tomorrow
¿Vendrás a mi casa pasado mañana?	I'll come by tomorrow morning

Exercise 2.1

*Fill in the following sentences with the correct form of the verb **pensar** and the verb that follows.*

1. Yo ____ (pensar/comer) con ustedes mañana por la mañana.
2. Ellos ____ (pensar/ir) a la feria la siguiente semana.
3. Nosotros ____ (pensar/jugar) videojuegos esta noche con nuestros amigos.
4. María y Juan ____ (pensar/ir) a un restaurante lujoso esta noche.
5. Pasado mañana, Roberto y yo ____ (pensar/salir) a pasear.
6. Rodrigo y Ángel ____ (pensar/jugar) fútbol con sus amigos mañana por la mañana.
7. Iván ____ (pensar/escribir) una carta a su esposa mañana.
8. Mañana, mi esposa ____ (pensar/salir) con nuestros hijos.
9. Mi mamá ____ (pensar/ir) al hospital mañana por la mañana
10. Elsa ____ (pensar/cocinar) para sus amigas que vendrán esta noche.

Exercise 2.2

*Fill in the following sentences with the correct form of the verb **ir**. See the example below.*

- *Yo voy a comer con mis padres esta noche.*
- *Ellos van a jugar mañana por la mañana.*

1. Mis amigos ____ (ir/buscar) a alguien que los pueda llevar a la feria.
2. Yo ____ (ir/tomar) el bus luego de salir de mi trabajo.
3. Nosotros ____ (ir/ver) una película mañana.
4. María ____ (ir/ayudar) a sus padres a reparar el televisor.
5. Mi hermano ____ (ir/visitar) a su amigo mañana por la tarde.
6. Juan ____ (ir/comprar) su nueva mochila.
7. Yolanda ____(ir/traer) más dinero.

Reading Comprehension

Cuando sea grande

When I grow up

Me llamo Iván. Yo nací en Zaragoza hace 13 años. Mi mamá no es de Zaragoza, mi papá si lo es. Todos los veranos visitamos a mis abuelos que viven en Perú. Es siempre súper divertido visitarlos. Ellos me llevan a lugares que nunca he visto en mi vida. Este verano cuando los visité, mis abuelos me preguntaron si yo ya había decidido que es lo que quiero ser cuando sea grande. Al principio no entendí la pregunta, así que respondí que no sabía lo que quería ser cuando sea grande.

Cuando volvimos a Zaragoza, empecé a preguntarme a mí mismo lo que yo quería hacer cuando sea grande.

"Puedo ser un doctor. Sí, eso puedo ser. Voy a ser un doctor, el mejor de todos."

Estaba a punto de levantarme de la silla y preguntarle a mis padres lo que necesito para convertirme en un doctor, cuando de repente recordé que a mí nunca me gustó ver sangre, y hasta donde yo sé, los doctores tienen que ver sangre todo el tiempo. Pero al menos puedo ser un astronauta. Eso es lo que yo siempre decía cuando era más pequeño. Las películas sobre aventuras espaciales siempre me han parecido muy interesantes.

"Voy a ser un astronauta, entonces. Pero también puedo convertirme en un policía, como mi tío. Él es un gran policía. Entonces, ¿qué le diré a mi abuelo la siguiente ocasión que lo visité? ¿Seré un astronauta o un policía?"

Quería buscar a alguien que me pueda ayudar a decidir. Por eso, fui a buscar a mi papá. Busqué y busqué a mi papá y no lo pude encontrar por ningún lugar de la casa. Finalmente lo encontré en el garaje.

"Papá, no sé qué quiero hacer cuando sea grande"

"¿Qué es lo que te gusta?"

"Me gusta jugar fútbol, cuidar a los animales y ayudarte a reparar los aparatos electrónicos"

"¿Entonces, qué crees que podrías ser, ahora que sabes lo que te gusta?"

"Seré un jugador de futbol profesional"

"Los jugadores de futbol profesional tiene que entrenar mucho para saber jugar muy bien"

"Entonces, entrenaré bastante y muy duro"

"¿No quisieras convertirte en un veterinario?"

"No lo he pensado mucho, pero sería genial. Voy a buscar más información sobre como los veterinarios."

"Puedes preguntar al veterinario la siguiente ves que vayas a llevar al perrito"

"Eso haré, gracias papá"

Mientras regresaba a mi habitación, veía a mi papá como seguía reparando la radio que un vecino le había traído hace unas horas. Fue ahí, cuando me di cuenta que me había olvidado que yo también podría ser un electricista, como mi papá.

"La siguiente ocasión le preguntaré diré a mi abuelo que ya sé lo que quiero ser cuando sea grande"

Verbs

Nací	Was Born
Visitamos	Visited
Llevan	Take
Preguntaron	Asked
Entendí	Understood
Respondí	Asnwered
Levantarme	Get Up
Convertirme	Become
Parecido	Seemed
Busqué	Searched
Encontré	Found
Jugar	To Play
Cuidar	To Take Care Of
Ayudar	To Help
Entrenar	To Train
Pensar	To Think
Reparar	To Fix
Di Cuenta	Realised

Nouns

Zaragoza	A City In Northeast Spain
Veranos	Summers
Lugares	Places
La Pregunta	The Questions

460

Doctor	Doctor
Silla	Chair
Sangre	Blood
Astronautas	Astronauts
Aventuras	Adventures
Garaje	Garage
Fútbol	Soccer
Animales	Animals
Jugador De Fútbol Profesional Player	Professional Soccer

Expressions

Mi papá si lo es (fromZaragoza)	My dad is
Al principio	At first

Preguntas

1. ¿De dónde viene Iván?
2. ¿Dónde viven los abuelos de Iván?
3. ¿Le gusta a Iván visitar a sus abuelos?
4. ¿Qué le preguntan a Iván sus abuelos?
5. ¿Qué es lo primero que piensa ser Iván?
6. ¿A quién pregunta Iván por ayuda?
7. ¿Qué le responde su papá?
8. ¿Qué le gusta hacer a Iván?
9. ¿Qué es lo Iván quiere ser cuando sea grande?

Preguntas

1. ¿Qué harás tú mañana por la tarde?
2. ¿Piensas viajar dentro de poco? ¿A dónde?
3. ¿Qué quieres hacer mañana? ¿Y la siguiente semana?
4. ¿Qué planeas hacer el siguiente verano?
5. ¿A dónde irás en tus siguientes vacaciones?
6. ¿Saldrás con tus amigos este fin de semana? ¿A dónde?

Chapter 4: *Objeto Directo e Indirecto*: Direct and Indirect Object

Part 1: Direct Object

The direct and indirect object, are, as their names imply, things or people that receive the action of the sentence.

Some verbs in Spanish need the direct object to function properly. These types of verbs are called *verbos transtivos* (transitive verbs). On the other hand, those that don't need the direct object to make sense are called *verbos intransitivos* (intransitive verbs). It's important to have this in mind as you'll see with the following verbs.

Subject + verb	Direct object
Yo leo	Un libro
Yo estoy comprando	Los ingredientes
Ella está mirando	La televisión
Tu cantarás	Una canción
Juan tendrá	El dinero
Nadie necesita	Tu ayuda
José traerá	Su ropa
Yo ganaré	El concurso

The object direct can also be "abbreviated." Object direct pronouns can help us with that.

Object direct pronouns replace the direct object with a pronoun. These are different and each one has to be used according to the object direct that's going to replace. Let's see the object direct pronoun.

Personal pronoun	Object direct pronoun	Translation
Yo	Me	Me
Tú	Te	You
Usted	Lo/La	You
Él	Lo	Him
Ella	La	Her
Eso	Lo	It
Esa	La	It

Nosotros	Nos	Us
Ustedes	Los/las	You
Vosotros	Os	You
Ellos	Los	Them
Ellas	Las	Them

To identify the direct object you have to find the answer to the questions:

- *¿Qué?*
- *¿Quién?*
- *¿A quién?* (This is not always the case, only certain transitive verbs can answer that question)

Answering these questions can help us identify the direct object.

Let's see how these can replace the object direct:

Fabiana **me** ordena a lavar los platos.	Fabiana orders me to wash the dishes
¿A quién ordena Fabiana?	Whom is Fabiana ordering?
A *mi*.	Me.
She's ordering *me,* that is, she's ordering the first person to do something. If you see in the table above, the direct object pronoun for the first person is *me*.	

Fabiana **te** olvidó.	She forgot you
¿A quién olvidó Fabiana?	Whom did Fabiana forget?
A *ti*.	You

Yo tengo **el dinero.**	I have the money
¿Qué tengo yo?	What do I have?
El dinero.	**The money**
Yo **lo** tengo.	I have it.dd

¿Tienes **el dinero**?	Do you have the money?
Sí, **lo** tengo	Yes, I have **it.**

Quiero ver **pelicula**	I want to see a movie
Quiero ver**la**	I want to see **it**.

Mi mamá **nos** trajo a la fiesta.	My mom brought **us** to the party.
Ella **nos** llamará	She will call us

¿Puedes ver las aves?	Can you see the birds?
Sí, puedo ver**las.**	Yes, I can see them.

Debemos cuidar a los perritos.	We should take care of the puppies.
Yo **los** cuidaré.	I will take care of them.

As you have seen, all object direct pronouns replace the object or person that's been previously mentioned. How can you know you're using it correctly?

How to Use the Direct Object Pronouns

- Direct object + verb

The direct object pronoun is usually placed before the conjugated verb. Let's see some examples.

¿Tienes mi billetera? / Do you have my wallet?	
Presente	Sí, yo **lo** tengo.
Futuro	Sí, yo **lo** tendré
Pretérito (pasado)	Sí, yo **lo** tuve
Presente continuo	Yo **lo** estoy teniendo
Presente continuo	Yo estoy teniéndo**lo**

In negative sentences, they appear after **no**

¿Tienes mi billetera? / Do you have my wallet?	
Presente	No, yo no **lo** tengo.
Futuro	No, yo no **lo** tendré
Pretérito (pasado)	No, yo no **lo** tuve
Presente continuo	No **lo** estoy teniendo
Presente continuo	Yo no estoy teniéndo**lo**

- Infinitive + direct object

You can place the direct object after the infinitive.

Ganar la competencia es muy difícil.	Winning the competition is very hard.
Ganar**la** es muy difícil.	Winning it is very hard

Tener el dinero en la mano es lo importante.	Having the money in hand is the important thing.
Tener**lo** en la mano es lo importante.	Having it in hand is the important thing.

Llamar a María es súper sencillo.	Calling María is very simple.
Llamar**la** es super sencillo.	Calling her is very simple.

Remember that the verb in infinitive and the direct object pronoun form make up one word.

- Imperative + infinitive

You can place the direct object pronoun after the imperative form of the verb.

¿Quieres que traiga huevos?	Do you want me to bring eggs?
Sí, por favor. Tráe**los**.	Yes, please. Bring them.

¿Quieres que **te** ayude?	Do you want me to help you?
Sí, por favor. Ayúda**me.**	Yes, please. Help me.

¿Quieren saber lo que hizo Martín?	Do you want to know what Martin did?
Sí, di**nos.**	Yes, tell us.

Have in mind that these also make up just one word.

This changes when forming negative imperative sentences. The direct object pronouns appear after **no** and before the verb.

¿Quieres que traiga huevos?	Do you want me to bring eggs?
No **los** traigas.	Don't bring them.

¿Quieres que **te** ayude?	Do you want me to help you?
No, gracias. No **me** ayudes.	No, thank you. Don't help me.

¿Quieren saber lo que hizo Martín?	Do you want to know what Martin did?
No. No **nos** digas.	No. Don't tell us.

Gerund + Direct Object

The direct object can be placed before the verb to be, like in these examples:

Lo estoy llamando.	I'm calling him
Te estamos buscando	We're calling you
Nos están viendo.	They're watching us.
¿**Me** estás entendiendo?	Are you understanding me?

But it can also be placed after the gerund. In that case, they form just one word, like in these examples:

Estoy llamándo**lo**	I'm calling him
Estamos buscándo**te**	We're calling you
Están viéndo**nos**	They're watching us.
¿Estás entendiéndo**me?**	Are you understanding me?

Note that the verbs have a written accent on them. This occurs in all verbs in gerund that have the direct object pronoun added.

Conjugated Verb + Infinite

Sentences, where more than one verb appear, are very common. You can place the direct object before the first verb, like in these examples:

¿**Lo** vas a regalar?	Are you going to give it away?
Las voy a hacer en un momento.	I'm going to do them in a moment.
La voy a comer	I take her to eat.
Los voy a comprar	I'm going to buy them.

The object direct pronouns can also be placed after the infinitive.

¿Vas a regalar**los**?	Are you going to give it away?
Voy a hacer**las.**	I'm going to do them in a moment.
Voy a comer**la**	I take her to eat.
Voy a comprar**los**	I'm going to buy them.

To have in mind:

In some parts of Spain, the object direct pronoun **lo** is changed to **le.** This anomaly is called *leísmo*. This is not the case in Latin America.

So you might hear in Spain:

- **Le** vi en el mercado.

But in Latin America:

- **Lo** vi en el mercado.

Verbs That Use the Direct Object.

You have already seen some verbs that use the direct object. These verbs are called transitive verbs and they need to have the direct object to have the full meaning. They can sometimes work without it but it might lack sense in most cases.

The most common transitive verbs are:

1.	Tener	Yo no **lo** tengo	I don't have it
2.	Guardar	¿Puedes guardar**lo**?	Can you keep it?
3.	Llevar	Lleva**los** a casa.	Take them home.
4.	Tomar	No quiero tomar**los**.	I donot want to take them.
5.	Obtener	**La** obtuve el año pasado.	I obtained it last year.
6.	Recibir	**Lo** recibiré mañana	I will receive it next year
7.	Aceptar	Ella **lo** aceptará	She will accept it
8.	Encontrar	Nosotros **lo** encontramos	We found it.
9.	Adquirir	Ellos **lo** adquirirán	They will adquire ir.
10.	Comprar	Nosotros compraremos **los libros.**	We will buy the books.
11.	Ganar	Ellos ganarán **el premio.**	They will win the prize.
12.	Robar	Él robo **mi cellular.**	He stole my phone.
13.	Dar	No me des **las noticias.**	Don't give me the news.
14.	Ofrecer	Ellos me ofrecieron **un trabajo.**	They offered me a job.
15.	Prestar.	Mi amigo me prestará **dinero.**	My friend will lend me **money.**

16. Pagar	Yo pagaré **la cuenta.**	I will pay the bill.
17. Abandonar	No **te** abandonaremos.	We will not abandon you.
18. Dejar	Déja**me** en paz.	Let me in peace.
19. Vender	¿Dónde venden **celulares?**	Where are cellphones sold?
20. Ver	¿**La** puedes ver?	Can you see her?
21. Entender	No entiendo **la clase.**	I don't understand the class
22. Esuchar	No puedo **escucharte.**	I can't hear you
23. Examinar	El doctor está examinando **las pruebas.**	The doctor is examining the evidence
24. Aprender	Estamos aprendiendo **a hablar un nuevo idioma.**	We're learning a new language.
25. Amar	Amo los **veranos en Mallorca**	I love summers in Majorca
26. Desear	Siempre deseo **lo mejor para ti.**	I always wish the best for you.
27. Odiar	Odio **este clima**	I hate this weather
28. Corregir	La profesora está corrigiendo **los exámenes.**	The teacher is correcting the exams.
29. Aumentar	El comerciante aumentó **el costo del gas.**	The merchant increased the cost of the gas.
30. Mejorar	Hay que mejorar **las notas**	You need to improve your grades
31. Meter	¿Puedes meter **mi ceular** en mi cartera?	Can you put my cellphone in my purse?
32. Continuar	Ellos están continuando **la conversación**.	They are continuing the conversation.
33. Celebrar	Mis padres están celebrando **su**	My parents are celebrating their

	aniversario.	anniversary.
34. Subir	Tenemos que subir **las escaleras**	We have to walk up the stairs
35. Construir	Veo que están construyendo **nuevos rascacielos**	They're building new skyscrapers.
36. Inventar	Él inventó **el internet.**	He invented the internet.
37. Decir	¿Vas a decir**me** lo que pasó?	Are you going to tell me what happened?
38. Repetir	¿Podrías repetir **lo que dijiste?**	Could you repeat what you said?
39. Pedir	Quiero pedir **dinero** a mi papa.	I want to ask my dad for money
40. Causar	Sus palabras **me** causaron mucho dolor.	Her words caused me a lot of pain.

Exercise 1.1

The direct object is highlighted in every sentence, replace it with the right direct object pronoun

1. No entiendo **la tarea**
2. Quiero escuchar **música.**
3. ¿Puedes prestarme **dinero?**
4. Han abandonado esos **perritos.**
5. ¿Me vas a decir **la verdad?**
6. Llevaré **mi celular** a la clase.
7. Estoy aprendiendo **a jugar fútbol.**
8. Odio **la comida chatarra**
9. Ellos están celebrando **su aniversario.**
10. Ya encontré **las llaves del auto.**

Reading Comprehension

¿Tienes mi dinero?

Do you have my money?

Hace dos semanas, yo presté 20 dólares a mi amigo Esteban. No sé exactamente para que quería el dinero, pero supongo que debe ser para algo muy importante. He estado esperando que me pagué. Él me dijo que él me iba a pagar el viernes, pero ya es domingo y aún no me ha pagado.

Lo bueno es que hoy día él viene a jugar fútbol con mis vecinos, y de seguro él vendrá a pagarme. Tendré que esperar a que él venga. Yo también iré a jugar.

Ya es hora de jugar y Esteban ya llegó. Es mejor que vaya y le pregunte sobre el dinero que le presté.

"¿Qué pasó con el dinero que te presté, Esteban?" – pregunté

"Hola, Roberto. Gracias por esperar. Disculpa que me haya demorado en pagarte. Toma, aquí está el dinero que te presté. También añadí 5 dólares más. Gracias por prestarme."

"Pero, ¿y qué hiciste con el dinero?"

"Me compré un videojuego."

"Pensé que iba a ser para algo muy importante"

"Si lo fue. Fue algo muy importante para mí. Lo compré para que mi hermano menor y yo jugáramos juntos."

"O, ya veo. Pero, ¿realmente te costó 20 dólares? Pensé que esos juegos costaban más que sólo 20 dólares"

"Sí, eso es cierto. El juego me costó 100 dólares. Sólo necesitaba 20 dólares más para poder comprarlo."

"Bueno, al menos ya me diste el dinero que te presté."

"Gracias, de nuevo. Si algún día tienes un poco de tiempo libre, puedes venir a jugar conmigo y mi hermano."

"Sería genial. Pero esta semana no tengo tiempo para jugar. Tal vez la siguiente semana."

"No hay problema, sólo avísame cuando estés libre, ¿vale?"

Después de la conversación, empezamos a jugar fútbol con todos nuestros vecinos. Por un momento pensé que Esteban no me quería pagar. Al menos me dio el dinero y cinco dólares más.

Me olvidé por completo preguntarle sobre el juego que compró. Yo no sé jugar videojuegos, pero creo que iré a su casa para jugar con él y su hermano. Después de todo, el compró ese videojuego con mi dinero.

Verbs

Presté		Lend
Sé		Know
Quería	Want	
Supongo		Suppose
Pagar		Pay
Vendrá	Come	
Vaya		Go
Esperar		Wait
Demorado		Delayed
Añadí		Add
Compré	Buy	
Fue		Was
Costó		Cost
Necesitaba		Need
Diste		Give
Olvidé		Forgot

Nouns

Semanas		Weeks
Dólares	Dollars	
Amigo		Friend
Viernes	Friday	
Domingo		Sunday
Vecinos	Neighbors	
Videojuego		Videogames
Tiempo Libre	Free Time	
Conversación	Conversation	

Preguntas

1. ¿Qué prestó el protagonista?
2. ¿A quién prestó el protagonista?
3. ¿Hace cuánto tiempo el protagonista prestó?
4. ¿Cuándo dijo Esteban que iba a pagar?

5. ¿Qué va a hacer Esteban el domingo?
6. ¿Con quiénes van a jugar Esteban u el protagonista?
7. ¿Cuánto devolvió Esteban?
8. ¿Qué compró Esteban con el dinero que se prestó?
9. ¿Cuánto costó lo que Esteban se compró?
10. ¿Qué invitación hace Esteban al protagonista?

Part 2: The Indirect Object

The indirect object answers the question *"To whom?"* Just like the direct object, it can be replaced with **indirect object pronouns.**

The Direct Object for Every Personal Pronoun

Before learning the indirect object pronouns for every personal pronoun, let's see some examples where the indirect object is present so that you can see how it's used.

- Mis padres regalaron flores **a María.**
- My parents gave flowers to Maria

Direct object: flores

Indirect object: María

As you may recall, the direct object answers the question *"What?"* In this case, if we want to identify the direct object, we would have to ask:

"What did my parents give?"	*Flowers*
"¿Qué regalaron mis padres?"	*Flores*

Now that the direct object has been identified, the question we should ask to identify the indirect object is:

"¿A quién regalaron las flores mis padres?"	*A María*
"¿To whom did my parents give the flowers?"	*To Maria*

As you have seen, direct and indirect objects can appear in a sentence. The right questions will help us identify the direct and indirect objects.

- Mi amigo está dando dinero **al policía.**
- My friend s giving money to the policeman.

Direct object: el dinero

Indirect object: policía

To get the direct object, we should ask:

"What is my friend giving to the police officer?"	*Money*
"¿Qué está dando mi amigo al policía?"	*El dinero*

And to get the indirect object, we should ask:

"To whom is my friend giving the money?"	*To the police officer*

"¿A quién está dando mi amigo el dinero?"   *Al policía*

- Mi papá enseño **a mi hermano** a hablar francés.
- My dad taught my brother to speak french.

To get the direct object, we have to ask:

"¿Qué enseñó mi papa?"   *A hablar francés*

"What did my dad teach?"   *To speak French*

To get the indirect object, we have to ask:

"¿A quién enseñó mi papa?"   *A mi hermano*

"¿To whom did my dad teach?"   *To my brother.*

Every personal pronoun has a different indirect object pronoun:

Yo	Me	Me
Tú	Te	You
Él	Le	Him
Ella	Le	Her
Eso	Le	It
Nosotros	Nos	Us
Ustedes	Les	You
Vosotros	Os	You
Ellos	Les	Them
Ellas	Les	Them

Some of the indirect object pronouns look like the direct object direct pronouns. This doesn't mean that these pronouns can replace both the direct and indirect object, as we will see.

The only indirect object pronouns that are different from the direct object pronouns are those of the third person, both singular and plural.

Having in mind the example sentences, let's see how the indirect object can be replaced with their respective pronouns.

Mis padres regalaron flores a María.	My parents gave flowers to María
Mis padres **le** regalaron flores.	My parents gave her flowers

In this case, *a María* was replaced with the indirect object pronoun **le.**

Now, let's see some more examples.

Mi amigo está dando dinero **al policía.**	My friends are giving money to the pólice officer
Mi amigo **le** está dando dinero.	My friend is giving him money.

In this case, *al policía* was replaced with the pronoun **le.**

And now let's see the last example

Mi papá enseño **a mi hermano** a hablar francés.	My dad taught my brother to speak French
Mi papá **le** enseñó a hablar francés.	My dad taught him to speak French.

In this case, *a mi hermano* was replaced with the pronoun **le.**

Le is not the only pronoun, as you read on, you'll find the other indirect object pronouns being used.

How to Use the Indirect Object Pronouns

¿Diste el dinero a mi hermano? / *Did you give the money to my brother?*	
Presente	Sí, yo **le** doy
Presente continuo	Yo **le** estoy dando.
Pretérito (Pasado)	Yo **le** di
Futuro simple	Yo **le** daré
Futuro inmediato	Yo voy a dar**le**.
Futuro inmediato	Yo **le** voy a dar.
Infinitivo	Dar**le**

What should you have in mind if you also want to use the direct object pronouns and the indirect object pronouns in the same sentence?

- The order

The indirect object pronouns always precede the direct object pronouns:

- Escríbe**melo**   Write it for me
- No **me lo** digas   Don't tell me
- Da**melo**   Give it to me
- Tóma**telo**   Take it

There are few rules that you should follow if you want to successfully use the indirect object pronouns, let's see some of them.

Repetition of the Pronouns

There are cases when some indirect object pronouns are repeated. This is actually very common in the Spanish language. You have already seen this with the verb ***gustar (like)***

A ella **le** gusta el chocolate.	She likes ice cream
Le estoy cantando una canción **a mi mamá.**	I'm singing a song to my mom.
Ella **les** está dándo las galletas **a sus hermanos.**	She's giving the cookies to her brothers.
Da**le** el abrigo a mi amigo	Give the sweater to my friend.

- **Permanence of** *le*

The indirect object pronoun used for the third person (***le***) always appears in sentences unless the indirect object is a name.

Le di mi tarea **al profesor.**	I gave my homework to my teacher
Di mi tarea al **Sr. Montenegro**.	I gave my homework to Mr. Montenegro

Le entregaré el dinero **a mi amiga.**	I'll give the money to my friend.
Entregaré el dinero **a María.**	I'll give the money to Maria.

Change of *Le* into *SE*

Third-person indirect objects (*le, les*) turn into *se* when there's third-person direct object (*lo/la/los/las*)

Voy a dar el dinero a Juana	I'm going to give the money to Juana
Voy a dár**selo**	I'm going to give it to her

Ellos venderán los mapas a mis padres.	They will sell the maps to my parents.
Ellos **se los** venderán.	They will sell them to them

Ella escribió una carta a Francisco	She wrote a letter to Francisco
Ella **se lo** escribió.	She wrote it to him.

Ellos comprarán unos juguetes para sus hijos.	They will buy some toys for their kids
Ellos **se los** comprarán.	They will buy them for them.

More Than Just One Way to Identify It

So far, you've seen that one of the questions used to identify the indirect object is *"¿a quién?" (to whom)*. There are also other questions we can use in Spanish to identify the indirect object.

One question we can use is *¿De quién?*

- **Le** robaron el juguete **a mi amigo.**
- My friend's toy was stolen.

¿De quién era el juguete?

Whose was the toy?

- De mi amigo.
- My friend's.

- **Le** compraré chocolates a mi esposa.

¿Para quién serán los chocolates?

For whom will the chocolates be?

- Para mi esposa
- For my wife

Se Has More Than One Use

Se is also used as an impersonal pronoun. As such, it appears alongside other indirect object pronouns mostly to emphasize the act or interest of the doer of the action.

La computadora **se me** malogró	The computer broke down.
In this case, **me** conveys the idea that the one who owned the computer was me, or it broke down while I was using it.	

Se le perdió el juguete a Ricardo.	Ricardo's toy is lost.
In this case, **le** conveys the idea that the toy may have belonged to Ricardo or that it belonged to someone else but Ricardo lost it.	

As you can see, some of these phrases may convey more than one idea. Context is key in determining the real meaning behind the use of the indirect object pronoun and the impersonal pronoun.

Mi celular **se me** perdió.	I lost my cellphone-
In this case, **me** conveys the idea that the one who owned the keys was me or I lost other person's keys.	

Also, you may have noticed that the English sentences are not word-for-word translations. The impersonal pronouns and the indirect object

479

pronouns can be difficult to translate, so you are mostly seeing the message rather than a word-for-word translation, at least in this section.

Verbs That Use the Indirect Object Pronouns

Verbo	Ejemplo	Traducción
1. Encantar	**Me** encanta jugar fútbol	I love playing soccer
2. Dar	Ya **les** di las gracias.	I thanked them
3. Regalar	Yo **se los** he regalado	I gave them to them
4. Prestar	No **le** prestes tu gorro.	Don't lend him your hat.
5. Enviar	Voy a enviar una carta **a mi mamá.**	I'm going to send a letter to my mom.
6. Devolver	**Se lo** devolví hace dos semanas.	I gave it back to him two weeks ago
7. Preparar	Yo **les** preparé un rico postré.	I made a delicious dessert for you
8. Traer	Ellos **me** trajeron ropa.	They brought me clothes
9. Poner	No **les** pongas sal.	Don't put salt on them
10. Comprar	Yo **se los** compraré	I'll buy them for him
11. Decir	Ya **te lo** dije.	I already told you
12. Pagar	**Te** pagaré mañana	I'll pay you tomorrow
13. Escribir	Yo **le** escribí ayer por la tarde.	I wrote to her yesterday afternoon.

Exercise 2.1

Fill in the following sentences with the correct indirect object pronouns

1. Yo ____ (a ellos) di mi abrigo.
2. Ella ____ (a mi) dio un beso.
3. Ellos ____ (a ti) darán un abrazo.
4. ¿Qué ____ (a ustedes) dieron sus padres?
5. ¿Qué ____ (para ti) compraste?
6. ____ (a ella) escribiré una carta.
7. Yo nunca ____ (a él) entregué la tarea.
8. Ellos ____ (a mi) enviaron un mensaje de texto.
9. ____ (a ellos) vendieron un televisor
10. Nosotros ____ (a ustedes) trajimos unas galletas.

Exercise 2.2

Interpret the following sentences. Have in mind that no need for a word-for-word translation.

1. Yo le di un regalo a mi mamá
2. Ellos no me escribieron.
3. El profesor me entregó
4. Te vendieron un mapa nuevo
5. Ella me pagará mañana
6. Yo le entregué la tarea al profesor.

Exercise 2.3

Answer these questions as you see fit

1. ¿A quién das tu tarea?
2. ¿Para quién trabajas?
3. ¿A quién pagas la luz y el cable?
4. ¿A quién debes dinero?
5. ¿Para quién compras regalos?

Reading Comprehension

Las flores
The flowers

Iván sigue caminando por las calles de Zaragoza. Él ha estado caminando ya por más de tres horas buscando una florería. ¿Por qué está Iván buscando una florería?

Iván tiene una novia. La novia de Iván se llama Vanesa. Ellos se conocieron en el último año de la secundaria. Mañana es su aniversario. Ellos cumplen un año de novios. Iván no puede creer como el tiempo ha pasado tan rápido. Las flores van a ser un regalo que Iván quiere dar a Vanesa.

Darle flores no será tan difícil para Iván, lo difícil será encontrar al menos una florería abierta. El día de hoy es feriado, así que ninguna tienda está abierta en el centro de la ciudad. La novia de Iván, Vanesa, siempre le da muchos regalos a Iván, y en esta ocasión él quiere darle un ramo de rosas rojas. Esas son las flores favoritas de Vanesa.

Son casi las 5 de la tarde y Iván finalmente encontró una florería abierta. Él entra en la tienda y se da con la sorpresa de que están a punto de cerrar. Antes de que puedan cerrar, Iván entra a la tienda y les pide las flores rojas que él anda buscando.

"¿Podría darme un ramo grande de rosas rojas, por favor?" – pregunta Iván

"¿Solamente un ramo de rosas rojas?" – pregunta la vendedora de la tienda

"Si, por favor"

"Aquí tiene"

"Gracias, ¿podría decirme cuánto cuesta?"

"Este ramo de flores sólo le costará 15 dólares"

"¿Acepta tarjeta de crédito?"

"Sí. Pero recuerde que hay un pequeño cargo de 2 dólares"

"Entiendo"

Iván finalmente compra las flores y sale de la tienda. Pero antes de eso da las gracias a la vendedora. Después de agradecerle, Iván corre al paradero de bus para poder el último bus hacia su casa. Él sabe bien que en feriado los buses no funcionan todo el día. Después de esperar unos minutos, él sube al bus. Las personas notan que él trae un ramo de rosas muy grande y le empiezan a preguntar. Iván, un poco avergonzado, responde las preguntas de los pasajeros, y al final, llega a su casa.

Mañana será un día muy bonito para Iván. Él ya planeó todo lo que va hacer en la cita. Ahora él sólo está esperando a que todo lo que está haciendo le guste a Vanesa.

Verbs

Sigue	Continues
Caminando	Walking
Buscando	Searching
Conocieron	Met
Puede	Can
Creer	Believe
Encontrar	Find
Cerrar	Close
Dar	Give
Cuesta	Cost
Acepta	Accept
Recuerde	Remember
Planeó	Planned
Darme	Give To Me
Entiendo	Understand
Compra	Buy
Agradecerle	Thank Her
Corre	Run
Sabe	Know
Funcionan	Work
Sube	Gets On
Responde	Answer
Llega	Arrive
Será	Will Be
Va	Go
Hacer	Do
Esperando	Waiting

Nouns

Calles	Streets

Florería	Flower Shop
Novia	Girlfriend
Ultimo Año	Last Year
Secundaria	High School
Aniversario	Anniversary
Regalo	Gift
Rosas	Roses
Ramo	Bouquet
Vendedora	Seller
Tienda	Strore
Paradero De Bus	Bus Stop
Bus	Bus
Personas	People
Casa	House
Cargo	Fee

Expressions

Se da con la sorpresa	He finds that

Preguntas

1. ¿Dónde está caminando Iván?
2. ¿Por cuánto tiempo ha estado caminando Iván?
3. ¿Qué está buscando Iván?
4. ¿Cómo se llama la novia de Iván?
5. ¿Cuándo se conocieron Iván y su novia?
6. ¿Qué quiere regalar Iván?
7. ¿A quién quiere regalar las flores Iván?
8. ¿Qué problema encuentra Iván en la ciudad?
9. ¿Por qué ninguna tienda está abierta?
10. ¿Cuánto cuestan las flores?
11. ¿Por qué está avergonzado Iván?

Part 3: Negative Sentences with Direct and Indirect Objects

How to Form Negative Sentences

You already know how to form negative sentences. This time you need to learn how to form negative sentences using direct and indirect objects. You'll see that this easy to do.

Let's see first some negative sentences with the indirect object

¿Pagaste a María? / Did you pay Maria?	
Presente	No, no le pago.
Presente continuo	No le estoy pagando
Presente continuo	No estoy pagándole
Pasado (pretérito)	No le pagué
Futuro	No le pagaré
Futuro inmediato	No le voy a pagar
Futuro inmediato	No voy a pagarle
Infinitivo	Pagarle

Imperativo	Tú	Usted	Nosotros	Ustedes
Pagar	No le pagues	No le pague	No le paguemos	No le paguen

But how these phrases would be if both the direct and indirect objects appear in the same sentence.

¿Diste el dinero a María?	
Presente	No, no se lo doy
Presente continuo	No se lo estoy dando
Presente continuo	No estoy dándoselo
Pasado (pretérito)	No se lo di
Futuro	No se lo daré
Futuro inmediato	No se lo voy a dar
Futuro inmediato	No voy a dárselo.
Infinitivo	Dárselo

Imperativo	Tú	Usted	Nosotros	Ustedes
Pagar	No se lo des	No se lo de	No se lo demos	No se lo den.

As a rule of thumb, the indirect object always precedes the direct object.

Special attention should be given to the present tense, and *futuro inmediato* since these have 2 different forms, both acceptable.

The Present Tense:

As you have been able to see, there are 2 ways to use the direct and indirect object with the present tense.

The first way is to write the direct and indirect object before the verb *estar*:

Se lo estoy dando.	I'm giving it to him.
No se lo estoy dando	I'm not giving it to him

The second way is to write to add direct and indirect objects to the verb in present tense. Remember that the indirect object has to come before the direct object. Also, when the direct and indirect objects are added to the verb in present tense, these make up one word.

Estoy dándoselo	I'm giving it to him.
No estoy dándoselo.	I'm not giving it to him

El Futuro Inmediato

The first way is to write the direct and indirect objects before the verb *estar:*

Se lo voy a dar	I'm going to give it to him
No se lo voy a dar.	I'm not going to give it to her

The second way is to add the objects to the verb in infinitive. Remember that they also make up just one word.

Voy a dárselo	I'm going to give it to him.
No voy a dárselo	I'm going to give it to him.

Aside from those two cases, mastering the use of the direct and indirect objects might not prove to be too difficult.

You may have noticed that there are written accents on both the present tense and the infinitive every time objects are added to them. This is because these words are now *stressed on the third-to-last syllable.* In Spanish, these words are called **esdrújulas**, and they always have a written accent on them. Keep this in mind every time you add the objects to some verbs.

Let's see how some verbs change and how they become **esdrújulas.**

Se lo estoy dando	Estoy dándoselo	I'm giving it to him
Lo estoy ayudando	Estoy ayudándolo	I'm helping him
Le estoy trayendo	Estoy trayéndolo	I'm bringing it to him
Se lo voy a decir	Voy a decírselo	I'm going to tell him
Me lo vas a dar	Vas a dármelo	You're going to give it to me.

Exercise 3.1

Write the right direct or indirect object pronouns in the sentences. Don't fail to remember to write the written accent if required.

1. ¿Vas a comer____ (eso)?
2. No puedo ayudar____ (a ti)
3. Ellos no podrán traer____ (a ti, eso).
4. ¿Cómo puedo yo ayudar____ (a ustedes)?
5. ¿Están ellos seguros de que van a traer____ (a mí, eso)?
6. No quiero compartir____ (eso) contigo
7. No ____ (a nosotros) dirán nada
8. No ____ (eso) tengo en mi bolsillo
9. Mis padres irán a dar____ (a mí, eso)

Exercise 3.2

Answer the following questions as you see fit.

1. ¿Le has escrito una carta a alguien?
2. ¿Le has dicho a alguien que sabes hablar español?
3. ¿Te acuerdas del libro que compraste?

Reading Comprehension

Comprando ropa

Buying clothes

Mi novia y yo fuimos a comprar algo en la tienda cerca de mi casa. Salimos muy temprano: a las 10 de la mañana. Yo llevé un poco de dinero porque también quería comprarme algo de ropa para mí. No pensaba que iba a dárselo todo a mi novia y que ella iba a gastárselo en ropa. Pero bueno, al menos no fue bastante dinero.

Cuando llegamos a la sección de hombres, empecé a escoger lo que quería comprar. Ella me dijo que era mejor esperar a que ella comprara primero y después viniéramos, ya que en la tienda de ropa de mujeres hay demasiadas personas y era mejor ir allí primero para salir más rápido.

Cuando llegamos a la sección de mujeres, me di cuenta que la habían remodelado. No era la primera vez que la visitaba, pero era la primera vez que me daba cuenta que le habían hecho bastantes cambios. A mi novia le encantó todos los cambios que la tienda había hecho.

Antes de ir al centro comercial, mi novia había buscado por internet qué es lo que quería comprar. Así que ella fue inmediatamente a buscar esa prenda de vestir. Cuando finalmente la encontró, ella me la mostró. Era un vestido azul muy largo. El modelo era sencillo y parecía de su talla, así que se lo probó. Cuando salió del cambiador, miramos juntos el precio y me sorprendí que estaba más caro de lo que pensaba.

Mi novia me miró a los ojos y me pidió que le ayudara a pagar. Yo ya le había dicho que yo quería ir a comprar algo de ropa para mí también. Así que le dije que si yo le ayudaba a comprar ese vestido, yo no podría comprar nada para mí. Ella me dijo que me iba a devolver el dinero y que a siguiente semana ella me iba a acompañar nuevamente al centro comercial a comprar algo para mí. Incluso ella me prometió que ella me iba a regalar algo.

No pude resistirme ante tantas palabras así que acepté. Le di el dinero que ella necesitaba para comprar ese vestido. Después de comprarlo, fuimos a comer algo. Esta vez mi novia pagó por todo la comida, incluyendo el postre. Honestamente, no me lo esperaba. Cuando le pregunté cuánto costaba toda la comida, ella me dijo que no necesitábamos pagar porque la dueña del restaurante era una de sus mejores amigas.

Después de eso, partimos hacia casa. De seguro la siguiente semana volveré con mi novia, pero esta vez seré yo quien compré la ropa.

Verbs

Salimos	Go Out
Está	To Be
Llevé	Took
Comprar	Buy
Llegamos	Arrived
Escoger	Choose
Viniéramos	Come
Me Di Cuenta	Realised
Remodelado	Remodeled
Mostró	Showed
Parecía	Looked Like
Miramos	Saw
Sorprendí	Surprised
Ayudaba	Helped
Podría	Could
Acompañar	Accompany
Prometió	Promised
Resistirme	Resist
Acepté	Accept
Comer	Eat
Pagó	Payed

Nouns

Novia	Girlfriend
Centro Comercial	Mall Center
Dinero	Money
Ropa	Clothes
Sección De Hombres	Male Section
Tienda De Ropa De Mujeres	Women's Clothing Store
Prenda De Vestir	Article Of Clothing
Palabras	Words
Vestido	Dress

Preguntas

1. ¿A dónde se van Iván y su novia?
2. ¿A qué hora salió Iván?
3. ¿A qué sección llegaron primero?
4. ¿A qué sección llegaron después?
5. ¿De qué se da cuenta Iván cuando entra a la tienda de ropa de mujeres?
6. ¿Qué fue a buscar la novia de Iván?
7. ¿Qué pidió su novia a Iván?
8. ¿A dónde se fueron después de comprar el vestido?
9. ¿Cuánto pagaron por la comida

Chapter 5: *Los Grados*: the Grades of Adjectives, The Comparative Form, and the Superlative Form

Part 1: The Positive Form

How to Form the Positive Form

Do you know what an adjective is? Adjectives are just simple words that tell us much about the noun. In a few words, adjectives qualify and modify the noun. In this whole chapter, we will focus only on *adjetivos calificativos*.

The positive form is the easiest of all the forms. Why? Because the positive form is just the adjective as it appears. In other words, the positive form is the normal, neutral form of an adjective. You already know many adjectives in their positive forms, such as:

Guapo	Handsome
Rápido	Fast
Triste	Sad
Hermoso	Beautiful
Lento	Slow
Moderno	Modern
Nuevo	New
Viejo	Old

We can go on and on with the adjectives, but the point here is not to show you just a list, but for you to understand more about the positive form.

Exercise 1.1

Use the adjectives you know in the following sentences.

1. He visto una ____ mujer.
2. Ese animal es muy ____.
3. Tu hermano mayor es ____.
4. Tu ____ habitación debe ser limpiada.
5. La caja que estás cargando parece muy ____.
6. El muchacho luce ____.
7. Ella no quiere tener ____ perritos.
8. Me encanta jugar con mis ____ mascotas.
9. No escucho muy bien. Debe ser porque el sonido está muy ____.
10. No tenemos flores ____.

In Spanish, adjectives can go before or after the noun:

Son flores hermosas	Those are beautiful flowers
Son hermosas flores	Those are beautiful flowers

Tengo un peludo perro.	I have a hairy dog
Tengo un peludo perro.	I have a hairy dog

Ella escribió una bonita carta.	She wrote a beautiful letter
Ella escribió una carta bonita.	She wrote a beautiful letter

There are exceptions, of course. Some adjectives cannot be placed before or after the noun without changing their meaning.

Él es una persona grande.	He's a big person
Él es una gran persona.	He's a great person
In this case, the adjective *grande* turns into *gran* when it's placed before the noun and at the same time its meaning changes. While the first one is talking about height or size, the second one is referring to a person who has a noble, kind attitude.	

Mi mejor amigo es Daniel.	My best friend is Daniel.
Daniel es uno de mis mejores amigos.	Daniel is one of my best friends.

In this case, *mejor* cannot be placed after the noun *friend*. Actually, *mejor* is always written before any noun.

Adjectives also have to conform to the nouns' gender and number, this is called *concordancia* in Spanish.

	Adjective	
Es una mujer muy alta	Alta	She's a very tall woman
El edificio que estoy viendo es muy alto.	Alto	The building that I'm seeing is very high
Mis amigos son muy altos	Altos	My friends are very tall
Mis primas son muy altas.	Altas	My cousins are very tall

	Adjetivo	
La comida es muy cara.	Cara	The food is very expensive
El vestido es muy caro	Caro	The dress is very expensive
Estas computadoras son muy caras.	Caras	These computers are very expensive
Los libros no resultaron ser muy caros.	Caros	The books didn't end up being too expensive.

Estoy muy avergonzado por lo que pasó.	Avergonzado	I am very ashamed of what happened.
Ellos están avergonzados por lo que pasó	Avergonzado	They're embarrassed for what happened.
Ellas están avergonzadas por lo que pasó	Avergonzadas	They're embarrassed for what happened.
Ella está avergonzada por lo que pasó	Avergonzada	She's embarrassed for what happened.

Remember:
- **M**ost of the time, masculine adjectives ends with –o.

Blanco	White
Negro	Black
Alto	Tall
Avergonzado	Embarrassed
Enojado	Angry

- **A**nd feminine adjectives ends with –a

Blanca	White
Negra	Black
Alta	Tall
Avergonzada	Embarrassed
Enojada	Angry

- **A**djectives that ends with –e only have one form for masculine and feminine nouns.

Fuerte	Strong
Cobarde	Coward
Amable	Kind

- **S**ome verbs that ends with consonant only need an –a added to form the feminine form.

Francésa	French
Habladora	Talkative

- **O**ther verbs that ends with consonant have only one form for both masculine and feminine nouns.

Cortés	Polite
Gris	Gray
Útil	Useful

- **I**f the adjective is used for many nouns, and at least one of them is a masculine noun, then the adjective has to be in its masculine form.

Mi mamá y papá son muy altos.	My mom and dad are very tall.
Mi hija y mi sobrino son muy habladores	My daughter and cousin are very talkative.
María y Daniel estaban muy avergonzados.	María and Daniel were very embarrassed.

- **T**he plural form of the adjectives is formed by adding an −s at then of the adjective.

Esos productos son muy caros.	Those products are very expensive
Mis amigos son muy altos	My friends are very tall
Tus perros son muy obedientes	Your dogs are very obedient.

- **If** the adjective ends with −a consonant or in −í or −ú, then you have to add −es to form the plural form of the adjective

Me gusta mucho el pan francés.	I like French bread a lot.
No me gustan los panes franceses.	I don't like French breads.

Mi amiga es muy respetuosa.	My friend is very respectful.
Mis amigos son muy corteses.	My friends are very polite.

- If the adjective ends with −z, that terminations have to be replaced with −ces

Me siento muy feliz.	I feel very happy.
Estamos muy felices de verte.	We're very happy to see you.

Reading Comprehension

El Perro

The dog

Baxter es el perro que mi papá me regaló hace dos años. Cuando mi papá lo trajo, Baxter era muy pequeño. Su pelaje era marrón y largo. Recuerdo también que él era muy juguetón y travieso. A él le gustaba romper los muebles de la casa y también destruía mis zapatillas y hacía hoyos en mis calcetines.

Ahora que Baxter ha crecido, ya no hace tanto desorden y ya dejó de destruir todas las cosas en la casa. Pero aún le gusta salir a pasear todas las mañanas. Antes de irme a la escuela, me levanto muy temprano para sacar a pasear a Baxter por al menos media hora. Baxter siempre está esperándome en la puerta de mi habitación para ir al parque a pasear.

Hace poco, tuve que llevar a Baxter al veterinario porque se sentía mal. Él no quería comer ni tampoco tomaba agua. Cuando finalmente el veterinario lo vio, ella me dijo que Baxter estaba enfermo y que necesitaba vacunas lo más pronto posible. Yo le pregunté si Baxter iba a mejorar y ella me aseguró que todo iba a estar bien y que no había nada que preocuparse.

La veterinaria también me preguntó si Baxter tenía sus vacunas contra las pulgas. Mi papá le había puesto las vacunas contra las pulgas pero la veterinaria me dijo que ya había pasado suficiente tiempo como para poner una vacuna más. Baxter no es un perro pulgoso, pero de todas maneras le pusimos la vacuna que faltaba.

Después de la visita al veterinario, llegamos a casa y Baxter se fue a descansar. La verdad es que yo estaba muy preocupado por él. Después de unas horas, Baxter se puso mejor y empezó a comer nuevamente la deliciosa comida para perros que siempre le damos. El agua estaba tibia para que la pueda tomar tranquilamente. No comió mucho, pero al menos comió algo.

Espero que Baxter se recupere pronto. Quiero volver a pasearlo en el parque todas las mañanas. Realmente espero a que se mejore completamente.

Verbs

Regaló	Gave
Trajo	Brought
Recuerdo	Remember
Romper	Break

497

Destruía	Destroy
Ha Crecido	Has Grown
Pasear	Walk
Comer	Eat
Tomaba	Drank
Mejorar	Improve/Get Better
Descansar	Rest
Preocuparse	Worry

Adjectives

Marrón	Brown
Largo	Long
Juguetón	Playful
Travieso	Naughty
Mal	Bad
Enfermo	Sick
Preocupado	Worried
Tibia	Lukewarm
Deliciosa	Delicious

Nouns

Muebles	Furniture
Hoyos	Holes
Calcetines	Socks
Desorden	Mess
Parque	Park
Pulgas	Fleas
Agua	Water
Vacuna	Vaccine
Veterinario	Vet

Preguntas

1. ¿Cómo se llama el perro del protagonista?
2. ¿Quién trajo al perro?

3. ¿Cómo era el perro cuando era pequeño?
4. ¿Qué le gusta hacer al protagonista todas las mañanas con el perro?
5. ¿Por qué Baxter tuvo que ser llevado al veterinario?
6. ¿Qué dijo el veterinario sobre Baxter?
7. ¿Qué hizo Baxter después de regresar a casa?
8. ¿Qué es lo que espera el protagonista?

Part 2: The Comparative Form

Comparative of Superiority

The comparative form is divided into three different forms. The first is known as comparative of superiority or *comparativo de superioridad* in Spanish.

The name itself reveals the meaning of this form of comparative. It's used to compare two or more objects or people and show that one of them has an advantage or greater quality than the others.

Let's see how this form of comparative is formed.

Sustantivo	Verb	Más	Adjetivo	Que	Sustantivo
Iván	Corre	Más	Rápido	Que	Juan

Fabiana canta mejor que Rocío	Fabiana sings better than Rocio
Rosa es más bonita que Fabiana	Rosa is more beautiful than Fabiana
Diego es más alto que Iván	Diego is taller than Ivan
Daniel escribe más rápido que Jorge	Daniel writes faster than Jorge.

Have in mind that:

- Some verbs have a special comparative form:

Más bueno	Mejor
Más grande	Mayor
Más malo	Peor
Mas pequeño	Menor

La película que vimos la semana pasada es mejor que esta.	The movie that we saw last week is better than this one.
Yo soy mayor que mi hermano.	I'm older than my brother.
Esos alumnos de esa escuela son peores que los de la mía	This school's students are worse than mine.
Mi hermana es más joven que yo.	My sister is younger than me.

- You can also compare more than just adjectives:

You can compare nouns too:

Joe tiene más amigos que Fransisco	Joe has more friends than Francisco
Fabiana tiene más dinero que Roberto	Fabiana has more money than Roberto
Roberto come más comida que Fabiana	Roberto eats more food than Fabiana
José tiene más celulares que yo.	José has more cellphones than me.

You can compare verbs:

Fabiana gana más que Roberto	Fabiana earns more than Roberto
Joe conversa más que Francisco	Joe talks more than Francisco
Roberto come más que Fabiana	Roberto eats more than Fabiana
José compra más que yo	José buys more than me.

You can compare quantities with numbers. To form this, you need this structure:

Sujeto	Más de	Cantidad	Complemento

Tengo más de dos perros en mi casa	I have more than 2 dogs in my house
Ella tiene más de 5 amigos.	She has more than 5 friends
La profesora enseña a más de 50 estudiantes.	The teacher teaches more than 50 students.

Now you can also form some comparative sentences. Let's see how well you can do it.

Exercise 2.1

Complete the missing words in each sentence

1. Yo escribo más ____ que mi hermano.
2. Mi hermano es más ____ que yo.
3. Juan es ____ alto ____ José.
4. José corre ____ rápido ____ que Juan.
5. Mi celular costó más ____ el tuyo.
6. Mi computadora es ____ pesada que mi celular.
7. El televisor es ____ moderno ____ la radio.
8. Mis padres son ____ bajos ____ mi hermano.
9. Mis amigos son ____ tranquilos ____ yo.
10. María es ____ alta ____ Ivón.

Tranlsate the following sentences

1. José es más alto que María
2. María es más rápida que Fabiana
3. José tiene más amigos que Diego
4. Iván come más que yo
5. Yo soy más bajo que mi hermano
6. El libro de matemáticas es más pesado que el de ciencias.
7. Mi perro es más peludo que el tuyo
8. Mis amigos cantan mejor que yo.
9. Mis manos son más largas que las manos de mi mamá
10. Mis amigos son más estudiosos que yo.

Reading Comprehension

La carrera

The race

Esta semana, la escuela está organizando una carrera entre todos los estudiantes. El entrenador estuvo ayudando a Benjamín entrenar. Benjamín ha estado entrenando duro.

Su rutina es la misma todos los días: se levanta temprano y va a la escuela antes que comiencen las clases. Durante media hora, el entrena con algunos compañeros más, pero es obvio que Benjamín entrena más duro que sus demás compañeros. Sus compañeros también están entrenando para la carrera y esperan poder ganar el premio.

La escuela está ofreciendo bastante dinero para el ganador de la carrera. Muchos alumnos se han enlistado para participar, y entre ellos hay alumnos de varias edades. Algunos son mayores que otros y algunos alumnos han entrenado más que otros. Benjamín es uno de ellos. Él ha entrenado más que la mayoría de los alumnos.

Es viernes, es el día de la carrera. Por fin, Benjamín va a correr y participar en la carrera. Antes de salir a correr, él tiene que calentar y estirarse. Mientras va calentando, él se da cuenta que hay más alumnos participando de lo que esperaba. Algunos de los participantes lucen mayores que él. Otros lucen más musculosos que Benjamín. A benjamín le entra la duda y se pone un poco nervioso.

Es ahí cuando su entrenador va a animarlo y a decirle que no hay que sentirse nervioso. Que él ya ha llegado hasta aquí y que es hora de demostrar que él puede ganar la carrera. Benjamín agradece las palabras del entrenador y va a correr.

La carrera empieza y parece que Benjamín está perdiendo. Está cuarto en la carrera. Después de unos segundos, Benjamín se recupera y empieza a correr más rápido. Ahora está segundo. El entrenador lo anima desde los asientos.

Ahora Benjamín está primero. Es obvio que él es más rápido que los demás. Los estudiantes que están viendo la carrera empiezan a gritar y a animarlo. Finalmente, Benjamín cruza la línea de llegada y la carrera llega a su fin.

Todos aplauden a Benjamín. El entrenador va a saludarlo. Él es declarado el ganador de la carrera y le dan el trofeo. Él también recibe el dinero que se prometió. Tal parece que todo el esfuerzo que Benjamín puso al entrenamiento valió la pena.

Ahora que Benjamín ha ganado esta carrera, él es invitado a participar en una carrera aún más grande. Esta vez, es una carrera entre varias escuelas. Benjamín dice que lo va a pensar.

Verbs

Organizando	Organazing
Ayudando	Helping
Entrenando	Training
Correr	Run
Participar	Participate
Calentar	Warm Up
Estirarse	Stretch
Demostrar	Show/Demonstrate
Ganar	Win
Recupera	Recover
Perdiendo	Losing

Adjectives

Más Duro	Harder
Mayores	Older
Musculosos	Muscular
Nervioso	Nervous
Segundo	Second
Cuarto	Fourth
Primero	First
Rápido	Faster
Declarado	Declared

Nouns

Rutina	Routine
Carrera	Race
Alumnos	Students
Trofeo	Prize

Expression

Le entra la duda

He starts to doubt

Es obvio que

It's obvious that

Preguntas

1. ¿Qué está organizando la escuela?
2. ¿Quién está entrenando para la carrera?
3. ¿Cuál es la rutina de Benjamín?
4. ¿Qué hace Benjamín antes de correr?
5. ¿Qué le dice su entrenador cuando Benjamín se pudo nervioso?
6. ¿En qué puesto llega Benjamín?
7. ¿Qué le dan a Benjamín por ganar la carrera?
8. ¿A qué es invitado Benjamín?

Part 3: Comparative of Inferiority

How to Form the Comparative of Inferiority

To form the comparative of inferiority, you only need to replace the word *más (more)* with the word *menos (less)*.

The structure of the comparative of inferiority is as follows

Sustantivo	Menos	Adjetivo	Que	Sustantivo

María es menos alta que Fabiana	María is less tall than Fabiana
Daniela es menos amigable que Rosa	Daniela is less friendly than Rosa
Rosa es menos gorda que Daniela	Rosa is less fat than Daniela

Have in mind that:

- You can compare quantities too.

To compare quantities you need to this structure

Sujeto	Menos de	Cantidad	Complemento

Rosa tiene menos de 3 perros en su casa.	Rosa has less than 3 dogs in her house
Jorge tiene menos de 5 clases.	Jorge has less than 5 classes
Juan tiene menos de 3 años estudiando	Juan has less than 3 years studying

- You can compare verbs, too

Yo como menos que tú	I run faster than you.
Ellos corren menos rápido que Benjamín	They run less fast than Benjamin
Benjamín es menos musculoso que ellos	Benjamin is less muscular than them

- You can compare nouns, too

Juan tiene menos amigos que José	Juan has less friends than Jose
Ellos comen menos postres que yo	They eat less desserts than me
Fabián tiene menos celulares que yo	Fabián has less cellphones than you

Let's see some more sentences where the comparative of inferiority appears

- Jennifer es menos gorda que yo.
- Jennifer is less fat than me.

- Mis padres son menos altos que los tuyos
- My parents are less tall than yours.

- Mis amigos son menos musculosos que yo.
- My friends are less muscular than me.

- José tiene menos mascotas que yo.
- Jose has less pets than me.

- Daniela tiene menos años trabajando que yo.
- Daniela has less years working than me.

- Diego es menos estudioso que su hermano.
- Diego is less studious than his brother.

Exercise 2.1

Fill in the following sentences with the missing words.

1. Ellos tienen _____ lapiceros _____ nosotros.
2. Nosotros tenemos _____ amigos _____ que ustedes.
3. Mi hermano mayor es _____ alto _____ yo.
4. Mi tía tiene menos _____ que mi mamá.
5. Mi mamá es menos _____ que mi profesora.
6. Mi amiga es _____ rápida que _____.
7. Mis amigos son menos _____ que mis padres.
8. Este perrito es menos _____ que el mío.
9. Tu gato es menos _____ que mi gato.
10. Este parque es menos _____ que el otro.

Exercise 2.2

Answer the following questions as you see fit.

1. ¿Qué es lo que tus amigos tienen menos que tú?
2. ¿Tienes más años que tu mejor amigo?
3. ¿Eres menor que tu profesor?
4. ¿Cuántos hermanos mayores tienes?
5. ¿Quién tiene más mascotas que tú?
6. ¿Quién corre más que tú?
7. ¿Quién habla más rápido que tú?

Reading Comprehension

Las Clases de Baile

Dance classes

José y Fabiana están a punto de ir a su clase de baile. Ellos han estado yendo a las clases de baile por más de dos meses. Cuando llegaron por primera vez a la clase de baile, ellos no sabían bailar para nada. Y ahora ellos bailan mejor que los demás estudiantes.

Al principio, José estaba más nervioso que Fabiana. Fabiana estaba menos preocupada porque ella ya sabía bailar un poco. El profesor llega a la clase de baile y les dice a los estudiantes que se pongan en sus lugares. ¿Qué tipo de baile están aprendiendo José y Fabiana?

Ellos están aprendiendo a bailar salsa. Salsa es un baile muy popular en Latinoamérica, pero fue inventado en Nueva York. Hoy en día, millones de personas alrededor del mundo bailan salsa, en especial en los países donde se habla el español.

La salsa puede ser un baile muy difícil de aprender, como José y Fabiana se están dando cuenta. La verdad es que puede ser muy frustrante aprender a bailar salsa ya que tiene muchos movimientos y a algunas personas no les gusta moverse tanto en la pista de baile. Ahora mismo, José está intentando hacer una maniobra dónde él da vueltas a Fabiana. Él sabe muy bien que Fabiana se marea más rápido que él. Felizmente, nada malo le pasa a Fabiana.

Durante la clase, los alumnos intentan imitar a la profesora. Ella siempre les está diciendo:

"No tengan vergüenza de intentar este paso"

José y Fabiana siempre están intentando imitar a la profesora también, pero a veces resulta muy difícil. Y con mucha razón es difícil. La profesora es una profesional. Tiene más años bailando que José y Fabiana. Fabiana tiene menos tiempo estando en la clase que algunos de sus compañeros y José tiene menos valor que algunos de sus compañeros.

"¿Cómo podemos bailar tan bien como usted, profesora?" – pregunta José

"Bueno, tienes que practicar mucho. Intenta practicar con Fabiana todos los días." – le dice la profesora

"Pero profesora, no tengo mucho tiempo libre"

"Tendrás que organizarte mejor para tener un poco de tiempo para practicar"

Ahora José ya sabe lo que tiene que hacer. Él le cuenta a Fabiana y ambos acuerdan separar un poco de tiempo para que ambos puedan practicar uno de estos días.

Verbs

Yendo	Going
Llegaron	Arrived/Came
Sabían	Knew
Bailar	Dance
Inventado	Invented
Moverse	Move
Aprender	Teach
Marea	Make/Be Dizzy
Resulta	Results
Intentar	Try
Imitar	Imitate
Practicar	Rehearse/Practice
Acuerdan	Agree

Adjectives

Mejor	Better
Nervioso	Nervous
Popular	Popular
Frustrante	Frustrating
Difícil	Difficult
Profesional	Professional

Nouns

Clases De Baile	Dance Classes
Tipo De Baile	Types Of Dance
Salsa	Salsa
Millones	Millions
Movimientos	Moves

Maniobra	Move
Latinoamérica	Latin America
Profesora	Teacher

Expression

| En Sus Lugares | In Your Places |
| Separar Un Poco De Tiempo | Set Aside Some Time |

Preguntas

1. ¿Quiénes van a ir a sus clases de baile?
2. ¿Sabían ellos bailar cuando empezaron a tomar las clases?
3. ¿Quién estaba más nervioso?
4. ¿Qué tipo de baile están ellos aprendiendo?
5. ¿Dónde fue inventada la salsa, pero dónde se baila más?
6. ¿Es fácil aprender a bailar salsa?
7. ¿Por qué puede ser frustrante bailar salsa?
8. ¿Qué consejo les da la profesora a José y Fabiana?

Part 4: Comparative of Equality

How to Form the Comparative of Equality

The comparative of equality is used to compare two nouns, but rather than indicating that one of them is greater than the other, this comparative form is used to indicate that both nouns share the same level of quality. Let's see some examples.

The structure of the comparative of equality is as follows:

Sustantivo	Verbo	Tan	Adjetivo	Como	Sustantivo
María	Es	Tan	Alta	Como	Rosa

José es tan rápido como Pedro.	José is as fast as Pedro.
Pedro es tan amigable como Iván.	Pedro is as friendly as Ivan
Alicia es tan flaca como Fabiana.	Alicia is as thin as Fabiana
Juan es tan alto como Diego	Juan is as tall as Diego

Have in mind that:

- You can compare **verbs**

But you need to exchange the word *tan* for *tanto*

Sustantivo	Verbo	Tan	Como	Sustantivo
María	Come	Tanto	Como	Rosa

José corre tanto como Pedro	José runs as much as Diego
Pedro estudia tanto como Iván	Pedro studies as much as Iván
Alicia juega tanto como Fabiana	Alicia plays as much as Fabiana
Juan crece tanto como Diego	Juan grows as much as Diego

- You can compare **nouns**

But you need to write *tanto* instead of *tan*. Also, *tanto* has to conform to the gender and number of the nouns you're comparing.

Yo tengo tantos amigos como mi hermano.	I have as many friends as my brother
Mi hermano tiene tanto dinero como mi primo.	My brother has as much money as my cousin
Mi prima tiene tantas sillas como mi mamá	My cousin has as many chairs as my mom
Mi mejor amigo tiene tanta comida como yo.	My best friend has as much food as me.

Exercise 4.1

Fill in the following sentences with the correct words

1. Yo tengo ____ amigos como mi primo.
2. Mi perro tiene ____ crías como mi gato.
3. Mi amigo es ____ guapo como yo.
4. Mi hermano menos corre ____ como mi mejor amigo.
5. Ella canta ____ bien como yo.
6. Yo no hablo el español tan ____ como yo.
7. Ella habla ____ idiomas como yo.
8. Yo tengo ____ discos como yo.
9. Nosotros tenemos ____ profesores como ustedes.

Reading Comprehension

Mi casa

My house

¡Bienvenidos a mi casa! Yo me llamo Roberto y vivo aquí en un vecindario en el centro de la ciudad. He vivido aquí casi toda mi vida. La casa donde antes vivía estaba muy lejos. Yo no he vivido en este vecindario tanto como mis vecinos. Ellos han vivido por muchos más años que yo.

Tal vez te estés preguntando quienes viven conmigo. ¿Crees que puedes adivinarlo? Yo vivo con mis padres, mis abuelos, mi hermano mayor, mi hermana menor y mi perrito. En total, somos 7 viviendo en esta casa.

No creas que porque somos 7 aquí, la casa nos queda muy pequeña. Todo lo contrario, la casa es tan grande como un campo de fútbol pequeño. Claro, no es una mansión, pero al menos es del tamaño que necesitamos.

En este vecindario hay muchas cosas divertidas que siempre están ocurriendo. A veces mis vecinos traen pasteles y nos los regalan. Debo ser honesto y decir que ellos hacen pasteles muy deliciosos. Ni mi mamá hace pasteles tan deliciosos como los de ellos. Una vecina mía también se ha convertido en una de mis mejores amigas. Cuando llegue por primera vez a este barrio, ella me enseñó todas las tiendas dónde podía comprar lo que yo quería. Ella también me enseñó dónde están la veterinaria, el centro comercial y el aeropuerto. No están tan lejos como yo pensaba.

Ahora que estoy en la secundaria, ella y yo estudiamos en la misma escuela. A veces regresamos juntos de la escuela. Ella no es tan alta como parece. En realidad, ella es más baja que yo. Lo importante es que ella es una de mis mejores amigas y creo que al final del día el tamaño no importa.

Ahora que estoy en la secundaria y tengo mucha tarea que hacer, ya no puedo salir tanto como quisiera. Al menos la profesora de matemáticas no deja tanta tarea como el profesor de química. Hoy día ya acabé toda mi tarea, así que creo que llamaré a mi amiga para salir juntos a jugar esta tarde.

Cuando llegué a la casa de mi amiga, sus padres me dijeron que ella había salido al centro comercial. Tengo su número de teléfono pero dejé mi teléfono celular en mi casa. Ni modo, creo que tendré que regresar y llamarla.

Verbs

Me Llamo	My Name Is
Vivo	Live
Preguntando	Asking
Adivinarlo	Guess It
Decir	Say
Ocurriendo	Happening
Comprar	Buy
Parece	Seems/Looks Like
Salido	Go Out
Estudiamos	Study
Regresar	Go Back
Llamarla	Call Her

Adjectives

Lejos	Far
Pequeña	Short/Small
Grande	Big/Large
Pequeño	Small
Honesto	Honest
Divertidas	Funny
Deliciosas	Delicious
Alta	Tall
Baja	Short
Misma	Same
Pensaba	Think
Quisiera	Would Like To

Nouns

Vecindario	Neighborhood
Centro De La Ciudad	City Center
Padres	Parents
Abuelos	Grandparents

Mi Hermano Mayor	My Older Brother
Mi Hermana Menor	My Younger Brother
Perrito	Puppy
Casa	House
Campo De Fútbol	Soccer Field
Mansión	Mansion
Vecina	Neighbor
Pasteles	Cakes
Barrio	Neighborhood
Tiendas	Stores
Veterinaria	Vets
El Centro Comercial	Malls
Aeropuerto	Airports
La Secundaria	High School
Profesora	Teacher
Número De Teléfono	Telephone Number
Escuela	School

Expressions

Ni mi mamá	Not even my mom

Preguntas:

1. ¿Cómo se llama el protagonista, y qué nos está mostrando?
2. ¿Es la casa donde ahora vive la única donde ha vivido?
3. ¿Quiénes viven con el protagonista?
4. ¿Es la casa del tamaño ideal?
5. ¿Qué es lo que traen los vecinos a la casa del protagonista?
6. ¿Quién es la mejor amiga del protagonista?
7. ¿Qué lugares le enseñó su mejor amiga?
8. ¿Quién deja más tarea?
9. ¿Qué pasó cuando el protagonista fue a la casa de su mejor amiga?

Part 5: The Superlative Form

The superlative form has two forms. The first one is called the relative superlative, or *el superlativo relativo.*

The Relative Superlative

This is formed with the following structure in mind:

Sustanti vo	Verb o	Artícu lo	(sustantiv o)	Má s	Adjeti vo	D e	Compleme nto
Juan	Es	El	(muchach o)	Má s	Fuerte	D e	Su escuela

Remember that the article has to conform to the gender and number of the noun.

Diego es el más inteligente de la clase	Diego is the smartest in the class
Fabiana es la mujer más hermosa que he visto	Fabiana is the most beautiful woman I've ever seen.
Iván es el muchacho más alto del salón	Ivan is the tallest guy ni the class
Elsa es la mejor madre del mundo.	Elsa is the greatest mother in the whole world
Eres el único amigo cercano que he tenido	You are the only close friend I've ever had
Mi perro es el más fiel de todos	My dog is the most loyal of all
Mi papá es el hombre más fuerte que conozco	My dad is the strongest man that I know
Él es el mejor tocando la guitarra	He's the best playing the guitar

Remember that there are some adjectives that have an irregular form:

Adjective	Comparative	Superlative	Translation
Grande (If it refers to age)	Mayor	El mayor	Old
Grande (if it refers to size)	Más grande Menos grande	El más grande	Big
Pequeño (if it	Menor	El menor	Young

referes to age)			
Pequeño (if it refers to size)	Menos pequeño Más pequeño	El más pequeño	Small
Bueno	Mejor	El mejor	Good
Poco	Menos	-	Less/ a little/ a few
Malo	Peor	El peor	Bad
Mucho	Más	-	More/ a lot/much/many

Es la mejor bailarina del mundo.	She is the greatest dancer in the whole world
Él es el mayor de mis hijos.	He's my oldest son
Fabián es el menor de todos mis hermanos.	Fabián is the youngest of my brothers.

Exercise 5.1

Fill in the following sentences with the correct form of the relative superlative

1. Ella es la mujer más ____ del mundo.
2. Nosotros somos los ____ cantantes del mundo.
3. Él es el ____ de mis hermanos.
4. Yo soy el ____ amigo de Fabián.
5. Mi hermana es la más ____ de toda la familia.
6. Tatiana es la ____ corredora de la escuela
7. Sean es muchacho más ____ que conozco
8. Juan no es el ____ gordo de la clase.
9. Juan es el ____ flaco de la casa.
10. Mi amigo es el ____ travieso de nuestro grupo.
11. Eleonor es la más ____ de la clase.
12. Tu relación es la ____ larga que he visto.
13. Nosotros somos los ____ jovenes en esta clase.
14. Esa bebida es la ____ fuerte que he probado
15. Esa comida es la más ____ salada que he visto.

Also have in mind that this form of superlative is called *relative superlative of superiority*. This means that there's also another type of *relative superlative*

The Relative Superlative of Inferiority

There's not really too much to say about this type of relative superlative other than you only need to replace *más* with *menos*. Let's see its structure and then some examples.

Sustantivo	Verbo	Artículo	(sustantivo)	Menos	Adjetivo	De	Complemento
Juan	Es	El	(muchacho)	Menos	Fuerte	De	Su escuela

519

Mi amigo es el menos fuerte de la clase.	My friend is the least strong in the class
Ivan es el menos confiable del salón.	Ivan is the least trustworthy in the class
Yo soy el menos alto de mi familia.	I'm the least tall in my family
Mi perro es el menos obediente que he tenido	My dog is the least obedient that I've had
Mis amigos son los menos tranquilos que yo haya tenido	My friends are the least quiet that I've had
Mi prima es la menos guapa de la familia.	My cousin is the least pretty in my family
Mi amiga es menos alta del vecindario	My friends is the least tall in my neighborhood
Mi hermana es la más joven de mi familia.	My sister is the youngest in my family.
Mis amigos son los peores.	My friends are the worst

Exercise 5.2

Fill in the following sentences with the correct form of the relative superlative. Some sentences might have more than one possible answer.

1. Ella es la ____ confiable.
2. Nosotros somos los ____ altos.
3. Mi mamá es la más ____ de la familia.
4. Mis tíos son los más ____ de la familia.
5. Mi perro es el menos ____ de todos los perros que he tenido.
6. Mi mejor amigo es el menos ____.
7. Yo soy el mejor ____.
8. Ellos son los peores ____.
9. Él es el ____ cantante.
10. Ellos son los ____ bailarines.
11. Ella es la mejor____.
12. Nosotros somos los mejores ____.
13. Mi clase es la mejor ____.
14. Mi profesor es el peor ____.
15. Mi mamá es la mejor ____.

The Absolute Superlative

There's also the absolute superlative. Its structure is as it follows

Sustantivo	Verbo	Muy	Adjetivo
Fabián	Es	muy	guapo

Muy means can be translated into English as *very*.

Javier es muy alto	Javier is very tall
Fabián es muy guapo	Fabián is very handsome
Mi doctor es muy inteligente	My doctor is very intelligent
Mi abuelo es muy bueno	My granddad is very good
Mi amigo es muy sabio	My buddy is very wise
Mi escuela es muy buena	My school is very good
Mi papá es muy grande	My dad is very big

There's also another way to form the absolute superlative, and this is formed by adding –ísimo to the adjective. Let's see some examples:

Mi padre es grandísimo	My dad is the biggest
Mi tío es altísimo	My uncle is very tall
Mi abuela es viejísima	My grandmom is very old
Mi amigo es bonísimo	My buddy is very good
Mi país es larguísimo	My country is very large
Yo soy gordísimo	I am very fat
Mi hermano es flaquísimo	My brother is very thin
Mi computadora es lentísima	My computer is very slow

There are some exceptions to this rule:

amplio	*amplísimo*
fuerte	*fortísimo*
valiente	*valentísimo*
bueno	*bonísimo*
pobre	*paupérrimo*
antiguo	*antiquísimo*
sagrado	*sacratísimo*
fiel	*fidelísimo*

Have in mind that every adjective that has the –ísimo added to it needs to conform to the gender and number of the noun.

Also, you cannot use both *muy* and an adjective that ends with –ísimo in the same sentence.

Some verbs that ends with –ble, need to replace that termination with –*bilísimo*

amable	amabilísimo
noble	nobilísimo

There are also some adjectives that do not accept superlative forms, in part because they already convey the idea of absoluteness. Some of these verbs are

eterno	eternal
ilimitado	unlimited
muerto	dead
inmortal	immortal
infinito	infinite
único	unique

If the adjectives ends with –ca or –co, then they need to change to a –c or –qu

rico	riquísimo
rica	riquísima

There are some words that can also help form the superlative, such as *super, requete and extra*. Many of these are very informal and you might only hear them in conversations.

- Esta súper deliciosa
- It's super delicious

- Esta requiterica
- It's very delicious

Exercise 5.3

Fill in the following sentences with the correct form of the superlative

1. Tengo _____ (mucho) dinero
2. Ellos son los ____ (bueno)
3. Yo soy ____ (valiente)
4. Ellas son ____(feas)
5. Nosotros trabajamos ____ (duro)
6. Hemos estado trabajando el día y ahora estamos ____ (cansados)
7. Mi perro tiene tanta hambre. Creo que es ____ (comelon)

Reading Comprehension

La talla

The size

Cuando finalmente Roberto llegó al centro comercial para poder encontrar a su novia, él se dio cuenta que muchas tiendas estaban cerradas. Él no entendía por qué, al fin y al cabo, era un día normal. Ni siquiera era feriado. Sea como sea, Roberto entra a la tienda y empieza a buscar a su novia.

La novia de Roberto se llama Elsa. Ella siempre va de compras los jueves por la mañana. Ella tiene una tienda favorita a donde a ella le gusta ir. Roberto sabe bien que si quiere encontrarla, él tiene que ir a esa tienda primero.

A pesar de que Roberto la ha estado buscando ya por más de media hora, él no puede encontrarla en la tienda. Es normal, la tienda a la que ella va es la tienda más grande de toda la ciudad. Y el centro comercial donde está la tienda es modernísimo. El centro comercial tiene la última tecnología, como cámaras de vigilancia muy modernas, alarmas muy ruidosas y agentes de seguridad súper entrenados para cualquier emergencia.

Roberto sabe bien que no puede llamar as u novia. Después de todo, él ya intentó hace eso y ella no le contestaba. Todo dependía de poder hallarla en la tienda de ropa.

Mientras él la buscaba, una vendedora se le acerca y le pregunta:

"Hola, ¿no quisieras probarte el nuevo modelo de camisa que tenemos?"

"muchas gracias, pero no vengo a comprar ropa. Vengo a buscar a una persona que creo que debe estar en la sección de mujeres"

"la sección de mujeres está al otro lado de la tienda"

"Gracias"

"Si desea probar los nuevos modelos, no dude en buscarme. Todos los modelos están a mitad de precio."

"¿A mitad de precio?"

"Así es, a mitad de precio"

"Bueno, en ese caso, quisiera ver los nuevos modelos"

"En un momento se los traigo"

Roberto se queda sentado esperando por los modelos de camisa que están en descuento. Después de un rato, la vendedora viene y trae muchísimas camisas. Roberto se prueba uno por uno y se da cuenta que ninguna es de su talla.

"¿No tiene alguna otra talla? Estas están muy pequeñas. Y esta otra está ajustadísima"

"Se lo traigo dentro de un momento, señor"

Mientras Roberto se queda esperando. Su novia aparece. Ellos empiezan a conversar y ella se da cuenta de que Roberto está ahí para poder comprar algo. Ella se acuerda que los todos los descuentos sólo están disponibles si es que él paga con tarjeta de crédito. Roberto pregunta eso a la vendedora y ella se lo confirma. Roberto le dice que él no tiene tarjeta de crédito así que se va de la tienda con su novia sin haber comprado nada.

Verbs

Llegó	Arrived
Poder	Can
Encontrar	Find
Dio Cuenta	Realised
Va De Compras	Go Shopping
Buscando	Searching
Intentó	Tried
Hacer	Do
Contestaba	Picked Up

Adjectives

Ruidosas	Noisy
Ultima	Latest
Modernas	Modern
Entrenados	Trained

Nouns

Cámaras	Cameras
Tecnología	Technology
Alarmas	Alarms
Agentes De Seguridad	Security Agents

Preguntas

1. ¿Para qué va el protagonista al centro comercial?
2. ¿De qué se da cuenta cuando llega al centro comercial?
3. ¿Qué tiene de especial la tienda?
4. ¿Qué tiene de especial el centro comercial?
5. ¿Qué le ofrece la vendedora a Roberto?
6. ¿Cómo reacciona Roberto al principio? ¿Cómo reacciona después?
7. ¿Qué lo hizo cambiar de opinión a Roberto?
8. ¿Dónde se encuentran Roberto y su novia?
9. ¿Qué le dice su novia a Roberto?
10. ¿Qué deciden hacer Roberto y su novia?

Conclusion

You know difficult it can be for anyone to learn a new foreign language. But you dared take the first step towards fluency by having this book in your hands and actively reading it. This book is the tool you needed to solidify what you previously learned, and that's going to be very useful for you.

Some of the subjects here might seem a little familiar to you. And that's no chance. *Learn Spanish For Intermediate Level The Fast Way* was designed for those who already made the first move. Even though you might think that some of the subjects here are familiar, they appear in this book so that you can expand on previous knowledge. That way, you will be prepared when the time comes for you to speak and show your language skills.

Learn Spanish For Intermediate Level The Fast Way also provided you with many useful conversations. These conversations reflect how the language is used on a day-to-day basis by native speakers. Use that to your advantage. Practice and imitate how these are structured, how the verbs, nouns, adjectives, and expressions are used in the way they appear in these conversations.

Since you're learning how a native speaker talks in his native language, why not you try the same? Why don't you try to practice with a native speaker? You don't need to be aware of it all. You don't need to know all the grammar rules and exceptions to really speak with a Spanish native speaker. Most of the time, that person will be delighted to hear another person trying to learn and speak their language. They will surely help you if you really express yourself in a very kind, respectful and polite manner.

Don't give up. If you feel you need to practice more in order to speak as you would like to, keep practicing. Remember that learning a language is not a difficult task, but that doesn't mean that it has to impossible or frustrating. Keep practicing and looking for help if you need it. in the meantime, you can always rely on *Learn Spanish For Intermediate Level The Fast Way* to help you have the best foundation in the Spanish language.

1001 Top Spanish Words in Context

How to Speak
Intermediate-Level Spanish
in Less than 21 Days

[Michael Navarro]

Introduction

Congratulations on purchasing *1001 Top Spanish Words in Context: How to Speak Intermediate-Level Spanish in Less than 21 Days*, and thank you for doing so.

In this book, we will focus on providing you with words written in Spanish and English. These words will be used in a sentence in Spanish, which we will also translate into English so that you can analyze the context in both languages. Through this, you will be able to compare the meaning of each of the words, focusing on just one at a time. For example:

Hola / Hello

Hola, ¿Cómo estas? / Hello, how are you?

Here, the main word is *hola*, which is the word initially mentioned, while the rest of the words are what we call context. Thanks to this method, you will learn to use the main word in context and also the meaning of the secondary words.

In the following chapters, you will find words from different topics, such as verbs, adjectives, adverbs, polysemous words, home, household chores, clothes, garments, accessories, nature, animals, professions, family, relationships, numbers, and many more. Learning these words and knowing how to use them will upgrade your Spanish language to the intermediate level.

We recommend reviewing the words provided here in the book at least once every two months so that you can remember them and put them into practice in your everyday life.

There are plenty of books on this subject on the market, so thank you again for choosing this one! Every effort was made to ensure it is full of as much useful information as possible. Please enjoy!

Chapter 1: Grammar

¡Felicitaciones! You have purchased a book to learn the Spanish language. In this book, we will provide a word in Spanish, as well as a sentence where it is used in context.

Verbs

In this section, we will provide you words that define actions; those words are known as verbs. Please remember that the verbs have a lot of different tenses. In the list, we will put the infinitive form of the verb, but in the context, we will use any of its tenses.

1. Ser / To be

Cuando crezca quiero ser un gran professional / When I grow up, I want to be a great professional

2. Estar / To be

Más tarde voy a estar en clases, no interrumpas / Later, I am going to be on clases; do not interrupt

3. Traer / To bring

¿Crees que puedas traer contigo un poco de dinero extra? / Do you think you could bring a little extra cash with you?

4. Caer / To fall

Ayer me resbalé y caí, pero hoy no vuelvo a caer / Yesterday, I slipped and fell, but today, I won't fall again.

5. Cortar / To cut

Mañana tengo que ir a cortar el árbol, ya está muy alto / Tomorrow, I have to go to cut the tree; it's already very high.

6. Amar / To love

Sabes muy bien que yo te voy a amar por siempre / You know very well that I'm going to love you forever.

7. Escribir / To wirte

Llegó la hora de escribir todo lo que querido escribir / It's time to write everything I wanted to write.

8. Leer / To read

Todas las mañanas me despierto y empiezo a leer durante una hora / Every morning, I wake up and start reading for an hour.

9. Nadar / To swim

Me encantaría saber nadar pero le tengo muchísimo miedo al agua / I would love to know how to swim, but I am very afraid of water.

10. Ir / To go

Ahora en un rato voy a ir a comprar merienda, ¿Quieres venir? / In a little while, I'm going to buy a snack; do you want to come?

11. Bailar - Danzar/ To dance

A mi prima le encanta ir a fiestas porque puede bailar toda la noche / My cousin loves to go to parties because she can dance all night.

12. Hacer / To do

Tengo que hacer un montón de tarea este fin de semana, no podré jugar / I have a lot of homework to do this weekend; I won't be able to play.

13. Pensar / To think

A veces me gusta pensar que no somos los únicos seres vivos en el universo / Sometimes, I like to think we're not the only living beings in the universe.

14. Llamar / To call

Si necesitas llamar, hazlo ahora, luego no podré atenderte / If you need to call, do it now; later, I won't be able to pick up the phone.

15. Manejar / To drive

A Lindsey le regalaron un carro, pero no lo usa porque aún no sabe manejar / Lindsey was given a car, but she doesn't use it because she doesn't know how to drive yet.

16. Preguntar / To ask

Nunca es malo preguntar algo que no sabemos / It's never bad to ask something we don't know.

17. Aceptar / To accept

Debemos aceptar que somos un peligro para el planeta y comenzar a cambiar / We must accept that we are a danger to the planet and start changing.

18. Permitir / To allow

No pienso permitirle a mi hijo que se vaya a una fiesta con esas personas / I'm not allowing my son to go to a party with those people.

19. Surgir / To arise

Muy pronto va a surgir un nuevo dragón que destruirá todo / Soon, a new dragon will arise and will destroy everything.

20. Despertar / To awake

Todas las mañanas debo despertar a mi hijo para que vaya a la escuela / Every morning, I have to wake up my son to go to school.

21. Vencer / Defeat – To Beat - Expire

Sé que esta noche si venceremos a los jugadores de tenis rivales / I know that tonight, we will beat the rival tennis players.

Esta leche que compré ya se va a vencer / This milk I bought is about to expire.

No me dejaré vencer tan fácilmente / I won't let myself be defeated so easily.

22. Creer / To Believe

Yo creo en Dios y en todo lo que está escrito en la biblia / I believe in God and all that is written in the Bible.

23. Convertir / To Become

No me quiero convertir en todo eso que siempre critiqué / I don't want to become all that that I've always criticized.

24. Pedir prestado / To Borrow

Yo no suelo pedir prestado nada, pero hoy en realidad es una emergencia / I don't usually borrow anything, but today is actually an emergency.

25. Doblar / To Bend – To double

Para que esa estructura quede bien, es necesario doblar un poco más el metal / In order for the structure to look good, it is necessary to bend the metal a little more.

Cuando juego póquer me gusta doblar la apuesta para presionar / When I play póker, I like to double the bet to push.

26. Apostar / To Bet

Yo soy un hombre de mucho apostar porque el que mucho apuesta, mucho gana / I am a man of many bets because whoever bets a lot wins a lot.

27. Morder / To Bite

Estaba jugando con el perro de la vecina cuando empezó a morder mi mano / I was playing with the neighbor's dog when he started biting my hand.

28. Sangrar / To Bleed

Después de varias mordidas, mi mano evidentemente comenzó a sangrar / After several bites, my hand evidently began to bleed.

29. Romper - Destruir / To Break

Tengo que romper con mi novia, ya no me siento cómodo con ella / I have to break up with my girlfriend. I'm not comfortable with her anymore.

Es muy fácil hacer que el vidrio se destruya / It's very easy to make the glass break.

30. Comprar / To Buy

Tengo que comprar pan y huevos para la cena de esta noche / I have to buy bread and eggs for dinner tonight.

31. Construir / To Build

Cuando juego con los Lego, me fascina construir cosas nuevas cada vez / When I play with the Lego, I love building new things every time.

32. Quemar / To Burn

Al cocinar hay que tener cuidado de no quemar la comida porque sabrá mal / When cooking, you have to be careful not to burn the food because it will taste bad.

33. Estallar / To Burst

Las granadas fueron diseñadas para estallar y provocar el mayor daño posible / The grenades were designed to burst and cause as much damage as possible.

34. Poder / Can

Realmente espero poder ir a la fiesta de cumpleaños de Martha, es mi amiga / I really hope I can go to Martha's birthday party; she's my friend.

35. Ser capaz de / Be able to

Realmente espero ser capaz de levantar más peso en el gimnasio la próxima vez / I really hope to be able to lift more weight in the gym next time.

36. Atrapar / To Catch

Es genial cómo la policía pudo atrapar al ladrón con esa maniobra secreta / It's great how the police could catch the thief with that secret maneuver.

37. Cancelar / To Cancel

Tendré que cancelar la suscripción anual de la revista, está muy costosa / I'll have to cancel the magazine's annual subscription; it's very expensive.

38. Cambiar / To Change

Huele muy mal, creo que ya es hora de cambiar el pañal del bebé / It smells really bad. I think it's time to change the baby's diaper.

39. Limpiar / To Clean

El nieto de mi tía no soporta que lo manden a limpiar la casa, lo detesta / My aunt's grandson can't stand being sent to clean the house; he hates it.

40. Peinar / To Comb

Tengo el cabello tan largo que me lo tengo que peinar cada veinte o treinta minutos / My hair is so long that I have to comb it every twenty or thirty minutes.

41. Escoger / To Choose

Siempre se me hace difícil escoger un sabor de helado cuando voy a la tienda de helados, todos me gustan mucho / I always find it difficult to choose an ice cream flavor when I go to the ice cream store; I like all of them very much.

42. Aferrarse / To Cling

Juan se iba a caer del árbol y tuvo que aferrarse de una rama para no hacerlo / Juan was going to fall from the tree and had to cling to a branch in order not to do it.

43. Venir / To Come

Mi papá va a venir a visitarme la próxima semana, le haré una gran bienvenida / My dad's coming to visit me next week; I'll give him a big welcome.

44. Quejarse / To Complain

Que incómodo es estar con alguien que lo único que hace es quejarse por todo / How uncomfortable it is to be with someone who only complains about everything.

45. Toser / To Cough

Tenía gripe pero ya no quería toser más en la clase, todos me estaban viendo / I had the flu, but I didn't want to cough in class anymore; everyone was watching me.

46. Cavar / To dig

Científicos van a cavar en varios lugares para buscar pozos de petróleo / Scientists will dig several places looking for oil wells.

47. Zambullir / To dive

No puedo esperar a llegar a la piscina, apenas llegue me voy a zambullir en ella / I can't wait to get to the pool. As soon as I get there, I'm gonna dive into it.

48. Dibujar / To draw

Mi hermano es bastante hábil para dibujar y nunca ha estado en clases para ello / My brother is pretty good at drawing, and he has never been to class for it.

49. Beber / To drink

Todas las mañanas me levanto a beber café antes de hacer cualquier otra cosa / Every morning, I wake up to drink coffee before doing anything else.

50. Soñar / To dream

Mi jefe me dijo que dejara de soñar con ser millonario y comenzara a trabajar para serlo / My boss told me to stop dreaming about being a millionaire and start working to be one.

51. Comer / To eat

La mejor sensación que existe es llegar a tu casa y comer la comida favorita que hace tu mamá / The best feeling is to get home and eat your favorite food made by your mom.

52. Explicar / To explain

No sé cuantas veces debo explicarle que no excedí el límite de velocidad / I don't know how many times I have to explain to you that I didn't exceed the speed limit.

53. Explotar / To explode

Si las baterías de los artefactos reciben electricidad en exceso, pueden explotar / If the batteries in the appliances receive excess electricity, they can explode.

54. Llenar / To fill

Debo ir a casa de mi tía a llenar la piscina para la reunión familiar del sábado / I have to go to my aunt's house to fill the pool for Saturday's family reunion.

55. Alimentar / To feed

Juan se fue de vacaciones y me dejó a cargo de alimentar a sus mascotas esta semana / Juan went on vacation and left me in charge of feeding his pets this week.

56. Sentir / To feel

Es bastante desagradable sentir que ya no le importas a alguien que quieres / It's pretty unpleasant to feel that you no longer matter to someone you love.

57. Pelear / To fight

Me parece graciosa la manera en que los cangrejos pelean entre ellos / I think it's funny the way crabs fight each other.

58. Encontrar / To find

He buscado esa llave durante una semana y ahora es que la vengo a encontrar / I've been looking for that key for a week, and now, I'm just coming to find it.

59. Encajar / To fit

A pesar de que parecía más grande que la pieza anterior, si logró encajar en el lugar / Although it looked bigger than the previous piece, it did manage to fit into place.

60. Arreglar / To fix

Tengo que arreglar mi carro para irme de viaje a la playa el próximo fin de semana / I have to fix my car to go on a trip to the beach next weekend.

61. Poner / To set

Debo poner mínimo tres alarmas en mi celular para poder despertarme y llegar a tiempo / I have to put at least three alarms on my cell phone, so I can wake up and be on time.

62. Firmar / To sign

Buenas tardes, tiene que firmar aquí para aceptar el paquete que le enviaron / Good afternoon, you have to sign here to accept the package sent to you.

63. Huir / To flee

Aunque el ladrón intentó huir, la policía fue inteligente y lo atrapó a tiempo / Although the thief tried to flee, the police were clever and caught him in time.

64. Volar / To fly

Siempre pienso que si yo fuese un ave, no dejaría de volar por los cielos todos los días / I always think that if I were a bird, I wouldn't stop flying through the skies every day.

65. Olvidar / To forget

Espero no olvidar que tengo que llamar a Alice dentro de dos horas / I hope I don't forget I have to call Alice in two hours.

66. Prohibir / To forbid

Voy a tener que prohibir escuchar música en esta casa, ya los vecinos se han quejado varias veces / I'm going to have to forbid listening to music in this house; the neighbors have already complained several times.

67. Deletrear / To spell

No entiendo qué palabra estás diciendo, ¿Puedes deletrearla, por favor? / I don't understand what word you're saying. Can you spell it, please?

68. Gastar / To spend

Tengo que dejar de gastar en cosas innecesarias y ahorrar dinero para mi viaje / I have to stop spending on unnecessary things and save money for my trip.

69. Empezar / To start

Nunca es muy tarde para empezar a hacer algo que de verdad te gusta / It's never too late to start doing something you really like.

70. Soportar / To stand

No creo que pueda soportar al bebé de mi prima todo el viaje en el carro / I don't think I can stand my cousin's baby all the way in the car.

71. Perdonar / To forgive

Para seguir adelante sin rencor, es necesario aprender a perdonar de verdad / To move forward without grudge, it is necessary to learn to truly forgive.

72. Congelar / To freeze

Muchos tipos de comida se tienen que congelar para que no se dañen / Many types of food have to be frozen so that they are not damaged.

73. Obtener / To get

Si me esfuerzo bastante lograré obtener una medalla de primer lugar en tenis / If I try hard enough, I'll get a first-place medal in tennis.

74. Decir / To tell

No es fácil decirle a alguien la verdad, y menos aún cuando ésta puede herir / It's not easy to tell someone the truth, especially when it can hurt.

75. Enseñar / To teach

Yo quiero ser profesor, mi gran pasión es enseñar a las demás personas muchas cosas / I want to be a teacher; my great passion is to teach other people many things

76. Dar / To give

Para tener mucho éxito en la vida, debemos siempre dar sin esperar recibir nada a cambio / To be very successful in life, we must always give without expecting to receive anything in return.

77. Crecer – Cultivar / To grow

Estoy desesperado por crecer cinco centímetros para el próximo verano, así podre entrar en la montaña rusa / I'm desperate to grow five centimeters by next summer, so I can get on the roller coaster.

Mi abuela está preparando su jardín para cultivar albahaca / My grandmother is preparing her garden to grow basil.

78. Tener / To have

La semana que sigue voy a tener mi nuevo teléfono, estoy ansioso porque llegue / Next week, I'm going to have my new phone; I'm looking forward to it.

79. Esperar / To wait

Odio tener que esperar a alguien que me dijo que ya estaba en camino / I hate to have to wait for someone who told me he was already on his way.

80. Querer / To want

Yo voy a querer un mes de descanso para ir a España estas vacaciones con mi familia / I want a month of a break to go to Spain this vacation with my family.

81. Observar / To watch

Me encanta observar televisión en las noches después de cenar con mis hijos / I love watching TV at night after dinner with my kids.

82. Oir / To hear

Cuando estoy sola en casa suelo prender el radio para oír algo que me distraiga / When I'm home alone, I usually turn on the radio to hear something distracting.

83. Esconder / To hide

A veces tengo que esconder los controles de los videojuegos de mis hijos, porque pueden jugar todo el día si los dejo / Sometimes, I have to hide my kids' video game controls because they can play all day if I let them.

84. Golpear / To hit

Ayer jugando béisbol, Alex no fue capaz de golpear la pelota ni una sola vez en todo el partido / Yesterday, playing baseball, Alex wasn't able to hit the ball once in the entire game.

85. Herir – Lastimar / To hurt

Cuando estaba caminando no pude evitar lastimar a un cachorro que estaba acostado y no lo vi / When I was walking, I couldn't avoid hurting a puppy who was lying down because I didn't see it.

Espero que no me vayas a herir con tus palabras / I hope you won't hurt me with your words.

86. Aguantar – Sostener / To hold

Necesito aguantar las ganas de gastar dinero en tonterías, ya se me va a acabar / I need to hold back the urge to spend money on nonsense; I'm going to run out.

Sostente fuerte de mí, no quiero que te caigas / Hold on tight to me; I don't want you to fall.

87. Saber / To Know

¿Tú sabes si mañana en la escuela veremos el nuevo tema de química? / Do you know if tomorrow, at school, we'll see the new chemistry theme?

88. Quedar / To Keep – To Stay

Me voy a quedar con tu teléfono hasta que logren arreglar el mío / I'm gonna keep your phone until they can fix mine.

Quédate conmigo aquí en la casa hasta mañana, ya es muy tarde para salir / Stay with me here in the house until tomorrow; it's too late to go out.

89. Arrodillar / To Kneel

Él se arrodilló ante ella en la oficina después de cinco años para pedirle matrimonio / He knelt before her in the office after five years to ask her to marry him.

90. Tejer / To Knit

A mi abuela le fascina tejer cualquier tipo de accesorio para bebés y niños / My grandmother is fascinated by knitting any kind of accessory for babies and children.

91. Guiar / To Lead

Soy su guía turístico, los voy a guiar aquí en Madrid mientras estén en su paseo / I am your tour guide; I will lead you here in Madrid while you are on your tour.

92. Poner - Colocar/ To Lay – To put

Yo puse los libros en la mesa antes de salir y ya no están / I put the books on the table before I left, and they're gone.

Yo coloqué los libros en la mesa antes de salir y ya no están / I laid the books on the table before I left, and they're gone.

93. Salir – irse / Leave

Me voy a salir del grupo de lectura, están discutiendo mucho últimamente / I'm going to leave the reading group; they've been arguing a lot lately.

94. Aprender / To learn

Siempre he querido aprender español, espero que este libro me ayude a hacerlo / I've always wanted to learn Spanish; I hope this book will help me do it.

95. Prestar / To lend

Le voy a prestar el carro este fin de semana al hermano de mi novia para que invite a su novia al cine / I'm lending the car this weekend to my girlfriend's brother to invite his girlfriend to the movies.

96. Dejar / To let

Debemos dejarlo llorar para que pueda tranquilizarse y luego hablar con él / We have to let him cry, so he can calm down and then talk to him.

97. Escuchar / To listen

En ocasiones, las personas solo necesitan alguien que las escuche sin juzgarlos / Sometimes, people just need someone to listen to them without judging them.

98. Vivir / To live

Me iré a vivir a Barcelona unos meses, espero que me vaya bien y no tener ningún inconveniente / I'm going to live in Barcelona for a few months. I hope it goes well and I do not have any inconvenience.

99. Mirar / To look

Los sábados voy al parque a mirar las aves y los árboles, es bastante relajante / On Saturdays, I go to the park to look at the birds and the trees; it's quite relaxing.

100.   Perder / To lose

No quiero perder la apuesta que hice contra mi primo, se burlaría de mi por siempre / I don't want to lose the bet I made against my cousin. He'd make fun of me forever.

101.Significar / To mean

¿Qué significa que una palabra sea polisémica? / What does it mean when a word is polysemic?

102.   Necesitar / To need

Necesito comprar pasta de dientes y cepillo de dientes para mí urgentemente / I need to buy toothpaste and toothbrush for myself urgently.

103.   Notar / To notice

Es importante notar que las palabras que hemos visto hasta ahora siguen siendo verbos / It is important to notice that the words we have seen so far are still verbs

104.   Abrir / To open

Mañana es día no laboral, pero creo que voy a abrir la tienda de todas maneras / Tomorrow's a non-working day, but I think I'm going to open the store anyway.

105.   Organizar / To organize

Es necesario organizar una reunión de emergencia para hablar sobre los gastos mensuales / It is necessary to organize an emergency meeting to discuss monthly expenses.

106.   Ordenar / To order

Tienes que ordenar la sala, vienen visitas en la tarde a ver a tu papá / You have to order the room; visitors are coming in the afternoon to see your dad.

Hay que ordenar los nuevos cheques antes de que estos se acaben / You have to order the new checks before they run out.

107.   Pagar / To pay

Ya se está acabando el mes, paga la nueva mensualidad de la escuela de Mike / The month is coming to an end; pay Mike's new monthly school fee.

108.   Probar / To prove

Debemos probar que somos inocentes para que nos dejen salir de aquí / We have to prove we're innocent, so they'll let us out of here.

109.   Pasar / To pass

El partido estuvo muy bueno gracias a que el equipo pasó bastante el balón / The match was very good because the team passed the ball quite a lot

Voy a pasar a través del centro comercial para llegar más rápido hasta allá / I'm going to pass through the mall to get there faster.

110. Llover / To rain

Según el pronóstico del clima, esta tarde lloverá por tres horas seguidas / According to the weather forecast, it's going to rain for three hours in a row this afternoon.

111. Montar / To ride

Me encanta montar a caballo, es una experiencia única y es algo bastante divertido / I love horseback riding; it's a unique experience, and it's a lot of fun.

112. Sonar / To ring- To sound

El teléfono comenzó a sonar pero no pude agarrar la llamada porque estaba ocupado cocinando / The phone started ringing, but I couldn't take the call because I was busy cooking.

Eso va a sonar muy fuerte si le pones tanto volumen / That's going to sound pretty loud if you put so much volume in it.

113. Responder / To reply

Disculpa que no respondí antes, había dejado el teléfono olvidado en una tienda y tuve que regresar a buscarlo / Sorry, I didn't reply before; I had left the phone forgotten in a store, and I had to go back to look for it.

114. Correr / To run

Es importante correr por lo menos una o dos horas a la semana para mantener saludable el cuerpo / It is important to run at least one or two hours a week to keep your body healthy.

115. Decir / To say

Te noto extraño, ¿Tienes algo que decirme? / I notice you are strange; do you have something to say to me?

116. Ver / To see

Me gusta desayunar mientras veo el amanecer / I like to have breakfast while I see the sunrise.

117. Vender / To sell

Para hacer buenos negocios, es mejor vender con poca ganancia pero en mayor cantidad / In order to do good business, it is better to sell with little profit but in greater quantity.

118. Enviar / To send

Necesito ir a la oficina postal para enviarle un paquete a mi madre que está en otro estado / I need to go to the post office to send a package to my mother who's in another state.

119. Sentar / To sit

Estaba tan cansado ayer después de correr que al llegar a casa me senté por quince minutos / I was so tired yesterday after running that when I got home, I sat for fifteen minutes.

120.   Dormir / To sleep

Si las personas supieran que lo más me gusta hacer es dormir, no me invitarían a salir tanto / If people knew that the best thing I like to do is sleep, they wouldn't ask me out so much.

121. Hablar / To talk

Para que una relación funcione es importante hablar sobre las cosas que nos molestan / For a relationship to work, it's important to talk about the things that bother us.

122.   Estudiar / To study

Es realmente importante estudiar bastante para salir bien en los exámenes / It's really important to study hard enough to do well in exams.

123.   Nadar / To swim

Nadar para mí es una de las actividades más relajantes que puedes hacer / Swimming for me is one of the most relaxing activities to do.

124.   Tomar / To Take

Voy a tomar el autobús de las seis y media de la mañana para llegar a tu casa aproximadamente a las siete y quince / I'll take the six-thirty in the morning bus to get to your house at approximately seven-fifteen.

125.Traducir / To Translate

Gracias a este libro serás capaz de traducir un montón de palabras en español y usarlas en contexto / Thanks to this book, you will be able to translate a lot of Spanish words and use them in context.

126.   Entender / To Understand

Para aprender algo nuevo, lo primero que debemos hacer es entenderlo y luego analizarlo / To learn something new, the first thing we have to do is to understand it and then analyze it.

127.Usar / To use

Usar hilo dental después de cepillarse los dientes es necesario para el cuidado de la boca / Using dental floss after brushing teeth is necessary for mouth care.

128.   Despertar / To wake up

Odio despertarme antes de que suene la alarma del teléfono, luego no me puedo volver a dormir / I hate waking up before the phone alarm rings. Then, I can't go back to sleep.

129.   Trabajar / To work

Mañana trabajaré todo el día y horas extras para estar libre pasado mañana y salir a pasear / Tomorrow, I'll work all day and overtime to be free the day after tomorrow and go for a walk.

130.   Escribir / To write

Escribimos historias de terror para niños, adultos y ancianos / We write horror stories for children, adults, and the elderly.

Polysemous Words

As we know, there are some words that, despite being written identically, have different meanings. In Spanish, these kinds of words exist, and we will provide you examples of some of them.

131. Aparato / Device – Tract

Este es un aparato que se usa para calibrar la frecuencia / This is a device that is used to calibrate the frequency.

El aparato digestivo es un conjunto de órganos que procesan los alimentos / The digestive tract is a set of organs that process food.

132.   Armar / Assemble – Arm

Este juguete trae las instrucciones para armar / This toy comes with instructions on how to assemble it.

La idea de esta compra es armar a la policía del estado / The idea of this purchase is to arm the state police

133.   Banco / Bank – Bench

En la mañana tengo que ir al banco a depositar un dinero / In the morning, I have to go to the bank to deposit some money.

Me agrada sentarme en el banco del parque a desestresarme un poco / I like to sit on the park bench and de-stress a little.

134.   Bolsa / Bag – Stock exchange

Hijo, recuerda que tienes que sacar la bolsa de basura antes de irte / Son, remember, you have to take out the garbage bag before you go.

Tengo un amigo que ha hecho millones gracias a la bolsa / I've got a friend who's made millions, thanks to the stock market.

135.Bomba / Bomb – Pump

En las noticias dicen que la explosión fue causada por una bomba / The news says the explosion was caused by a bomb.

A mi carro se le daño la bomba de agua y así no puedo usarlo / My car's water pump has been damaged, so I can't use it.

136.   Botón / Button

Me compre una linda camisa de botones para la fiesta / I bought a nice button-down shirt for the party.

No debes nunca presionar el botón rojo de ningún aparato / You must never press the red button on any device.

137.Café / Coffee (Color, drink, and shop)
No es bueno tomar café en las noches porque provoca insomnio / It's not good to drink coffee at night because it causes insomnia.

Ella se compró una linda camisa color café / She bought herself a nice coffee-colored shirt.

Iré al café a merendar, ¿Quieres venir? / I'll go to the coffee shop and have a snack. Do you want to come?

138.   Calculadora / Calculator – Calculating

Estoy preocupada, mañana tengo el examen de matemáticas y no consigo mi calculadora / I'm worried. Tomorrow, I have the math test, and I can't find my calculator.

Clara es una persona muy calculadora, siempre piensa en todo / Clara is a very calculating person; she always thinks of everything.

139.   Canal / Channel – Canal

Hoy a las nueve de la noche en el canal 45 van a pasar una buena película / Today, at nine o'clock at night on Channel 45, they're going to have a good movie.

Mi tío es uno de los ingenieros que construyó el canal de Panamá / My uncle is one of the engineers who built the Panama Canal.

140.   Capa / Cloak – Layers

Casi todos los superhéroes usan capas, aunque parezcan incómodas / Almost all superheroes wear cloaks, even if they seem uncomfortable.

Las cebollas tienen bastantes capas / Onions have quite a lot of layers.

141. Columna/ Column (Newspaper article – Vertebral – Constructions)

Debería ir al quiropráctico, tengo un dolor en la columna desde hace varios días / I should go to the chiropractor. I have had a column pain for several days.

¿Leíste la columna de la pagina tres del periódico? La escribí yo / Did you read the column on page three of the paper? I wrote it.

El edificio tiene buenos cimientos, aparte tiene bien ubicadas las columnas / The building has good foundations, and it has well-located columns.

142.   Cometa / Comet – Kite

El niño estaba volando su cometa fuera de su casa cuando vió pasar el cometa / The boy was flying his kite out of his house when he saw the comet pass.

143.   Crema / Cream (Food- Skin – Color)

La crema de calabaza que hace mi mamá es dulce y muy sabrosa / My mom's pumpkin cream is sweet and very tasty.

Me compré una crema para la piel, la tengo reseca desde el viaje a la playa / I bought a cream for my skin; it has been dry since the trip to the beach.

Los nuevos zapatos color crema de Amy están horribles / Amy's new cream shoes look awful.

144.   Cuadro / Frame – Painting – Square

En la galería de arte tenían cuadros muy famosos e interesantes de observar / In the art gallery, they had very famous and interesting paintings to observe.

Cuando choqué en la moto se dobló un poco el cuadro y no se puede arreglar / When I crashed on the bike, the frame bent a little and can't be fixed.

En la clase de geometría de hoy, dibujaremos un cuadro / In today's geometry class, we'll draw a square.

145.Cubo / Bucket – To the cube – Cube

No me fijé y pateé el cubo de agua que tenía mi mamá en la cocina, se va a molestar mucho / I didn't notice, but I kicked the bucket of water my mom had in the kitchen. She's going to be very upset.

Si elevamos el número dos al cubo, obtendremos ocho / If we raise number two to the cube, we get eight.

La figura geométrica que representa al dado es el cubo / The geometric figure representing the dice is the cube.

146.   Cura / Priest – Heal

El cura es una excelente persona / The priest is an excellent person.

Él cura excelente a las personas / He heals, excellently, the people.

147.Dado / Give – Dice

No le he dado el regalo porque no he tenido la oportunidad perfecta / I haven't given him the gift because I haven't had the perfect opportunity.

Deja de pelear por el juego y lanza el dado de una vez / Stop fighting about the game, and roll the dice at once.

148.   Derecho / Law – Straight – Right

Él esta estudiando derecho en la Universidad del sur / He's studying law at the University of the South.

Sigue derecho por esta vía hasta que encuentres una farmacia / Go straight this way until you find a pharmacy.

Yo tengo el derecho a un abogado / I have the right to an attorney.

149.   Destino / Destiny – Destination

Si algo tiene que pasar, pasará, el destino no se puede cambiar / If something has to happen, it will happen; destiny cannot be changed.

Señores pasajeros, les informamos que dentro de veinte minutos llegaremos a su destino / Passengers, we inform you that, in twenty minutes, we will arrive at our destination.

150.   Don / Mister – Gift

Don Miguel siempre es bastante atento y cuidadoso con su esposa / Mr. Miguel is always quite attentive and careful with his wife.

Mi cuñada tiene el don de la música, es una prodigiosa del piano / My sister-in-law has a gift for music; she's a piano prodigy.

151. Entrada / Entrance (Food – Place)

Ya llegue, ¿Tú estas en la entrada sur o en la norte? / I'm here. Are you at the south entrance, or are you at the north entrance?

Buenas noches caballero, ¿Ya desea ordenar la entrada? / Good evening, sir. Would you like to order the entrance?

152. Frente / Forehead – Front

Cuando jugaba quemados me pegaron un pelotazo en la frente y me dio dolor de cabeza / When I was playing dodgeball, I got hit in the forehead with a ball, and it gave me a headache.

Al frente de mi casa se están peleando tres personas por un mango / In front of my house, three people are fighting for a mango.

153.Gato / Cat – Jack

Mi gato está loco, el otro día no sabemos cómo pero se subío al techo / My cat is crazy; the other day, we don't know how, but she climbed on the roof.

Pásame el gato que está en el maletero para poner la rueda de repuesto / Hand me the jack in the trunk to put the spare wheel on.

154.General / General (Military - General)

Las órdenes del General Martínez es que sigamos trotando hasta las diez de la mañana / General Martinez's orders are to keep jogging until ten o'clock in the morning.

No se porqué, pero tengo un malestar general desde hace varias semanas / I don't know why, but I've had a general discomfort for several weeks.

155.Globo / Balloon – Earth Globe

Mi juego favorito en las ferias es el de explotar los globos con los dardos / My favorite game at fairs is to explode balloons with darts.

Hace muchos años se tenía la creencia de que el globo terráqueo era plano / Many years ago, there was a belief that the Earth's globe was flat.

156. Local / Shop – Local

Aunque quede más lejos, voy al local del este, hay una cajera muy bonita allá / Even if it's farther east, I'm going to the east shop; there's a very pretty cashier there.

La operación fue espantosa, la anestecia que me pusieron fue local y sentí todo / The operation was awful, the anesthesia was local, and I felt everything.

157. Mango / Mango – Handle

La fruta más sabrosa que he probado hasta ahora es el mango / The tastiest fruit I've tasted so far is mango.

Agarra bien el mango del cuchillo porque si se te resbala te puedes cortar / Hold the handle of the knife well because if it slips, you can cut yourself.

158. Manzana / Apple – Square

Esther prepara un pie de manzana que es mejor que el de cualquier repostería / Esther makes an apple pie that is better than the ones made in any bakery.

Debes darle la vuelta a la manzana para llegar a mi casa / You have to go around the square to get to my house.

159. Merengue / Meringue – Cake

A los latinos les encanta bailar merengue, es bastante divertido / Latinos love to dance merengue; it's pretty fun.

Para preparar el merengue de la torta se necesitan tres huevos, mantequilla y azúcar / In order to prepare the meringue of the cake, three eggs, butter, and sugar are needed.

160.   Mono / Monkey – Sweatpants

Estaba en el zoologico cuando un mono bajó del árbol y me robó el pan que estaba comiendo / I was at the zoo when a monkey came down from the tree and stole the bread I was eating.

Está haciendo tanto frío en las mañanas que salgo a trotar usando un mono / It's so cold in the mornings that I go out jogging wearing sweatpants.

161. Muñeca / Doll – Wrists

Estaba corriendo el otro día y me caí, me golpeé en las muñecas / I was running the other day, and I fell. I hit my wrists.

La tía de mi mamá tiene una colección de muñecas desde que era pequeña / My mom's aunt has had a doll collection since she was little.

162.   Nada / Swim – Nothing

Él nada todas las mañanas porque se está preparando para una competencia / He swims every morning because he's getting ready for a competition.

Nada va a hacer que cambie mi opinión respecto al aborto / Nothing's gonna change my mind about abortion.

163.   Órgano / Organ (Music – Body)

El órgano tiene un sonido particular, es diferente al piano / The organ has a particular sound; it is different from the piano

El hígado es uno de los órganos del cuerpo más importante / The liver is one of the most important organs in the body.

164.   Pata / Legs – Paw

Le enseñé a mi perra a darme la pata cuando era cachorra / I taught my dog to give me her paw when she was a puppy.

Quiero una mesa de tres patas, se ven más a la moda / I want a three-legged table; they look more fashionable.

165.Pendiente / Earrings – Pending

Los pendientes que vimos en la joyería estaban bonitos, pero demasiado caros / The earrings we saw at the jewelry store were nice but too expensive.

Sé que me transferiste, pero está en el balance pendiente / I know you transferred me, but it's on the pending balance.

166.   Pico / Beak – Pickaxe – Peak

Las águilas mudan el pico cada cierto tiempo / Eagles molt their beaks from time to time.

El pico para minar se rompió ayer mientras lo usaba / The mining pickaxe broke yesterday while I was using it.

Juan subió al pico de la montaña en tres días / Juan climbed to the peak of the mountain in three days.

167.Planta / Plant, factory, Sole of the foot

Las plantas son las encargadas de hacer la fotosíntesis y así proporcionan oxígeno / The plants are responsible for photosynthesis and thus provide oxygen.

La planta de gas contamina muchísimo el medio ambiente / The gas factory pollutes the environment very much.

Estaba caminando descalzo cuando me clavé una espina en la planta del pie / I was walking barefoot when I got a thorn in the sole of my foot.

168.　　　Pluma / Feather – Pen

Las plumas de los loros son preciosas / The parrots' feathers are precious.

¿Tienes una pluma que me prestes para firmar? / Do you have a pen I could borrow to sign?

169.　　　Prenda / Clothe – To start

Las prendas de ropa de la colección de verano están muy coloridas / The clothes of the summer collection are very colorful.

Espero que el carro prenda después de haberlo arreglado / I hope the car starts after I've fixed it.

170.　　　Radio / Radio - radius

En el radio escuché la canción que te gusta / On the radio I heard the song you like

El radio de esa circunferencia es de cinco centímetros / The radius of that circumference is five centimeters.

171. Ratón / Mouse (Animal – computer)

El ratón de la casa se está comiendo los cables de los electrónicos / The house mouse is eating the wires from the electronics.

Papá, ¿Has visto el ratón que utilizo para mi computadora? / Dad, did you see the mouse I use for my computer?

172.Regla / Ruler - Rule- Period

Medí con la regla la longitud de mi celular / I measured with the ruler the length of my cell phone.

Las reglas de tránsito prohíben conducir bajo efectos del alcohol / Traffic rules prohibit driving under the influence of alcohol.

El día que iba a ir a la playa me vino la regla / The day I was going to the beach I got my period.

173.Sal / Go out – Salt

Sal de mi casa / Get out of my house.

Le falta un poco más de sal / It is missing a little more salt.

174.Salsa / Sauce – Salsa

La salsa de la pasta está exquisita / The pasta sauce is exquisite.

Bailar salsa es súper complicado / Dancing salsa is super complicated.

175.Serie / Tv serie – Set of numbers

La serie de números consecutivos del uno al cinco / The series of consecutive numbers from one to five.

Todas las noches en la televisión veo mi serie favorita / Every night on TV I watch my favorite series

176.Sobre / Above – Envelope

Todas las opciones están sobre la mesa si sigues comportándote mal / All options are above the table if you continue to behave badly.

Te llegó un sobre desde Alabama por el correo / You got an envelope from Alabama in the mail.

177. Taco / Taco – Football shoes

Me gustaría cenar un taco con mucha guasacaca / I'd like to have a taco with a lot of guasacaca.

Para poder jugar bien futbol necesito unos nuevos tacos / To be able to play good football, I need new football shoes.

178. Teclado / Piano – Keyboard

El teclado que compró mi mamá es marca Yamaha y suena espectacular / The piano my mom bought is Yamaha, and it sounds spectacular.

Al teclado de mi computadora no le sirve la letra "M" / The "M" letter doesn't work on my computer keyboard.

179. Saber / To know – Taste

Es bueno saber un segundo idioma para obtener buenos trabajos / It's good to know a second language to get good jobs.

Esta sopa va a saber a pollo / This soup's gonna taste like chicken.

180.   Arco / Goal – Bow – Arc

Si el radio vale 15 centímetros, ¿Cuánto vale el arco de circunferencia? / If the radius is 15 centimeters, how much is the arc of circumference worth?

Él pateó la pelota hacia el arco y casi anotó / He kicked the ball into the goal and almost scored.

Me gustaría practicar más con el arco y flecha / I would like to practice more with the bow and arrow.

181. Barra / Bar (Long bar – Bars)

Para hacer el edificio se utilizaron muchas barras de hierro / A lot of iron bars were used to make the building.

Ella es la chica que atiende en la barra / She's the girl who serves at the bar.

182.   Chile / Chile – Chili

Chile es un país muy bonito ubicado en América del Sur / Chile is a very beautiful country located in South America.

Los mexicanos comen todo con chile picante / Mexicans eat everything with spicy chili.

183.   Cinta / Tape – Strips

Necesito la cinta adhesiva para pegar el pedazo de plástico que se despegó / I need the tape to stick the piece of plastic that came off.

Me fascina la cinta de color azul que tienes, se ve muy bien con tu atuendo / I love the blue strip you have; it looks great with your outfit.

184.   Copa / Cup – Top

Para hacer el arroz, se recomienda utilizar dos tazas de agua por una de arroz / To make rice, it is recommended to use two cups of water for one cup of rice.

En la copa del árbol hay una pelota atorada / At the top of the tree, there's a ball stuck

185.   Corredor / Runner – Hallway

Nick es el mejor corredor del equipo, si se lesiona, vamos a perder / Nick's the best runner on the team. If he gets hurt, we're gonna lose.

Si está interesado en nuestras promociones acérquese al corredor numero tres / If you are interested in our promotions, go to hallway number three.

186.   Cuarto / Room – Forth – Quarter

Estaba en mi cuarto escuchando música cuando me llamaste / I was in my room listening to music when you called me.

Este fue el cuarto estornudo en diez minutos, tengo alergia / This was the fourth sneeze in ten minutes. I have allergies.

La mitad de una mitad es conocida como un cuarto / Half of one half is known as a quarter.

187.Masa / Mass – Dough – Weight

La masa de personas viene corriendo rápidamente a la capital / The mass of people comes running quickly to the capital.

Mira, masa para pizza lista para hornear, ¿Compramos? / Look, pizza dough is ready to bake; shall we buy?

Mi masa es de 76 kilogramos / My weight is 76 kilograms.

188.   Plano / Flat – Plans

Me gusta manejar bicicleta en esta zona porque aquí es plano / I like to ride a bike in this area because it's flat here.

Los planos del edificio quedaron muy bien, te felicito / The plans of the building were very good; I congratulate you.

189.   Pie / Foot – Pie

Jugando futbol ayer me lesioné el pie y debo ir al doctor / Playing football yesterday, I hurt my foot, and I have to go to the doctor.

El pie de limón es mi postre favorito, la combinación de dulce y ácido es excelente / Lemon pie is my favorite dessert; the combination of sweet and sour is excellent.

190.   Portero / Door keeper – Goal keeper

Tuve problemas con el portero, casi no me dejaba entrar al edificio / I had problems with the doorkeeper; he almost wouldn't let me in the building.

El portero del equipo de futbol de mi hermano es excelente, nunca le hacen gol / The goalkeeper of my brother's football team is excellent; he never gets a goal.

191. Tienda / Tent – Store

La tienda de campaña de Luis está genial, yo quiero una así / Luis's tent is great; I want one like that.

Iré a la tienda de zapatos a comprarme unos nuevos / I'm gonna go to the shoe store and get some new ones.

192.   Listo / Done – Smart

El trabajo que me pediste está listo, ¿Te lo envío? / The job you asked for is done. Shall I send it to you?

Ese chico, aunque no lo parezca, es muy listo / That boy, even if he doesn't seem like it, is very smart.

Adjectives

Adjectives are used to describe characteristics of certain objects or subjects.

193.   Aburrido / Boring

Salí con el chico nuevo, pero es bastante aburrido / I dated the new guy, but he's pretty boring.

194.   Ácido / Sour

Me comí una naranja y estaba muy ácida / I ate an orange, and it was very sour.

195.Alegre / Cheerful

Ella es perfecta para estar en el grupo de las animadoras, siempre está alegre / She's perfect to be in the cheerleading group; she's always cheerful.

196.   Alto / Tall

Mi novio John es el más alto de la clase de biología / My boyfriend John is the tallest boy in biology class.

197.Amarillo / Yellow

Cuando estaba paseando ayer en el centro comercial vi un paragua amarillo precioso / When I was walking around the mall yesterday, I saw a beautiful yellow umbrella.

198.   Amargo / Bitter

No me gusta tomar café sin azucar porque me parece muy amargo / I don't like to drink coffee without sugar because I think it's too bitter.

199.   Anaranjado / Orange

Lo que más me gusta de las motos KTM es su color anaranjado / What I like most about KTM motorcycles is their orange color.

200.   Ancho / Wide

Para disminuir el tráfico debieron hacer la autopista más ancha / To decrease traffic, they had to make the highway wider.

201.   Atrevido / Daring

Me encanta la personalidad de Brad, es muy atrevido y tambien es guapo / I love Brad's personality; he's very daring, and he's also handsome.

202.   Azul / Blue

Siempre me ha gustado ver el cielo porque dicen que todo lo de color azul es relajante / I've always liked to see the sky because it is said that all things blue are relaxing.

203.   Bajo / Short – Low

Ella quería alcanzar una fruta de un árbol pero no podía por ser muy baja / She wanted to reach for a fruit from a tree, but she couldn't because she was too short.

204.   Blanco / White

Mi prenda de ropa favorita es el sueter blanco que compré en Italia / My favorite piece of clothing is the white sweater I bought in Italy.

205.   Blando / Soft

La gelatina es un postre muy rico, además de ser bastante blando / Jell-O is a very tasty dessert, and it's quite soft.

206.   Bonito / Pretty – Beautiful

Los zapatos que me regaló mi tía están extremadamente bonitos, ella conoce mis gustos / The shoes my aunt gave me are extremely pretty; she knows my tastes.

207.   Bueno / Good

Aunque parezca oscuro y misterioso, él en realidad es bastante bueno / Although he may seem dark and mysterious, he's actually quite good.

208.   Caliente / Hot

Me fascina el té de manzana y canela bien caliente / I love apple and cinnamon tea very hot.

209.   Calvo / Bald

Mi abuelo está tan viejo que ya esta completamente calvo / My grandfather is so old that he's already completely bald.

210.   Capaz / Able- Capable

La nueva computadora con tecnología de última generación es capaz de correr todos los nuevos juegos / The new computer with the latest generation technology is able to run all the new games.

211. Ciego / Blind

El novio de mi hermana, perdió por completo la visión y ahora es ciego por una enfermedad / My sister's boyfriend completely lost his vision and is now blind because of a disease

212.   Colorido / Colorful

El arcoíris es algo muy espectacular por ser tan colorido / The rainbow is something very spectacular for being so colorful.

213.   Común / Common

Este libro para aprender español tiene tantas palabras, que lo hacen un libro poco común / This book for learning Spanish has so many words that make it a not-so-common book.

214.   Conocido / Known

¿Cómo es posible que no sepas quien es él? Es uno de los músicos más conocidos en la actualidad / How is it possible that you don't know who he is? He is one of the most-known musicians today.

215.Contento - Felíz / Happy

Estoy muy felíz por el resultado que obtuve en mi examen / I'm very happy with the result I got on my exam.

216.   Corto / Short

Pensaba comprarme la camisa que vi en oferta, pero me quedaba muy corta / I thought about buying the shirt I saw on sale, but it was too short.

217.Débil / Weak

Santiago es demasiado débil como para poder levantar una bolsa de cemento / Santiago is too weak to lift a bag of cement.

218.   Delgado / Thin

Él pudo entrar a la casa a través de la reja porque es muy delgado / He was able to get into the house through the fence because he's very thin.

219.   Derecho / Right

El papá de mi compañero era derecho antes de perder la mano en un accidente / My partner's dad was right before he lost his hand in an accident.

220.   Diferente / Different

Hay algo especial en él que hace que sea diferente a los demás / There's something special about him that makes him different from the others.

221.   Difícil / Difficult

Muchas personas encuentran muy difícil aprender un nuevo idioma, yo no / Many people find it very difficult to learn a new language; I don't.

222.   Divertido / Funny

Puede que me haya dolido el golpe que me dí cuando caí, pero fue divertido / I may have been hurt by the hit I got when I fell, but it was funny.

223.   Dulce / Sweet

La receta secreta para hacer pollo de mi mamá es muy dulce / My mom's secret recipe for making chicken is very sweet.

224.   Duro / Hard

Hacer el examen sin haber estudiado fue realmente duro / Taking the test without having studied was really hard.

225.   Enfermo / Ill

Ya sé porque estaba actuando tan extraña, ella estaba enferma / I know why she was acting so weird; she was sick.

226.   Estrecho / Tight

El callejón es demasiado estrecho como para poder pasar con la moto por allí / The alley is too tight for the bike to pass through.

227.   Exterior / Outside

Estoy interesado en el carro, tiene un buen aspecto en su exterior / I'm interested in the car; it looks good on the outside.

228.   Fácil / Easy

Estudié toda la noche para el examen de hoy, quizás por eso me pareció fácil / I studied all night for today's exam; maybe that's why I found it easy.

229.   Falso / False

En la sección de selección simple de la prueba yo puse que todo era falso / In the simple selection section of the test, I put that everything was false

230.   Famoso / Famous

Mira, este es el video del gato más famoso de internet esta semana / Look, this is the video of the most famous cat on the internet this week.

231.   Feo / Ugly

La comida estaba deliciosa, aunque la presentación estaba un poco fea / The food was delicious, although the presentation was a little ugly.

232.   Final / Final

Después de muchos intentos, este es el documento final / After many attempts, this is the final document.

233.   Fresco / Fresh

La brisa en la playa de noche resulta ser bastante fresca / The breeze on the beach at night turns out to be quite fresh.

234.   Frío / Cold

No te recomiendo dormir afuera, hoy hace muchísimo frío / I don't recommend sleeping outside; it's very cold today.

235.   Fuerte / Strong

Si fue lo suficientemente fuerte para levantar la bolsa de cemento, no lo esperaba / He was strong enough to lift the bag of cement; I didn't expect it.

236.   Gordo / Fat

De tanto comer y jugar videojuegos, Daniel se puso gordo / From so much eating and playing video games, Daniel got fat.

237.   Grande – Gran / Big

Yo soy tu más grande fan, ¿Me das tu autógrafo? / I'm your biggest fan; can I have your autograph?

Creo que esto es un gran error, no deberíamos estar aquí / I think this is a big mistake. We shouldn't be here.

238.   Guapo / Handsome

¿Vieron al chico nuevo? Está bastante guapo para tener 15 años / Did you see the new guy? He looks handsome enough to be 15 years old.

239.   Genial – Cool / Cool

Encontrarme 200$ en el piso del estacionamiento ha sido lo más genial de esta semana / To find $200 on the parking lot floor was the coolest thing this week.

Me considero un chico bastante cool para la edad que tengo / I consider myself a pretty cool guy for the age I am.

240.   Gris / Gray

Las canas de mi mamá hacen parecer que tuviera el cabello gris / My mom's gray hairs make it look like she had gray hair.

241.   Húmedo / Damp

Para utilizar ciertos productos para el cabello, es recommendable tenerlo húmedo / When using certain hair products, it is recommended to have damp hair.

242.   Igual / Same – Equal

Este lápiz es igual al otro, ¿Cómo sabes que es el tuyo? / This pencil looks equal to the other. How do you know it's yours?

No me importa cuál te quedes, dame uno y ya, de todas maneras son iguales / I don't care which one you keep. Just give me one; they're the same anyway.

243.   Imposible / Impossible

Pasar todos los exámenes de esta semana e ir a la fiesta de Michelle parecen una misión imposible / Passing all this week's exams and going to Michelle's party seems like an impossible mission.

244.   Interesante / Interesting

Resulta muy interesante la manera en que los científicos explican la creación del universo / It is very interesting how scientists explain the creation of the universe.

245.   Inútil / Unsuccessful – Useless

Aunque me trasnoché estudiando, fue inútil hacerlo, reprobé el examen / Even though I stayed up studying, I was unsuccessful; I failed the exam.

Por más que me esfuerce para mejorar, es inútil / No matter how hard I try to improve, it's useless.

246.   Zurdo / Left

Leo Messi es el mejor delantero que hay, y es zurdo igual que yo / Leo Messi is the best striker out there, and he's left-handed just like me.

247.   Jóven / Young

El nuevo mesero del restaurante donde acabamos de comer se ve bastante joven / The new waiter at the restaurant where we just ate looks pretty young.

248.   Largo / Long

Mi cuñada tiene el cabello tan largo que le llega a las rodillas / My sister-in-law's hair is so long it reaches her knees.

249.   Lento / Slow

Perdón por llegar tan tarde, tuve que venir en autobús y venía realmente lento / Sorry I'm so late; I had to come by bus, and it was really slow.

250.   Listo / Smart

No importa que tan listo seas, siempre alguien logrará engañarte / It does not matter how smart you are; someone will always fool you.

251.Malo / Bad

Si caperucita cuenta la historia, el lobo siempre será el malo / If Little Red Riding Hood tells the story, the wolf will always be the bad guy.

252. Malvado / Evil

Fue muy malvado de tu parte engañar al conductor de taxi para pagarle con un billete falso / It was very evil of you to trick the taxi driver into paying him with a fake ticket.

253. Marrón / Brown

Mamá, ¿Has visto mi cinturón favorito? El que es marrón / Mom, have you seen my favorite belt, the one that's brown?

254. Mayor / Older – Bigger

Mi hermano mayor siempre pelea conmigo por el control de la televisión / My older brother always fights me for the TV remote.

Claro que 4x4 es mayor que 3x5, haz la multiplicación para que veas / Of course, 4x4 is bigger than 3x5; do the multiplication, and you will see.

255. Mejor / Best

Mi amigo se compró el nuevo juego de aliens y me invitó a jugar, es el mejor/ My friend bought the new game of aliens and invited me to play; he is the best.

256. Menor / Younger – Smaller

Mi hermano menor es un llorón, me molesta mucho / My younger brother's a crybaby; it bothers me a lot.

El menor entre 6, 4 y 3 es el 3 / The smallest between 6, 4, and 3 is 3.

257. Mojado / Wet

No debes interactuar con nada eléctrico si estás mojado / You shouldn't interact with anything electrical if you're wet.

258. Morado / Purple

Se pisó el dedo con la puerta del carro y se le puso morado / He smashed his finger in the car door, and it turned purple.

259. Muerto / Dead

Las zariguellas a veces se quedan tan quietas que parece que estan muertas / The opossums sometimes stay so quiet that they seem to be dead.

260.   Musical / Musical

El ringtone de ese teléfono es extraño, me recuerda a algo musical / The ringtone on that phone is strange; it reminds me of something musical.

261.   Nacional / National

El mejor chocolate que he probado es el nacional / The best chocolate I've ever tasted is the national one.

262.   Natural / Natural

Es impresionante la alta calidad que tienen los productos de origen natural / The high quality of natural products is impressive.

263.   Negro / Black

Los zapatos negros son los mejores, combinan con todo / Black shoes are the best; they go with everything.

264.   Nuevo / New

No hay nada mejor que el olor a carro nuevo / There's nothing better than the smell of a new car.

265.   Peor / Worse

De todas las mermeladas que hay, la de fresa es la peor / Of all the jams out there, strawberry is the worst.

266.   Pequeño / Little

Pensaba comprar un reloj pequeño, este es incómodo / I was thinking of buying a little watch; this is uncomfortable.

267.   Pelirrojo / Redhead

¿Viste que Jonathan ahora es pelirrojo? / Did you see Jonathan's redhead now?

268.   Perfecto / Perfect

Un sanduche relleno de mantequilla de maní y jalea es perfecto / A sandwich filled with peanut butter and jelly is perfect.

269.   Pobre / Poor

Si no se hubiese endeudado tanto con el banco no habría quedado pobre / If he hadn't been so indebted to the bank, he wouldn't have gone poor.

270.   Poco / Little – Few

Yo hablo solo un poco de Español / I speak only a little Spanish.

Yo pienso que es muy poco para la fiesta / I think it's too few for the party.

271. Popular / Popular

Ella piensa que como viajó ahora es la más popular / She thinks that, as she has traveled now, she is the most popular.

272.   Posible / Possible

Con dedicación y enfoque, todo es posible / With dedication and focus, anything is possible.

273.   Primer – Primero / First

Mi primer beso fue con ella / My first kiss was with her.

Yo soy el primero en terminar el examen siempre / I'm the first one to always finish the exam.

274.   Principal / Principal – Main

Ella es la cantante principal de la obra / She's the principal singer of the show

El principal objetivo de estudiar es aprender / The main objective of studying is to learn.

275.   Próximo / Next

Yo me graduaré de la Universidad el próximo año / I'm graduating from college next year.

276.   Rápido / Fast

La nueva moto de mi vecino es extremadamente rápida / My neighbor's new bike is extremely fast.

277.   Raro / Rare – Weird

Este es un material muy raro de encontrar en la naturaleza / This is a very rare material to find in nature.

No se porqué él es tan raro / I don't know why he's so weird.

278.   Real / Real

Mis lentes Gucci no son falsos, son reales / My Gucci glasses aren't fake; they're real.

279.   Recto / Straight

Mira esta línea que hice sin usar regla, quedó bastante recta / Look at this line I made without using a ruler; it is pretty straight.

280.   Rico / Rich

Él supo invertir muy bien sus ahorros y ahora es rico / He knew how to invest his savings very well, and now, he's rich.

281.   Rojo / Red

La sangre de los insectos es de distintos colores, pero no rojo / Insect blood is of different colors but not red.

282.   Rubio / Blonde

Adam Levine se ve demasiado bello así rubio / Adam Levine looks too beautiful being blond like that.

283.   Salado / Salty

El arroz de ayer me cayó mal, estaba muy salado / Yesterday's rice made me sick; it was very salty.

284.   Sano / Healthy

Comer de cualquier cosa en exceso tampoco es sano / Eating too much of anything isn't healthy either.

285.   Seco / Dry

Revisa si la ropa de la secadora está seca / Check if the clothes in the dryer are dry.

286.   Segundo / Second

Dejé de ser el primero por flojo, ahora soy el segundo / I stopped being the first because I was lazy; now, I'm the second.

287.   Simple / Simple

Los momentos que más se disfrutan en la vida son los simples / The most enjoyable moments in life are the simple ones.

288.   Sinvergüenza / Shameless

Que sinverguenza, vino sin camisa a mi casa / So shameless, he came to my house without a shirt.

289.   Social / Social

Vamos, sera un experimente social / Come on; it'll be a social experiment.

290.   Solo / Alone

Cuando estoy muy molesto o triste, prefiero estar solo / When I'm very upset or sad, I prefer to be alone.

291.   Tímido / Shy

Al principio es tímido, pero luego entra en confianza / At first, he's shy, but then he comes into confidence.

292.   Tonto / Silly

Que tonto, estaba bromeando, no era para que te molestaras / So silly, I was joking; it wasn't to bother you.

293.   Turquesa / Turquiose

El turquesa es el color más perfecto que existe / Turquoise is the perfect color there is.

294.   Triste / Sad

La situación fue bastante triste, nadie lo esperaba / The situation was pretty sad; nobody expected it.

295.   Útil / Useful

Esperamos que este libro te sea útil para aprender español / We hope that this book will be useful for you to learn Spanish.

296.   Verdadero / True

Espero que lo que me dices sea verdadero o vamos a tener problemas / I hope what you're telling me is true, or we're gonna have troubles.

297.   Verde / Green

Los colores de la navidad son el rojo y el verde / The colors of Christmas are red and green.

298.   Viejo / Old

La manzana que está en la mesa tiene allí como una semana, ya está vieja / The apple that's on the table has been there for about a week; it's already old.

299.   Vivo / Alive

A pesar del accidente que tuvo, gracias a dios sigue vivo / Despite the accident he had, thank God, he's still alive.

Adverbs

300.   Ahora / Now

Si quieres salir de fiesta con tus amigos, tienes que hacer las tareas de la casa ahora / If you want to party with your friends, you have to do the housework now.

Ahora iré a tomar una merengada, ¿Te traigo una? / Now, I'm going to have a snack. Can I get you one?

301.   Antes / Before

Antes de salir de la casa me gusta cepillarme los dientes y echarme perfume / Before I leave the house, I like to brush my teeth and spray myself perfume.

302.   Después / After

Después de salir del trabajo siempre paso por la panadería a buscar merienda / After work, I always stop by the bakery for a snack.

303.   Ayer / Yesterday

Lo único que podemos hacer con el ayer es aprender de nuestros errores / The only thing we can do with yesterday is to learn from our mistakes.

304.   Hoy / Today

Hoy tengo una muy importante conferencia a la que no puedo faltar o seré despedido / Today, I have a very important conference that I can't miss, or I will be fired.

305.   Mañana / Tomorrow

Mañana salgo de viaje con la empresa al congreso anual de economistas / Tomorrow, I'm going on a trip with the company to the annual congress of economists.

306.   Temprano / Early

Temprano, cuando me desperté, aún no había salido el sol / Earlier, when I woke up, the sun had not yet risen.

307.   Pronto / Soon

Si no cambiamos nuestros hábitos, la Tierra pronto colapsará por la contaminación / If we don't change our habits, the Earth will soon collapse because of the pollution.

308.   Tarde / Late

Ya es demasiado tarde para pedir disculpas, el daño está hecho / It's too late to apologize; the damage is done.

309.   Aquí – Acá / Here

Aquí en mi casa tengo unos zapatos que te pueden servir / Here, in my house, I have shoes that you can use.

Acá donde trabajo hay una señora que siempre me pregunta por ti / Where I work, there's a lady who always asks me about you.

310.   Allí – Ahí – Allá / There

¿Allí en la cafetería no se me olvidó un paraguas negro? / Didn't I forget a black umbrella there in the coffee shop?

Ahí en la esquina venden los mejores tacos mexicanos que he probado en mi vida / There, on the corner, they sell the best Mexican tacos I've ever tasted in my life.

Allá en aquella librería tienen la edición especial del comic que te gusta / In that bookstore over there, they have the special edition of the comic you like.

311. Cerca / Close

No estés tan cerca de mí porque me pongo nervioso / Don't be so close to me because I get nervous.

312. Lejos / Far

El control de la televisión está demasiado lejos para agarrarlo, creo que seguiré viendo esto / The TV's remote is too far to grab; I think I'll keep watching this.

313. Dentro / Inside

¿Segura que las llaves del carro no están dentro de tu cartera? Yo las guardé ahí / Are you sure the car keys aren't inside your purse? I stored them there

314. Fuera / Outside

Toma, ya las conseguí, estaban fuera de mi cartera, se deben haber salido / Here, I got them. They were outside my purse; they must have gotten out.

315. Alrededor / Around

Amo cuando me abrazas y pones tus brazos alrededor de mi cintura, es muy romantico / I love it when you hug me and put your arms around my waist, it's very romantic.

316. Encima / On

Yo siempre pongo mi teléfono a cargar encima de la mesa, así no olvido donde está / I always put my phone to charge on the table, so I don't forget where it is.

317. Detrás / Behind

El gato estaba persiguiendo a un ratón y se quedó atorado detrás de la nevera / The cat was chasing a mouse and got stuck behind the fridge.

318. Delante – En frente/ In front

Estaba delante de ti en el atasco de tráfico y no te diste cuenta / I was right in front of you in the traffic jam, and you didn't notice.

En frente de ti está la chica más inteligente de la escuela, voltea disimuladamente / In front of you is the smartest girl in school; turn around.

319.   Despacio - Lentamente / Slowly

La hermana de mi padrastro maneja tan despacio que es desesperante salir con ella / My stepfather's sister drives so slowly that it makes me desperate to go out with her.

¡QUIETO! Ponga el arma en el suelo lentamente y alce las manos / FREEZE! Put the gun on the ground slowly and raise your hands

320.   Deprisa – Rápido – Rápidamente / Quickly

Entra a la casa deprisa, se cayó un panal de abejas y vienen a picarnos / Get in the house quickly. A beehive fell, and they are coming to sting us.

Él siempre responde muy rápido a las preguntas que hace el profesor en clase / He always responds very quickly to questions asked by the teacher in class

Rápidamente todo cambió entre nosotros / Quickly, everything changed between us.

321.   Bien / Well

Prefiero mil veces los productos artesanales, siempre están bien hechos / I prefer handcrafted products a thousand times; they are always well-made.

322.   Mal / Badly

Hubo una tormenta en la ciudad, y la gente la tomó mal. / There was a storm in the city, and the people took it badly.

323.   Mucho / A lot - Very much

Me gustas mucho / I like you a lot.

Muchas gracias / Thank you very much

324.   Poco / Not much

No me gusta mucho / I like him but not much.

325.   Muy / Very

Estamos en una situación muy complicada / We're in a very complicated situation.

326.   Casi / Almost

No es posible que estes casi todo el día jugando videojuegos / It's not possible that you spend almost all day playing video games.

327.   Todo / All

Todo el helado era de tu hermana y te lo comiste / All the ice cream was from your sister,and you ate it.

328.   Nada / Nothing at all

La nevera está vacia, no hay nada / The fridge is empty; there's nothing at all

329.   Algo / Some – A Little

Solo he sido capaz de estudiar algo, he estado muy ocupado / I've only been able to study a little. I've been very busy.

330.   Medio / Half

Solo me queda medio sanduche, ¿Quieres un poco? / I only have half a sandwich left; do you want some?

331.   Demasiado / Too much

Esto de los vapeadores ha ido demasiado lejos / This vapers thing has gone too far.

332.   Más / More

Mi café tiene poca azúcar, ¿Puedes traerme más? / My coffee's low on sugar; can you get me some more?

333.   Menos / Less

Estuvo muy rico, aunque me gusta con menos salsa / It was really good, although I like it with less sauce.

334.   Además / Besides

Además de ser buen estudiante, es buen atleta / Besides being a good student, he's a good athlete.

335.   Incluso / Even

Incluso después de dormir, seguía con mucho sueño / Even after I slept, I was still very sleepy.

336.   También / Also – Too

Yo también te amo / I love you too

Trae refrescos y también cervezas / Bring sodas and also beers.

337.   Sí / Yes

Le propuse matrimonio y me dijo que sí / I proposed to her, and she said yes.

338.   No / No

La invite a salir y me dijo que no / I asked her out, and she said no.

339.   Tampoco / Neither, nor

El entrenador no se rinde y los jugadores tampoco / The coach doesn't give up, neither do the players.

Mi hermano no es muy alto, y yo tampoco / My brother's not very tall, nor am I.

340.   Jamás / Never, ever

Jamás iré al desierto / I'll never go to the desert.

341.   Nunca / Never, ever

Nunca en mi vida perdonaré a ese estúpido / I'll never forgive that stupid person in my life.

342.   Tal vez – Quizás / Perhaps – Maybe

Tal vez podamos salir mañana, depende de si termino mi tarea / Maybe we can go out tomorrow; it depends on whether or not I finish my homework.

Quizás sea el indicado para mí / Perhaps he's the one for me.

Numbers

343.   Uno / One

Quería dos jugos, pero dame solo uno / I wanted two juices, but just give me one.

344.   Primero / First

Él ganó de primero la carrera / He won the race as the first placer.

345.   Dos / Two

Los seres humanos tenemos dos ojos / Human beings have two eyes.

346.   Segundo / Second

Casi llega de primero, pero al final se tropezó y quedó de segundo / He almost finished first, but in the end, he stumbled and finished second.

347.   Tres / Three

Contandome a mí, somos tres hermanas / Counting me, we're three sisters.

348.   Tercero / Third

¿Por cuál trimestre voy? Creo que es el tercero / Which trimester am I going for? I think it's the third.

349.   Cuatro / Four

La mayoría de animales tienen cuatro patas / Most animals have four legs.

350.   Cuarto / Fourth

El cuarto lugar casi nunca recibe premio / Fourth placers almost never get a prize.

351.Cinco / Five

En las manos y en los pies tenemos cinco dedos / In the hands and feet, we have five fingers.

352.   Quinto / Fifth

Es curioso que el quinto grado sea el más difícil / It's curious that fifth grade is the hardest.

353.   Seis / Six

Tenía seis llamadas perdidas de mi mamá / I had six missed calls from my mom.

354.   Sexto / Sixth

Deje de llamarte en la sexta llamada / I stopped calling you on the sixth call.

355.   Siete / Seven

Me compre siete juegos de video nuevos / I bought seven new video games.

356.   Séptimo / Seventh

Tenían una oferta, si llevabas seis, el séptimo juego era gratis / They had an offer; if you bought six, the seventh game would be free.

357.   Ocho / Eight

Con este perro ya son ocho adoptados, no puedes seguir así / Including this dog, you have already adopted eight; you can not do it anymore.

358.   Octavo / Eighth

Según la tabla de clasificaciones, quedaron de octavos / According to the table of classifications, they finished eighth.

359.   Nueve / Nine

Mi hermanita tiene nueve años / My little sister is nine years old.

360.   Noveno / Nineth

En su noveno cumpleaños le regalamos una bicicleta / On his ninth birthday, we gave her a bicycle.

361.   Diez / Ten

Según la biblia, hay diez mandamientos / According to the Bible, there are ten commandments.

362.   Décimo / Tenth

El décimo mandamiento también es muy importante / The Tenth Commandment is also very important.

363.   Once / Eleven

Hace once años tuve el accidente / Eleven years ago, I had an accident.

364.   Décimoprimero / Eleventh

El décimo primero de la competencia fue mi primo / The eleventh in the competition was my cousin.

365.   Doce / Twelve

El día se divide en dos períodos de doce horas / The day is divided into two periods of twelve hours

366.   Décimosegundo / Twelfth

Contar hasta el decimosegundo motivo es algo innecesario / Counting to the twelfth motive is unnecessary.

367.   Trece / Thirteen

Este viernes será viernes 13 / This Friday will be Friday the 13th.

368.   Décimo tercero / Thirteenth

Hoy es el decimotercer jueves del año / Today is the thirteenth Thursday of the year.

369.   Veinte / Twenty

Mi hijo mayor se fue de vacaciones hace veinte días / My eldest son went on vacation twenty days ago.

370.   Vigésimo / Twentieth

Hoy es el vigésimo día fuera de casa y ya extraño a mis padres / Today is the twentieth day away from home, and I already miss my parents.

371. Treinta / Thirty

Abril es un mes de treinta días / April is a month of thirty days.

372.   Cuarenta / Forty

Estudios demuestran que a partir de los cuarenta años empiezan los problemas de la visión / Studies show that from the age of forty, vision problems begin.

373.   Cincuenta / Fifty

¿Sabías que cincuenta es la mitad exacta de cien? / Did you know that fifty is exactly half of a hundred?

374.   Cien / A hundred

Un siglo es la manera de expresar que ya han pasado cien años / A century is the way to express that a hundred years have passed.

375.   Doscientos / Two hundred

La moto de Jake alcanza doscientos kilómetros por hora / Jake's bike reaches two hundred miles an hour.

376.   Mil / A Thousand

El carro que me quiero comprar cuesta mil dólares, ¿Está a buen precio? / The car I want to buy costs a thousand dollars; is it a good price?

377.   Millón / A Million

Yo quiero ganar la lotería, con un millón de dólares haría muchas cosas nuevas / I want to win the lottery; with a million dollars, I would do many new things.

Chapter 2: Home

In this chapter, you will find words related to the home.

378.   Casa / House

Yo vivo en una casa grande de color verde que queda cerca de la farmacia / I live in a big, green house near the pharmacy.

379.   Apartamento / Apartment

En este edificio hay diez apartamentos, todos del mismo tamaño / There are ten apartments in this building, all of the same size.

380.   Edificio / Building

Todos los edificios de la urbanización tienen salón de fiesta y parque infantil / All the buildings in the city have a party room and children's playground.

381.   Condominio / Condo

Ella es la encargada de llevar el condominio / She's in charge of running the condo.

382.   Cabaña / Cabin

Para las vacaciones vamos a alquilar una cabaña con capacidad para 8 personas / For the holidays, we are going to rent a cabin with a capacity for 8 people.

383.   Granja / Farm

La vida en el campo es muy tranquila, trabajar en la granja me ha permitido desestresarme / Life in the countryside is very quiet; working on the farm has allowed me to de-stress.

384.   Casa de campo / Country house

Prefiero pasar navidad en la casa de campo, en esa época el clima es muy agradable / I would rather spend Christmas in the country house; at that time the weather is very pleasant.

385.   Mansión / Mansion

Casi todos los artistas de Hollywood viven en mansiones lujosas / Almost every Hollywood artist lives in luxurious mansions.

386.   Property / Propiedad

La granja, los tractores y el ganado son de mi propiedad / The farm, the tractors, and the animals are my property.

387.   Planta baja / Ground floor

Se alquila planta baja de un condominio, consta de una habitación, baño, cocina y sala de estar / The ground floor of a condominium for rent consists of a bedroom, bathroom, kitchen, and living room.

388. Primer piso / First floor

Las oficinas que usted busca están en el primer piso / The offices you are looking for are on the first floor

389. Alojamiento – Hospedaje / Accommodation

En esta temporada es dificil conseguir hospedaje / In this season, it is difficult to get accommodation.

390. Techo / Roof

Me gustan las casas con techo alto / I like houses with high roofs.

391. Chimenea / Chimney

Necesito reparar la chimenea antes de que llegue el invierno / I need to repair the chimney before winter arrives.

392. Piso / Floor

El piso de la cocina es diferente al piso de la sala / The kitchen floor is different from the living room floor.

393. Sótano / Basement

La decoracion de Halloween esta guardada en el sotano / The Halloween decorations are stored in the basement.

394. Balcón / Balcony

Asomate al balcón para que veas el desfile / Look out on the balcony to see the parade.

395. Escaleras / Stairs

¿Por donde quedan las escaleras mecánicas? / Which way are the moving stairs?

396. Piedra / Stone

Debemos escoger el tipo de piedra que queremos para el jardín / We must choose the type of stone we want for the garden.

397. Teja / Tile

Las tejas han ido deteriorándose, ya debemos cambiarlas / The tiles have been deteriorating, and we must change them.

398. Dormitorio / Bedroom

Esperame en tu dormitorio para que conversemos / Wait for me in your bedroom so we can talk.

399. Comedor / Dining room

¿Qué te parece este juego de muebles para nuestro comedor? / How about this set of furniture for our dining room?

400. Sala / Living room

Esta alfombra quedaría perfecta en la sala de tu casa / This carpet would fit perfectly in your living room.

401. Estudio / Study

Acabo de mudarme, aún no he organizado el estudio / I just moved in; I haven't set up the studio yet.

402. Baño / Bathroom

Olvidé mi paraguas en el baño del cine / I forgot my umbrella in the cinema bathroom.

403. Ático / Attic

Hace mucho tiempo que no subo al ático, debe estar muy sucio / It has been a long time since I've been in the attic. It must be very dirty.

404. Cocina / Kitchen

La cocina es mi sitio preferido de la casa, siempre nos reunimos allí / The kitchen is my favorite place of the house; we always meet there.

405. Espejo / Mirror

Recomiendan tener espejos en espacios pequeños para dar la sensación de amplitud / It is recommended to have mirrors in small spaces to give the sensation of amplitude.

406. Lavar / Wash

Prefiero lavar mi traje de baño a mano y con detergente suave / I prefer to wash my bathing suit by hand and with mild detergent.

407. Limpiar / Clean

Samuel debe limpiar su cuarto una vez por semana / Samuel must clean his room once a week.

408. Cepillar / Brush

El odontologo recomienda cepillar los dientes 3 veces al dia / The dentist recommends brushing your teeth 3 times a day.

409. Peinar / Comb

Ella dura mucho tiempo peinándose, tiene el cabello muy largo / She takes a long time combing her hair; she has very long hair

410. Cepillo de dientes / Toothbrush

Mi marca preferida de cepillo de dientes es Oral B / My favorite brand of toothbrush is Oral B.

411. Fachada / Facade

Ellos quieren arreglar la fachada de la tienda pero es muy costoso / They want to fix the facade of the store, but it is very expensive.

412.   Pasillo / Hallway

Tenía miedo, el pasillo estaba muy solo y oscuro / I was afraid; the hallway was very lonely and dark.

413.   Sala / Hall

Por favor diles a los niños que no dejen juguetes en la sala / Please tell the children not to leave toys in the hall.

414.   Ascensor / Elevator

Durante los temblores o terremotos no se debe usar el ascensor / The elevator should not be used during earthquakes or tremors.

415. Azotea / Rooftop

Podemos hacer la fiesta en la azotea / We can have the party on the rooftop.

416.   Jardín / Garden

Se mudaron a una casa con un jardín muy grande / They moved into a house with a very large garden.

417. Puerta / Door

La puerta principal se quedó abierta toda la noche / The main door stayed open all night.

418.   Calefacción / Heating

Todas las cabañas tienen calefacción / All cabins have heating.

419.   Aire acondicionado / Air conditioning

Por favor apaga el aire acondicionado que ya tengo mucho frio / Please turn off the air conditioning because I'm already very cold.

420.   Rascacielos / Skyscraper

En Nueva York hay muchos rascacielos famosos como el Empire Estate, la Catedral San Patricio, el Edificio Woolworth y otros / In New York, there are many famous skyscrapers, such as the Empire State, St. Patrick's Cathedral, Woolworth Building, and others.

421.   Garage / Garage

La puerta del garage esta dañada / The garage door is damaged.

422.   Patio trasero / Backyard

Me gustaría construir una piscina en el patio trasero / I'd like to build a pool in the backyard.

423.   Buzón / Mailbox

Dicen que lo dejarón en el buzón, pero no esta allí / They say they left it in the mailbox, but it's not there.

424.   Sillón / Armchair

No te sientes allí, es el sillón favorito de mi abuelo / Don't sit there; it's my grandfather's favorite armchair.

425.   Alfombra / Carpet

No me gusta usar alfombras en la habitación, acumulan mucho polvo / I don't like to use carpets in the room; they collect a lot of dust.

426.   Sofá / Couch

No dejes que la perrita se suba al sofá / Don't let the little dog get on the couch.

427.   Estante para libros – Biblioteca / Bookcase

Mientras esperas puedes tomar un libro de la biblioteca / While you wait, you can take a book from the bookcase

428.   Mesa de centro / Coffee table

La mesa de centro esta muy bonita pero no combina con mis muebles / The coffee table is very nice, but it doesn't match my furniture.

429.   Silla reclinable / Recliner

Nada mejor que una silla reclinable y buena música para relajarme / There's nothing better than a reclining chair and good music to relax.

430.   Lámpara / Lamp

Ese bombillo no le sirve a la lámpara / That light bulb doesn't fit the lamp.

431.   Cama / Bed

Todos los cuartos tienen camas matrimoniales / All the rooms have double beds.

432.   Armario / Closet

Tengo mucha ropa, necesito un armario más grande / I've got a lot of clothes; I need a bigger closet.

433.   Mesa de noche / Nightstand

Los libros que estoy leyendo en este momento están en mi mesa de noche / The books I'm reading right now are on my nightstand.

434.   Reloj despertador / Alarm clock

Voy a poner mi reloj despertador para tomarme las medicinas / I'm gonna set my alarm clock to take my meds.

435.   Almohada / Pillow

Las almohadas del hotel eran muy cómodas / The hotel pillows were very comfortable.

436.   Colchón / Mattress

Solo falta comprar los colchones para poder mudarnos / All we need to do is buy the mattresses so we can move in.

437.   Sábanas / Sheets

Ella prefiere sabanas blancas / She prefers white sheets.

438.   Cobija / Blanket

Mi hija lleva a todos lados su cobija de muñequitas / My daughter carries her doll's blanket everywhere.

439.   Estufa / Stove

No te acerques a la estufa que esta encendida / Don't go near the stove that's on.

440.   Lavaplatos (Jabón) / Dishwasher soap

Ninoska usa guantes para fregar, ella es alérgica al jabón / Ninoska wears gloves to wash the dishes; she's allergic to soap.

441.   Lavaplatos (Máquina) / Dishwasher

Mila tiene un lavaplatos pero casi no lo usa / Mila has a dishwasher but hardly uses it.

442.   Fregadero / Sink

Coloca todos los platos en el fregadero cuando acabes de comer / Put all the dishes in the sink when you finish eating.

443.   Especiero / Spice rack

El especiero que les compramos a los vecinos en la venta de garage quedó perfecto en nuestra cocina / The spice rack we bought from the neighbors at the garage sale fitted perfectly in our kitchen.

444.   Ducha / Shower

Me encanta tomar una ducha caliente antes de dormir, así duermo mejor / I love to take a hot shower before I go to sleep, so I sleep better.

445.   Bañera / Bathtub

Entró a la bañera y se resbaló, por lo que lo llevaron al hospital / He went into the bathtub and slipped, so they took him to the hospital.

446.   Poceta – Inodoro – Retrete / Toilet

En mi casa lavan la poceta todos los días, es un lugar que debe mantenerse aseado / In my house, they wash the toilet every day; it's a place that must be kept clean.

447.   Toalla / Towel

Los científicos recomiendan lavar las toallas del hogar cada semana / Scientists recommend to wash the household towels weekly.

448.   Cesta de ropa sucia / Laundry basket

Hijo, ¿Hasta cuándo tengo que decirte que no dejes que se llene la cesta de ropa sucia? / Son, how long do I have to tell you not to let the laundry basket fill up?

449.   Mesa de comedor / Dinner table

El especiero de los vecinos es perfecto porque combina muy bien con nuestra mesa del comedor / The spice rack of the neighbors is perfect because it combines very well with our dining table.

450.   Servilleta / Napkin

Es muy importante que cuando vayas a un restaurante tengas una servilleta a la mano / It is very important that when you go to a restaurant, you have a napkin at hand.

451.Cubiertos / Cutlery

Los restaurantes siempre deben tener bien presentable los cubiertos / Restaurants should always have good, presentable cutlery.

452.   Abrelatas / Tin opener

Es mejor tener un abrelatas y no necesitarlo que necesitarlo y no tenerlo / It's better to have a tin opener and not need it than to need it and not have it.

453.   Tazón / Bowl

Debiste poner las galletas en un tazón mas grande, aquí se van a romper / You should've put the cookies in a bigger bowl; they're gonna break here.

454. Cafetera / Coffee maker

Es increíble tener una cafetera, solo hay que encenderla y esperar por el café / It's amazing to have a coffee maker; you just have to turn it on and wait for the coffee.

455. Microondas / Microwave

Utilizar el microondas para descongelar los alimentos no es recomendable porque no se descongela de forma natural / Using the microwave to defrost food is not recommended because it does not defrost naturally.

456. Cuchara / Spoon

No sé que hacen con las cucharas de la casa, cada día hay menos / I don't know what they do with the spoons in the house; every day, there are less.

457. Tenedor / Fork

Este tenedor es de plata, me lo regaló mi abuela en un set de cubiertos hace muchos años / This fork is made of silver, my grandmother gave it to me in a set of cutlery many years ago.

458. Cuchillo / Knife

El mejor cuchillo para picar la carne es el que está en la segunda gaveta / The best knife for cutting meat is the one in the second drawer.

459. Nevera / Fridge

No podemos meter tanta comida en la nevera porque deja de enfriar / We can't put that much food in the fridge because it stops cooling.

460. Sacacorchos / Corkscrew

Traje una botella de vino para celebrar, ¿Tienen un sacacorchos para destaparla? / I brought a bottle of wine to celebrate. Do you have a corkscrew to open it?

461. Calentador de agua / Water heater

El nuevo calentador de agua que instalamos es genial, tiene agua caliente infinita / The new water heater we installed is great; it has infinite hot water

462. Destapador de botellas / Bottle opener

Desde que usamos el destapador de botellas el otro día, no lo consigo / Since we used the bottle opener the other day, I can't find it.

463. Escoba / Broom

Es curioso que en los cuentos las brujas utilicen las escobas para transportarse / It is curious that, in fairy tales, witches use brooms to transport themselves.

464. Trapeador / Mop

Para usar el trapeador así de sucio es mejor no utilizarlo, en lugar de limpiar está ensuciando / It is better not to use the mop that's so dirty. Instead of cleaning, it is soiling.

465. Guantes / Gloves

Siempre que voy a usar cloro tengo que utilizar guantes, la piel de mis manos es muy delicada / Whenever I use chlorine, I have to use gloves; my skin is very delicate.

466. Licuadora / Blender

La licuadora se dañó porque le echaron demasiado hielo el día de los batidos / The blender was damaged because too much ice was thrown in the milkshake.

467. Hacer la cama / Make the bed

Todas las mañanas estoy tan apurado que se me olvida hacer la cama / Every morning, I'm in such a hurry that I forget to make the bed.

468. Limpiar / Tidy up

Es hora de limpiar mi habitación, ya huele mal / It's time to tidy up my room; it already smells bad.

469. Aspirar - Aspiradora / Vacuum

Mamá, ¿Has visto la aspiradora? No está en el closet donde se guarda / Mom, have you seen the vacuum? It's not in the closet where it's kept.

Nunca está de más aspirar al perro para quitarle las pulgas / It never hurts to vacuum the dog to get rid of the fleas.

470. Lavar los platos / Wash the dishes

En casa de mi novia, el último que termina de comer es el que debe lavar los platos / At my girlfriend's house, the last one who finishes eating is the one who has to wash the dishes.

Chapter 3: Family and Relationships

In this chapter, we will take a closer look at words related to family and relationships.

471.Familia / Family

Mi familia, aunque esté separada, sigue siendo muy unida / My family, even though separated, is still very close.

472.   Mamá / Mother

Mi mamá es la mejor de todas porque siempre me trata bien y me cuida mucho / My mom is the best of all because she always treats me well and takes good care of me.

473.   Papá / Father

El papá de Lila es increíble, él crió a Lila y a sus dos hermanas sólo / Lila's dad is amazing; he raised Lila and her two sisters alone.

474.   Hijo / Son

Entonces, ¿Julio es o no el hijo del señor del kiosko? / So, is Julio the son of the kiosk man or not?

475.   Hija / Daughter

La Sra Clauss se ve tan joven que su hija pareciera su prima / Mrs. Clauss looks so young that her daughter looked like her cousin.

476.   Hermano / Brother

Aunque no seamos hijos de la misma mamá, yo lo quiero como a un hermano / Even if we're not children of the same mother, I love him like a brother.

477.   Hermana / Sister

La hermana menor de Sebastián tiene un coeficiente intelectual muy bajo / Sebastian's younger sister has a very low IQ.

478.   Tío / Uncle

Me encanta visitar al tío Ned, siempre nos da caramelos y dulces / I love visiting Uncle Ned; he always gives us candy and sweets.

479.   Tía / Aunt

La casa de la tía es muy aburrida, no hay televisión ni videojuegos / Our aunt's house is very boring; there is no television or video game.

480. Abuelo / Grandfather

Mi abuelo es un señor de 56 años, mientras que el abuelo de mi amigo tiene 73 / My grandfather is a 56-year-old man, while my friend's grandfather is 73.

481. Abuela / Grandmother

Mi abuela siempre teje cosas bonitas y me las regala en ocasiones especiales / My grandmother always knits nice things and gives them to me on special occasions.

482. Nieto / Grandson

Siempre intento ser el nieto que me gustaría tener / I always try to be the grandson I'd like to have.

483. Nieta / Granddaughter

A Carla la quieren mucho sus abuelos porque es su única nieta / Carla is loved very much by her grandparents because she is their only granddaughter.

484. Sobrina / Niece

La sobrina de mi abuelo es una persona muy conflictiva, no la soporto / My grandfather's niece is a very troubled person. I can't stand her.

485. Sobrino / Nephew

Amo que mi sobrino me venga a visitar, siempre es de mucha ayuda aquí en casa / I love that my nephew comes to visit me; he's always very helpful here at home.

486. Primo – Prima / Cousin

¿Entonces quieres decir que el hijo de mi tío es mi primo? / So you mean my uncle's son is my cousin?

487. Padrino / Godfather

Una de mis películas favoritas es "El padrino" / One of my favorite movies is "The Godfather."

488. Madrina / Godmother

Ella es mi madrina desde que fui bautizado en la iglesia hace seis años / She's been my godmother since I was baptized in church six years ago.

489. Padrastro / Stepfather

Mis padres se separaron cuando yo era pequeña y ahora tengo un padrastro / My parents separated when I was little, and now, I have a stepfather.

490. Madrastra / Stepmother

La madrastra de cenicienta era muy cruel con ella, espero que mi madrastra no sea así conmigo / Cinderella's stepmother was very cruel to her. I hope my stepmother is not so cruel to me.

491. Hermanastro / Stepbrother

Leo y Samanta son hermanastros, son hijos de padres diferentes/ Leo and Samanta are stepbrothers and stepsisters; they are children of different parents.

492. Hermanastra / Stepsister

Quiero a mi hermanastra más que a mi hermana / I love my stepsister more than I love my sister.

493. Cuñado / Brother – in – law

Le presté mi carro a mi cuñado y lo chocó / I lent my car to my brother-in-law, and he crashed it.

494. Cuñada / Sister – in – law

Mi cuñada siempre me pinta las uñas y arregla el pelo, nos llevamos muy bien / My sister-in-law always paints my nails and does my hair; we get along very well.

495. Suegro / Father – in – law

Ayer peleé con mi suegro porque trató muy mal a su hija / Yesterday, I fought with my father-in-law because he treated his daughter very badly.

496. Suegra / Mother – in – law

No puedo ir, mi suegra me invitó a almorzar a su casa / I can't go. My mother-in-law invited me to lunch at her house.

497. Nuera / Daughter – in – law

Siempre me confundo, si tú eres la novia de mi hijo, ¿eres mi nuera? / I'm always confused; if you're my son's girlfriend, are you my daughter-in-law?

498. Yerno / Son – in – law

Despues de casarte con mi hija, seras mi yerno favorito / After you marry my daughter, you'll be my favorite son-in-law.

499. Novia / Bride

La novia lucía radiante entrando a la iglesia con ese vestido / The bride looked radiant entering the church in that dress.

500. Novio / Boyfriend

Mi novio siempre me trata de maravilla, es perfecto / My boyfriend always treats me great. He's perfect.

501.   Novia / Girlfriend

Antes de que fuera mi novia, ya estaba enamorado de ella / Before she was my girlfriend, I was already in love with her.

502.   Amigo – Amiga / Friend

Nos conocimos en preescolar y somos amigos desde entonces / We met in preschool, and we've been friends since then.

503.   Compañero – Compañera / Partner

Mi hermana es mi mejor compañera, va conmigo a todas partes / My sister is my best partner; she goes everywhere with me.

504.   Compañero de trabajo / Workmate

Angelo fue mi compañero de trabajo por diez años / Angelo was my workmate for ten years.

505.   Compañero de studio / Studymate

Si quieres ser mi compañero de studio debes ser responsable y comprometido / If you want to be my study-mate, you must be responsible and committed.

506.   Vecino – Vecina / Neighbor

Dicen que tu vecino puede llegar a ser tu familia más cercana / It is said that your neighbor may become your closest family.

507.   Exnovia / Ex-girlfriend

Su exnovia le devolvió todos los regalos / His ex-girlfriend gave him back all the presents.

508.   Exnovio / Ex-boyfriend

Carlos es su nuevo novio, es más buenmozo que su exnovio / Carlos is her new boyfriend. He's more handsome than her ex-boyfriend.

509.   Mascota / Pet

Nunca he tenido mascotas, no me gustan los animales / I've never had pets. I don't like animals.

510.   Adoptado / Adopted

No compres perros, adopta uno, los adoptados son fieles y agradecidos / Don't buy dogs; adopt one. Adopted ones are faithful and grateful.

511. Amistad / Friendship

Enseña el valor de la amistad a tus hijos desde pequeños / Teach the value of friendship to your children from an early age.

512.Antepasados / Ancestors

La tarea es hacer un árbol genealógico con mis antepasados / The homework is to make a family tree out of my ancestors.

513. Bisabuelo / Great-Grandfather

Mi abuelo nunca conoció a su padre por eso no me cuenta historias de mi bisabuelo / My grandfather never met his father, so he doesn't tell me stories about my great-grandfather.

514. Bisabuela / Great-Grandmother

Marta era la mamá de mi abuela, ella era mi bisabuela / Marta was my grandmother's mother; she was my great-grandmother.

515. Compromiso – Noviazgo/ Engagement

Su cena de compromiso será en un restaurante italiano / Her engagement dinner will be at an Italian restaurant.

516. Descendientes / Descendants

Mi hijo y mi nieto son mis descendientes, ellos heredarán mi dinero /My son and grandson are my descendants; they will inherit my money.

517. Gemelos / Twins

Esos hermanos se parecen mucho pero no son gemelos /Those brothers look a lot alike, but they're not twins.

518.   Heredero / Heir

Su hijo será el único heredero de toda la fortuna de su padre / His son will be the sole heir to his father's entire fortune.

519. Hijo ilegítimo / Illegitimate child

Julio es hijo ilegítimo, nunca conoció a su padre / Julio is an illegitimate son. He never met his father.

520.   Huérfano / Orphan

Ella es huérfana, su madre murió cuando ella tenía 3 años / She's an orphan; her mother died when she was 3.

521. Marido – Esposo / Husband

Ya se casaron, ahora son marido y mujer / They're married; now, they're husband and wife.

522.   Mujer (Comprometida) – Esposa / Wife

Mi esposa es el amor de mi vida, amiga y compañera / My wife is the love of my life, friend, and companion.

523.   Pariente / Relative

Todos los parientes cercanos asistieron al funeral / All close relatives attended the funeral.

524.   Prometido / Engaged

El prometido estaba nervioso por conocer a toda la familia / The engaged man was nervous about meeting the whole family.

525.   Abandono / Desertion

Estaba triste y desconsolada luego del abandono de su novio / She was sad and heartbroken after her boyfriend's desertion.

526.   Afecto / Affection

Siento un gran afecto por ti, son muchos años de compañerismo / I have a great affection for you; it has been many years of companionship.

527.   Amor / Love

El primer amor nunca se olvida / First love is never forgotten.

528.   Amante / Lover

Segun la historia de Egipto, Cleopatra era la amante de Marco Antonio / According to the history of Egypt, Cleopatra was Marco Antonio's lover.

529.   Amar – Querer / To love

"Amar es desear lo mejor para el otro, permitir que sea feliz" / "To love is to wish the best for the other, to allow him to be happy."

530.   Amigo íntimo / Intimate friend

Un amigo íntimo es aquel con el que mantienes una relación muy estrecha / An intimate friend is one with whom you have a very close relationship.

531.Amor a primera vista / Love at first sight

Lo ví y me enamoré, fue amor a primera vista / I saw him, and I fell in love; it was love at first sight

532.   Amor platonico / Platonic love

Zac Efron es mi amor platónico / Zac Efron is my platonic love.

533.   Amorío – Romance / Love affair

Se conocieron en vacaciones y tuvieron un amorío / They met on vacation and had an affair.

534.   Amoroso / Loving

Mi abuela siempre me hablaba en un tono amoroso, dulce y suave / My grandmother always spoke to me in a loving, sweet, and soft tone.

535.   Anillo de boda / Wedding ring

Los novios estaban indecisos para escoger sus anillos de boda / The bride and groom were hesitant to choose their wedding rings.

536.   Anillo de compromiso / Engagement ring

Si tu anillo de compromiso tiene diamantes debes escoger algo más sencillo para la boda / If your engagement ring has diamonds, you should choose something simpler for the wedding.

537.   Atracción / Atraction

¿Como saber si sientes atracción por alguien? / How do you know if you feel attraction for someone?

538.   Atracción sexual / Sexual attraction

La atracción sexual no es lo mismo que la atracción sentimental / Sexual attraction is not the same as sentimental attraction.

539.   Aventura / Affair

Tener una aventura es peligroso para tu matrimonio / Having an affair is dangerous for your marriage.

540.   Beso / Kiss

Dale besos y abrazos de mi parte / Give him kisses and hugs from me.

541.Boda / Wedding

La boda se realizará en la iglesia de su pueblo / The wedding will take place in the church of her village.

542.   Cariño / Darling – Honey

No te preocupes cariño, yo hago la cena hoy / Don't worry, honey. I'll make dinner today.

543.   Cariñoso / Affectionate

Siempre fue muy cariñoso y tierno con ella / He was always very affectionate and cute to her.

544.   Casado / Married

Aun no está casado, la boda es en un mes / He's not married yet; the wedding's in a month.

545.   Comprometido / Engaged

Ayer fue la cena con sus padres, ya están comprometidos formalmente / Yesterday was dinner with their parents; they are already formally engaged.

546.   Coquetear / Flirt

Le gusta coquetear con su novio / She likes to flirt with her boyfriend.

547.   Vivir juntos / To live together

Los abuelos se mudaron con nosotros, vamos a vivir juntos por un tiempo / The grandparents moved in with us; we're going to live together for a while.

548.   Corazón / Heart

Su corazón palpita cada vez que la ve / His heart beats every time he sees her.

549.   Enamorado / In love

Nunca ha tenido novios, no se ha enamorado / She's never had boyfriends; she hasn't fallen in love.

550.   Estar enamorado / To be in love

Estar enamorado es una sensación que no puedo describir / Being in love is a feeling I can't describe.

551. Indiferencia / Indifference

Ella lo amaba muchísimo, pero su indiferencia la alejó / She loved him very much, but his indifference pushed her away.

552.   Intimidad / Intimacy

En ciertas religiones está prohibido tener intimidad antes del matrimonio / In certain religions, it is forbidden to have intimacy before marriage.

553.   Juntos / Together

Ellos han estado juntos desde hace muchos años / They've been together for many years.

554.   Recién casados / Newlyweds

Los recién casados tuvieron su luna de miel en Barbados / The newlyweds had their honeymoon in Barbados.

555.   Matrimonio civil / Civil marriage

Al matrimonio civil solo asistieron los familiares y amigos íntimos / The civil marriage was only attended by family and close friends.

556.   Matrimonio religioso / Church wedding

Luego del matrimonio religioso hicieron una gran fiesta / After the church wedding, they had a big party.

557.   Mujeriego / Womanizer

Ese hombre no es mi tipo, es un mujeriego / That man isn't my type; he's a womanizer.

558.   Pasión / Passion

La pasión hacia una persona esta asociada con el deseo sexual / Passion for a person is associated with sexual desire.

559.   Pretendiente / Suitor

Tuvo muchos pretendientes en su juventud y lo escogió a él como su novio / She had many suitors in her youth and chose him as her boyfriend.

560.   Conexión / Connection

Hubo una conexión entre los dos, fue amor a primera vista / There was a connection between the two; it was love at first sight.

561.Relación / Relationship

En esta empresa no permiten tener relaciones entre los empleados / In this company, it is not allowed to have relationships between employees.

562.   Sensación / Feeling

Tengo la sensación de que me estoy enamorando / I have the feeling that I'm falling in love.

563.   Separación / Separation

Luego de una larga separación se reconciliaron / After a long separation, they reconciled.

564.   Divorcio / Divorce

Firmaron los papeles del divorcio y quedaron como amigos / They signed the divorce papers and remained as friends.

565.   Alma gemela / Soul mate

Si existe mi alma gemela aun no la he encontrado / If my soul mate exists, I haven't found her yet.

566.   Soltero / Single

Es el soltero mas codiciado de la oficina / He's the most wanted single guy in the office.

567.   Viudo / Widowed

Su esposa murió y el quedó viudo / His wife died, and he was widowed.

568.   Separado / Separated

Están separados por razones de trabajo / They are separated for work reasons.

569.   Cita / Date

Mi primera cita con un chico fue en la heladería / My first date with a guy was at the ice cream shop.

570.   Cita a ciegas / Blind date

No me gustan las citas a ciegas, me siento insegura / I don't like blind dates; I feel insecure.

571. Fidelidad / Faithfulness

En el altar, juras fidelidad hasta que la muerte los separe / On the altar, you swear faithfulness until death separates you.

572.   Infidelidad / Unfaithfulness

La infidelidad es el principal causante de los divorcios / Unfaithfulness is the main cause of divorces.

573.   Pareja / Couple – Partner

Mi pareja y yo cumplimos 5 años de casados / My partner and I have been married for 5 years.

574.   Merecer / To deserve

Te mereces un hombre que te respete y valore / You deserve a man who respects and values you.

575.   Enemigo / Enemy

Algunas parejas después del divorcio terminan como enemigos / Some couples, after divorce, end up as enemies.

576.   Llevarse / Get along

Pueden llevarse bien pero sino se aman no deben casarse / You can get along, but if you don't love each other, you mustn't get married.

577.   Celos / Jealous

Los celos le hacen mucho daño a una relación / Jealousy does a lot of damage to a relationship.

Chapter 4: Nature

This chapter contains words related to nature, natural phenomena, and the weather.

Weather

578.   Pronóstico del clima / Weather forecast

En las mañanas veo el pronóstico del clima por el canal de noticias / In the mornings, I see the weather forecast on the news channel.

579.   Lluvia / Rain

A Sofi le gusta jugar en la lluvia, incluso si atrapa un resfriado / Sofi likes to play in the rain, even if she catches a cold.

580.   Lluvioso / Rainy

Hoy no podre ir a la playa, el dia amaneció lluvioso / Today, I won't be able to go to the beach. The day started rainy.

581.   Sol / Sun

¿A qué hora se oculta el sol aquí en Madrid? / What time does the sun hide here in Madrid?

582.   Soleado / Sunny

Este dia soleado me encanta, quizá pueda broncearme / I love this sunny day; maybe I can get a tan.

583.   Clima / Weather

Mi nuevo telefono me permite ver como estará el clima / My new phone allows me to see what the weather will be like.

584.   Calor / Hot

Todos irán a la piscina porque hoy hace mucho calor / Everybody's going to the pool because it's very hot today.

585.   Frío / Cold

Aquí afuera hace mucho frio, entremos a la casa / It's so cold out here; let's go inside.

586.   Nieve / Snow

La nieve tapaba la entrada de la casa el día de navidad / The snow covered the entrance to the house on Christmas Day.

587.   Nevando / Snowing

Hoy no tendré clases, ha estado nevando todo el día / I won't have classes today. It's been snowing all day.

588.   Nube / Cloud

Aquel avión volaba muy cerca de las nubes / That plane flew very closely to the clouds.

589.   Nublado / Cloudy

Ha estado nublado hoy, no he podido ver el sol en todo el dia / It's been cloudy today; I haven't been able to see the sun all day.

590.   Viento / Wind

Se indica el viento a 8km/h esta tarde en Bogotá / The wind is indicated at 8km/h this afternoon in Bogota

591.Ventoso / Windy

Hoy tendremos un ventoso dia, fuertes vientos en toda la zona / Today, we'll have a windy day, with strong winds all over the area.

592.   Neblina / Fog

Había mucha neblina, parecía una pelicula de terror / There was a lot of fog; it looked like a horror movie.

593.   Ola de calor / Heat wave

La ola de calor afecta mayormente a la tercera edad / The heat wave mostly affects seniors.

594.   Ola de frío / Cold wave

Algunos animales pequeños mueren a causa de olas de frío / Some small animals die from cold waves.

595.   Granizo / Hail

El granizo de anoche dañó la pintura del auto / Last night's hail damaged the paint on the car.

596.   Temperatura / Temperature

El termómetro indica que su temperatura esta alta, podría tener fiebre / The thermometer indicates your temperature is high; you may have a fever.

597.   Grados / Degrees

Buenos Aires podriía alcanzar los 33 grados centígrados en las próximas horas / Buenos Aires could reach 33 degrees Celsius in the next few hours.

598.   Marea / Tide

En la playa hay un anciano que conoce a la perfección la marea / On the beach, there's an old man who knows the tide perfectly.

599.   Marea alta / High tide

Es peligroso ir en barco, a esta hora hay marea alta / It's dangerous to go by boat; at this time, it's high tide.

600.   Marea baja / Low tide

Los peces se ocultan hacia el mar cuando hay marea baja / Fish hide deep into the sea at low tide.

Nature

601.   Naturaleza / Nature

Muchos de los productos para el cabello vienen de la naturaleza / Many of the hair products come from nature.

602.   Ecosistema / Ecosystem

Los humanos no debemos intervenir en la perfección de los ecosistemas / Humans should not intervene in the perfection of ecosystems.

603.   Bosque / Forest

Cerca de mi casa hay un bosque muy bonito / Near my house, there is a very nice forest.

604.   Desierto / Desert

El desierto del Sahara es el más grande del mundo / The Sahara desert is the largest in the world.

605.   Prado / Meadow

En la casa de campo de mi tío tienen un prado lleno de flores / In my uncle's country house, they have a meadow full of flowers.

606.   Jungla / Jungle

Los monos viven principalmente en las junglas / Monkeys live mainly in the jungles.

607.   Colinas / Hills

Me gusta manejar bicicleta cerca de las colinas / I like to ride a bicycle near the hills.

608.   Montañas / Mountains

Las montañas de mi ciudad en invierno son extremadamente frías / The mountains of my city in winter are extremely cold.

609.   Cima / Peak

En la cima de la montaña a veces se ve nieve / At the peak of the mountain, snow can sometimes be seen.

610.   Cañon / Canyon

El gran cañón es uno de los monumentos naturales más increíble de todos / The Grand Canyon is one of the most incredible natural monuments of all.

611. Isla / Island

A veces quisiera vivir en una isla y no saber nada de nadie / Sometimes, I wish I could live on an island and know nothing about anyone.

612.   Oasis / Oasis

Tuve una alucinación de que veía un oasis / I had a hallucination that I saw an oasis.

613.   Bahía / Bay

Llegaré a la bahía mañana después del medio día / I'll arrive at the bay tomorrow afternoon.

614.   Costa / Coast

Ayer, mientras estaba en la playa, caminé por toda la costa / Yesterday, while I was on the beach, I walked all along the coast.

615. Volcán / Volcano

Hay muchas ciudades que están peligro por un volcán / There are many cities that are endangered by a volcano.

616.   Valle / Valley

Cuando fue a Holanda vió unos valles muy preciosos / When he went to the Netherlands, he saw some very beautiful valleys.

617. Río / River

No es bueno jugar en el río cuando se hace fuerte la corriente / It's not good to play in the river when the current is strong.

618.   Terremoto / Earthquake

Lo primero que debes hacer durante un terremoto es mantener la calma / The first thing you should do during an earthquake is to stay calm.

619.   Huracán / Hurricane

El huracán Dorian causó muchos daños en ciertas ciudades / Hurricane Dorian caused a lot of damage in certain cities.

620.   Tormenta / Storm

La tormenta de la semana pasada derribó tres árboles en mi urbanización / Last week's storm knocked down three trees in my city.

621.   Trueno / Thunder

Mi perro le tiene muchísimo miedo a los truenos / My dog is terribly afraid of thunder.

622.   Rayo / Lightning

El trueno siempre va después del rayo / Thunder always comes after lightning.

623.   Cascada / Waterfall

El salto ángel es la cascada más grande del mundo / Salto Angel is the largest waterfall in the world.

624.   Paisaje / Scener

Son increíbles los hermosos paisajes que se pueden observar volando en un avión / The beautiful sceneries that can be observed when flying in an airplane are incredible.

625.   Iceberg / Iceberg

El titanic se hundió a causa de una colisión con un iceberg / The Titanic sank due to a collision with an iceberg.

626.   Mar / Sea

Navegar en el mar es algo increíble, una experiencia que vale la pena vivir / Navigating the sea is something incredible, an experience worth living.

627.   Nivel del mar / Sea level

Si después de un terremoto, el nivel del mar retrocede, puede ocurrir un tsunami / If after an earthquake, the sea level recedes, a tsunami may occur.

628.   Océano / Ocean

En el océano hay miles de especies diferentes de animales marinos / In the ocean, there are thousands of different species of marine animals.

629.   Acantilado / Cliff

Esa foto increíble de la motocicleta es en el acantilado que esta cerca de la licorería / That incredible photo of the motorcycle is on the cliff near the liquor store.

630.   Lago / Lake

Algunas personas van a nadar y hacer kayak en lagos / Some people go swimming and kayaking in lakes.

631.   Dunas / Dunes

Las dunas de arena son bastante interesantes desde el punto de vista físico / The sand dunes are quite interesting from a physics point of view.

632.   Represa / Dam

Debemos concientizar a las personas sobre el uso del agua, ya la represa está casi vacia / We must make people aware of the use of water; the dam is almost empty.

633.   Piedra / Stone

La fachada de esa casa hecha de piedra hace que se vea muy elegante / The facade of that stone house makes it look very elegant.

634.   Pantano / Swamp

Shrek era el ogro del pantano en su película / Shrek was the swamp ogre in his movie.

635.   Piedritas / Pebbles

Estaba manejando bicicleta, y me caí a causa de unas piedritas / I was riding a bike, and I fell because of some pebbles.

636.   Horizonte / Horizon

La mejor obra de la naturaleza es ver al sol ocultarse por el horizonte al atardecer / Nature's best work is the sun hiding on the horizon at dawn.

637.   Arboleda / Grove

El jardinero de mi urbanización hace un trabajo excelente con la arboleda / The gardener of my city does an excellent job with the grove.

638.   Charco / Puddle

Acababa de bañar a mi perro y fue a lanzarse al charco / I had just bathed my dog, and he went to jump into the puddle.

639.   Amanecer / Sunrise

Todas las mañanas me levanto al ver el amanecer / Every morning, I wake up to see the sunrise

640.   Atardecer / Sunset

Estar en la playa después del atardecer es algo muy gratificante / Being on the beach after sunset is a very rewarding thing.

641.   Tierra / Earth

Fuera de la casa dejé tres sacos llenos de tierra para el jardín / Outside the house, I left three sacks full of the earth for the garden.

642.   Planeta Tierra / The Earth

El planeta tierra está muy deteriorado por causa de los seres humanos / The Earth is very deteriorated because of human beings.

643.		Metal / Metal

Es muy difícil conseguir un metal que sea capaz de soportar mucho calor / It is very difficult to get a metal that can withstand a lot of heat.

644.		Diamante / Diamonds

El diamante es el mineral más duro de toda la naturaleza / Diamond is the hardest mineral in all of nature.

645.		Carbón / Charcoal

Los diamantes provienen del carbón / Diamonds come from charcoal.

646.		Hierro / Iron

Muchas cosas de nuestro día a día están hechas o tienen partes de hierro / Many things of today are made or have parts of iron.

647.		Semillas / Seeds

Mi abuela me regaló unas semillas de girasol para que las sembrara en el jardín / My grandmother gave me some sunflower seeds to plant in the garden.

648.		Árboles / Trees

Los árboles proporcionan sombra y oxígeno y aún así hay personas que los talan / Trees provide shade and oxygen, and yet there are people who cut them down.

649.		Flores / Flowers

¿Sabes cuáles son las flores favoritas de la abuela? Hoy es su cumpleaños y quiero regalarle unas / Do you know what Grandma's favorite flowers are? Today is her birthday, and I want to give her some.

650.		Grama / Grass

El campo de futbol donde juegan los niños tiene la grama muy alta, ya es difícil jugar allí / The football field where the children play has very high grass; it is already difficult to play there.

651.Frutas / Fruits

Las frutas han salvado a miles de personas de morir de hambre a lo largo de la historia / Fruits have saved thousands of people from starvation throughout history.

652.		Vegetales / Vegetables

Una cantidad balanceada de vegetales es necesaria para una buena alimentación / A balanced amount of vegetables is necessary for a good diet.

653.   Pino / Pine

En la casa iremos a comprar el pino de navidad el primero de Diciembre / We will buy the Christmas pine on December 1st for the house.

654.   Palmera / Palm tree

Las palmeras son un tipo de árbol muy común en las playas y costas venezolanas / Palms are a very common type of tree on Venezuelan beaches and coasts.

655.   Capa de ozono / Ozone layer

Las pinturas y otros productos en aerosol son responsables del deterioro de la capa de ozono / Paints and other aerosol products are responsible for the deterioration of the ozone layer.

656.   Recycle / Reciclar

Como nada es infinito, debemos reciclar los materiales que utilizamos / As nothing is infinite, we must recycle the things we use.

657.   Reforestación / Reforestation

Al cancelar la construcción que habían planeado, comenzaron con el proceso de reforestación / When they canceled the construction they had planned, they began the reforestation process.

658.   Energía solar / Solar energy

La energía solar es una de las mejores fuentes alternativas de energía en la actualidad / Solar energy is one of the best alternative sources of energy today.

659.   Contaminar / Pollute

Si dejáramos de contaminar, el planeta comenzaría a mejorar lentamente / If we stopped polluting, the planet would slowly begin to improve.

660.   Cambio climático / Climate change

El cambio climático es producto de la acción humana sobre el planeta / Climate change is a product of human action on the planet.

661.   Calentamiento global / Global warming

Todas estas anomalidades que estamos viviendo son consecuencia del calentamiento global/ All these anomalies that we are experiencing are a consequence of global warming.

662.   Deforestación / Deforestation

Es necesaria la deforestación de esta área para el nuevo edificio que van a construir / Deforestation of this area is necessary for the new building they are going to build.

663.   Incendio forestal / Wild fire

El incendio forestal de Amazonia fue algo impactante y nunca antes visto / The Amazonia wildfire was something shocking and never seen before.

664.   Extinción / Extinction

El dodo es un animal que desde hace bastante tiempo está extinto / The dodo is an animal that has been extinct for quite some time.

665.   Especies en peligro de extinción / Endangered species

Las especies en peligro de extinción deben ser protegidas y monitoreadas por protección animal / Endangered species must be protected and monitored by animal protection.

666.   Animales / Animals

Hay millones de distintos animales en todo el mundo / There are millions of different animals all over the world.

667.   Especies / Species

Las especies son los distintos tipos de animales que existen / The species are the different types of animals that exist.

668.   Reino animal / Animal kingdom

El reino animal es algo tan grande, que aún hay muchos animales que no han sido descubiertos / The animal kingdom is so big that there are still many animals that have not been discovered.

669.   Animales domésticos / Domestic animals

Lo mejor de tener un animal doméstico es que ayudan a que no te sientas solo / The best thing about having a domestic animal is that they help you not to feel lonely.

670.   Perro / Dog

Como dice la gente: El perro es el mejor amigo del hombre / As people say, the dog is man's best friend.

671.Gato / Cat

¿Crees que sea cierto que los gatos siempre caen parados? / Do you think it's true that cats always fall on their feet?

672. Loro / Parrot

Es muy divertido enseñarle frases al loro para que las repita / It's very fun to teach the parrot phrases to repeat.

673. Conejo / Rabbit

Los conejos son animales muy adorables y tiernos / Rabbits are very adorable and tender animals.

674. Cabra / Goat

Hay países donde toman la leche de cabra como si fuese leche de vaca / There are countries where they drink goat's milk as if it were cow's milk.

675. Oveja / Sheep

Las ovejas recién afeitadas son bastante chistosas, cuando les quitan la lana / Freshly shaved sheep are pretty funny-looking when they get their wool off.

676. Paloma / Pigeon

Es increíble la cantidad de enfermedades que pueden transmitir las palomas, y pensar que hay miles de ellas en todos lados / It's incredible how many diseases pigeons can transmit and to think that there are thousands of them everywhere.

677. Animales salvajes / Wild animals

Ten cuidado cuando te vayas de excursión, no sabes que animales salvajes puedas encontrarte / Be careful when you go on an excursion; you don't know which wild animals you may encounter.

678. León / Lion

El león tiene fama de ser el rey de la selva / The lion has a reputation for being the king of the jungle.

679. Tigre / Tiger

Me gustan mucho las cintas que tiene el tigre, y en el tigre blanco se ven aún mejor / I like very much the stripes that the tiger has, and in the white tiger, they look even better.

680. Puma / Cougar

Los pumas son felinos muy poderosos también / Cougars are very powerful felines, too.

681. Gorila / Gorilla

Me gusta mucho la película donde sale un gorila gigante y se lo llevan a la ciudad, no recuerdo cómo se llamaba / I really like the movie where a giant gorilla comes out and is taken to the city; I do not remember what it was called.

682.   Mono / Monkey

Los científicos afirman que los humanos provenimos de la evolución del mono / Scientists claim that humans come from the evolution of the monkey.

683.   Cocodrilo / Crocodile

Aunque parezca extraño, en Florida es común encontrarse cocodrilos en las piscinas / As strange as it may seem, crocodiles are commonly found in swimming pools in Florida.

684.   Rinoceronte / Rhinoceros

Para mí, el rinoceronte es una bestia formidable, su gruesa piel y su cuerno lo hacen ser muy temible / For me, the rhinoceros is a formidable beast; its thick skin and horn make it very fearsome.

685.   Elefante / Elephant

En algunos países se utilizan elefantes como medios de transporte o como una mascota exótica / In some countries, elephants are used as a form of transport or as an exotic pet.

686.   Jirafa / Giraffe

Es curioso que a pesar de su largo cuello, las jirafas no emitan ningún tipo de sonido / It is curious that despite their long necks, giraffes do not emit any kind of sound.

687.   Tiburón / Shark

Dicen que el tiburón es peligroso, pero anualmente no mueren ni 80 personas a causa de ataques de tiburón / Sharks are said to be dangerous, but not even 80 people die from shark attacks every year.

688.   Ballena / Whale

Las ballenas se comunican mediante sonidos y frecuencias muy extraños / Whales communicate through strange sounds and frequencies.

689.   Camarón / Shrimp

Hay un refrán que dice: "Camarón que se duerme, se lo lleva la corriente" / There's a saying, "A shrimp that falls asleep is carried away by the current."

690.   Cangrejo / Crab

Hay una especie de cangrejo que solo tiene una de las dos pinzas de tamaño grande / There's a kind of crab that only has one of the two large-sized claws.

691.   Delfín / Dolphin

Mi sueño siempre ha sido nadar con los delfines, me encantaría hacerlo / My dream has always been to swim with dolphins; I would love to do it.

692.   Medusa / Jellyfish

Esta comprobado que es falso que orinar en la picadura de una medusa ayuda con la picazón / It's been proven false that urinating on the bite of a jellyfish helps with the itching.

693.   Pulpo / Octopus

Los tentáculos de los pulpos tienen algo parecido a unos chupones que les da muy buen agarre / The octopus tentacles have something like suckers that give them a very good grip.

694.   Tortuga / Turtle

No puedo creer que haya visto el nacimiento de una tortuga, fue algo inexplicable / I can't believe I saw the birth of a turtle; it was inexplicable.

695.   Calamar / Squid

Según las leyendas, hay un calamar gigante en el mar / According to legends, there's a giant squid in the sea.

696.   Caballito de mar / Seahorse

Si la pareja de un caballito de mar muere, el que queda vivo muere a los pocos días de tristeza / If the partner of a seahorse dies, the remaining one dies within a few days of sadness.

697.   Estrella de mar / Starfish

Por favor, no te tomes fotos con las estrellas de mar fuera del agua porque las matas / Please don't take pictures with the starfish out of the water because you kill them.

698.   Orca / Killer whale

Se han realizado estudios que indican que la orca es más o igual de agresiva que los tiburones / Studies has indicated that killer whales are more or equally aggressive than sharks.

699.   Águila / Eagle

El águila puede ver a su presa a una distancia de casi cuatro kilómetros / The eagle can see its prey at a distance of almost four kilometers.

700.   Dinosaurio / Dinosaur

Los dinosaurios eran animales inmensos que existieron hace miles de millones de años / Dinosaurs were immense animals that existed billions of years ago.

701. Murciélago / Bat

Los murciélagos son animales que tienen una pésima visión, ellos ven a través de ondas utilizando una especie de sonar / Bats are animals that have a terrible vision; they see through waves using a kind of sonar.

702. Mamíferos / Mammals

La mayoría de los animales que conocemos son mamíferos / Most of the animals we know are mammals.

703. Reptiles / Reptiles

Los repstiles son animales que se caracterizan por poseer escamas epidérmicas / Reptiles are animals characterized by epidermal scales.

704. Anfibios / Amphibians

Los anfibios son increíbles, pasan de respirar y vivir en el agua a hacerlo fuera de ella / Amphibians are incredible; they go from breathing and living in the water to living on land.

705. Insectos / Insects

No hay nada que me de mas asco y nauseas que los insectos / There's nothing more disgusting and nauseating than insects.

706. Mapache / Racoon

Incluso si parecen tiernos e inofensivos, los mapaches siguen siendo animales salvajes / Even if they seem cute and harmless, raccoons are still wild animals.

707. Ciervo / Deer

No encuentro ningún atractivo en decorar las casas con cabezas de ciervos / I don't find anything attractive in decorating houses with deer heads.

708. Ardilla / Squirrel

En muchos de los parques y árboles de ciertas zonas urbanas es posible ver ardillas / In many of the parks and trees of certain urban areas, it is possible to see squirrels.

709. Oso / Bear

Existen distintos tipos de osos y mi favorito es el panda, es muy diferente a los demás / There are different types of bears, and my favorite is the panda. It is very different from the others.

710. Halcón / Falcon

El halcón es un ave muy rápida y letal para pequeños mamíferos / The falcon is a very fast and lethal bird for small mammals.

711. Buitre / Vulture

¿Sabes cuáles son las aves que se comen a los animales muertos? Los buitres / Do you know which birds eat dead animals? The vultures.

712. Cuervo / Crow

Los espantapájaros de las granjas sirven para ahuyentar a los cuervos / The scarecrows of the farms serve to drive away the crows.

713. Mosca / Fly

Que increíble que la mosca solo vive veinticuatro horas y las usa para fastidiar en los hogares / I can't believe that the fly only lives for twenty-four hours and uses their lives to annoy homes.

714. Mariposa / Butterfly

Antes de ser bonitas, las mariposas son unas orugas que se encierran en un caparazón / Before being beautiful, butterflies are caterpillars enclosed in a cocoon.

715. Libélula / Dragonfly

La libélula hace un sonido muy desagradable cuando vuela / The dragonfly makes a very unpleasant sound when it flies.

716. Escarabajo / Beetle

El Volkswagen escarabajo fue inspirado por el insecto con mismo nombre / The Volkswagen beetle was inspired by the insect with the same name.

717. Caracol / Snail

Eres tan lento que pareces un caracol, apurate / You're so slow. You look like a snail; hurry up.

718. Araña / Spider

Si bien es cierto que algunas arañas son inofensivas, hay otras que son extremadamente letales / It is true that some spiders are harmless, but others are extremely lethal.

719. Abeja / Bee

La miel es producida por las abejas, y dependiendo de las flores y las abejas, pueden saber diferente / Honey is produced by bees, and depending on the flowers and bees, they may taste different.

720. Perezoso / Sloth

Quisiera ser un perezoso para comer y dormir todo el día / I'd like to be a sloth, so I can eat and sleep all day.

721.Koala / Koala

No lo sabía, pero los koalas comen eucalipto, que es una planta venenosa / I didn't know, but koalas eat eucalyptus, which is a poisonous plant.

722. Pingüino / Penguin

De todas las especies de pingüinos, mi favorito es el pingüino emperador / Of all the penguin species, my favorite is the emperor penguin.

723. Hipopotamo / Hippopotamus

Los hipopótamos parecen una mezcla extraña entre elefantes y rinocerontes / Hippos look like a strange mixture of elephants and rhinoceroses.

724. Buho / Owl

Los búhos son aves que cazan por las noches / Owls are birds that hunt at night.

725. Escorpión / Scorpion

Me parece que los escorpiones son los animales más desagradables que existen / I think scorpions are the most disgusting animals there are.

726. Caballo / Horse

Una patada de caballo puede fracturarte varias costillas, lo digo por experiencia / A horse's kick can fracture several ribs; I say that from experience.

727. Burro / Donkey

Un burro jamás será tan veloz como un caballo / A donkey will never be as fast as a horse.

728. Yegua / Mare

Esta es la yegua con la que sacaremos crías a nuestro caballo / This is the mare with which we will raise our horse.

729. Vaca / Cow

Muchos productos de consumo diario como el queso, la mantequilla y las cremas son hechos con leche de vaca / Many daily consumables, such as cheese, butter, and creams are made from cow's milk.

730. Toro / Bull

Es extremadamente injusto que existan las corridas de toros, es un deporte despiadado / It is extremely unfair that there are bullfights; it's a merciless sport.

731. Hormiga / Ant

El único animal de ser capaz de levantar tres mil veces su peso son las hormigas / The only animal capable of lifting three thousand times its weight is ants.

732. Ciempies / Centipedes

Siempre he querido contar las patas de un ciempiés a ver si en verdad son cien / I've always wanted to count the legs of a centipede to see if it really is a hundred.

733. Canguro / Kangaroo

En las películas dicen que en Australia hay muchos canguros / In the movies, they say that in Australia, there are many kangaroos.

734. Rana / Frog

Haz veinte saltos de rana / Make twenty frog jumps.

735. Sapo / Toad

El sapo estaba en la alcantarilla / The toad was in the sewer.

736. Pato / Duck

Dicen que el pato asado es muy sabroso / It is said that roasted duck is very tasty.

737. Camello / Camel

Los dromedarios tienen una joroba y los camellos dos / Dromedaries have one hump, and camels have two.

738. Camaleón / Chameleon

Tengo un camaleón de mascota y a veces me cuesta conseguirlo / I have a pet chameleon, and sometimes, I find it hard to find.

739. Dragón de komodo / Komodo dragon

Cuando escuché el nombre de dragón de komodo me asuste / When I heard the name of komodo dragon, I got scared.

740. Zorro / Fox

Debo cuidar a las gallinas de los zorros / I must take care of the hens from the foxes.

741. Cerdo / Pig

No sé porqué los cerdos son tan cochinos / I don't know why pigs are so filthy.

742. Puercoespín / Porcupine

Yo pensaba que el puercoesín era venenoso / I thought the porcupine was poisonous.

743.		Foca / Seal

Las focas son animals bastante ferozes / Seals are pretty fierce animals.

744.		Sardina / Sardine

Algunas personas prefieren comer sardina que atún / Some people prefer to eat sardines than tuna.

745.		Pez espada / Swordfish

Debes ser muy cuidadoso buceando, hay peces espada / You must be very careful diving; there are swordfishes.

746.		Chinche / Bedbug

El otro día estaba descalzo y pisé un chinche, olío terrible / The other day, I was barefoot, and I stepped on a bedbug. It smelled terrible.

747.		Piojo / Louse

Tengo que cortarle el cabello a mi hijo, tiene muchos piojos / I have to cut my son's hair; he's got a lot of lice.

748.		Garrapata / Tick

Le conseguí una garrapata a mi gato, espero que no esté enfermo / I found a tick on my cat. I hope he's not sick.

749.		Avispa / Wasp

Nunca he sido picado por una avispa / I've never been stung by a wasp.

750.		Pavo / Turkey

Es común cocinar un pavo para el día de acción de gracias / It's common to cook a turkey for Thanksgiving.

751. Luciernaga / Firefly

Las luciernagas son insectos bastante agradables / Fireflies are pretty nice insects.

752.		Castor / Beaver

La idea de la represa viene de los castores / The idea of the dam comes from the beavers.

753.		Lobo / Wolf

El lobo es mi animal favorite, me haré un tatuaje de uno / The wolf is my favorite animal; I'll get a tattoo of one.

754.		Cisne / Swan

En el lago cerca de mi casa hay tres cisnes / In the lake near my house, there are three swans.

Chapter 5: Professions

Here, you will find useful words for common and not so common professions.

755. Arqueólogo / Archaeologist

Es super interesante ser arqueólogo / It's super interesting to be an archaeologist.

756. Panadero / Baker

Me encantaría ser panadero, es muy sabroso el pan / I'd love to be a baker; the bread is very tasty.

757. Biólogo / Biologist

Mi tío es biólogo y sabe mucho sobre la naturaleza / My uncle is a biologist and knows a lot about nature.

758. Carnicero / Butcher

El carnicero siempre me regala un poco más de carne / The butcher always gives me a little more meat.

759. Cajero / Cashier

Soy el nuevo cajero de la tienda, aun estoy aprendiendo / I'm the new cashier at the store. I'm still learning.

760. Actor / Actor

Me engañó por completo, no sabía que era actor / He totally tricked me. I didn't know he was an actor.

761.Actriz / Actress

Es impresionante el buen papel de esa actriz / The role of that actress is impressive.

762. Astronauta / Astronaut

No creo que en el futuro haya más astronautas, todo será robotizado / I don't think there will be more astronauts in the future; everything will be robotized.

763. Youtuber / Youtuber

Debe ser genial ser youtuber, hacer videos y que te paguen por ello / It must be great to be a YouTuber, make videos, and get paid for it.

764. Community manager / Community manager

Ser community manager no es fácil como todos creen / Being a community manager isn't as easy as everyone thinks.

765. Conserje / Janitor

El conserje se esforzó muchísimo, todo quedó impecable / The janitor worked very hard; everything was impeccable.

766. Carpintero / Carpenter

Necesito llamar a mi carpintero, creo que tenemos termitas en casa / I need to call my carpenter. I think we have termites at home.

767. Albañil / Bricklayer

¿Conoces algún buen albañil en esta zona? / Do you know any good bricklayers in this area?

768. Conductor de autobus / Bus driver

El señor Luis tiene años como conductor de autobús / Mr. Luis has years as a bus driver.

769. Empresario / Businessman

Mi papá es un gran empresario, siempre se ha esforzado mucho / My dad's a great businessman. He's always tried so hard.

770. Cuidador / Caretaker

Necesitamos un cuidador para nuestro perro mientras nos vamos de viaje / We need a caretaker for our dog while we go on a trip.

771. Limpiador / Cleaner

Carlos es un limpiador professional / Carlos is a professional cleaner.

772. Dentista / Dentist

Mi dentista me recomendó cepillarme cuatro veces al día / My dentist recommended me to brush four times a day.

773. Economista / Economist

Según el economista, vienen tiempos muy duros / According to the economist, hard times are coming.

774. Electricista / Electrician

Si no fuera por el electricista, mi casa no tuviera electricidad / If it wasn't for the electrician, my house wouldn't have electricity.

775. Payaso / Clown

Soy el payaso del hospital para niños especiales / I'm the clown of the special children's hospital.

776. Granjero / Farmer

He sido granjero de esta casa durante veinticinco años / I've been a farmer in this house for twenty-five years.

777. Bombero / Firefighters

Los bomberos combatieron el incendio forestal antes que los daños fueran muchos / The firefighters fought the wildfire before the damage was too much.

778. Químico / Chemist

La mezcla esta saturada, lo sé porque soy químico / The mixture is saturated. I know that because I'm a chemist.

779. Bailarín / Dancer

Siempre haz lo que amas, yo soy bailarín / Always do what you love; I'm a dancer.

780. Asesor / Counselor

Él es el asesor escolar, si tienes alguna duda, habla con él / He's the school counselor. If you have any questions, talk to him.

781. Mecánico / Mechanic

No conozco un buen mecánico, todos son mentirosos / I don't know a good mechanic; they're all liars.

782. Cartero / Mailman

El cartero me dijo que perdió mi correo hace una semana / The mailman told me he lost my mail a week ago.

783. Cantante / Singer

Ella canta muy bien, debería ser cantante / She sings very well; she should be a singer

784. Científico / Scientist

Los científicos tienen muchos conocimientos que las otras personas no / Scientists have a lot of knowledge that other people don't.

785. Escritor / Writer

Yo sería un gran escritor de cuentos para niños / I would be a great children's story writer.

786. Limiador de ventanas / Window cleaner

Mira aquel edificio, el limpiador de ventanas está haciendo un gran trabajo / Look at that building; the window cleaner's doing a great job.

787. Camarera / Waitress

Disculpe, ¿Podría darle esta propina a la camarera? / Excuse me, could you give this tip to the waitress?

788.   Camarero / Waiter

Jóven, ¿Está interesado en ser mi camarero? / Young man, are you interested in being my waiter?

789.   Taxista / Taxi driver

Me compré un auto viejo para ser taxista / I bought an old car to be a taxi driver.

790.   Trabajador social / Social worker

La trabajadora social lleva muchos casos importantes de la zona / The social worker takes many important cases from the area

791. Psiquiatra / Psychiatrist

Estoy alucinando, debo ir al psiquiatra / I'm hallucinating. I have to go to a psychiatrist.

792.   Psicólogo / Psychologist

Me gusta ir al psicólogo de vez en cuando a hablar de mis problemas / I like to go to the psychologist once in a while to talk about my problems.

793.   Pintor / Painter

Que gran pintor fue Edvard Munch / What a great painter Edvard Munch was.

794.   Oficinista / Office worker

Aunque no sea muy emocionante, me gusta ser la oficinista / Although it's not very exciting, I like to be the office worker.

795.   Fotógrafo / Photographer

Para ser el mejor fotógrafo es necesario tener mucha imaginación / To be the best photographer, it is necessary to have a lot of imagination.

796.   Plomero / Plumber

Si tienes algún problema con las tuberías, llámame, soy plomero / If you have a problem with the pipes, call me. I'm a plumber.

797.   Zapatero / Cobbler

Llevaré tus zapatos rotos al zapatero / I'll take your broken shoes to the cobbler.

798.   Cocinero / Cook

Solicito cocinero para puesto de comida rápida / I'm seeking a cook for a fast-food stall.

799.   Cocinero professional / Chef

El chef preparó un plato exquisito en mi casa / The chef made a exquisite dish at my house.

800.   Programador / Programmer

Hice un proyecto como programador y cobré mil dólares / I did a project as a programmer and charged a thousand dollars.

801.   Recepcionista / Receptionist

Como recepcionista siempre debo atender bien al público / As a receptionist, I must always serve the public well.

802.   Presidente / President

Soy amiga del presidente de la compañía / I'm a friend of the president of the company.

803.   Niñera / Nanny

La niñera que tengo me está robando comida/ The nanny I have is stealing my food.

804.   Monje / Monk

Los monjes son muy tranquilos / The monks are very calm.

805.   Cura / Priest

El cura de la ciudad tiene muchos seguidores / The city priest has many followers.

806.   Político / Politician

No me gustaría ser politico, es una profesión muy sucia / I wouldn't want to be a politician. It's a very dirty profession.

807.   Policía / Policeman

Los policías arriesgan sus vidas por nosotros todo el tiempo / The policemen risk their lives for us all the time.

808.   Operador telefónico / Telephone operator

Buenas tardes, soy su operador telefónico, dígame como puedo ayudarle / Good afternoon, I am your telephone operator; tell me how can I help you.

809.   Conductor de camión / Truck driver

He viajado por todo el país siendo conductor de camión / I've traveled all over the country as a truck driver.

810.   Consultor / Consultant

No estoy muy seguro de lo que hace un consultor / I'm not quite sure what a consultant does.

811. Decorador / Decorator

Es buen momento para llamar al decorador, ya viene navidad / It's a good time to call the decorator. Christmas is coming.

812.   Estudiante / Student

Ya estoy harto de ser estudiante / I'm sick and tired of being a student.

813.   Abogado / Lawyer

Los abogados son geniales, siempre intentan protegerte / Lawyers are great; they're always trying to protect you.

814.   Administrador de base de datos / Database administrator

Soy el administrador de base de datos de Apple / I am Apple's database administrator.

815.   Administrador / Administrator

No sé, pregúntale al administrador por los cheques / I don't know; ask the administrator about the checks.

816.   Agente de ventas / Sales Agent

Si eres bueno convenciendo a las personas, entonces sé agente de ventas / If you're good at convincing people, then be a sales agent.

817.Vendedor / Seller

Como vendedor eres excelente / As a seller, you are excellent.

818.   Agricultor / Farmer

Soy el agricultor de la ciudad / I'm the city farmer.

819.   Alergista / Allergist

Deberías ir al alergista, esa alergia no es normal / You should go to the allergist. That is not a normal allergy.

820.   Analista financiero / Financial analyst

Mi analista financiero dice que no debería invertir en eso / My financial analyst says that I shouldn't invest in that.

821.   Anatomista / Anatomist

Según el anatomista, esa deformación no es perjudicial / According to the anatomist, that deformation is not harmful.

822.   Anestesiólogo / Anesthesiologist

Gracias a Dios el anestesiólogo usó anestecia general / Thank God, the anesthesiologist used general anesthesia.

823.   Antropólogo / Anthropologist

Si no fuera por los antropólogos, estaríamos en grandes problemas / If it weren't for the anthropologists, we'd be in big trouble.

824.   Artesano / Craftsman

Mi vecino, el artesano, hace cosas muy bonitas / My neighbor, the craftsman, does very pretty things.

825.   Artista / Artist

Son increíbles las grandes obras de algunos artistas / The works of some artists are incredible.

826.   Contador / Accountant

El contador que teníamos fue bastante malo, necesitamos uno nuevo / The counter we had was pretty bad; we need a new one.

827.   Asesor financiero / Financial adviser

Mi vecino me recomendó a un gran asesor financiero / My neighbor recommended a great financial advisor.

828.   Astrofísico / Astrophysicits

El astrofísico aplica sus conocimientos físicos a la astrología / The astrophysicist applies his physical knowledge to astrology.

829.   Astrólogo / Astrologer

Según los astrólogos, las estrellas revelan muchas cosas / According to astrologers, stars reveal many things.

830.   Bibliotecario / Librarian

El bibliotecario es un genio, sabe de memoria donde está cada libro / The librarian is a genius; he knows where each book stands by heart.

831.   Cardiólogo / Cardiologist

Por más que lo intentó, el cardiólogo no logró salvarlo / No matter how hard he tried, the cardiologist couldn't save him.

832.   Cirujano / Surgeon

El cirujano dijo que no era necesaria la cirugía / The surgeon said there was no need for surgery.

833.   Climatólogo / Climatologist

En el pronóstico del clima, el climatólogo siempre se equivoca / In the weather forecast, the climatologist is always wrong.

834.   Criminalista / Criminalist

La criminalista dará información importante mañana / The criminalist will give out important information tomorrow.

835.   Dermatólogo / Dermatologist

Mi dermatólogo recomienda usar protector solar diariamente / My dermatologist recommends daily use of sunscreen.

836.   Diseñador de moda / Fashion designer

La nueva diseñadora de moda es mucho mejor que la anterior / The new fashion designer is much better than the previous one.

837.   Diseñador de interior / Interior designer

Necesito que el diseñador de interiores me renueve este espacio / I need the interior designer to renovate this space for me.

838.   Diseñador de productos / Product Designer

Quiero crear un nuevo producto, por eso debemos contratar a un diseñador de productos / I want to create a new product, so we must hire a product designer.

839.   Diseñador web / Web designer

La página web de Amazon es genial, quiero su diseñador web / Amazon's website is great; I want your web designer.

840.   Educador / Educator

Mi pasión es ser un gran educador / My passion is to be a great educator.

841.   Egiptólogo / Egyptologist

Debe ser muy interesante ver y saber todo lo que sabe un egiptólogo / It must be very interesting to see and know everything an Egyptologist knows.

842.   Escultor / Sculptor

El escultor de "El pensador" fue un genio / The sculptor of "The Thinker" was a genius.

843.   Filósofo / Philosopher

Odio ir a clases de filosofía, mi profesor cree que todos seremos filósofos / I hate going to philosophy classes; my teacher thinks we'll all be philosophers.

844.   Fiscal / Prosecutor

El fiscal dio la orden de cerrar el caso / The prosecutor gave the order to close the case.

845.   Fisioterapeuta / Physiotherapist

La lesión de Vanessa mejoró rápido gracias al fisioterapeuta / Vanessa's injury improved quickly, thanks to the physiotherapist.

846.   Forense / Forensic

Forense, ¿Ya sabe la hora de la muerte? / Forensics, do you know the time of death yet?

847.   Geólogo / Geologist

Ser geólogo me parece algo un poco aburrido / Being a geologist seems a little boring to me.

848.   Músico / Musician

Michael Jackson fue el más grande músico de la historia / Michael Jackson was the greatest musician in history.

849.   Historiador / Historian

Mi abuelo es historiador y sabe muchas historias importantísimas / My grandfather is a historian and knows many very important stories.

850.   Informático / Informatic

Ese programa lo hizo mi amigo informático / That program was made by my informatic friend.

851.   Ingeniero civil / Civil engineer

Los arquitectos diseñan y los ingenieros civiles se encargan de lo demás / Architects design buildings, and civil engineers do the rest.

852.   Ingieniero de software / Software engineer

Se solicita ingeniero de software para proyecto de inteligencia artificial / Software Engineer requested for an Artificial Intelligence project.

853.   Ingeniero electrónico / Electronic engineer

Los ingenieros electrónicos sueñan con ser como Steve Jobs o Elon Musk / Electronic engineers dream of being like Steve Jobs or Elon Musk.

854.   Ingeniero mecánico / Mechanical engineer

Mi primo sabe bastante de termodinámica, él es ingeniero mecánico / My cousin knows a lot about thermodynamics; he's a mechanical engineer.

855.   Investigador / Researcher

Con toda la información que hay en internet, ser investigador debe ser fácil / With all the information on the Internet, being a researcher should be easy.

856.   Jardinero / Gardener

Amo la manera en que el jardinero arregla el jardín / I love the way the gardener tidies up the garden.

857.   Juez / Judge

La orden del juez fue de cárcel por cinco años / The judge's order was five years in jail.

858.   Locutor / Speaker

Richard es el locutor con mejor voz que conozco / Richard is the best-voiced speaker I know.

859.   Masajista / Masseur

Después de las visitas de mi masajista, me siento excelente / After my masseur's visits, I feel excellent.

860.   Meteorólogo / Meteorologist

El meteorólogo esta preocupado por el cambio climático / The meteorologists are concerned about climate change.

861.   Nutricionista / Nutritionist

Su nutricionista le dio una dieta para el embarazo / Her nutritionist gave her a diet for the pregnancy.

862.   Oceanógrafo / Oceanographer

Yo le temo al océano y él es oceanógrafo / I'm afraid of the ocean, and he's an oceanographer.

863.   Oftalmólogo / Ophthalmologist

Mi visión está empeorando, debo ir al oftalmólogo / My vision is getting worse; I have to go to the ophthalmologist.

864.   Otorrinolaringólogo / Otolaryngologist

Creo que tengo una infección en el oído, el otorrinolaringólogo me dirá / I think I have an ear infection; the otolaryngologist will tell me.

865.   Periodista / Journalist

El periodista le hizo una genial entrevista al ganador de la lotería / The journalist did a great interview with the lottery winner.

866.   Piloto / Pilot

Estoy muy preocupado, este sera el primer vuelo del piloto / I'm very concerned; this will be the pilot's first flight.

867.   Psicopedagogo / Educational Psychologist

Todas las escuelas necesitan un psicopedagogo, pero no todas tienen uno / Every school needs an educational psychologist, but not every school has one.

868.   Publicista / Advertiser

La campaña publicitaria fue un fracaso, despide al publicista / The advertising campaign was a failure; fire the publicist.

869.   Quiropráctico / Chiropractor

Tengo desgaste en las vertebras, dijo mi quiropráctico / I've got wear on my vertebrae, my chiropractor said.

870.   Relacionista público / Public relationist

Esa chica es muy buena como relacionista pública / That girl is very good as a public relationist.

871.Secretario / Secretary

Mi secretario trabaja desde las nueve hasta las doce / My secretary works from nine to twelve.

872.   Sexólogo / Sexologist

Hoy intentaremos unas cosas que me dijo el sexólogo / Today, we'll try some things the sexologist told me.

873.   Sismólogo / Seismologist

Ya el equipo de sismólogos estan evaluando la situación / The seismologist team is already assessing the situation.

874.   Teólogo / Theologist

Ella defiende muy bien su religión, es teóloga / She defends her religion very well; she's a theologist

875.   Traumatólogo / Traumatologist

Me fracturé el hombro y salí de emergencia al traumatólogo / I fractured my shoulder and went to the traumatologist in an emergency.

876.   Tutor / Tutor

El padre de Bernardo es tutor y le dijo que su tesis estaba mala / Bernardo's father is a tutor and told him that his thesis was bad.

877.   Webmaster / Webmaster

Ser webmaster es algo incredible / Being a webmaster is something incredible.

878.   Zoólogo / Zoologist

Los animales han mejorado bastante, debe ser gracias al zoólogo / The animals have improved a lot; it must be thanks to the zoologist.

879.   Aplicar / Apply

Me gustaría aplicar para este puesto / I would like to apply for this position.

880.   Empleo / Jobs

Me interesa el empleo, estoy disponible / I'm interested in the job; I'm available.

881.   Habilidades / Skills

Como pueden ver, mis habilidades son más que necesarias / As you can see, my skills are more than necessary.

882.   Cualidades / Qualities

Mis cualidades exceden sus expectativas / My qualities exceed your expectations.

883.   Salario / Salary

¿Cuánto es el salario? / How much is the salary?

884.   Tiempo extra / Overtime

No se preocupe, hoy me quedaré tiempo extra / Don't worry, I'll do overtime today.

885.   Jefe / Boss

Mi jefe dijo que pronto me iba a ascender / My boss said I was going to be promoted soon.

886.   Asistente / Asistant

El trabajo de asistente es agotador / The assistant's job is exhausting.

887.   Empleado / Employee

Solo soy un simple empleado de la empresa / I'm just a simple employee of the company.

Chapter 6: Clothing

In this chapter, we will take a look at words related to clothing.

Clothing and Styles

888.   Camisa / Shirt

Creo que iré con mi camisa favorita / I think I'll go with my favorite shirt.

889.   Camiseta / T-Shirt

¿Se verá mal si uso camiseta? / Would it look bad if I wore a T-shirt?

890.   Franela / Flannel

Me parece horrible esa franela / I find that flannel horrible.

891.   Franelilla / Tank top

A veces uso franelilla para ir al gimnasio / Sometimes, I use tank top to go to the gym.

892.   Camisa cuello en V / V-neck Shirt

Encuentro las camisas cuello en V muy sexys / I find the V-neck shirts very sexy.

893.   Camisa de botones / Button-down shirt

Esa camisa de botones te queda perfecta / That button-down shirt fits you perfectly.

894.   Camisa de cuadros / Cheked shirt

¿Crees qué sea mucho si voy en camisa de cuadros? / Do you think it's too much if I wore a checked shirt?

895.   Camisa manga larga / Long sleeve shirt

No usaré la camisa manga larga, hace mucho calor / I won't wear the long-sleeved shirt; it's too hot.

896.   Pantalones / Pants

Ponte unos pantalones y vas a comprar el desayuno / Put on some pants, and go buy breakfast.

897.   Jeans - Vaqueros / Jeans

Me gustan bastante los vaqueros negros / I like black jeans a lot.

898.   Leggins / Leggins

A Cyntia le lucen muy bien esos leggins / Cyntia looks great in those leggings.

899.   Joggers / Joggers

Si pudiera, siempre usaría joggers, son muy cómodos / If I could, I'd always use joggers. They're very comfortable.

900.   Falda / Skirt

Debo depilarme las piernas para usar falda el sábado / I have to shave my legs to wear a skirt on Saturday.

901.   Vestido / Dress

El vestido de la novia estaba precioso / The bride's dress was beautiful.

902.   Sueter / Sweater

Le presté mi sueter a mi amiga y se lo quedó / I lent my sweater to my friend, and she kept it.

903.   Blusa / Blouse

La tía de Susan le regaló esa blusa rosada / Susan's aunt gave her that pink blouse.

904.   Chaqueta – Jacket

Cuando salgo en moto, no salgo sin mi chaqueta / When I go out on a motorcycle, I don't go out without my jacket.

905.   Brassier / Bra

Mi brassier se rompió y me lastima / My bra broke, and it hurts.

906.   Pantaleta / Panty

Quiero desesperadamente esa pantaleta fucsia / I desperately want those fuchsia panties.

907.   Ropa interior / Underwear

Tiene un montón de ropa interior / She's got a lot of underwear.

908.   Abrigo / Coat

No olvides traer un abrigo / Don't forget to bring a coat.

909.   Gabardina / Gabardine

Te queda grande esa gabardine / That gabardine is big on you.

910.   Chaleco / Vest

Para trabajar de camarero debo usar chaleco / To work as a waiter, I must wear a vest.

911. Impermeable / Raincoat

Llovió temprano pero yo llevaba mi impermeable / It rained early, but I was wearing my raincoat.

912.   Bufanda / Scarf

En invierno, salir sin bufanda significa resfriado seguro / In winter, going out without a scarf means getting a cold.

913.   Guantes / Gloves

La abuela de Lily le tejió unos guantes muy bonitos / Lily's grandmother knitted her some very nice gloves.

914.   Orejeras / Earmuffs

Si no uso orejeras, el frió me hace doler los oídos / If I don't wear earmuffs, the cold would make my ears hurt.

915.Calzoncillos – Interiores / Underpants

Mamá, ¿Sabes donde están todos mis calzoncillos? / Mom, do you know where all my underpants are?

916.   Boxers / Boxers

Los boxers son mucho más comodos que los calzoncillos / Boxers are much more comfortable than underpants.

917.Shorts / Shorts

No consigo mis shorts de futbol y ya es tarde / I can't find my football shorts, and it's already late.

918.   Medias / Socks

Ella no usa medias y sus zapatos huelen mal / She doesn't wear socks, and her shoes smell bad.

919.   Pijama / Pyjamas

La pijama de Nataly es de conejos / Nataly's pyjama is of rabbit design.

920.   Corbata / Tie

Tengo la corbata muy ajustada, me lastima / My tie's too tight; it hurts.

921.   Corbata de lazo / Bow tie

La corbata de lazo es mejor para esta ocasión / The bow tie is better for this occasion.

922.   Gorra / Cap

El equipo de beisbol quiere hacer unas gorras / The baseball team wants to make some caps.

923.   Sombrero / Hat

Me quito el sombrero ante tal actuación / I take my hat off at such a performance.

924.   Cinturón / Belt

He adelgazado, lo noto por el cinturón / I've lost weight; I notice from the belt.

925.   Zapatos / Shoes

Estos zapatos ya me aprietan, toma, te los regalo / These shoes are already tight; here, I'll give them to you.

926.   Botas / Boots

De pequeña usaba botas para ir a todos lados / When I was a kid, I wore boots everywhere.

927.   Sandalias / Sandals

En casa me gusta usar sandalias, es más cómodo / At home, I like to wear sandals; it's more comfortable

928.   Tacones / Heels

Tengo diecinueve años y aún me cuesta caminar con tacones / I'm nineteen years old, and I still have a hard time walking in heels.

929.   Zapatos de correr / Running shoes

Salí anteayer a correr con los zapatos de correr y es mu diferente / I went out the day before yesterday to run in my running shoes; it's so different.

930.   Atuendo / Outfit

Amiga, te queda precioso ese atuendo / My friend, you look beautiful in that outfit.

931.   Zapatos deportivos / Sneakers

Yo solo uso zapatos deportivos / I only wear sneakers.

932.   Atar / Tie

Debo atar las trenzas de mis zapatos / I must tie my shoe laces.

933.   Desatar / Untie

Hice un nudo para que no se vuelva a desatar / I made a knot so it won't untie again.

934.   Vestir / Wear

Ya casi salgo, me tengo que vestir / I'm almost out. I have to wear some clothes.

935.   Ponerse / Put on

Mañana mi hermana va a ponerse su camisa negra / Tomorrow, my sister is going to put on her black shirt.

936.   Vestirse / Dress

Ellá aún tiene que vestirse, espera unos minutos / She still has to get dressed. Wait for a few minutes.

937.   Desvertirse / Undress

Ya terminó el primer show, todos a desvertirse para el próximo / The first show is over; everyone has to undress for the next one.

938.   Chándal / Tracksuit

Me compre un chándal gris / I bought a gray tracksuit.

939.   Ropa deportiva / Sport clothes

El profesor siempre usa ropa deportiva / The teacher always wears sports clothes.

940.   Ropa formal / Formal clothes

No creo que tengamos que usar ropa formal para el evento / I don't think we have to wear formal clothes to the event.

941.   Ropa casual / Casual clothes

Yo iré con ropa casual, es mejor / I'll go in casual clothes; it's better.

942.   Talla / Size

¿Qué talla es tu pantalón? / What size are your pants?

943.   Pequeño / Small

Yo soy talla pequeño en camisas / I'm a small size in shirts.

944.   Mediano / Medium

Mis boxers son medianos / My boxers are medium.

945.   Grande / Large

Mi tío usa pantalones grandes / My uncle wears large pants

946.   Extra grande / Extra Large

Algunas personas muy musculosas usan ropa extra grande / Some very muscular people wear extra large clothing.

947.   Collar / Necklace

Perdí mi collar en la piscina del hotel / I lost my necklace at the hotel pool.

948.   Zarcillos / Earrings

Quiero unos zarcillos nuevos para el viernes / I want a new pair of earrings by Friday.

949.   Anillos / Rings

Él me dio un anillo muy lindo / He gave me a very nice ring.

950.   Pulseras / Bracelet

Sin pulseras me siento desnuda / Without bracelets, I feel naked

951.Reloj / Watch

El reloj aporta mucho estilo en los hombres / The watch brings a lot of style to men.

952.   Billetera / Wallet

Amor, ¿Has visto mi billetera? / Honey, have you seen my wallet?

953.   Cartera / Purse – Handbag

Debe estar dentro de mi cartera, búscala / It must be in my purse; look for it.

954.   Bolso / Backpack

Olvidé que tenía una banana en mi bolso y se aplastó / I forgot I had a banana in my backpack, and it got crushed.

955.   Jarra de agua / Water jug

Es bueno llevar una jarra de agua para correr. / It is good to carry a water jug for jogging.

956.   Traje de baño / Swimsuit

¿Es muy atrevido este traje de baño? / Is this swimsuit too daring?

957.   Bikini / Bikini

Está súper sexy ese bikini / It's super sexy, that bikini.

958.   Traje de baño completo / One piece swimsuit

Si no uso traje de baño completo no voy a la playa / If I'm not wearning a one-piece swimsuit, I don't go to the beach.

959.   Maquillaje / Makeup

Quiero empezar a usar maquillaje / I want to start wearing makeup.

960.   Accesorios / Accessories

Se ven muy bien todos tus accesorios / All your accessories look great.

Hair

961.   Peinado / Hairstyle

Ya me cansé de este peinado, quiero uno nuevo / I am tired of this hairstyle. I want a new one.

962.   Estilista / Hair stylist

Mi estilista vendrá a pintarme el cabello / My hair stylist is coming to paint my hair.

963.   Corte de cabello / Haircut

Intentaré recrear el corte de cabello de algún actor famoso / I'll try to recreate some famous actor's haircut.

964.   Afeitar / Shave

Debería afeitarme las axilas antes de ir al gimnasio / I should shave my armpits before I go to the gym.

965.   Secar / Blow dry

Luego de bañarme, me voy a secar el pelo / After I bathe, I'm going to blow-dry my hair.

966.   Cortar las puntar / Trim

Tengo poco tiempo, solo me voy a cortar las puntas / I don't have much time. I'm just gonna trim my tips.

967.   Mechas / highlights

Vi una chica con mechas en instagram, me han encantado / I saw a girl with highlights in Instagram; I loved them.

968.   Flequillo / Fringe

Cuando era pequeña usaba un horrible flequillo / When I was little, I wore a horrible fringe.

969.   Raíces / Roots

Ese shampú me debilita las raíces / That shampoo weakens my roots.

970.   Rizar / Curl

Disculpe, ¿Podría decirme cuanto cuesta rizar mi cabello? / Excuse me, could you tell me how much it costs to curl my hair?

971.Alisar / Straighten

Martha no ha regresado de alisar su cabello en la peluquería / Martha hasn't come back from straightening her hair at the hairdressers.

972.   Ondular / Wave

Conozco una tecnica para ondular de forma natural / I know a natural technique to put waves on the hair.

973.   Peluquero / Hairdresser

El peluquero ha sido muy amable con nosotras / The hairdresser has been very kind to us.

974.   Barbero / Barber

Mis amigos me recomiendan siempre este barbero, dicen que es muy bueno / My friends always recommend me this barber; they say it's very good.

975.   Corto / Short

Que lindas son las chicas con el cabello corto / How cute girls are with short hair.

976.   Largo / Long

¿Por qué los chicos a los que les gusta el metal tienen el cabello largo? / Why do boys who like metal have long hair?

977.   Medio / Mid- length

Siempre me he visto mejor con el estilo medio, por la forma de mi cara / I've always looked better with the mid-length by the shape of my face.

978.   Encrespado / Frizzy

Al despertarme siempre tengo el cabellado encrespado, no importa lo que haga / When I wake up, my hair is always frizzy, no matter what I do.

979.   Acondicionador / Conditioner

Estoy probando una nueva marca de acondicionador, además, huele muy bien / I'm trying a new brand of conditioner; it smells great.

980.   Espuma / Foam

No puedo afeitarme sin la espuma, ire a compra una nueva / I can't shave without the foam. I'll buy a new one.

981.   Laca / Hairspray

La laca ayuda a mantener la forma del peinado / The hairspray helps to maintain the shape of the hairstyle.

982.   Gelatina / Gel

Nunca me ha gustado la gelatina, pienso que daña mucho el cabello / I've never liked gel. I think it damages the hair a lot.

983.   Bigote / Mustache

Los bigotes siempre han sido una excelente moda masculina / Moustaches have always been an excellent addition to male fashion.

984.   Barba / Beard

Que aspecto tan rudo le da una barba a un hombre / What a rough look a beard gives a man.

985.   Afeitado / Shaven

Para cuidar mejor la piel, es mejor mantenerse afeitado / To take care of your skin, it's better to stay shaven.

986.   Patillas / Sideburn

En la antigüedad, solían usar mucho las patillas largas / In the ancient times, they used long sideburns a lot.

987.   Pinchos / Spiky

Para entrar en la banda debes hacerte unos pinchos / To enter the band, you must have spiky hair.

988.   Rastas / Dreadlocks

Todos los raperos de hoy en día tienen rastas / Every rapper today has dreadlocks.

989.   Extensiones / Hair Extensions

Es una fiesta muy formal, me pondré extensiones para verme mejor / It's a very formal party. I'll wear extensions to look better.

990.   Longitud del hombro / Shoulder-Length

Solo dejo que me crezca el pelo hasta la longitud del hombro / I just let my hair grow to shoulder length.

991.   Moño / Bun

Para hacer ejercicio tengo que hacerme un moño, así no me molesta el cabello / In order to exercise, I have to make a bun, so my hair doesn't bother me.

992.   Giro francés / Frenchtwist

Que hermosa se veía la novia con el giro francés en el altar / How beautiful the bride looked on the altar with her frenchtwist.

993.   Trenza / Braid

Me agrada que venga mi prima porque se deja hacer una trenza / I'm glad my cousin's coming because she lets herself make a braid.

994.   Cola de caballo / Ponytail

Le pedí a mi hermana que me enseñara a hacerme una cola de caballo / I asked my sister to teach me how to make a ponytail.

995.   Trenzas / Pigtails

Siempre dejo que mis amigas me hagan trenzas, ya que soy la que tiene el cabello mas largo / I always let my friends do pigtails on me since I'm the one with the longest hair.

996.   Permanente / Perm

Creo que me haré una permanente en el cabello / I think I'll get a perm.

997. Capas / Layers

Quiero que mi corte de cabello sea por capas / I want my haircut to be layered.

998. Afeitadora / Razor

Se agotaron las baterias de la afeitadora mientras me afeitaba / I ran out of razor batteries while I was shaving.

999. Tijeras / Scissors

No utilices tijeras para cortarme el cabello / Don't use scissors to cut my hair.

1000. Crema de afeitar / Shaving cream

Es increíble la diferencia que proporciona la crema de afeitar / It's amazing what a difference shaving cream makes.

1001. Adiós / Goodbye

Adiós y gracias por leer completo el libro / Goodbye and thank for reading the whole book

Conclusion

Thank you for making it to the end of *1001 Top Spanish Words in Context: How to Speak Intermediate-Level Spanish in Less than 21 Days*. Let's hope it was informative and able to provide you with all of the tools you needed to achieve your goal.

Now that you have finished the book, we hope that you really liked it, and you have enjoyed and learned a lot with the words written here, We carefully chose and used each word so you could maximize your learning.

Felicitaciones, ya debes ser capaz de entender esta frase.

The next step to reach a more advanced level of the Spanish language would be to write about your daily activities using the sentences written here as a basis. To have an advanced level of the Spanish language is extremely important to study the verb tenses of the Spanish language because there are many more than those existing in English.

Once again, we want to remind you that this is not a book that you should read only once because it has a lot of content, and it is difficult to learn the first time you read it.

Hasta luego, sigue practicando tu español y muy pronto verás lo fácil que es .

Finally, if you found this book useful in any way, a review on Amazon is always appreciated!

One last thing to do

If you enjoyed this book or found it useful I'd be very grateful if you'd post a short review on it. Your support really does make a difference and we read all the reviews so we can get your feedback and make this book even better.

Thanks again for your support!

Printed by Amazon Italia Logistica S.r.l.
Torrazza Piemonte (TO), Italy

16959001R00373